THE SOVIET EXPERIENCE

THE SOVIET EXPERIENCE

Success or Failure?

Edited by DANIEL R. BROWER
University of California, Davis

HOLT, RINEHART AND WINSTON
New York • Chicago • San Francisco • Atlanta
Dallas • Montreal • Toronto • London • Sydney

Cover illustration: Bolsheviks captured in Bessarabia by Roumanians during the Russian Civil War. *(Photoworld)*

Library of Congress Catalog Card Number: 76–132153
SBN: 03–085001–0
Printed in the United States of America
1 2 3 4 008 9 8 7 6 5 4 3 2 1

CONTENTS

CHRONOLOGY

1917 October (November by new calendar)—Seizure of power by Bolshevik party

1918 Beginning of Civil War

First constitution for Russian Socialist Federated Soviet Republic

1919 Founding of Communist International

1920 End of Civil War

1921 March—Revolt of Kronstadt sailors against Communist regime

Introduction of New Economic Policy

All of Transcaucasia (Azerbaidjan, Armenia, Georgia) incorporated into Soviet state

1922 Declaration of Union of Soviet Socialist Republics; Stalin named General Secretary of the Central Committee of Communist party

1924 Death of Lenin; leadership controlled by triumvirate of Zinovev, Kamenev, and Stalin

Last of Central Asian lands (Khorezm and Bukhara) incorporated into U.S.S.R.

1927 Trotsky expelled from Communist party and exiled

Policy of rapid industrialization approved by Fifteenth Party Congress

1928 Beginning of five-year plans

1929 Leadership of Soviet Union under complete control of Stalin following expulsion of Bukharin from Politburo; massive collectivization drive begun

1934 Assassination of Sergei Kirov, followed by first wave of purges and arrests in party

1936 Stalin constitution adopted; Great Purges begin

1937 Officer corps of Red Army decimated by purges

1938 End of Great Purges with execution of last of Old Bolshevik leaders; Beria made head of secret police

1939 Signing of nonaggression pact with Germany; seizure of eastern region of Poland; outbreak of war with Finland

1940 Victory over Finland and seizure of eastern Finnish territory; annexation of Baltic states; seizure of Bessarabia and Bukhovina from Roumania

1941 German invasion of Soviet Union

1945 Soviet victory over Germany; war against Japan

1946 Beginning of new purges by secret police
1949 First nuclear bomb exploded by Soviet Union
1952 First party congress held since 1939
1953 Death of Stalin; Beria shot; collective leadership of party by Malenkov and Khrushchev
1955 Leadership in hands of Khrushchev
1956 Denunciation of Stalin's "cult of personality" by Khrushchev at Twentieth Party Congress
Revolt in Hungary suppressed by Soviet troops
1957 Launching by Soviet Union of first earth satellite *Sputnik*
1961 Declaration by Khrushchev that Soviet Union approaching the "first stage of communism"
First manned space flight by Soviet cosmonaut
1964 Khrushchev deposed; new leadership of Brezhnev and Kosygin
First application of new industrial policy ("Libermanism") of decentralization of decision making
1965 New agricultural policy of greater investments and incentives for collective farms
1966 New drive against dissident intellectuals; trial of Siniavsky and Daniel'
1967 Fiftieth anniversary of Bolshevik Revolution
1968 Soviet invasion of Czechoslovakia

Churchgoers who lost relatives in World War II attend a mass for the dead at the Kitskansk Monastery, Moldavia. *(Sovfoto)*

INTRODUCTION

The study of Soviet history has been a source of debate and controversy ever since Westerners began paying attention to the new regime in Russia. Events of great importance have taken place in the Soviet Union, yet there is still no agreement on their meaning or significance. The Bolsheviks introduced fundamental reforms in all fields of Soviet life and argued that they were creating a new society and a new man. Their arguments were based on the Marxist ideology adapted to Russian circumstances. The issues they raised cannot be dismissed as biased polemics, however. A human experiment of mammoth proportions has occurred in the Soviet Union. But what exactly were these innovations? Did they represent an original contribution to the historical experience of mankind, or were they a unique product of Russian traditions? Were they a step forward or backward in Russian history? These questions are at the heart of the debate over the significance of the Soviet experience.

The West could not avoid taking part in this controversy. The Marxist promise of a new life was familiar and attractive to many Europeans, hated and despised by others. The Soviet leaders claimed that this ideology had come alive in their land, and some Western Marxists, though far from all, felt that the Soviet Union was the new hope of mankind. The American journalist John Reed, witness and interpreter of the Bolshevik Revolution, recorded the promises of the Bolshevik leaders and himself proclaimed the glorious future ahead. He foresaw the building by the Russian people of a "kingdom more bright than any heaven had to offer, and for which it was a glory to die."[1] In the dark years of the 1930s, when the depression was causing hardship throughout the Western world and fascist movements were rising in many countries, the communist program offered the possibility of continued progress toward social justice and equality. Hitler's Germany and Stalin's Soviet Union stood at opposite poles in the political and ideological strife of those years.

Further heightening the importance of the debate over the Soviet Union was the fact that the pressures of rising international tensions in the 1930s required closer diplomatic contacts with the Soviet state. The U.S.S.R. was by then a force to be reckoned with on the international scene. Even the United States govern-

[1] John Reed, *Ten Days That Shook the World* (New York, 1967), p. 229.

ment had to accept this fact, finally extending diplomatic recognition to the Soviet Union in 1933. Yet the conduct of diplomatic relations could not remain free from the controversy over the Soviet experience. Some Western politicians urged strong ties with the "progressive" Soviet government, while others warned that the revolutionary ideas of the Soviet Union made it an untrustworthy partner in any diplomatic dealings. World War II put this issue at the forefront of public concern. The defeat of Germany brought Soviet power into the center of Europe. Westerners tried hastily to understand how it was that the Soviet Union had become so powerful. The cold war became inevitably an ideological debate for or against the Soviet experience.

At the same time the colonial revolts against the Asian and African empires of the European states brought out another issue relevant to the evaluation of Soviet history. From the start the Bolshevik leaders had pictured their revolution as a revolt against European imperialism and had offered aid and advice for similar revolts in colonial lands. Their experience in modernization offered a model for rapid change.

The development of the Soviet Union has thus raised major issues of importance for modern world history. Predictions of the imminent collapse of Bolshevism following Stalin's death proved false. The Soviet regime demonstrated that it had found the techniques for the peaceful transfer of power from one leadership to the next, first rather painfully after Stalin's death in 1953, then quite smoothly with the dismissal in 1964 of Khrushchev and the rise of Brezhnev and Kosygin. The celebration in 1967 of the fiftieth anniversary of the Bolshevik Revolution served to emphasize the permanence of Soviet institutions. It also reaffirmed the necessity of confronting the real issues raised by the Soviet experience of a half century of revolutionary change. But on what basis should the issues be judged?

Marxist theories have provided one framework of analysis. Soviet scholars have relied entirely on Marxism, as interpreted by their political leaders, to explain and justify the fundamental aspects of their country's development. Their people, under the leadership of the Communist party, embarked on the construction of socialism, prelude to the communist society. Marx had foreseen the inevitable historical progression from feudalism to capitalism and ultimately to communism. The Bolshevik Revolution had accelerated this advance by cutting short the capitalist period in Russia. The five-year plans for industrialization had further speeded up the tempo and had by the mid-1930s transformed the country into a socialist society, marked by the end of class antagonism. Ahead lay the full realization of communism. Khrushchev declared formally in 1961 that the Soviet Union would within twenty years enter the first stage of communism. Since his fall from power, the subject has been dropped. But the historical scenario remains basically unchanged and sets the context for all Soviet discussion of the country's revolutionary experience.

Marxists opposed to Bolshevism answer that Marx's dream of a new society has been perverted in the Soviet Union. In pushing their revolution from above, the Soviet leaders neglected the goal of a classless society to build up a new elite and had to strengthen, not weaken, the oppressive powers of the state. These measures meant the abandonment of true Marxism.

The usual Western approach has been to minimize the Marxist ideology in judging the Soviet transformation. For most scholars in the West, the important questions relate to the fate of the population under the Soviets. The concern of some lies with the loss of personal freedom in the Soviet totalitarian state. Others assert that the population has in the long run benefited enormously in terms of material well-being and social advancement. These advantages, in large part the fruits of industrialization and urbanization, outweigh the restrictions placed on political activities and freedom of expression.

A slightly different view is taken by those scholars who argue that the Soviet regime has actually revived traditional Russia in a new guise. The autocracy became the dictatorship of the proletariat; serfdom became collective farms; and the religious uniformity imposed by the Orthodox Church reappeared as Marxism-Leninism. In their opinion the Soviet Union moved into the industrial age by means of traditional Russian institutions and practices.

The rise of interest in the problems of developing societies has produced its school of Soviet specialists. From their perspective the Soviet experience appears as one important instance of the efforts by underdeveloped nations to catch up with the West. By implication they deny that Western concepts of liberalism and individualism are applicable to a country whose true character is non-Western. They see the Marxist ideology merely as one tool of political organization and social mobilization for modernization. Their evaluation of Soviet development depends on how successfully they believe the Soviets satisfied the needs of a modernizing country.

These are some of the major interpretations of Soviet history. In a field so subject to controversy, it is not surprising that there is a wide range of opinions. Yet this complicates the task of the student interested in the Soviet Union. He needs on the one hand to be aware of the variety of viewpoints on the subject, and on the other to define his own opinion. In the pages that follow a large sampling has been made of significant points of view covering many aspects of the Soviet experience. Both the supporting evidence and the views should be examined critically. Is the interpretation based on sound evidence, or does it rely on unproven assertions? Does it give a comprehensive picture of the subject, or does it distort or omit some facts? The selections can do no more, however, than to familiarize the reader with the historical problems which he, ultimately, must resolve to his own satisfaction.

The first group of readings deals with Soviet political developments. Central to the debate here is the character and the effect of the new political regime. What was new about it, and what impact did it have on the Soviet population? For the

Soviet Communist party, whose 1967 "Theses" in honor of the fiftieth anniversary of the Bolshevik Revolution open the readings, the answer is clear. The Soviet Union has progressed on the basis of a union between the people and their party, which has ruled in their interests. The party provided the necessary leadership for industrialization and collectivization, and for the Great Patriotic War against Nazi Germany. No one man, not even Joseph Stalin, deserves special mention, for the party collectively was responsible for the progress made. These "Theses" emphasize the positive side to the party's activities. Only briefly do they mention Stalin's "personality cult" and its terrible consequences for the Soviet population. The great achievements of the party in the end justify the sacrifices and outweigh the mistakes.

To this Milovan Djilas responds that the Soviet Communist party was pursuing in reality the defense of its own power, not the interests of the masses. Giving Marxist theories a new twist, he asserts that the ruling party bureaucrats enjoyed a monopoly on property and power in the Soviet Union. As such they became an exploiting class no better than the capitalists of nineteenth-century Europe. Though they professed to act in the name of the people, they were above all concerned with their own privileges. Before their power could be firmly established, they had to get rid of revolutionaries, such as Leon Trotsky, who fought their growing influence. Joseph Stalin, however, supported their views and encouraged their hold over the country. His triumph was thus the victory of the new class.

The role of Joseph Stalin is still the most controversial political issue of Soviet history. For Alec Nove, the Soviet dictator does not deserve a blanket condemnation. The situation in the Soviet Union in the late 1920s was a critical one requiring strong leadership. The general direction Soviet policies had to take was clear. Industrialization and collectivization were necessary, and so therefore was a "commander in chief." Stalin became that man. He personally exploited the position for his own power ambitions, although as leader he did fulfill the task demanded of him.

From the point of view of the political institutions of the Soviet Union, however, Stalin was only the central figure in a vast mechanism for dictatorial rule. He alone could have done little. Richard Lowenthal believes that these political institutions form the real contribution of the Soviet political experience. They were the fruit of Lenin's decision to use the state as the instrument to achieve his ideological goals. To do this, total political control was required. Out of this commitment developed Soviet totalitarianism. Lenin created the basic institutions, which Stalin used for his "permanent revolution from above."

In the second group of readings the issues relating to Soviet economic development are examined from four different perspectives. In the opinion of Nikolai Baibakov the key to the economic history of his country has been the system of socialist planning. The origins of planning lay in the Marxist ideology and in Lenin's practical application of these ideological goals. The establishment of state controls, first over industry then over agriculture and commerce, created the necessary economic foundations on which planning could operate to guide the Soviet economy. For Baibakov, proof of the success of socialist planning can be seen in the figures on Soviet economic growth.

The idea that rational ideological principles inspired this development of the Soviet economy is denied by Marshall Goldman. When he looks at Soviet economic history, he sees little influence of ideology. On the contrary, he finds a whole series of short-term, pragmatic decisions taken under the pressure of circumstances and without any real perception of what the consequences would be. War communism was just the first of a series of compromises. Planning had to function on the basis of these policies. Economic development in the Soviet Union was thus achieved through a procedure of trial and error.

When compared with the economic performance of the United States, the Soviet achievements lose some of their luster. Walt Rostow uses this comparative method to argue that the exceptional advances of the Soviet economy have been grossly exaggerated. He also feels that similar results could have been attained by another economic system. He finds, therefore, that the Soviet economic experience is mainly significant as an example of the ability of a dictatorial political regime to divert economic growth to its own ends.

The economic institutions which the Soviets created impress Charles Wilber as valid models for modernization. Taking the case of agriculture, he concludes that the collective farm organization which spread throughout the Soviet countryside in the 1930s was an effective tool for mobilizing agricultural resources for economic development. It provided a substantial surplus of farm commodities for the cities and for export, and released agricultural labor for other uses. Though the cost to the peasantry was high, this was an economic model which performed well.

The social aspect to the Soviet experience is discussed in the third group of readings. The issues here concern the extent of social change and the degree to which that change was guided from above. Alex Inkeles is interested in the Soviet attempt at "social experimentation and innovation" which led to radical social reforms. He argues that some of the new institutions did represent a fundamental alteration in social relations, such as the collective farms. But he also finds a considerable degree of conservatism, particularly strong in what he terms the "third phase of revolutionary development" beginning in the mid-1930s. He sees this stabilization as a natural development arising from the needs of the "day-to-day operation of a large-scale social system." This phase marked the end of planned social change.

Another social problem touches on the effect on the population of the Soviet experience. Isaac Deutscher makes a distinction between the working class in the cities and the peasantry. The latter were the great impediment to change in Russia, but were finally reduced to a subordinate position in society during the Soviet period. The workers, on the other hand, advanced in numbers and importance to the point where, in Deutscher's opinion, they may "challenge the bureaucracy" and "resume the struggle for emancipation" begun in 1917.

The nationalities represent a separate and very important issue in Soviet social history. Their experiences in the new Soviet society depended in large part on their own historical development. For the eastern peoples in the Transcaucasus and Central Asia, Alec Nove and J. Newth assert that the Soviet period has brought a mixture of colonialism and liberation. They present the arguments and evidence for both sides of the question, and defend their own compromise views. They see real evidence of Russian political controls over the region, but also convincing proof of the economic advantages Soviet rule has brought these peoples. These Asian groups, therefore, have not occupied a strictly "colonial" position in the Soviet Union.

The other side to the nationalities question is provided by the history of the Jews under the Soviets. Their problem under the Russian tsars was social discrimination and political persecution. Peter Grose argues that the problem has remained very alive in the Soviet period. Anti-Semitism was rampant under Stalin, and Jewish religious practice was effectively discouraged then and later. Officially opposed to any form of racial or national discrimination, the Soviet government continued to single out the Jews for harsh treatment.

The fourth group of readings examines the question of a new Soviet culture. Fedor Korolev presents the case for a real "transformation of the consciousness and behavior of people." He looks to the activities of the men who defended the Soviet Union in the Civil War, or who contributed to the industrialization drive in the 1930s, or who fought against Hitler's Germany in World War II for examples of the new Soviet man. The role of education has in his opinion been crucial in transmitting the ideals of public service, patriotism, and collectivism.

Looking at these ideals as embodied in Soviet literature, Andrei Siniavsky finds them artificial and unconvincing. The literary style of socialist realism was dictated not by realism but by socialist ideals as defined by the party. Novels became, therefore, forms of moral exhortation, with the positive hero the goal for which men were to strive. By definition, negative social attitudes must be unimportant and dissension a temporary aberration. What appeared new in Soviet literature was not a reflection of reality, only of a new literary style.

Perhaps the political evolution of the Soviet Union has left its mark on the population as well. In a highly speculative essay Lewis Feuer argues that the style of political leadership under the Soviets set a model for character formation for the Russian population at large. The liberating effects of the Revolution weakened the passive traits of Russians. Stalinist leadership from the 1930s provided a character model of cruelty and discipline in keeping with the personality required by the policies of the period. Perhaps, he suggests, this was the real "new Soviet man."

Fifty years of Soviet history have produced an abundance of views on the significance of the Soviet experience. Each one makes certain assumptions about what the most important changes in Soviet life have been and what impact these changes have had on the people of the Soviet Union. For Sidney and Beatrice Webb, the chief innovation was the introduction of a new morality based on a social ethic of justice and equality. Writing in the late 1930s, they judged these principles far superior to those of the West, for they created a "new civilization."

The readings which follow can assist the reader in coming to his own conclusion. The subject is vast and the issues are complex. One Westerner with considerable experience in Soviet affairs, Winston Churchill, wrote in October 1939 that Russia was "a riddle wrapped in a mystery inside an enigma." But the Soviet experience still deserves our close attention, for it has changed the course of human history.

In the reprinted selections footnotes appearing in the original sources have in general been omitted unless they contribute to the argument or better understanding of the selection.

The Soviet political experience is above all the history of the Communist party. In the Soviet Union the party sets the guidelines for the interpretation of its own past. It sees its activities since 1917 as the source of all creative leadership in the country. The people, in whose interests it acted, contributed significantly in the construction of socialism, the defeat of the German invaders, and in all other major achievements. But without the party none of these triumphs would have been possible. This is the view presented in the "Theses" prepared by the Central Committee of the Communist party at the occasion of the fiftieth anniversary of the Bolshevik Revolution.*

Communist Party of the Soviet Union

The Triumph of the Party

The Great October Socialist Revolution overthrew the system of exploitation and oppression. The proletariat fought for emancipation from wage slavery—it became the master of the factories and mills. The working peasantry suffered from land hunger—Soviet rule abolished the landed estates and turned the land over to the peasants. Soviet rule nationalized large-scale industry, the land, railroads and banks, and introduced a foreign-trade monopoly. For the first time in history all the natural resources and the principal means of production had become the property of the people. Public ownership of the means of production, which became the economic foundation of socialism, was established in the decisive branches of the economy. The oppressed nationalities inhabiting Tsarist Russia suffered from lack of political rights—Soviet rule proclaimed the equality of nations and their right to self-determination. The division of the population into social estates and the privileges possessed by these social estates were abolished; and the humiliating laws consolidating the unequal status of women were abrogated.

The Great October Socialist Revolution wrested our country from the abyss of the bloody imperialist war. The people passionately desired peace—the Decree on Peace was the very first decree of Soviet rule; the country was saved from the national catastrophe to which the

*"Fiftieth Anniversary of the Great October Socialist Revolution: Theses of the Central Committee of the Communist Party of the Soviet Union," *Pravda,* June 25, 1967. Translation from *The Current Digest of the Soviet Press,* June 12, 1967, pp. 3–7, published at The Ohio State University by the American Association for the Advancement of Slavic Studies. Copyright 1967 by *The Current Digest.* Reprinted by permission.

ruling classes had doomed it. The peoples of Russia were delivered from the threat of enslavement by foreign capital.

The Great October Socialist Revolution shook the world of capitalism to its foundations. The world split into two systems, socialist and the capitalist. The Soviet state began to apply new principles in the relations among peoples and countries. The economic, social and political emancipation of the masses became the goal of the workers' and peasants' regime born of the Revolution. Herein lies the profound meaning of the revolutionary humanism of the October Revolution. Mankind acquired a reliable bulwark in its struggle against predatory wars, for peace and the security of peoples, for social progress.

The world-historic significance of the October Revolution lies in the fact that it indicated the paths and discovered the forms and methods of revolutionary transformation, and they acquired an international character. The experience of the Great October Socialist Revolution is an inexhaustible treasure-house of the theory and practice of revolutionary struggle, a model of scientific strategy and tactics. . . .

After the foreign interventionists were driven out and the Civil War ended, it became possible for the Party and the people to concentrate their efforts on solving the main task of the Revolution, the construction of socialism.

The imperialists failed to destroy the Soviet Republic by military force, but they ruined our country to such an extent that, as V. I. Lenin put it, they "half achieved their aim." We had to begin peaceful construction from such a low level that the output of large-scale industry was one-seventh of the prewar level, and the output of steel was less than 5% of the prewar level. Agricultural output fell by almost half. All this created enormous difficulties in the transition to socialist construction.

It is the historic service of the Communist Party, headed by V. I. Lenin, that it armed the Soviet people with a scientific plan for building socialism, which took account of economic and social conditions in the country. Lenin's ideas provided for the country's industrialization, socialist cooperation in agriculture and the accomplishment of a cultural revolution. These ideas conformed to the basic interests of the masses, who sought to put an end to the economic dislocation, economic backwardness, poverty and ignorance.

Under V. I. Lenin's direct leadership, the Party elaborated and, at its Tenth Congress, adopted the New Economic Policy, an important and necessary stage on the road to socialism. The purpose of this policy was to overcome the economic dislocation, to create the foundation for a socialist economy, develop large-scale industry, establish economic integration of town and country, strengthen the alliance between the working class and the peasantry, squeeze out and liquidate capitalist elements and achieve the victory of socialism. The ways of fulfilling these tasks were: all-out development of cooperatives, broad expansion of trade and the use of material incentives and economic accountability. For the purpose of rehabilitating the economy, the enlistment of private capital was accepted, while the commanding heights were kept in the hands of the proletarian state.

The basic principles of the New Economic Policy are of international significance; they are used in the process of building socialism in other countries.

The policy of building socialism was upheld and pursued by the Party and the working class in a fierce class struggle against remnants of the deposed exploiting classes, against capitalist elements in town and country and against "left" and right opportunists who attempted to divert us from the Leninist path.

Of great importance was the ideological and political program of Trotskyism,[1] which sowed distrust in the powers of the working class of the U.S.S.R. by maintaining that the victory of socialism in our country was impossible without the prior victory of the proletarian revolution in the West. The Trotskyites sought to deprive our party and people of the prospect of building socialism successfully in the U.S.S.R. and denied its importance to the world revolutionary movement. Using ultrarevolutionary "left" phraseology as a cover, the Trotskyites sought to impose an adventurist policy of artificially "promoting" revolution in other countries, while dooming the building of socialism to defeat in our country. They demanded a shift to antidemocratic, militarized methods of leadership of the masses within the country, rejected the Leninist principle of democratic centralism, insisted on "freedom" of factional struggle within the Party, and, on this road, slid toward anti-Sovietism.

The Party also had to wage a resolute struggle against the right opportunists who reflected the ideology of the exploiting kulak strata[2] in the countryside and opposed rapid industrialization, collectivization of agriculture and liquidation of the kulaks as a class.[3]

Sweeping aside the petty-bourgeois adventurism of the Trotskyites and the capitulationism of the right opportunists, our party firmly and confidently led the Soviet people along the Leninist path.

[1] Referring to policies defended by Leon Trotsky (1883–1940), party leader defeated by Stalin in 1927. —Ed.

[2] Prosperous peasants.—Ed.

[3] Defended by Nikolai Bukharin (1888–1938) and his supporters, ousted from power by Stalin in 1929. —Ed.

Socialist industrialization was the key task in the construction of socialism. . . . Socialist industrialization proceeded in the circumstances of capitalist encirclement and constant threat of attack by the aggressive forces of imperialism. This determined the extremely accelerated pace of the transformations and required the utmost mobilization of efforts and resources. In the U.S.S.R. industrialization was carried out without outside help, through internal resources and rigid economy. . . .

The successful fulfillment of the First Five-Year Plan at a time when the capitalist countries were in the grip of the most destructive world economic crisis vividly demonstrated the superiority of the socialist over the capitalist economic system. This victory raised high the U.S.S.R.'s international prestige.

Industrialization created the necessary material base for strengthening our country's economic independence, for the technical reconstruction of all branches of the national economy and for reorganizing agriculture on a new socialist foundation. Industrialization had enormous social-political significance. It consolidated public ownership in the decisive branches of the economy; ensured the ousting of capitalist elements in the towns, the triumph of the socialist mode of production in industry and the growth of the working class; and helped to strengthen the working class's role in society and to consolidate the U.S.S.R.'s economic and defense might. The socialist industry built by the people largely predetermined our victory in the Great Patriotic War.[4]

The reorganization of agriculture on socialist lines was the most complicated and difficult task after the seizure of power by the proletariat. It was necessary to overcome the age-old force of habit in

[4] German-Soviet war of 1941–1945.—Ed.

the petty proprietor, change his psychology and convince the peasantry of the advantages of the new life. . . .

Millions of small, private, peasant producers united in collective farms and embarked upon the path of socialism. In the course of collectivization a logical form of social farm management was found, the agricultural artel,[5] which made it possible to combine the peasants' social and personal interests; leftist attempts to introduce egalitarian distribution were overcome; and instances of violation of the principle of the peasants' voluntary enrollment in the cooperatives were eliminated. The establishment of the collective farms proceded in fierce struggle against the kulaks. The resistance of the exploiters in the countryside was broken by the efforts of the working class and the rural poor in close alliance with the middle peasants. On the basis of complete collectivization throughout the country, the last and most numerous exploiting class was liquidated.

The creation of large state enterprises in agriculture—the state farms and the Machine and Tractor Stations[6]—played a big role in the socialist transformation of the countryside. . . .

The experience of industrialization and collectivization in the U.S.S.R. has passed the test of history brilliantly and is being creatively utilized by many socialist countries, with due account for their own features and specific conditions.

For the successful building of socialism, it was necessary to carry out a cultural revolution. The Party was guided by Lenin's instructions that socialist culture can be established on the basis of assimilation and critical reworking of the spiritual heritage of the past, of all the treasures of world culture, while resolutely overcoming the exploiting classes' reactionary ideology and the survivals and prejudices of the past, on the basis of profoundly instilling the ideas of scientific communism in the consciousness of the working people.

A cultural revolution is an intricate and long process. Despite the difficult conditions of the country's cultural backwardness and the acute shortage of skilled cadres and resources, the state created a new system of public education, which ensured universal literacy, a rapid upswing of science and culture and the upbringing of the rising generation in the spirit of socialism. The best representatives of the old intelligentsia went over to the service of the people, and a new workers' and peasants' intelligentsia, dedicated to the cause of socialism, emerged.

A socialist, genuinely people's culture was established in the course of the cultural revolution. The greatest achievement of this revolution was the formation of the socialist consciousness of the masses of millions of working people.

In the process of socialist construction Lenin's Program on the national question was implemented, and the socialist fraternity of all the peoples of our ho. ıeland was established. Overcoming economic and cultural backwardness and the traces of former national friction, the Party and the Soviet regime patiently and consistently built up all-round cooperation of the peoples, who in December, 1922, voluntarily united in the Union of Soviet Socialist Republics. The formation of the U.S.S.R., recorded in the Soviet Con-

---

[5] Form of collective farm in which land, labor, and farm implements are owned in common but peasants keep their own houses and plots of land.—Ed.

[6] State farms are run as industrial enterprises with workers receiving regular wages; Machine and Tractor Stations, until dissolved in 1959, managed and operated the heavy farm machinery needed by the collective farms.—Ed.

stitution of 1924, was an event of enormous historical importance.

The October Revolution and the construction of socialism awakened and stirred into independent historical creativity formerly backward peoples, some of whom were saved from physical extinction. In the course of building socialism they acquired their own statehood, put an end to their economic and cultural backwardness and adapted to higher socialist forms of economy and culture. This triumph was all the more notable in that peoples who prior to the Revolution had been at the stage of feudalism or even the patriarchal-clan system bypassed capitalism in their progress toward socialism. All the peoples of the Soviet Union recognize that the Russian working class, the Russian people, had a big role in the implementation of the Leninist national policy.

Socialism ensures the peoples of the U.S.S.R. genuine equality in political, economic and cultural respects. Peoples at a lower level of economic development were given enormous economic assistance, and large capital investments were made to accelerate the development of industry, agriculture and culture. The reunification of the Ukrainian, Belorussian and Moldavian peoples, the restoration of Soviet rule in the Baltic republics and their entry into the Union of Soviet Socialist Republics were important milestones in the solution of the national question. . . .

The state of the dictatorship of the proletariat was the principal instrument for the building of socialism in the U.S.S.R. The supreme principle underlying the dictatorship of the proletariat is the alliance between the working class and the peasantry, with the working class in the leading role. The Soviet state has been an extremely great force, capable of organizing the creative labor of millions of people and ensuring the establishment of a new economy and culture and an upswing in the people's well-being. . . .

Soviet people did not stint their efforts; they consciously accepted hardships and set examples of courage and self-sacrifice in their work on behalf of overcoming the economic backwardness of the country and turning it into a great socialist power. The building of Magnitogorsk, the Kuznetsk Basin, the Turkestan-Siberian Railroad, the Dnieper Hydroelectric Station, the city of Komsomolsk-on-Amur and many other projects and the broad unfolding of socialist competition and shock work—all these were manifestations of the new, socialist attitude toward work. . . .

The triumph of socialism was formally recorded in the U.S.S.R. Constitution adopted in December, 1936, by the Extraordinary Eighth Congress of Soviets. The Constitution affirmed the socialist principles underlying the social and state organization of the U.S.S.R. and the broad social freedoms and rights of citizens, instituted a system of direct, equal and universal suffrage by secret ballot for elections to ruling bodies and expanded the representation in the supreme governing body of all the Union and autonomous republics, autonomous provinces and national regions. The political superstructure was brought into line with the economic foundation of socialism.

The development of the Soviet Union proceeded in a complicated international situation, in conditions of constant danger of imperialist aggression. This danger was particularly intensified when fascism, a barefaced terroristic and chauvinistic dictatorship of the most reactionary and aggressive forces of imperialism, seized power in Germany. Fascism entrenched itself and was able to carry out the rearming of Germany with the help of the American and British monopolies, which regarded it as the assault force of anti-communism.

The Communist Party and the Soviet government saw the danger represented by the policy of the fascist states, reckoned with the situation and took steps to strengthen the country's defense capacity. The Party carried out important measures to reorganize the work of industry and transportation in the light of the growing war danger. The defense industry built in the prewar years provided the country's armed forces with modern military equipment.

The Soviet government made energetic efforts to create a system of collective security in Europe in order to bar the way to war. These efforts encountered the resistance of Western politicians, the "men of Munich," who sought to direct fascist aggression against the U.S.S.R. and enter into an alliance with Hitler. In this complicated situation the Soviet Union concluded a nonaggression treaty with Germany, which upset the calculations of the imperialists and made it possible to win time for strengthening the country's defenses. But it proved impossible to avert war in the given circumstances. With the connivance of ruling circles in the West, Hitler Germany unleashed the second world war. After seizing many European states, it invaded the U.S.S.R.

The war forced upon the Soviet Union by German fascism on June 22, 1941, was the largest military clash between socialism and the assault forces of imperialism. It became the Great Patriotic War of the Soviet people for the freedom and independence of the socialist homeland, for socialism.

German imperialism set itself the objective of destroying the world's first socialist state, annihilating millions of people and enslaving the peoples of the Soviet Union and many other countries.

The Great Patriotic War was the most severe and brutal of all the wars ever experienced by our homeland. Particularly grim trials fell to our lot at the beginning of the war. The huge army of the Hitlerites and their satellites, mobilized beforehand and intoxicated with the poison of chauvinism and racism, cut deep into our territory. The enemy reached the foothills of the Caucasus, broke through to the Volga, laid siege to Leningrad and threatened Moscow. Mortal danger hung over the Soviet land.

The Hitlerites took advantage of their temporary advantages: the militarization of the German economy and all life in Germany; the long preparation for a war of aggrandizement and the experience gained in military operations in the West; their superiority in armaments and in the size of troops concentrated beforehand in the border zones. They had at their disposal the economic and military resources of almost the whole of Western Europe. In the European countries Hitler Germany had seized a whole arsenal of military equipment, huge stocks of metal, strategic raw materials and metallurgical and military plants. The Soviet Union had to enter into single combat with a colossal military machine.

Miscalculations in judging the timing of a possible attack against us by Hitler Germany and consequent shortcomings in the preparation for repelling the first blows played their part. Besides, at that time Soviet troops lacked experience in conducting large-scale operations in conditions of modern warfare. But even the early period of the war showed that the Hitlerites' military adventure was doomed to failure. The defeat of the Germans before Moscow was the beginning of the turning point in the course of the war. The Hitlerite plan for a Blitzkrieg was buried once and for all; the spurious legend of the Hitler army's "invincibility" was destroyed before the eyes of the whole world.

The entire Soviet people rose to the defense of their homeland. The country became a huge armed camp, with the single desire of smashing the enemy, driving him from Soviet soil and destroying fascism. The Party slogan "Everything for the front, everything for victory!" became an absolute law of life for the Soviet people. The Party took energetic steps in organizing the rout of the enemy and uniting the efforts of front and rear. The State Defense Committee was set up under the chairmanship of J. V. Stalin.[7] In the republics, territories and provinces the Party, Soviet, trade union and Young Communist organizations performed an enormous amount of work in mobilizing all forces and resources for defense.

Our heroic people, under the leadership of the Communist Party, succeeded in surmounting the difficulties of the early period of the war and in 1942–43 turned the tide against the enemy. The victory in the gigantic Battle of Stalingrad, the rout of the Hitler troops at Kursk and their major defeats in other battles were historic milestones on the road to the Soviet Union's victory over fascist Germany. The German fascist invaders were completely driven from the Soviet Union in 1944, and the offensives of the Soviet Army in the last year of the war played a decisive role in delivering the peoples of Austria, Albania, Bulgaria, Hungary, Norway, Poland, Rumania, Czechoslovakia and Yugoslavia from fascist occupation and in the final victory over the fascist coalition.

The Soviet people upheld the socialist homeland and the gains of the Great October Socialist Revolution. Fascism was overthrown. The war ended where it had originated. The shattered German fascist armies surrendered unconditionally. Militarist Japan was also put to rout. The U.S.S.R. gave military-political assistance to the revolutionary forces of China and Korea. The principal war criminals were tried, and received well-deserved punishment. World civilization was saved from the plague of fascism.

The victory over the German fascist invaders was won through the joint efforts of many peoples. A mighty anti-Hitler coalition took shape in the course of the war. Powerful blows were dealt the enemy by the armies of the Western Allies, and the allied troops of Poland, Czechoslovakia and Yugoslavia fought courageously. But it was the Soviet people and their heroic army that bore the main burden of the war and played the decisive role in the victory over Hitler Germany.

The war cost the Soviet people huge losses of life and great destruction. More than 20,000,000 Soviet people died on the battlefields, were buried beneath the ruins of cities and villages, were executed by the fascist bandits or were tortured to death in the Hitlerite concentration camps. It would be difficult to find a family that did not suffer the death of its nearest and dearest during the war. The bitterness of the losses inflicted in the war was boundless.

The material loss caused by the war was huge. The fascists razed more than 70,000 of our cities, settlements, towns and villages. The country lost nearly 30% of its national wealth. The mass barbarism and outrages committed on our soil by the fascist occupiers had no precedent in history.

[7] Special executive committee in charge of the conduct of the war and of related economic needs, set up by Stalin in July 1941.—Ed.

In this vast military collision with imperialism and its most monstrous creation, fascism, the socialist social and state system was victorious. The Soviet Union drew its strength from the socialist economy, the social-political and ideological unity of the society, Soviet patriotism, the friendship of the U.S.S.R.'s peoples, the solidarity of the people with the Communist Party and the unexampled heroism and courage of the Soviet troops. It was a victory of socialist ideology over the misanthropic ideology of imperialism and fascism.

In this war the Soviet people were victorious. As one man they rose to defend their homeland. This was unparalleled mass heroism, truly of the entire people.

In this war the Soviet Armed Forces were victorious. Created to defend the gains of the October Revolution, they have honorably held their battle standards high throughout the history of the Soviet state. The feats accomplished by the Soviet warriors during the Great Patriotic War shall never be forgotten. The great victory over fascism was also ensured by the superiority of Soviet military science and military art.

A struggle of the entire people was waged against the fascist occupiers behind enemy lines. . . .

The victory in the war was also a victory of the toilers who worked at the Soviet rear. . . . More than 1,360 large industrial enterprises were evacuated to eastern regions and quickly put into operation there. The eastern industrial base bore the main burden of supplying our army with armaments and equipment. During the war Soviet industry produced almost twice as much modern military equipment as Hitlerite Germany. . . .

During the years of severe war ordeals, the Communist Party stood at the head of the fighting people. It organized, inspired and ideologically armed the Soviet people for the struggle against the enemy. The finest sons of the Communist Party were in the forefront of the armed struggle against fascism. The Party reared and brought to the fore a galaxy of brilliant military leaders. Political workers, who included prominent figures in the Party and government, conducted extensive organizational, Party and political work in the army. By the end of the war there were more than 3,000,000 Communists at the front. The greatest influx of fighting men into the Party occurred during the hardest months of 1941 and 1942. Ours was truly a fighting Party.

The Soviet Union's victory in the Great Patriotic War was of world-historic significance. Conditions conducive to the development and triumph of socialist revolutions in European and Asian countries, for the emergence of the world socialist system, were created. The national-liberation struggle of peoples unfolded on a wide scale. The international forces of socialism and democracy grew stronger, and the positions of imperialism and reaction were weakened.

The outcome of the Soviet Union's Great Patriotic War most convincingly demonstrated that there are no forces on earth capable of crushing socialism, of bringing to their knees a people dedicated to the ideas of Marxism-Leninism, loyal to the socialist homeland and united around the Leninist party. This outcome is a stern warning to the imperialist aggressors and a stern and unforgettable lesson of history.

After winning the historic victory over a mortal enemy, the Soviet people set about further accomplishment of the plans of peaceful construction. The Party and government took energetic steps for the rapid rehabilitation of the cities and villages that had suffered most in the war years. Reconstruction of the national economy was carried on as soon as occupied regions were liberated. There was nothing in history to match the simultaneous large military offensives and rehabilitation work on such a huge scale. . . . By 1948 the prewar level of industrial output had been achieved in the main. . . .

Matters were much more complicated in agriculture, which had suffered particularly heavily in the war years. The collective-farm peasantry and the state farm workers displayed a high sense of duty and selflessness in labor by rehabilitating the war-ruined farms in a short period. By 1950 gross industrial output reached the prewar level. However, in the next few years the rate of growth in this important branch of the economy slowed down, causing certain difficulties in the supply of food for the public and of raw materials for light industry. This was to some extent explained by the fact that the possibilities of financing agriculture and providing it with material and technical supplies were limited in the initial postwar period. Also, the reserves inherent in the socialist mode of production for developing the collective and state farms were not fully utilized. The September, 1953, plenary session of the Party Central Committee adopted measures to give agriculture material and technical assistance and to increase the material interest of the collective farms and their members in the results of their labor. The development of the virgin and idle lands[8] was an additional source for increasing grain output.

The growth of material production made it possible to carry out a number of measures aimed at raising the public well-being. The wages of workers and employees were raised, old-age and disability pensions were increased considerably, the working week was reduced without cutting wages, and large-scale housing construction developed throughout the country. Fresh successes were achieved in science and technology and in the development of culture. In scope and level of education the Soviet land firmly took one of the leading places in the world.

The postwar conditions of development of Soviet society confronted the Communist Party with complicated and responsible tasks. Life confirmed the correctness of the Party's political course and showed its ability to give theoretical generalization to the experience of the masses, to put forward correct political slogans and to disclose mistakes and right them. In pursuing the course of further development of socialist democracy, the Party, at the 20th Congress, firmly condemned Stalin's personality cult, which had been expressed in glorification of the role of one person, something alien to the spirit of Marxism-Leninism, in departures from the Leninist principle of collective leadership, and in unwarranted repressions and other violations of socialist legality which inflicted harm on our society. These distortions, for all their gravity, did not alter the nature of socialist society, did not shake the pillars of socialism. The Party and the people believed deeply in the cause of communism, they worked with enthusiasm, carrying out the Leninist ideals and overcoming difficulties, temporary setbacks and mistakes.

The Party carried out measures to overcome the consequences of the personality cult in all spheres of Party, state and ideological work, and to secure the observance of the Leninist norms and prin-

[8] Program begun in 1954 for agricultural exploitation of semiarid regions of southern Siberia and northern Kazakhstan.—Ed.

ciples of Party life. The powers of the Union republics, territories and provinces in deciding matters of economic and cultural construction and the rights of executives of enterprises were extended. All this led to an activization of the country's social-political and spiritual life and of work at all levels of the Party, state and economic apparatus. The Soviet social and state system was further strengthened and developed, the social-political and ideological unity of the workers, peasants and intelligentsia became firmer, the friendship of the peoples of the Soviet Union grew, and they rallied closer around the Leninist party.

The complete, final victory of socialism is the principal result of the Soviet people's revolutionary transforming activity under the leadership of the Communist Party.

The formation of the world socialist system and the strengthening of the Soviet Union's economic and defense power changed the balance of forces in the world arena in favor of socialism, created a firm guarantee against the restoration of capitalism in the U.S.S.R. and ensured the complete victory of socialism. . . .

All the generations of Soviet people invested their labor, courage and wisdom in socialist construction. Mankind will always preserve the memory of the historic achievements of those who pioneered in the construction of socialism.

MILOVAN DJILAS (b. 1911) argues that the new political regime set up in the Soviet Union after 1917 was not really a class dictatorship of the proletariat led by the Communist party but rather a class dictatorship of the Communist bureaucracy. It managed the nationalized industry and commerce and collectivized agriculture, and thus held a virtual monopoly on the country's property. By Marxist criteria it was a class. Its exclusive control of political power produced, therefore, a new class dictatorship. Djilas, a leading Yugoslav Communist until 1954, was imprisoned in 1956 for having written *The New Class.* Freed in 1961, he was again arrested in 1962 following publication in the United States of his next book, *Conversations with Stalin.* He was finally released in 1966.*

Milovan Djilas

The New Class Dictatorship

Everything happened differently in the U.S.S.R. and other Communist countries from what the leaders—even such prominent ones as Lenin, Stalin, Trotsky, and Bukharin—anticipated. They expected that the state would rapidly wither away, that democracy would be strengthened. The reverse happened. They expected a rapid improvement in the standard of living—there has been scarcely any change in this respect and, in the subjugated East European countries, the standard has even declined. In every instance, the standard of living has failed to rise in proportion to the rate of industrialization, which was much more rapid. It was believed that the differences between cities and villages, between intellectual and physical labor, would slowly disappear; instead these differences have increased. Communist anticipations in other areas—including their expectations for developments in the non-Communist world—have also failed to materialize.

The greatest illusion was that industrialization and collectivization in the U.S.S.R., and destruction of capitalist ownership, would result in a classless society. In 1936, when the new Constitution was promulgated, Stalin announced that the "exploiting class" had ceased to exist. The capitalist and other classes of ancient origin had in fact been destroyed, but a new class, previously unknown to history, had been formed.

It is understandable that this class, like

*From Milovan Djilas, *The New Class: An Analysis of the Communist System* (New York: Frederick A. Praeger, 1957), pp. 33–39, 42–44, 48–51. Reprinted by permission. Footnotes omitted.

those before it, should believe that the establishment of its power would result in happiness and freedom for all men. The only difference between this and other classes was that it treated the delay in the realization of its illusions more crudely. It thus affirmed that its power was more complete than the power of any other class before in history, and its class illusions and prejudices were proportionally greater.

This new class, the bureaucracy, or more accurately the political bureaucracy, has all the characteristics of earlier ones as well as some new characteristics of its own. Its origin had its special characteristics also, even though in essence it was similar to the beginnings of other classes.

Other classes, too, obtained their strength and power by the revolutionary path, destroying the political, social, and other orders they met in their way. However, almost without exception, these classes attained power *after* new economic patterns had taken shape in the old society. The case was the reverse with new classes in the Communist systems. It did not come to power to *complete* a new economic order but to *establish* its own and, in so doing, to establish its power over society.

In earlier epochs the coming to power of some class, some part of a class, or of some party, was the final event resulting from its formation and its development. The reverse was true in the U.S.S.R. There the new class was definitely formed after it attained power. Its consciousness had to develop before its economic and physical powers, because the class had not taken root in the life of the nation. This class viewed its role in relation to the world from an idealistic point of view. Its practical possibilities were not diminished by this. In spite of its illusions, it represented an objective tendency toward industrialization. Its practical bent emanated from this tendency. The promise of an ideal world increased the faith in the ranks of the new class and sowed illusions among the masses. At the same time it inspired gigantic physical undertakings.

Because this new class had not been formed as a part of the economic and social life before it came to power, it could only be created in an organization of a special type, distinguished by a special discipline based on identical philosophic and ideological views of its members. A unity of belief and iron discipline was necessary to overcome its weaknesses.

The roots of the new class were implanted in a special party, of the Bolshevik type. Lenin was right in his view that his party was an exception in the history of human society, although he did not suspect that it would be the beginning of a new class.

To be more precise, the initiators of the new class are not found in the party of the Bolshevik type as a whole but in that stratum of professional revolutionaries who made up its core even before it attained power. It was not by accident that Lenin asserted after the failure of the 1905 revolution that only professional revolutionaries—men whose sole profession was revolutionary work—could build a new party of the Bolshevik type. It was still less accidental that even Stalin the future creator of a new class, was the most outstanding example of such a professional revolutionary. The new ruling class has been gradually developing from this very narrow stratum of revolutionaries. These revolutionaries composed its core for a long period. Trotsky noted that in pre-revolutionary professional revolutionaries was the origin of the future Stalinist bureaucrat. What he did not detect was the beginning of a new class of owners and exploiters. . . .

When Communist systems are being critically analyzed, it is considered that their fundamental distinction lies in the fact that a bureaucracy, organized in a special stratum, rules over the people. This is generally true. However, a more detailed analysis will show that only a special stratum of bureaucrats, those who are not administrative officials, make up the core of the governing bureaucracy, or, in my terminology, of the new class. This is actually a party or political bureaucracy. Other officials are only the apparatus under the control of the new class; the apparatus may be clumsy and slow but, no matter what, it must exist in every socialist society. It is sociologically possible to draw the borderline between the different types of officials, but in practice they are practically indistinguishable. This is true not only because the Communist system by its very nature is bureaucratic, but because Communists handle the various important administrative functions. In addition, the stratum of political bureaucrats cannot enjoy their privileges if they do not give crumbs from their tables to other bureaucratic categories.

It is important to note the fundamental differences between the political bureaucracies mentioned here and those which arise with every centralization in modern economy—especially centralizations that lead to collective forms of ownership such as monopolies, companies, and state ownership. The number of white-collar workers is constantly increasing in capitalistic monopolies, and also in nationalized industries in the West. In *Human Relations in Administration,* R. Dubin says that state functionaries in the economy are being transformed into a special stratum of society.

> . . . Functionaries have the sense of a common destiny for all those who work together. They share the same interests, especially since there is relatively little competition insofar as promotion is in terms of seniority. In-group aggression is thus minimized and this arrangement is therefore conceived to be positively functional for the bureaucracy. However, the esprit de corps and informal social organization which typically develops in such situations often leads the personnel to defend their entrenched interests rather than to assist their clientele and elected higher officials.

While such functionaries have much in common with Communist bureaucrats, especially as regards "esprit de corps," they are not identical. Although state and other bureaucrats in non-Communist systems form a special stratum, they do not exercise authority as the Communists do. Bureaucrats in a non-Communist state have political masters, usually elected, or owners over them, while Communists have neither masters nor owners over them. The bureaucrats in a non-Communist state are officials in modern capitalist economy, while the Communists are something different and new: a new class.

As in other owning classes, the proof that it is a special class lies in its ownership and its special relations to other classes. In the same way, the class to which a member belongs is indicated by the material and other privileges which ownership brings to him.

As defined by Roman law, property constitutes the use, enjoyment, and disposition of material goods. The Communist political bureaucracy uses, enjoys, and disposes of nationalized property.

If we assume that membership in this

bureaucracy or new owning class is predicated on the use of privileges inherent in ownership—in this instance nationalized material goods—then membership in the new party class, or political bureaucracy, is reflected in a larger income in material goods and privileges than society should normally grant for such functions. In practice, the ownership privilege of the new class manifests itself as an exclusive right, as a party monopoly, for the political bureaucracy to distribute the national income, to set wages, direct economic development, and dispose of nationalized and other property. This is the way it appears to the ordinary man who considers the Communist functionary as being very rich and as a man who does not have to work. . . .

Although he did not realize it, Lenin started the organization of the new class. He established the party along Bolshevik lines and developed the theories of its unique and leading role in the building of a new society. This is but one aspect of his many-sided and gigantic work; it is the aspect which came about from his actions rather than his wishes. It is also the aspect which led the new class to revere him.

The real and direct originator of the new class, however, was Stalin. He was a man of quick reflexes and a tendency to coarse humor, not very educated nor a good speaker. But he was a relentless dogmatician and a great administrator, a Georgian who knew better than anyone else whither the new powers of Greater Russia were taking her. He created the new class by the use of the most barbaric means, not even sparing the class itself. It was inevitable that the new class which placed him at the top would later submit to his unbridled and brutal nature. He was the true leader of that class as long as the class was building itself up, and attaining power.

The new class was born in the revolutionary struggle in the Communist Party, but was developed in the industrial revolution. Without the revolution, without industry, the class's position would not have been secure and its power would have been limited.

While the country was being industrialized, Stalin began to introduce considerable variations in wages, at the same time allowing the development toward various privileges to proceed. He thought that industrialization would come to nothing if the new class were not made materially interested in the process, by acquisition of some property for itself. Without industrialization the new class would find it difficult to hold its position, for it would have neither historical justification nor the material resources for its continued existence.

The increase in the membership of the party, or of the bureaucracy, was closely connected with this. In 1927, on the eve of industrialization, the Soviet Communist Party had 887,233 members. In 1934, at the end of the First Five-Year Plan, the membership had increased to 1,874,488. This was a phenomenon obviously connected with industrialization: the prospects for the new class and privileges for its members were improving. What is more, the privileges and the class were expanding more rapidly than industrialization itself. It is difficult to cite any statistics on this point, but the conclusion is self-evident for anyone who bears in mind that the standard of living has not kept pace with industrial production, while the new class actually seized the lion's share of the economic and other progress earned by the sacrifices and efforts of the masses.

The establishment of the new class did not proceed smoothly. It encountered bitter opposition from existing classes and from those revolutionaries who could not reconcile reality with the ideals of their struggle. In the U.S.S.R. the opposition of revolutionaries was most evident in the Trotsky-Stalin conflict. The conflict between Trotsky[1] and Stalin, or between oppositionists in the party and Stalin, as well as the conflict between the regime and the peasantry, became more intense as industrialization advanced and the power and authority of the new class increased.

Trotsky, an excellent speaker, brilliant stylist, and skilled polemicist, a man cultured and of excellent intelligence, was deficient in only one quality: a sense of reality. He wanted to be a revolutionary in a period when life imposed the commonplace. He wished to revive a revolutionary party which was being transformed into something completely different, into a new class unconcerned with great ideals and interested only in the everyday pleasures of life. He expected action from a mass already tired by war, hunger, and death, at a time when the new class already strongly held the reins and had begun to experience the sweetness of privilege. Trotsky's fireworks lit up the distant heavens; but he could not rekindle fires in weary men. He sharply noted the sorry aspect of the new phenomena but he did not grasp their meaning. In addition, he had never been a Bolshevik. This was his vice and his virtue. Attacking the party bureaucracy in the name of the revolution, he attacked the cult of the party and, although he was not conscious of it, the new class.

Stalin looked neither far ahead nor far behind. He had seated himself at the head of the new power which was being born—the new class, the political bureaucracy, and bureaucratism—and become its leader and organizer. He did not preach—he made decisions. He too promised a shining future, but one which bureaucracy could visualize as being real because its life was improving from day to day and its position was being strengthened. He spoke without ardor and color, but the new class was better able to understand this kind of realistic language. Trotsky wished to extend the revolution to Europe; Stalin was not opposed to the idea but this hazardous undertaking did not prevent him from worrying about Mother Russia or, specifically, about ways of strengthening the new system and increasing the power and reputation of the Russian state. Trotsky was a man of the revolution of the past; Stalin was a man of today and, thus, of the future.

In Stalin's victory Trotsky saw the Thermidoric reaction[2] against the revolution, actually the bureaucratic corruption of the Soviet government and the revolutionary cause. Consequently, he understood and was deeply hurt by the amorality of Stalin's methods. Trotsky was the first, although he was not aware of it, who in the attempt to save the Communist movement discovered the essence of contemporary Communism. But he was not capable of seeing it through to the end. He supposed that this was only a momentary cropping up of bureaucracy, corrupt-

[1] Marxist revolutionary from 1897, member of the Bolshevik party from 1917 and one of the leaders of the party between 1917 and 1924, expelled from the party in 1927, and assassinated by a Soviet secret police agent in 1940 in Mexico.—Ed.

[2] Defeat of the radical Jacobin leadership during the French Revolution and end of the period of revolutionary reforms.—Ed.

ing the party and the revolution, and concluded that the solution was in a change at the top, in a "palace revolution." When a palace revolution actually took place after Stalin's death, it could be seen that the essence had not changed; something deeper and more lasting was involved. The Soviet Thermidor of Stalin had not only led to the installation of a government more despotic than the previous one, but also to the installation of a class. This was the continuation of the other side of the coin, the violence of the revolution which had given birth and strength to the new class. . . .

Abstract logic would indicate that the Communist revolution, when it achieves, under different conditions and by state compulsion, the same things achieved by industrial revolutions and capitalism in the West, is nothing but a form of state-capitalist revolution.[3] The relationships which are created by its victory are state-capitalist. This appears to be even more true because the new regime also regulates all political, labor, and other relationships and, what is more important, distributes the national income and benefits and distributes material goods which actually have been transformed into state property.

Discussion on whether or not the relationships in the U.S.S.R. and in other Communist countries are state-capitalist, socialist, or perhaps something else, is dogmatic to a considerable degree. However, such discussion is of fundamental importance.

Even if it is presumed that state capitalism is nothing other than the "antechamber of socialism," as Lenin emphasized, or that it is the first phase of socialism, it is still not one iota easier for the people who live under Communist despotism to endure. If the character of property and social relationships brought about by the Communist revolution is strengthened and defined, the prospects for liberation of the people from such relationships become more realistic. If the people are not conscious of the nature of the social relationships in which they live, or if they do not see a way in which they can alter them, their struggle cannot have any prospect of success.

If the Communist revolution, despite its promises and illusions, is state-capitalist in its undertakings with state-capitalist relationships, the only lawful and positive actions its functionaries can take are the ones that improve their work and reduce the pressure and irresponsibility of state administration. The Communists do not admit in theory that they are working in a system of state capitalism, but their leaders behave this way. They continually boast about improving the work of the administration and about leading the struggle "against bureaucratism."

Moreover, actual relationships are not those of state capitalism; these relationships do not provide a method of improving the system of state administration basically.

In order to establish the nature of relationships which arise in the course of the Communist revolution and ultimately become established in the process of industrialization and collectivization, it is necessary to peer further into the role and manner of operation of the state under Communism. At present, it will be sufficient to point out that in Communism the state machinery is not the instrument which really determines social and prop-

[3] Defined by Marxists as the appropriation of the means of production by the bourgeois state, either by means of nationalization or through agreements with capitalist industry.—Ed.

erty relationships; it is only the instrument by which these relationships are protected. In truth, everything is accomplished in the name of the state and through its regulations. The Communist Party, including the professional party bureaucracy, stands above the regulations and behind ever single one of the state's acts.

It is the bureaucracy which formally uses, administers, and controls both nationalized and socialized property as well as the entire life of society. The role of the bureaucracy in society, i.e., monopolistic administration and control of national income and national goods, consigns it to a special privileged position. Social relations resemble state capitalism. The more so, because the carrying out of industrialization is effected not with the help of capitalists but with the help of the state machine. In fact, this privileged class performs that function, using the state machine as a cover and as an instrument.

Ownership is nothing other than the right of profit and control. If one defines class benefits by this right, the Communist states have seen, in the final analysis, the origin of a new form of ownership or of a new ruling and exploiting class.

In reality, the Communists were unable to act differently from any ruling class that preceded them. Believing that they were building a new and ideal society, they built it for themselves in the only way they could. Their revolution and their society do not appear either accidental or unnatural, but appear as a matter of course for a particular country and for prescribed periods of its development. Because of this, no matter how extensive and inhuman Communist tyranny has been, society, in the course of a certain period—as long as industrialization lasts—has to and is able to endure this tyranny. Furthermore, this tyranny no longer appears as something inevitable, but exclusively as an assurance of the depredations and privileges of a new class.

In contrast to earlier revolutions, the Communist revolution, conducted in the name of doing away with classes, has resulted in the most complete authority of any single new class. Everything else is sham and an illusion.

The 1967 "Theses" of the Communist party scarcely mention the role of Joseph Stalin in the victory of socialism in the Soviet Union. After Khrushchev's denunciation of Stalin in 1956, he passed from hero of all Soviet citizens to virtual nonperson. Yet his contributions to the transformation of the Soviet Union are too great to be ignored. Though he did tremendous harm to millions of Soviet citizens, within the party and without, the country under his leadership achieved great economic growth and contributed decisively to the defeat of the mightiest military power of the time, Nazi Germany. ALEC NOVE (b. 1915), professor of international economics at the University of Glasgow, examines the conditions which, in his opinion, made Stalin "necessary."*

Alec Nove

The Necessity for a Dictator

Stalin has suffered a dramatic post-mortem demotion, and a monument to his victims is to be erected in Moscow. The present Soviet leadership is thus dis-associating itself publicly from many of the highly disagreeable features of Stalin's rule, while claiming for the Party and the Soviet system the credit for making Russia a great economic and military power. Is this a logically consistent standpoint? How far was Stalin, or Stalinism, an integral, unavoidable, "neccessary" part of the achievements of the period? How much of the evil associated with the Stalin system is attributable to the peculiar character of the late dictator, and how much was the consequence of the policies adopted by the large majority of the Bolshevik party, or of the effort of a small and dedicated minority to impose very rapid industrialisation on a peasant country.?

To ask these questions is of interest from several standpoints. Firstly, in trying to answer them we might be able to see a little more clearly the meaning of such misused terms as "determinism," causality, or the role of personality in history, and so continue to explore some of the problems which E. H. Carr presented in so stimulating a way in his Trevelyan lectures. Secondly, an examination of the circumstances which brought Stalin to power and led to—or provided an opportunity for—crimes on a massive scale is

*From Alec Nove, "Was Stalin Really Necessary?" *Encounter* (April, 1962), pp. 86–92. Reprinted by permission of the publisher and of the author. Footnotes omitted.

surely of very practical interest, since it might help in understanding how to avoid a repetition of these circumstances, particularly in those under-developed countries which are being tempted by their very real difficulties to take the totalitarian road.

To some people, the word "neccessary" smacks of "historicism," of a belief in inevitability, or suggests that the author wishes to find some historic justification, a whitewash to be applied to Stalin and his system. This is far from being my intention. "Necessity" is used here with no moral strings attached. If I say that to travel to Oxford it is necessary to go to Paddington station, this implies no approval, moral or otherwise, of the service provided by the Western Region of British Railways, still less of the project of making the journey to Oxford. It is simply that *if* I wish to do A, it involves doing B.

It is true that there may be alternatives. One might, for instance, do not B but C, or D. Thus I could go to Oxford by car, or by bus. However, it could be that these physically possible methods are not in fact open to me; I may not own a car, and shortage of time precludes taking the bus. Thus a judgment on the "necessity" or otherwise of an action in pursuit of a given purpose requires some consideration of what could have been done instead.

The range of choice is not, in practice, limited only by what is *physically* possible. There are also actions which are excluded by religious or ideological principle. For example, it is not in fact open to a rabbi to eat a ham sandwich or an orthodox Hindu to eat cow-meat. Thus if an "alternative" happens to involve such acts, it is not *for them* an alternative at all. This is because, were they to act otherwise, they would cease to be what they in fact are. A rabbi does not eat pork; were he to do so, he would not be a rabbi. The fact that he is a rabbi would also affect his outlook, his "freedom" to choose between alternative modes of conduct, where religious law is less strict: for instance, there is nothing in the Talmud or in Deuteronomy about smoking on the Sabbath, but rabbis would tend to be the kind of people who, faced with this "new" problem, would give the answer "no."

Thus, to come nearer our subject, there may have been a number of solutions to the problems posed by Russia of the 'twenties which the Communists could not have chosen because they were Communists, and in considering the practical alternatives before them we have to bear this in mind. In doing so, we are by no means driven to any generalisations about the "inevitability" of the Russian revolution or of the Bolshevik seizure of power, and *a fortiori* we need not assume that non-Bolsheviks could not have found some other ways of coping with the problems of the period. (Indeed, though the problems would still have been acute, they might in important respects have been different.) Before his assassination in 1911, the last intelligent Tsarist prime minister, Stolypin, expressed the belief that his land reform measures would create in about twenty years a prosperous peasantry which would provide a stable foundation for society and the throne. No one will know if he would have been right, if he had not been murdered, if the Tsar had been wise, if Rasputin had not existed, if the war had not broken out. . . . But of what use is it to indulge in such speculations? A 19th-century Russian blank-verse play provides, if somewhat inaccurately, a relevant comment:

If, if, if grandma had a beard,
She would be grandpa. . . .

In assessing the choices open to the Bolsheviks in, say, 1926, the events before that date must be taken as given. The real question, surely, is to consider the practical alternatives which Stalin and his colleagues had before them.

In doing so, we should certainly not assume that what happened was inevitable. "Necessity" and "inevitable" are quite distinct concepts, though some critics seem to confuse them. Two simple and probably uncontroversial propositions will illustrate this: it was neccessary for 18th-century Poland to make drastic changes in its constitution if she were to survive as an independent state; and for China around 1890 a strong, modernising government was urgently necessary if many disasters were to be avoided. Yet the "necessary" steps were not taken and the disasters occurred. Unless we believe that whatever was not avoided was for that reason unavoidable, we would wish to examine the actions which men took, their choices between *available* alternatives, and see whether viable alternatives in fact existed. . . .

Now on to Stalin, or rather to Stalinism, since the idea of "necessity" does not of course mean that the leader had to be a Georgian with a long moustache, but rather a tough dictator ruling a totalitarian state of the Stalinist type. What were the practical alternatives before the Bolsheviks in the late 'twenties, which contributed to the creation of the Stalinist régime, or, if one prefers a different formulation, gave the opportunity to ambitious men to achieve so high a degree of absolutism?

The key problem before the Bolsheviks concerned the linked questions of industrialisation and political power. They felt they had to industrialise for several reasons, some of which they shared with non-Bolshevik predecessors. Thus the Tsarist minister, Count Witte,[1] as well as Stalin, believed that to achieve national strength and maintain independence, Russia needed a modern industry, especially heavy industry. The national-defence argument, re-labelled "defence of the revolution," was greatly strengthened by the belief that the Russian revolution was in constant danger from a hostile capitalist environment, militarily and technically far stronger than the U.S.S.R. Then there was the belief that the building of socialism or communism involved industrialisation, and, more immediately, that a "proletarian dictatorship" was insecure so long as it ruled in an overwhelmingly petty-bourgeois, peasant, environment. There had to be a large increase in the number and importance of the proletariat, while the rise of a rich "kulak" class in the villages was regarded as a dangerous (or potentially dangerous) resurgence of capitalism. It was clear, by 1927, that it was useless to wait for "world revolution" to solve these problems. These propositions were common to the protagonists of the various platforms of the middle 'twenties. Thus even the "moderate" Bukharin[2] wrote: "If there were a fall in the relative weight of the working class in its political and its social and class power, . . . this would subvert the basis of the proletarian dictatorship, the basis of our government." He too spoke in prin-

[1] Minister of Finance under Nicholas II from 1892 to 1903.—Ed.

[2] Leading party theoretician and defender in the 1920s of a policy of restrained industrialization. —Ed.

ciple of the "struggle against the kulak, against the capitalist road," and warned of the "kulak danger." He too, even in the context of an attack on Zinoviev and the "left" opposition,[3] argued the need for "changing the production relations of our country."

Until about 1927, a rapid rise in industrial production resulted from (or, "was a result of") the reactivation of pre-revolutionary productive capacity, which fell into disuse and disrepair in the civil war period. However, it now became urgent to find material and financial means to expand the industrial base. This at once brought the peasant problem to the fore. The revolution had distributed land to 25 million families, most of whom were able or willing to provide only small marketable surpluses. Supplies of food to the towns and for export fell, peasant consumption rose. Yet the off-farm surplus must grow rapidly to sustain industrialisation, especially where large-scale loans from abroad could scarcely be expected. As the "left" opposition vigorously pointed out, the peasant, the bulk of the population, had somehow to be made to contribute produce and money, to provide the bulk of "primitive Socialist accumulation."[4]

The arguments around these problems were inextricably entangled in the political factional struggles of the 'twenties. The moderate wing, led by Bukharin, believed that it was possible to advance slowly towards industrialisation "at the pace of a tortoise," a pace severely limited by what the peasant was willing to do voluntarily. This was sometimes described as "riding towards socialism on a peasant nag." The logic of this policy demanded priority for developing consumers' goods industries, to make more cloth to encourage the peasants to sell more food. At first, Stalin sided with the moderates.

The case against the Bukharin line was of several different kinds. Firstly, free trade with the peasants could only provide adequate surpluses if the better-off peasants (*i.e.*, those known as *kulaks*) were allowed to expand, since they were the most efficient producers and provided a large part of the marketable produce. Yet all the Bolshevik leaders (including, despite momentary aberrations, Bukharin himself) found this ideologically and politically unacceptable. A strong group of independent, rich peasants was Stolypin's[5] dream as a basis for Tsardom. It was the Bolshevik's nightmare, as totally inconsistent in the long run with their rule or with a socialist transformation of "petty-bourgeois" Russia. But this made the Bukharin approach of doubtful internal consistency. This was understood at the time by intelligent non-party men. Thus the famous economist Kondratiev, later to perish in the purges, declared in 1927: "If you want a higher rate of accumulation . . . then the stronger elements of the village must be allowed to exploit (the weaker)," in other words that the "kulaks" must expand their holdings and employ landless labourers. The "peasant nag" could not pull the cart; or it, and the peasant, would pull in the wrong direction.

A second reason concerned the pace of the tortoise. The Bolsheviks were in a hurry. They saw themselves threatened by "imperialist interventionists." Even though some war scares were manufac-

[3] Opposed in 1925–1927 to policies of Stalin and Bukharin of support for the private peasant economy.—Ed.

[4] Investment capital to be used by Soviet state for industrialization.—Ed.

[5] Minister of the Interior under Nicholas II from 1906 to 1911.—Ed.

tured for factional reasons, the Party as a whole believed that war against them would come before very long. This argued not merely for speed, but also for priority to *heavy* and not light industry, since it provided a basis for an arms industry. Still another reason was a less tangible but still very real one: the necessity of maintaining political *élan,* of not appearing to accept for an indefinite period a policy of gradualism based on the peasant, which would have demoralised the Party and so gravely weakened the régime. It was widely felt, in and out of Russia, that by 1927 the régime had reached a *cul-de-sac.* I have in front of me a contemporary Menshevik[6] pamphlet published abroad, by P. A. Garvi, which describes its dilemma quite clearly, and indeed the political and economic problem was extremely pressing: to justify its existence, to justify the Party dictatorship in the name of the proletariat, a rapid move forward was urgent; but such a move forward would hardly be consistent with the "alliance with the peasants" which was the foundation of the policy of the moderates in the 'twenties. Stalin at this point swung over towards the left, and his policy of all-out industrialisation and collectivisation was a means of breaking out of the *cul-de-sac,* of mobilising the Party to smash peasant resistance, to make possible the acquisition of farm surpluses without having to pay the price which any free peasants or free peasant associations would have demanded. He may well have felt he had little choice. It is worth quoting from the reminiscences of another Menshevik, who in the late 'twenties was working in the Soviet planning organs: "The financial base of the first five-year plan, *until Stalin found it in levying tribute on the peasants, in primitive accumulation by the methods of Tamerlane,* was extremely precarious. . . . (It seemed likely that) everything would go to the devil. . . . No wonder that no one, literally no one, of the well-informed economists, believed or could believe in the fulfilment (of the plan)."

[6] Moderate Marxist party in Russia opposed to the Bolsheviks.—Ed.

It does not matter in the present context whether Stalin made this shift through personal conviction of its necessity, or because this seemed to him to be a clever power-manoeuvre. The cleverness in any case largely consisted in knowing that he would thus strengthen his position by becoming the spokesman of the view which was widely popular among Party activists. The "leftists," destroyed organisationally by Stalin in earlier years, had a considerable following. Stalin's left-turn brought many of them to his support—though this did not save them from being shot in due course on Stalin's orders. It is probably the case that he had at this time genuine majority support within the Party for his policy, though many had reservations about certain excesses, of which more will be said. But if this be so, the policy as such cannot be attributed to Stalin personally, and therefore the consequences which flowed from its adoption must be a matter of more than personal responsibility.

Let us examine some of these consequences. Collectivisation could not be voluntary. Rapid industrialisation, especially with priority for heavy industry, meant a reduction in living standards, despite contrary promises in the first five-year plans. This meant a sharp increase in the degree of coercion, in the powers of the police, in the unpopularity of the régime. The aims of the bulk of the people were bound to be in conflict with the aims of the Party. It should be added that this conflict is probably bound to arise in some form wherever *the state* is responsible for financing rapid industrialisation; the sacrifices are then imposed by political authority, and the masses of "small" people do not and cannot provide voluntarily the necessary savings, since in the nature of things their present abstinence cannot be linked with a future return which they as individuals can identify. However, this possibly unavoidable unpopularity was greatly increased in the U.S.S.R. by the sheer pace of the advance and by the attack on peasant property, and, as we shall see, both these factors reacted adversely on production of consumers' goods and so led to still further hardships and even greater unpopularity. The strains and priorities involved in a rapid move forward required a high degree of economic centralisation, to prevent resources from being diverted to satisfy needs which were urgent but of a non-priority character. In this situation, the Party was the one body capable of carrying out enormous changes and resisting social and economic pressures in a hostile environment; this was bound to affect its structure. For a number of years it had already been in process of transformation from a political into a power machine. The problems involved in the "revolution from above" intensified the process of turning it into an obedient instrument for changing, suppressing, controlling.

This, in turn, required hierarchical subordination, in suppression of discussion; therefore there had to be an unquestioned commander-in-chief. Below him, toughness in executing unpopular orders became the highest qualification for Party office. The emergence of Stalin, and of Stalin-type bullying officials of the sergeant-major species, was accompanied by the decline in the importance of the cosmopolitan journalist-intellectual type of party leader who had played so prominent a role earlier.

The rise of Stalin to supreme authority was surely connected with the belief among many Party members that he was the kind of man who could cope with this kind of situation. Of course, it could well be that Stalin tended to adopt policies which caused him and his type to be regarded as indispensable, and he promoted men to office in the Party because they were loyal to him. Personal ambition, a desire for power, were important factors in shaping events. But this is so obvious, so clearly visible on the surface, that the underlying problems, policy choices and logical consequences of policies need to be stressed.

Let us recapitulate: the Communists needed dictatorial power if they were to continue to rule; if they were to take effective steps towards industrialisation these steps were bound to give rise to problems which would require further tightening of political and economic control. While we cannot say, without much further research, whether a Bukharinite or other moderate policy was impossible, once the decision to move fast was taken this had very radical consequences; the need for a tough, coercive government correspondingly increased. Given the nature of the Party apparatus, the mental and political development of the Russian masses, the logic of police rule, these policies were bound to lead to a conflict with the peasantry and to excesses of various kinds. Thus, given the premises, certain elements of what may be called Stalinism followed, were objective "necessities." In this sense, and to this extent, Stalin was, so to speak, operating within the logical consequences of Leninism.

It is an essential part of Lenin's views that the Party was to seize power and use it to change Russian society; this is what distinguished him from the Mensheviks who believed that conditions for socialism should ripen within society. Lenin also suppressed opposition parties and required stern discipline from his own followers. (It is impossible to ban free speech outside the Party without purging the Party of those who express "wrong" views within it.) Indeed Lenin promoted Stalin because he knew he was tough, would "prepare peppery dishes," though he had last-minute regrets about it. While it would be going too far to describe Stalin as a true Leninist, if only because Lenin was neither personally brutal nor an oriental despot, Stalin undoubtedly carried through some of the logical consequences of Lenin's policies and ideas. This remains true even though Lenin thought that the peasant problem could be solved by voluntary inspiration, and would probably have recoiled at the conditions of forced collectivisation.

Is it necessary to stress that this does not make these actions right, or good? Yes, it is, because so many critics assume that to explain is to justify. So it must be said several times that no moral conclusions follow, that even the most vicious acts by politicians and others generally have causes which must be analysed. We are here only concerned to disentangle the special contribution of Stalin, the extent to which Stalinism was, so to speak, situation-determined. This is relevant, indeed, to one's picture of Stalin's personal responsibility, but in no way absolves him of such responsibility. If in order to do A it proves necessary to do B, we can, after all, refuse to do B, abandon or modify the aim of attaining A, or resign, or, in extreme circumstances—like Stalin's old comrade Ordzhonikidze—commit suicide.

But Stalin's personal responsibility goes far beyond his being the voice and leader of a party majority in a given historical situation. For one cannot possibly argue that all the immense evils of the Stalin era flowed inescapably from the policy decisions of 1928–29. In assessing Stalin's personal role in bringing these evils about, it is useful to approach the facts from two angles. There was, first, the category of evils which sprang from policy choices which Stalin made and which he need not have made; in other words we are here concerned with consequences (perhaps necessary) of unnecessary decisions. The other category consists of evil actions which can reasonably be attributed to Stalin and which are his direct responsibility.

Of course, these categories shade into one another, as do murder and manslaughter. In the first case, the evils were in a sense situation-determined, but Stalin had a large hand in determining the situation. In the second, his guilt is as clear as a politician's guilt can be.

The most obvious examples of the first category are: the brutality of collectivisation and the madly excessive pace of industrial development. In each case, we are dealing with *"excessive excesses,"* since we have already noted that collectivisation without coercion was impossible, and rapid industrialisation was bound to cause stresses and strains.

Take collectivisation first. Some overzealous officials were presumably bound to overdo things, especially since the typical Party man was a townsman with no understanding or sympathy for peasants and their problems. But these officials received orders to impose rapid collectivisation, to deport *kulaks,* to seize all livestock, and Stalin was surely the source of these orders. The deportation of the *kulaks* (which in reality meant anyone who voiced opposition to collectivisation) removed at one blow the most efficient farmers. There had been no serious preparation of the measures, no clear orders about how a collective farm should be run. Chinese experience, at least before the communes, suggests that milder ways of proceeding are possible. In any event, the attempt to collectivise all private livestock ended in disaster and a retreat. It is worth reproducing the figures from the official handbook of agricultural statistics:

Livestock Population
(Million of Head)

	1928	*1934*
Horses	32.1	15.4
Cattle	60.1	33.5
Pigs	22.0	11.5
Sheep	97.3	32.9

Yet already by 1934 private livestock holdings were again permitted, and in 1938 over three-quarters of all cows, over two-thirds of all pigs, nearly two-thirds of all sheep, were in private hands. This is evidence of a disastrous error.

Its consequences were profound. Peasant hostility and bitterness were greatly intensified. For many years there were in fact no net investments in agriculture, since the new tractors merely went to replace some of the slaughtered horses. Acute food shortage made itself felt—though the state's control over produce ensured that most of those who died in the resulting famine were peasants and not townsmen. But once all this happened, the case for coercion was greatly strengthened, the need for police measures became more urgent than ever, the power of the censorship was increased, freedom of speech had still further to be curtailed, as part of the necessities of remaining in power and continuing the industrial revolution in an environment grown more hostile as a result of such policies. So Stalin's policy decisions led to events which contributed greatly to the further growth of totalitarianism and the police state.

The same is true of the attempt to do the impossible on the industrial front in the years of the first five-year plan. Much of the effort was simply wasted, as when food was taken from hungry peasants and exported to pay for machines which rusted in the open or were wrecked by untrained workmen. At the same time, the closing of many private workshops deprived the people of consumers' goods which the state, intent on building steelworks and machine-shops, was quite unable to provide. Again, living standards suffered, the hatred of many citizens for the régime increased, the N.K.V.D.[7] had to be expanded and the logic of police rule followed. But Stalin had a big role in the initial decisions to jump too far too fast. (It is interesting to note that Mao, who should have learnt the lessons of history, repeated many of these mistakes in China's "great leap forward" of 1958–59, which suggests that *there are certain errors which Communists repeatedly commit,* possibly due to the suppression, in "anti-rightist" campaigns, of the voices of moderation and common sense.)

One of the consequences of these acute hardships was isolation from foreign countries. Economists often speak of the "demonstration effect," *i.e.,* of the effect of the knowledge of higher living standards abroad on the citizens of poor and under-developed countries. This knowl-

---

[7] Soviet secret police.—Ed.

edge may act as a spur to effort—but it also generates resistance to sacrifice. Stalin and his régime systematically "shielded" Soviet citizens from knowledge of the outside world, by censorship, by cutting off personal contacts, by misinformation. The need to do so, in their eyes, was greatly increased by the extent of the drop in living standards in the early 'thirties.

But we must now come to Stalin's more direct contribution to the brutality and terrorism of the Stalin era.

There was, firstly, his needless cruelty which showed itself already in the methods used to impose collectivisation. The great purges were surely not "objectively necessary." To explain them one has to take into account Stalin's thirst for supreme power, his intense pathological suspiciousness, *i.e.,* matters pertaining to Stalin's personal position and character. These led him to massacre the majority of the "Stalinist" central committee elected in 1934, who had supported or at the very least tolerated Stalin's policies up to that date. The facts suggest that they believed that relaxation was possible and desirable; many of them seem to have died for the crime of saying so. Nor was there any "police logic" for the scale and drastic nature of the purges. Indeed, the police chiefs figured prominently among the victims. True, there was a kind of "snowballing" of arrests, which might have got out of control in 1938, but this was due largely to the effect of the terror on the police, who had to show zeal or go under. Nor can any "necessity" explain the post-war repressions, the death of Voznesensky, the so-called "Leningrad affair," the shooting of the Jewish intellectuals, the "doctors' plot." Stalin played so prominently a personal role in establishing a reign of terror in the Party and the country that he must bear direct responsibility even where executions were the result of false information supplied to him by his subordinates for reasons of their own. . . .

Of much more general significance is the fact that the events prior to 1934, including the building up of Stalin into an all-powerful and infallible dictator (by men many of whom he afterwards massacred), cannot be disassociated with what followed; at the very least they provided Stalin with his opportunity. This is where the historian must avoid the twin and opposite pitfalls of regarding what happened as inevitable, and regarding it as a chapter of "personalised" accidents. At each stage there are choices to be made, though the range of possible choices is generally much narrower than people suppose. In 1928 any practicable Bolshevik programme would have been harsh and unpopular. It might not have been *so* harsh and unpopular but for choices which need not necessarily have been made. If before 1934, *i.e.,* in the very period of maximum social coercion, Stalin truly represented the will of the Party, and Khrushchev argues that he did, some totalitarian consequences logically follow. One of these, as already suggested, is the semi-militarised party led by a *Fuehrer,* a dictator, because without an unquestioned leader the consequences of the policies adopted could not be faced.

But, even if it is true that the triumph of a dictator may be explained by objective circumstances which certainly existed in the Soviet situation, the acts of a dictator once he has "arrived" involve a considerable (though of course not infinite) degree of personal choice. Those who gave him the opportunity to act in an arbitrary and cruel way, who adopted policies which involved arbitrariness and coercion on a big scale, cannot ascribe subsequent events to the wickedness of one man or his immediate associates and claim that their hands are clean, even indeed if they were shot themselves on Stalin's orders. The whole-hog Stalin, in other words, was not "necessary," but the possibility of a Stalin was a necessary consequence of the effort of a minority group to keep power and to carry out a vast social-economic revolution in a very short time. And *some* elements of Stalinism were, in those circumstances, scarcely avoidable.

The serious problem for us is to see how far certain elements of Stalinism, in the sense of purposefully-applied social coercion, imposed by a party in the name of an ideology, are likely or liable to accompany rapid economic development even in non-Communist countries.

For it is surely true that many of the problems tackled by Stalin so brutally are present elsewhere, though events in the U.S.S.R. were, of course, deeply affected by peculiar features of Russia and of Bolshevism. The West should indeed emphasise the high cost in human and material terms of a Stalin, and show that the rise of such a man to supreme power in the Soviet Union was, to use the familiar Soviet-Marxist jargon phrase, "not accidental." Indeed, some Western historians who normally write "personalist" and empiricist history will begin to see the virtues of an approach they normally deride as "historicist"; they will analyse Soviet history to establish patterns, regularities, "necessities" which lead to Stalin. By contrast, an embarrassed Khrushchev will be—is being—forced to give an un-Marxist emphasis to personal and accidental factors.

But, of course, we must not confine our search for "necessities" in history only to instances which happen to serve a propagandist purpose. This would be a typically Soviet approach to historiography, only in reverse. It is particularly important to think very seriously about the inter-relationship of coercion and industrialisation, about the nature of the obstacles and vicious circles which drive men to think in totalitarian terms. Unless we realise how complex are the problems which development brings, how irrelevant are many of our ideas to the practical possibilities open to statesmen in these countries, we may unconsciously drive them towards the road which led to Stalin. They cannot be satisfied with "the pace of a tortoise."

Stalin's individual contribution may be less important than the political institutions and practices by which he ruled the Soviet Union. There were many formidable tasks confronting the Bolsheviks after November 1917 for which their own prerevolutionary political life gave them no preparation. RICHARD LOWENTHAL (b. 1908), professor of international relations at the Free University of Berlin and author of *World Communism: The Disintegration of a Secular Faith* (1964), stresses the importance of the Bolsheviks' decision to convert their revolutionary dictatorship into a "totalitarian single-party state." These new political institutions were created to "twist the development of society in the preconceived direction indicated by the ideology." However, the victory of totalitarianism meant the defeat of the original Bolshevik ideological goals.*

Richard Lowenthal

The Rise of the Totalitarian State

In the completed form which it reached in Russia from about 1921, and in which it has made its way around the world, the totalitarian single-party State may be defined by four main institutional characteristics. The first is the monopolistic control of the State by the ruling party, excluding the toleration of other, independent parties in opposition or even as genuine partners in coalition, and leading logically also to a ban on the formation of organized tendencies of "factions" *within* the ruling party; this amounts in effect to a monopoly of political initiative and decision for the inner leadership of that party, and ultimately to a monopoly of decision for a single leader. The second is the party's monopolistic control of all forms of social organization, depriving these organizations of their role as independent interest groups as exercised in non-totalitarian, "pluralistic" societies and converting them into as many tools for the mobilization, education, and control of their members by the ruling party; this enables the totalitarian regime to supplement the levers of the state bureaucracy for controlling the actions of its subject "from above" with a network of organizations enveloping them from cradle to grave, while preventing the formation of any independent groups. The third is the monopolistic control of all channels of public communication, from the press and other mass media to all forms of education, of literature and art,

*From Richard Lowenthal, "The Model of the Totalitarian State," in *The Impact of the Russian Revolution, 1917–1967* (New York: Oxford University Press, 1967), pp. 275–276, 279–280, 282–291. Footnotes omitted.

with the aim not merely of preventing the *expression* of hostile or undesirable opinions by a kind of censorship, but of controlling the *formation* of opinion at the source by planned selection of all the elements of information. The fourth is what Lenin himself used as the definition of dictatorship—"the removal of all legal limitations on state power," in other words, the possibility to use state power in arbitrary and terroristic ways whenever this is deemed expedient for the purposes of the regime. It is essentially the combination of these four characteristics which has enabled the totalitarian regimes of our time to extend the effectiveness of state power beyond anything that was deemed possible before 1917.

This institutional scheme had not been conceived by the Bolsheviks in advance. We may apply to it the words of J. L. Talmon about another regime with which their rule has often been compared: "Jacobin dictatorship was an improvisation. It came into existence by stages, and not in accordance with a blueprint. At the same time, it corresponded to, and was the consequence of, a fixed attitude of mind of its authors, intensified and rendered extreme by events."

In the Bolshevik case, however, this attitude of mind had long created its appropriate body in the centralistic organizational structure of the party that seized power on 7 November 1917. Lenin had consciously created his "party of a new type" as an instrument for the revolutionary conquest of power; and even though, in writing *What is to be Done,*[1] he had been far from envisaging the concrete forms that party's domination was to take fifteen or twenty years later, the possibility of a totalitarian party dictatorship was implied in the shape of that instrument. Without the pre-existing "party of a new type," the first State of the new type could not have been built up; with that party once victorious, the tendency for its leaders to establish dictatorial, monopolistic rule was given—to be brought out "by events". . . .

Even so, Lenin at first sincerely rejected the implication that he was aiming at a party dictatorship in Russia. We do not know just when he came to regard such a regime as the necessary political form for the "dictatorship of the proletariat," but we do know that up to the First World War he considered that a dictatorship of the proletariat was not yet on the agenda of Russian history. During the revolution of 1905, he aimed at the overthrow of Tsarism by an alliance of workers and peasants, and at the formation of a coalition government of Social-Democrats and Social-Revolutionaries[2] as its political expression. It was only the shock of the war of 1914 that convinced Lenin that a socialist revolution had become an immediate task internationally, and that it was therefore the duty of socialists even in backward Russia to go beyond the overthrow of Tsarism and the establishment of a "bourgeois-democratic" regime and to set up the power of the proletariat in order to contribute to the fulfilment of the international task.

When Lenin, after his return to Russia in April 1917, began to propagate this new concept, first within and then beyond his party, he did so under the slogan "All Power to the Soviets." Yet while he emphasized the Soviets[3] as the direct organs of proletarian rule, the opposition of all other socialist parties to this programme convinced him that the establishment of

[1] Written in 1902.—Ed.

[2] Revolutionary party defending the peasantry.—Ed.

[3] Councils representing the workers and soldiers in the cities.—Ed.

that rule depended on the Bolsheviks acquiring control of the Soviets first. In the course of 1917, the Bolsheviks ceased in Lenin's mind to be merely the most enlightened and energetic representatives of the interests of the Russian working class and became, to him, the *only* party of the Russian proletariat; and this implied that the "dictatorship of the proletariat" must in fact take the form of a Bolshevik party dictatorship.

This crucial identification of party and class appears as a matter of course in all Lenin's writings during the months immediately preceding the seizure of power. It becomes most explicit on the very eve of victory in his pamphlet *Can the Bolsheviks Retain State Power?*, in which the Soviets—the directly elected representatives of the workers, soldiers, and peasants—are openly and unceremoniously treated as the new "state apparatus" by means of which the victorious Bolsheviks will exercise and maintain *their* power and carry out *their* policy. It was a consequence of this outlook, not yet understood at the time even by many leading Bolsheviks, that Lenin after 7 November consistently rejected all proposals for a coalition with the Mensheviks and accepted as temporary partners in the new regime only those Left Social-Revolutionaries whom he regarded as representing the peasants in the process of agrarian revolution. It was another consequence that he dispersed the Constitutent Assembly,[4] elected *after* the Bolshevik assumption of power, when its large non-Bolshevik majority refused to vote a blanket endorsement of all the revolutionary measures already enacted by the new regime.

By the time of the October Revolution, then, Lenin was determined to establish a revolutionary dictatorship of his party. But this did not mean that he had, even then, a plan or blue-print for a totalitarian single-party State. What was clear in his mind was the last of our four characteristics of such a State—the rejection of any legal limitations on the revolutionary power. This was sufficient to enable him to suppress resistance to his policy as the need arose. But as resistance developed into civil war, determination to break it was no longer enough: to maintain and defend the revolutionary government, a new state machine had to be created. . . .

Yet while the Bolshevik regime of the Civil War years was clearly a terrorist dictatorship—"Red Terror" was officially proclaimed as a policy after the attempt on Lenin's life in August 1918— and while the dictatorial party increasingly merged with the new state machine in process of construction, it did not yet create a totalitarian single-party State as we have come to know it since. As late as 1920, there were many hundreds of Mensheviks in the provincial Soviets, and Martov[5] himself was able in the Moscow Soviet to voice their protest against the arbitrary suppression of "working-class democracy" and to advocate their programme for economic recovery that anticipated the later New Economic Policy of the Bolsheviks. Important trade unions were still under Menshevik control, and the Bolshevik leaders were under no illusion that the influence of their critics among the workers was increasing as the Civil War drew to a close. Discontent and indiscipline had moreover affected so many of the Bolsheviks' own militants that spontaneous co-operation between Mensheviks and

[4] Originally called to prepare a new constitution for Russia and made up of representatives elected by universal suffrage.—Ed.

[5] Leader of the Menshevik party and Marxist intellectual.—Ed.

those undisciplined Bolsheviks produced surprise majorities against the "party line" in Soviets or trade unions more than once. It was only after the end of the Civil War, in early 1921, at a time of growing unrest among both workers and peasants culminating in the Kronstadt rising,[6] and simultaneously with the decision to introduce the New Economic Policy, that Lenin decided to put his regime on a more secure institutional basis. To understand the decision that produced the first modern totalitarian regime, we must try to envisage the problems that faced him.

The classical tasks of a Jacobin revolutionary dictatorship had been fulfilled. The counter-revolution had been defeated, the power of the former ruling classes broken for good. But the expectation that the Bolshevik victory in Russia would be the immediate prelude to socialist revolutions in the advanced countries of Europe had not come true: the "dictatorship of the proletariat"—in fact of a minority party claiming to represent the proletariat—had remained isolated in a backward country in which the proletariat formed a minority, and in which, as Lenin knew and recognized, the economic and cultural preconditions for a socialist system were lacking. To overcome the discontent born out of economic paralysis, to begin the work of recovery after the devastations of war and civil war, major economic concessions to all the remaining non-proletarian strata—to the peasant majority above all, but also to the traders and technicians—were inevitable; the "war communist" fantasies of a straight leap into Utopia had to give way to a policy of patiently creating, in cooperation with all classes, the productive resources which elsewhere had been created by capitalism, and which alone could eventually form the basis for a socialist economy. It seemed the typical situation for a "Thermidor"—for liquidating the revolutionary dictatorship that had done its work; and that was indeed what the Mensheviks suggested with growing confidence in their own judgment.

Yet Lenin drew a different conclusion. He agreed on the need for a break with utopian dreams, for material concessions to all productive classes, for shifting the emphasis in Russia from political revolution to economic evolution; but he insisted that the 'proletarian' dictatorship must be maintained during the new phase as well, in order to ensure that evolution was accomplished by what he termed state capitalism—under the control of a State which would maintain Russia's independence from the capitalist world and prevent the restoration of a class of capitalist owners, even while accomplishing the task which capitalism had fulfilled in the advanced countries, and would thus preserve the foundations for the later transition to socialism as well as a stronghold for the international revolutionary movement. The Bolsheviks must hold on to their dictatorial power—no longer primarily as a revolutionary dictatorship, but as a special type of a dictatorship of development. It is from this decision that the truly unique course of the Russian Revolution begins; it is from this decision, too, that the need to create a system of totalitarian institutions has resulted.

The new need, as Lenin saw it, was no longer the comparatively simple one of fighting the class enemy arms in hand: it was to harness the economic energies of non-proletarian classes for a constructive task, to grant them a place in society for a whole period—yet to prevent them from influencing the direction of eco-

[6] Revolt of the radical sailors of the Kronstadt naval base near Leningrad against the Bolshevik regime.—Ed.

nomic and social development. As Lenin had once conceived the "party of a new type" as an instrument to make the social forces of discontent converge in a revolutionary direction which they might not otherwise take, so now he conceived the State of a new type as an instrument to guide the millions of independent peasants, the private traders, the industrial technicians of bourgeois origin, in a socialist direction which ran counter to their natural tendency to evolve a capitalist social structure. To foil that tendency, it was not enough that the State kept firm control of the "commanding heights" of the economy; the alien classes must be permanently excluded from any possible access to the levers of political power. The unique purpose of forcing an entire society to develop not in the direction corresponding to its inherent trend, but in the direction dictated by the ideology of its ruling party, required a unique institutional form, closing all channels of political expression to the existing social forces: no plurality of political parties, however vestigial; no organized interest groups or publishing media free from party control; and finally, as a logical extension of this principle, no plurality of organized tendencies *within* the ruling party, as in the absence of opposition parties such factions would tend to become the channels for the pressure of non-proletarian class interests.

Oddly enough, no formal ban on all remnants of non-communist parties was passed even then. But mass arrests of their central and local leaders destroyed their organizations for good in the early months of 1921, so that in the summer of 1922 even the Menshevik leadership, by then in exile, explicitly renounced any further attempt to put up candidates for Soviet elections. Moreover, a formal ban on factions within the ruling party *was* passed at its tenth congress in March 1921—the same congress that introduced the NEP—on Lenin's proposal, and explicitly based on the grounds stated above—thus showing that the final destruction of the other parties at this moment was a deliberate decision. By November, on the fourth anniversary of the Bolshevik seizure of power, Zinoviev could state publicly that the Bolsheviks had been "the only legal party" in Russia for some time past. The remaining Menshevik-controlled trade unions were "reorganized" under appointed communist leaders during the same year, thus proving that the regime could in fact not afford to tolerate the independent advocacy of the interests of the industrial workers any more than of any other class; and by the time of the twelfth party conference of the Bolsheviks, in August 1922, the need to extend the principle of *Gleichschaltung*[7] to all "so-called social organizations", as well as to the universities and publishing firms, was proclaimed on the ground that otherwise those legal channels could be used by the now illegal "anti-Soviet parties" for their dangerous propaganda.

The first totalitarian State thus did not arise either as an automatic result of revolution and civil war, or as a mere instrument for the accelerated economic development of a backward country: it was the product of the decision to use the dictatorship resulting from the revolution in order to twist the development of society in the preconceived direction indicated by the ideology of the ruling party. As Lenin saw it, however, that politically directed development would henceforth proceed by evolutionary methods, with-

[7] "Coordination" of all organizations to create a monopoly of political power.—Ed.

out further violent upheavals. The emphasis in the writings of his final years was on the need to raise the economic and cultural level of the Russian people—including in particular the cultural level of the new bureaucracy—by steady, patient efforts within the given political framework; Lenin's last pamphlet on the agricultural co-operatives in particular, which Bukharin was later to describe as his political testament, pointed to the growth of co-operation rather than capitalist differentiation in the countryside as decisive for the evolution of Russia in a socialist direction, but envisaged that growth as taking place voluntarily on the basis of the peasants' material self-interest, parallel with the progress of the agricultural machine industry on one side and of the peasants' educational level on the other.

This evolutionary vision of the state-guided development of Russian society was also generally accepted by Lenin's heirs, at least as long as the problem of post-war recovery dominated economic life. As for Stalin in particular, he continued to oppose the idea of reviving the internal class struggle against the peasants for several years after first Trotsky and then Zinoviev and Kamenev had called for it. When, in 1925, he undertook to define the task of the totalitarian regime in terms of a distinction between the "bourgeois" and the "proletarian" revolution, he explained that the former had only had to remove the pre-capitalist "political superstructure" after the new capitalist economic and social "basis" was already fully developed, whereas in the case of the latter the political seizure of power—the creation of the new "socialist" superstructure—was a *precondition* for the development of the new basis, the socialist economy and society. But while this formula brought out with striking clarity the originality of the task bequeathed by Lenin and the extent of his departure from the Marxist tradition, it contained no hint that the creation of the new basis would require further crises of a revolutionary character.

Yet as the period of recovery drew to a close and the problem of financing Russia's industrialization—of the primitive socialist accumulation of capital—pressed to the fore, the hidden, inner contradiction of Lenin's vision of the guided socialist evolution of a society containing a majority of small, independent producers became obvious and confronted his heirs with a dilemma. The financing of socialist industrialization by peaceful, evolutionary methods—by encouraging the peasants to earn surpluses and to lend their savings to the State—as advocated by Bukharin, was *economically* possible and indeed rational; but, as experience showed by 1928, it was bound to increase the *social* weight of the individualist peasantry and to lead to a growing dependence of the formally all-powerful party-state on the informal but effective organizations of the village, typically led by the most efficient, near-capitalist peasants. The more successful the evolutionary road in terms of production and savings, the less likely was it to lead in the desired direction of preventing a capitalist development of the village and its growing impact on Russian society as a whole—the more it would therefore undermine the purpose and ultimately the power of the totalitarian regime. Conversely, the alternative road of financing socialist industrialization at the expense of the peasants, by syphoning off their surpluses more or less forcibly, as originally advocated by the "Left Opposition," might effectively stifle the tendency towards capitalist development in the village and maintain the course required by the regime's ideology; but it was bound to provoke peasant resistance to an extent that could be broken only by the massive use of state power—in other words by the abandonment of peaceful evolution.

In launching the "liquidation of the kulaks as a class" and the forced collectivization of agriculture, which he himself later described as a revolution "equivalent" to that of October 1917, but distinguished from it by being "accomplished from above, on the initiative of the State," Stalin decided in favour of the primacy of the totalitarian regime and its ideological goal: he recognized what Lenin had not foreseen—that a totalitarian regime can fulfill its task of diverting the development of society from its "spontaneous" course in an ideologically preconceived direction only by repeated recourse to revolutionary violence. The dynamics of the permanent, or at any rate recurrent, revolution from above as developed by Stalin are the necessary complement to the ideological goals set and to the totalitarian institutions created by Lenin: they, too, were not part of a blueprint, but they grew out of a fixed attitude of mind—and out of the institutions in which it had been embodied—under the pressure of events.

There is no need for us at this point to discuss the later development of Soviet totalitarianism under Stalin and its post-Stalinist fate; for it is the form given to the single-party State in the final years of Lenin's rule and the early period of Stalin's that has become effective as an international model and that is still regarded as "classic" in the Soviet Union today. What concerns us here is the degree of success obtained by the Bolsheviks by means of those institutions in achieving their objectives, the impression made by that success in different regions of the world, and the reasons both for the domestic success and for the spread of the model.

To begin with a negative statement: the Bolsheviks clearly did *not* succeed in achieving the goals that had originally inspired their revolutionary dictatorship—in establishing the social power of the proletariat or in approaching an egalitarian society. Both ideological goals were, of course, strictly incompatible with the immediate task of state-directed primitive accumulation, which required massive material sacrifices on the part of all productive classes, including the industrial working class; and the ruling party, being potentially independent of its original proletarian basis by its centralistic structure, used its dictatorial power to impose these sacrifices on workers and peasants alike, and to identify itself in outlook and composition increasingly with the "new class" of bureaucrats and technicians who were both indispensable for the process of state-directed industrialization and few in numbers, and therefore had to be privileged.

But the Bolsheviks *did* succeed in achieving the goals that had inspired their transformation of the original revolutionary dictatorship into a totalitarian single-party State: in maintaining their own dictatorial power, far beyond the revolutionary crisis that had enabled them to seize it, by turning it into an engine for the state-directed modernization of their country, and in changing the direction of Russian social development to a considerable extent from the course it would otherwise have taken. Their experience showed that even the most powerful State could not force society to conform to aims that were inherently utopian; but it also proved that a new type of State specifically geared to the purpose of directing social development could alter the "natural" course of that development far more effectively than had previously been believed possible.

Ever since, in the eighteenth century, the first western thinkers began to conceive of the economy as a self-regulating mechanism, and of the development of society as following immanent historical laws, modern thought about the relation between State and society had been dominated by the concept of the limits of political force. However much Liberals and Marxists might later disagree about the *content* of the laws that controlled social life, they did agree that these laws were objectively given and could not be altered by political fiat; nor did either school show much awareness that their supposedly universal laws were in fact generalizations based on the experience of modern western societies alone. Conservative thinkers, too, while more wary of this type of generalization, tended to minimize the "manageable" element in society by their emphasis on the limits of legislation and on the necessary ineffectiveness of any attempt to interfere with the organic growth of a historical entity. To all of them, the Bolshevik experiment seemed foredoomed to failure—because it violated the canons of economic rationality, because it tried to leap ahead of the stage reached in Russian social development, or because it was contrary to the character and traditions of the Russian people.

Yet the Bolshevik regime, by following political investment priorities and by brutally forcing the mass of the people to bear the cost of its often grossly irrational economic methods, succeeded in building up the industrial apparatus of a modern great Power with remarkable speed—at the price of depressing the standard of living of the Russian people for decades. By deporting millions of "kulak" families to break peasant resistance, it succeeded in suppressing the inherent tendency of the individualist peasantry to competition and capitalist differentiation, and in shepherding the bulk of the rural population into state-controlled collectives—at the price of causing a catastrophic loss of livestock and condemning Russia's agriculture to abysmal stagnation for a quarter of a century. By exposing an entire generation to a combination of harsh bureaucratic pressures, based on the threat of dire penalties for trifling offences against labour discipline or for failure to fulfill the delivery quotas, with intense educational remoulding through an all-embracing network of party-controlled organizations and publications, it succeeded in changing the "Russian character," the typical attitudes to work and leisure, to rationality and superstition, to family and State, far more quickly than the combination of Reformation, Counter-Reformation, and Enlightenment with the brutalities of early capitalism had brought about comparable changes in the West—at the price of creating a "reserve army' of state slaves in its labour camps and of drastically narrowing the mental horizon of the entire nation.

Moreover, the unprecedented concentration of political, economic, and ideological power by the totalitarian institutions (which caused Trotsky to write at the end of his life that Stalin could truly make the claim *"La Société c'est moi"*), did not only enable the ruling party to create a social structure of a completely new type, consisting of the four classes of the ruling and managing bureaucracy, the state workers, the collective peasants, and the labour slaves in the camps. It also enabled it to combine the prevention of any organized resistance to state-imposed sacrifices and party-directed mental remoulding with the active mobilization of the people to share in the society's transformation and their own. The party-controlled Soviets, trade unions, and other mass organizations, long deprived of any independent role as organs of self-government or of the advocacy of group interests, proved effective organs for broadening mass participation in the administrative execution of decisions handed down from the top; the institutions of the Union Republics and the smaller national units, barred from attempting independent national policies or even from developing a true cultural autonomy at the risk of countermeasures ranging from wholesale purges of political and intellectual leaders to the verge of genocide, proved nevertheless effective in giving large numbers of members of these nationalities, including not a few who had been illiterate only yesterday, the chance to learn to help administer their own affairs in their own language—always in accordance with central directives. In the end, totalitarian oppression proved compatible with, if not conducive to the growth of a truly felt "Soviet patriotism," a genuine allegiance of the citizen to the State in whose greatness his blood, sweat, and tears had been invested by the rulers.

Last and not least, the party regime has succeeded in maintaining for half a century, in the face of several crises of leadership succession, dramatic policy turns, murderous purges, and the supreme test of a world war, both its power over its subjects and its internal cohesion. No ancient or modern dictatorship of revolutionary origin can boast of a similar record. The Russian achievement has been all the more remarkable because, while the nature of the totalitarian single-party State requires a single leader with uncontested authority (so as to stop the inevitable disagreements within the inner circle from leading to the growth of organized factions), the nature of communist ideology has prevented the Bolsheviks from admitting this need and seeking an institutional solution for the problem of succession. Yet on the other hand it is that same ideology, the common faith inspiring the cadres of the ruling party, that must be regarded as to an important degree responsible for the longevity of the regime—not only because it has helped again and again to maintain its *political* cohesion in the face of crises, power struggles, and tyrannical crimes that would have been intolerable to non-believers, but also because it has helped to maintain its *moral* cohesion in the face of the innumerable temptations of dictatorial rule. Soviet bureaucracy, including the party bureaucracy, has of course had its full share of the corruption inseparable from the exercise of arbitrary power, but a comparison with some other modern dictatorships will at once show the vital difference of degree: in fifty years of Bolshevik rule, corruption has never reached the point of endangering the cohesion of the system. For an ideology that has had to be adapted to such far-reaching changes of situation, policy, and generation as the communist one, that, too, is a remarkable achievement.

From the communist point of view, the key to development under the Soviets has been the planned growth of the economy. First introduced during the 1920s, planning was extended to cover the entire economy by the mid-1930s. It thus became possible to make the objectives of the plans binding on the economic system and to punish those who failed to fulfill their part in the plans. Public ownership of property and planning together assured rapid advances of the economy and answered the needs of socialism, in the opinion of NIKOLAI BAIBAKOV (b. 1911), Chairman of the State Planning Commission of the U.S.S.R.*

Nikolai Baibakov

The Superiority of Planning

The October Revolution laid the foundations for the creation of a socialist society, a tremendous political, social, and economic transformation unparalleled in the history of mankind. In the economic field this has meant the introduction of socialized production on the basis of a plan. Summing up the lessons of historical development, we can conclude that "the theory and practice of the planned supervision of the economy of the U.S.S.R. is a major contribution to the historical experience of mankind and to the construction of communism."

The development of the socialist economy was dependent upon long-term and current plans[1] which reflected the economic policies of the Communist party. Planning made possible effective controls over the national economy on a nationwide scale and the rational distribution of productive forces. Socialist planning has proved itself historically; it has served as the most important tool for the solution of the major tasks of each step of communist development. The fifty-year experience of the economic growth of the Soviet Union has established conclusively the

[1] Long-term plans present the economic goals covering periods of several years; current plans prepare the detailed instructions for economic activity of a brief period of two years or less.—Ed.

*Nikolai Baibakov, "Economic Planning—The Fundamental Advantage of Socialism," *Planovoe khoziaistvo* (November, 1967), pp. 5–6, 7–11. Translated by Daniel R. Brower. Footnotes omitted.

overwhelming superiority of planning to guide national production. As a result of the systematic development of the economy, our country has transformed itself in a historically short period of time into a mighty industrial power with advanced agriculture and a high standard of living for the people. . . .

The systematic regulation of the production of a society cannot be achieved under conditions of capitalism, since private property and its corrolary, the conflict of interests among monopolies, independent enterprises, and private individuals, constitute an unavoidable obstacle to such policies. The founders of Marxism indicated that only the abolition of private property and the introduction of public ownership of the means of production could create a firm foundation for the planned regulation of the national economic system and the development of the economy on the basis of a national plan. Friedrich Engels wrote that the political power won by the proletariat would be used to convert the means of production into the property of the whole society. In that manner the means of production are freed from their capitalistic restraints and can develop freely according to their social nature. It is then possible to conduct socialized production on the basis of a preconceived plan. The possibility for controlled centralized planning of the economy by means of a system of state planning agencies is one of the most important advantages of socialism. . . .

The organization of a system of economic planning is directly associated with the name of the great founder of the Communist party and the Soviet Union, Vladimir Ilich Lenin. On his initiative the State Planning Commission[2] was set up in 1921. Lenin was both inspirer and organizer of the first perspective economic plan in history, the State Plan for the Electrification of Russia.[3] For the first time the Marxist goal of heavy industry as the material foundation of socialism was brought to life as a concrete task for the socialist reorganization and the technological reconstruction of an economy, based on electrification.

The GOELRO plan, which foresaw the accelerated development of heavy industry, the electrification of the country, and on this foundation the advance of all branches of the economy, was directly coordinated with immediate policies for the realization of these aims. They were successfully accomplished, thanks to the heroic efforts of the Soviet people. By 1926–1927 the 1913 economic level had been reached and in certain sectors surpassed. But the goals of socialist construction could not be satisfied by attaining the level of economic activity of prerevolutionary Russia. On the eve of the Revolution Lenin declared that Russia was still an unbelievably backward country, miserable and semibarbarous, whose supply of industrial machinery was one-fourth that of England, one-fifth that of Germany, and one-tenth that of the United States.

The difficult tasks of the technological reequipment of the entire economy and the creation of the foundations of the socialist economic system still had to be undertaken. For the time being the country's industrial development remained backward in comparison with that of the major capitalist countries. In 1928 electric power production in the U.S.S.R. was 4 percent, iron and steel output 8 percent, and fuel production 7 percent of the American level. . . . There still lay ahead

[2] Russian abbreviation "Gosplan."—Ed.

[3] Russian abbreviation "GOELRO."—Ed.

the job of overcoming the country's backwardness and of outdoing the capitalist countries not only in their rate of growth but also in their actual level of production.

The distinctive qualities of the GOELRO plan were its scientific precision and its comprehensive survey of the regional and sectoral peculiarities of the economy. In the preparation of the target figures of the plan, use was made of all available statistical material on the condition of the economy, on the country's natural resources—the extent of their exploration and readiness for industrial exploitation—and on all aspects of the development of the economic system of the country. . . . Lenin remarked that plans for separate sectors of production should be carefully coordinated, connected, and altogether constitute a single economic plan. He also underlined the necessity for a proper combination of perspective and current economic plans, in order that all current plans flow from the perspective plan.

The fundamental Leninist ideas concerning economic planning were developed in the resolutions of the congresses and conferences of the Communist party of the Soviet Union, the plenary meetings of its Central Committee, and in the edicts of the Soviet government. Under the direction of the party, plans were worked out for the development of the Soviet economic system. They succeeded in a short time in accomplishing the socialist industrialization of the country, in applying the Leninist plan for agricultural cooperatives, and in attaining the final and complete victory of socialism.

The crucial aspect of the construction of socialism was the socialist industrialization of the country. The application of the Leninist GOELRO plan and the early five-year plans secured the rapid economic development of the Soviet state and its transformation into a major industrial power. The first five-year plan (1928–1932) reflected the policy of industrialization of the country, of the reconstruction of the economy, and of the socialist reorganization of agriculture. Its basic political-economic task consisted in the development of heavy industry—the foundation of the technological reequipment of all sectors, including light industry—the creation of the material basis for the socialist reorganization of agriculture, the raising of the standard of living, and the securing of the defense preparedness of the country.

In the years of the first five-year plan the volume of industrial production grew steadily—on an average 19.2 percent a year. The plan was completed in four years and three months. The increase of industrial production occurred primarily because of the growth of heavy industry. During this period many new branches of heavy industry were founded—electric power production, machine-tool construction, the automobile, defense, and chemical industries, and so on. The production of farm machinery grew at a high rate, permitting the mechanization of agriculture. . . .

The country was firmly on the path of industrial development. The success of socialist industry created the prerequisites for the planned control of agriculture and prepared the basis for the widespread introduction of collectivization. The victory of the new system based on collective farms greatly strengthened the agriculture of the Soviet Union. The success of socialism in all economic sectors permitted the growth of the standard of living of the population; unemployment, the scourge of laborers in capitalist countries, disappeared.

Striking evidence of the advantages of socialism over capitalism in those years was, on the one hand, the unparalleled tempo of growth of the economic system of the U.S.S.R., and, on the other, the catastrophic decline of production in the capitalist world. In 1929 the capitalist world was struck by an economic crisis of unprecedented intensity and strength. Its characteristics were the decline of production, massive unemployment, and the impoverishment of millions of laborers. The crisis spread over the major capitalist countries, especially the United States. The level of industrial production in 1932 as compared to 1929 was down 46 percent in the United States, 16 percent in England, and 41 percent in Germany. . . . In the U.S.S.R. industrial production grew in those years by 69 percent.

The fulfillment of the first five-year plan made it possible in the following period to complete the technological reconstruction of the country. In the years of the second five-year plan the capitalist elements in the rural and urban areas were definitely liquidated, and the collectivization of the peasant economy was brought to a successful end. By 1937 the socialist sector had become the dominant element throughout the economy. Its share of the national income was 99.1 percent; it contributed 99.8 percent of gross industrial production, 98.5 percent of agricultural production, and 100 percent of the retail trade of commercial enterprises (including the food industry). . . .

In the years of the third five-year plan the possibility grew of reaching the basic economic goal: the attaining and surpassing of the major capitalist countries in terms of total per-capita production. Together with this goal, the third five-year plan also aimed at further strengthening the defense preparedness of the country, the development of the defense industry, and the stockpiling of important reserves [for possible wartime use].

The expansion of the Soviet economic system in the prewar years raised the country to a fundamentally new level of development. State planning totally directed an increasingly large number of sectors of the economy. The rise in industrial production by 600 percent in those years was accompanied by a major alteration in its structure, namely, the increasing importance of the electrical, machine-tool, and chemical industries. The growing preponderance of these sectors permitted the marked increase of the most important types of industrial production in both absolute and per-capita terms. This allowed the U.S.S.R. to liquidate its economic and technological backwardness and to occupy in 1940 second place in the world by its volume of industrial production.

Another very important result of the development of the Soviet economic system in the prewar years was the significant growth of the material standard of living of the working classes. While the population increased 30 percent between 1927 and 1939, the production of consumer goods rose almost 5 times and the physical volume of trade 2.3 times.

Such were some of the results of the socialist transformation during the first two decades of peaceful economic construction in the U.S.S.R.

The successful completion of the third five-year plan was interrupted by the treacherous attack of Hitler's Germany on the Soviet Union. The war did tremendous damage. The country lost 20 million people; tens of thousands of cities, towns, and villages were turned into ruins. Approximately 30 percent of the national wealth was destroyed. Under the leadership of the Communist party our people were victorious over fascism, brought freedom to many nations of Europe, raised cities and towns out of ruins, and in a short time restored the war-devastated economy. Three years after the war the prewar level of industrial production was attained; agriculture reached its prewar production by 1950. The standard of living of the population also rose. By 1950 the real wages of workers and employees had increased by 26 percent in comparison with 1940, and the real income of the peasants by 19 percent.

Having achieved the revival and reconstruction of the economy, the Soviet Union entered a new phase of economic development whose fundamental aspect was the transition to the construction of the material-technological base of communism. The fulfillment of this task depended on the further industrialization of the national economy of the country.

The expansion of production in this period required as before that emphasis be placed on the growth of heavy industry, especially electric power, machine-tool, and chemical output. Between 1951 and 1965 production of machine tools and metallurgical products increased at a significantly more rapid pace than industry as a whole. The widening and strengthening of the process of industrialization permitted the development of electric power to catch up with other branches of industry. The volume of production of electric power grew about 3 times in the period 1956–1965, while all industrial production increased by 2.5 times. . . .

The successful development of these very important branches of heavy industry created a solid foundation for the subsequent rise of production in the light and food industries and for the marked increase in the output of consumer goods. In the period 1951–1965 production of light-industry products rose by 2.8 times, and the food industry by 3.4 times.

The marked growth of the standard of living of the population has been one of the most significant achievements of the Soviet Union in the postwar years. It can be seen in the shortening of the length of the working day,[4] in the increase in the wages of laborers in various categories (especially in the lowest paid categories), in the decrease of prices for items of mass consumption, and in the accelerated construction of living quarters. The average monthly pay of workers and employees (including wages and fringe benefits) increased over the years 1951–1965 by 1.6 times; the real income of workers and employees (account taken of the decline of prices) grew almost 2 times, and that of collective farm workers by 2.7 times. . . .

Considerable means were devoted to the development of the eastern regions of the country.[5] Almost 35 percent of the state's productive investments were directed during the years of Soviet power to the eastern regions, including the Ural mountains. As a result the share of these regions in the national production of many important types of industrial products increased several times.

The Soviet Union became a country of advanced machine-tool production, electric power output, metallurgy, fuel production, chemical and electronics production. In 1966 the U.S.S.R. produced almost one-fifth of the world's output of industrial products; in 1913 its share had been slightly over four percent. . . .

One of the outstanding advantages of the planned socialist economy has been the constantly high rate of economic

[4] In 1967 Soviet industry went over to the five-day work week.—Ed.

[5] The Siberian, Central Asian, and Pacific Coast regions.—Ed.

growth. Over a period of almost a half century (1918–1966) the average growth of industrial production of the U.S.S.R. was 9.9 percent, of the United States 3.7 percent, of England 2.1 percent, and of France 3.7 percent. Over the past 38 years (1929–1966) the tempo of development of Soviet industry has been even higher: the average yearly growth of industrial production of the U.S.S.R. reached 11.1 percent, while that of the United States was 4 percent. . . .

The tempo of development of Soviet industry has remained high in recent years. On an average the yearly growth of industrial production between 1959 and 1966 reached 9.2 percent, as compared to 5 percent for the United States. The Soviet Union has recently outdistanced the United States in absolute growth of a series of important types of products. This qualitatively new stage in the peaceful economic competition between the U.S.S.R. and the United States is evidence of the inevitability of the triumph of the planned economic system.

Soviet economic policies were primarily a response to pressures for economic development, in the opinion of MARSHALL GOLDMAN (b. 1930), professor of economics at Harvard University. The Marxist ideology was of little use to a regime confronted with a backward country and a conservative peasantry. The Soviet leaders sought pragmatic solutions to difficult economic problems. Only the institutions for planning grew out of a desire for rational economic decision making, and even this was not originally a Marxist idea. By implication, Goldman suggests that the Soviet type of economic development was a unique product of circumstances in Russia.*

Marshall Goldman

The Needs of Economic Development

Myth: *Upon coming to power, the Bolsheviks adopted a Marxist blueprint for action which they have been following ever since.*

If it is difficult to determine in which countries Marx said the revolution would take place, it is even more difficult to decide what Marx expected would happen once the revolution had occurred. The confusion multiplies when the revolution erupts in a country other than one of those selected by Marx.

The reason for all this uncertainty is that Marx seldom concerned himself with the operations and problems of a communist society. He was primarily a student of capitalism. Consequently his main concern was the revolution and the disintegration of an economic system, not its construction and expansion. Only rarely did Marx make any comments about what the new communist society would be like. Perhaps the best example of such a study is *The Critique of the Gotha Program,*[1] and even that is only a rough sketch.

With such an incomplete blueprint, it is sometimes hard to argue that a particular action would or would not have fit into Marx's scheme. Yet clearly there are some economic activities he presumably would have opposed, even if they were explained away as being only a temporary expedient. As we shall see, temporary

[1] Written in 1874.—Ed.

*From Marshall I. Goldman, *The Soviet Economy: Myth and Reality,* © 1968, pp. 19–25, 26–29. Reprinted by permission of Prentice-Hall, Inc., Englewood Cliffs, New Jersey. Footnotes omitted.

expedients have a way of becoming permanent encumbrances, especially when the Marxist revolution takes place in a country which is not among the economically advanced. Then the state becomes responsible for building up the industrial framework which theoretically should already have been completed. As we have seen, this usually forces the state to assume the role of a forceful accumulator, a role which it never seems to want to give up. Inevitably democratic rights are sacrificed in the process and only slowly if ever regained. . . .

One of the first actions after the revolution was the expropriation of private property. Seemingly this was in line with Marxist ideology. However, Marxism had little to do with what happened. For the most part confiscation tended to take place almost spontaneously. Returning home from the battlefront, the peasants simply threw out the landlords and took over the acreage they had previously rented. But this amounted to no more than substitution of one form of ownership for another. The peasants instead of the landlords became the owners. This often meant the new owner was just as conservative as his predecessor.

Ideology was similarly upended in industry. Prior to the revolution, Lenin called for complete nationalization, but immediately after the revolution most of the communist leaders changed their minds and called for moderation and patience. In the reaction and civil war that ensued, there was widespread chaos. The communists wanted all the production and stability they could find. Therefore they opposed confiscation because they feared it would lead to further disruption of the economy. Furthermore, they recognized that some of the old managers would support the new government if the transition to state control was not violent. Actually, the old managers were needed to run the factories. There was a shortage of skilled managers who were also communists. Not many members of the proletarian class had training enough to take over the managerial function.

Pleas for moderation however were of little or no avail. To some extent the factory workers were caught up in the same emotional tide as the peasants. They, too, wanted to throw out the old owners. Unfortunately, there was a big difference between taking over a farm which was much more of a self-contained unit and a factory which depended on other sources for its raw materials as well as its customers. If nothing else, the peasant could always consume his produce himself. But the factory had to sell to and buy from others. Accordingly, when some workers took over their factories and tried to set themselves up as self-contained units, they ran into immediate problems. It was ridiculous to expect that the rest of the world would unconditionally meet the terms called for by the new factory committees. Increasingly the Soviet leaders began to realize that the workers were reacting in a syndicalist fashion.[2] Their attitudes verged on anarchy. The workers were urging that each factory should be a castle unto itself. This was hardly a course that could be maintained in a society which was attempting to complete the process of industrialization.

For a time Lenin tried to fight these syndicalist tendencies, and decrees were issued in February, 1918, prohibiting the confiscation of factories without specific permission from the ruling authorities in Moscow. Ultimately, Lenin decided he

[2] The syndicalist program called for worker control of the factories.—Ed.

could not hold back the tide. Therefore he decided to roll with it and thereby attempt to guide and control it. Still it was not until June 28, 1918, that a decree was finally adopted ordering the nationalization of all large-scale industry. It was like turning off the lights after the power has gone off. Only in retrospect could it possibly have been argued that confiscation of property was in accord with Marxist precepts. Even then, such rationalization amounted to nothing more than trying to make the best out of a bad situation.

Following the period from 1917 to 1921, which was subsequently called *War Communism,* the Communists made a major shift in policy. By 1921, Lenin had managed to eliminate most of the opposition of the more conservative segments of society. However, he encountered a new form of opposition. Lenin suddenly found that many of his early supporters such as the poorer peasants and even the sailors at the Kronstadt Naval Base outside of Leningrad were beginning to protest the policies of his government in agriculture and its inability to provide enough food in the cities. This hurt because these same sailors had been the source of Lenin's main support during the November attack on the Czar's Winter Palace in Leningrad. When allies like the militant Kronstadt sailors defected, it was clear to Lenin that he must be doing something wrong.

Recognizing that some radical changes were necessary, Lenin proclaimed a New Economic Policy (NEP) for the country in March, 1921. He decided that it would be necessary to take one step backward in order to make what he promised would be two steps forward. But the steps were so far backward that some critics were convinced that Lenin had stepped back into capitalism.

To bring some order out of the economic chaos that existed, Lenin realized that one of the first things he would have to do would be to restore the flow of consumer goods, including nonfood products. Food was in short supply in the urban areas, and what few products were produced in the urban factories somehow never found their way to the peasants. Finding there was nothing they could exchange for their food, the peasants had simply cut down on the amount of food they offered to exchange. When Lenin sent out troops to confiscate the food, the peasants decided to resist even more.

Because he felt that further pressure by the state and further monopolization of trade through state-controlled stores would do nothing to alleviate this situation, Lenin decided to reverse himself. First, he decreed that henceforth peasants would only have a fixed quota of food to deliver. Everything above that could be sold freely at higher prices. Like a progressive piece rate in its impact, the more the peasant produced, the higher the price he was paid for that extra output. This was meant to stimulate the peasants to extra effort, and in a very short period of time it did. Second, he decided to permit the reappearance of private traders. In this way he hoped that profit-seeking merchants would dig out hidden stocks of goods and encourage the production of new ones. Together this would lead to a rebirth of commerce and retail sales. Lenin was right. Private merchants opened up small shops in the cities and peddlers, called *Nepmen,* spread through the countryside selling factory-made products for food.

Throughout the whole NEP period, the state maintained control over what Lenin called "the commanding heights." Thus heavy industry and the banks were retained under state ownership to ensure that there could be no major subversion of communist control. Nonetheless, private ownership in the fringe areas of the economy was encouraged to get the economy moving again. As we have seen, this policy was highly successful. By 1928, recovery from the damage of the civil war and revolution had been completed. Still, no matter how Lenin's steps are rationalized, certainly the NEP period cannot be considered part of any Marxist blueprint. If anything, it was recognition that Russia was not ready for any jump into complete state ownership, a step which presumably a Marxist state would have had to take.

Lenin died in the course of the New Economic Policy, and Stalin assumed control. No one knows what course Lenin would have taken had he lived, but his moderation in the NEP period suggests his subsequent policies might have been more temperate than Stalin's. Certainly it is hard to see how they could have been any more intemperate.

With reconstruction completed, Stalin addressed himself to the problem of the Soviet Union's future. He and his advisers were worried that growth in the future would not be as easy. Economic growth in a period of reconstruction is usually quite rapid. In some cases, all that is needed to set an idle factory in motion is to find a new source of raw materials. In other cases, more extensive repairs may have to be made. For the most part, however, there is no need to make extensive capital investments. Therefore the capital-output ratio is very low, which means a little capital investment in the form of inventory and repairs will generate an impressive rate of growth. But with reconstruction completed, it was anticipated that the capital–output ratio would increase in industrial output. Along with several economists of the time, Stalin began to wonder whether or not the Soviet Union would be able to generate the much larger quantities of capital he now thought would be necessary to build brand new projects. If not, then the growth rate would fall. In the debate that was generated over this problem, apparently there was little mention of the fact that Russia had managed rapid growth with new projects (albeit with some help from foreign investments) in the 1890s and from 1905 to 1913. . . .

Stalin had other problems as well. Because of the concessions that were made to win peasant support for the Revolution, the state found that it was not enough to issue a decree that the harvest be a certain tonnage of grain. As long as the peasants were in possession of their own little farms, they could not be relied upon to supply a steady flow of grain to market. Even later, when the state assumed ownership of the farms, Stalin found that decrees to the peasants had little impact. It was easy for the peasant to cut himself off from the market. By planting just enough for his own family, he could be assured of an adequate food supply and some homemade clothes. He could do without almost everything else, except salt. The peasant had displayed this kind of independence during the period of War Communism, when many of them refused to market any of their produce. The NEP reforms were meant to change this. As the peasants began to respond to the improved incentives, their output increased. This, however, had the effect of bringing down the price of food. Simultaneously, after an initial drop, the price of industrial goods rose as factories found their needs mounting rapidly. The rise in the prices of manufactured goods was accelerated by a rapid increase in the flow of currency from the printing press, which led inevitably to inflation. The divergence in industrial and agricultural prices came to be known as the *scissors crisis.* As the peasants saw that the harder they worked, the less they were able to buy, they began to hold back their surpluses again. This jeopardized the flow of food to the cities and to export markets.

With time, as the NEP reforms brought about increased factory production and improved distribution, price levels returned to more balanced levels, but government officials decided that they could not depend on a smooth flow of marketed output from the peasants. Furthermore, the road ahead would probably be particularly bumpy because of a decision by the government about future price policy. After some debate, it was decided to hold down prices on agricultural products. At first, supporters of the peasant had argued that higher prices would stimulate higher outputs and higher marketings. Critics of this position asserted that this would amount to turning over the fruits of the revolution to the peasants, and, after all, the proletariat were expected to enjoy some of the benefits. It was realized that the urban worker would not have been very pleased to find that the price of his food and therefore his cost of living had increased. There seemed to be little appreciation of the fact that after a time, an increase in farm output would probably have led to a natural fall in prices. Those who did see this were not pacified either since they feared a fall in prices might in itself set off another peasant boycott. All in all, unless something was done to revoke the concessions that had been made to the peasants at the time of the revolution, Stalin felt that the state would forever be at their mercy. So it was that Stalin became displeased with the agricultural situation as it existed in the 1920s. He concluded that something would have to be done to break the hammerlock of the peasants on the future of the rest of the country. . . .

The fear of [a food crisis] plus his desire to eliminate the stranglehold of the peasants once and for all led Stalin to call for the collectivization of agriculture. Under this policy, Russian peasants were urged and ultimately compelled to form collective farms *(kolkhozy).* To do this, they had to give up their land (except for a small area which they were later allowed to farm privately), almost all their livestock, and any machinery they might have had. Henceforth all farming was to be done collectively with the work and the profits shared jointly.

The reaction of the peasants to this new proposal was one of tremendous hostility and resistance. Millions of lives were lost in what was later called the *Second Russian Revolution.* For centuries the peasants had been serfs and tenants. During all those years they yearned for the ownership of what, after a time, they considered their land. Then suddenly, in the emotional wave of 1917 and 1918, they attained what they had sought for so long. In the years that followed, there were pressures and problems, but the land was theirs. Their conservative yearnings were finally satisfied. Suddenly all of this was taken away. They had been double crossed. The land had been given to them in exchange for their support during the Revolution; then it was nationalized by the state and they had lost it all.

Again the question arises: Did the collectivization of agriculture fit into the Marxist blueprint? Conceivably it could have. Collectivization meant the end of private ownership. But the destruction that ensued was certainly a high price to pay. If anything, there is good reason to believe that economic progress, if not ideological purity, would have been advanced with only slightly more moderate policies. Moreover, the increased production that a slightly higher price for grain would have stimulated would probably not have resulted in a transfer of economic wealth from the urban to the rural sector as Stalin feared. On the contrary, if there had been no collectivization, there would not have been so much suffering and protest. This in turn would have meant increased production on the farm and a better standard of living for the urban residents.

It is not just that Stalin's agricultural policy created a drag on the economy that even now has not been completely remedied; it is also that he acted more out of pragmatism than ideology to eliminate what he though to be an impending agricultural crisis. In the process, of course, he created his own crisis, but it is hard to see how ideology more than pragmatism was the main guide to his actions.

Marxist ideology seems to have been more of an influence in the industrial sector. Lenin sought complete ownership by the state of private industry. Stalin gradually reduced the amount of private ownership that had been permitted during the New Economic Policy and, in the crop year 1927–1928, announced the inauguration of the first of a series of Five Year Plans. Variations of these plans have continued to the present day, interrupted only by war and by over-and under-fulfillment. . . .

Today, planning is considered a hallmark of a Marxist society. Lenin took the first hesitant steps in this direction with his GOELRO (State Commission for Electrification) introduced in March, 1920. This group was to draw up a plan for the electrification of the country. In Lenin's words "Communism is the Soviet system (councils or the new forms of government administration) plus the electrification of the entire country." Of course, it took much more than that, but this was a way of focusing attention on the need to promote electrification.

Subsequently, GOLERO was merged into Gosplan (the State Planning Commission) in February, 1921. It was Gosplan which drew up the preliminary work and ultimately the first complete Five-Year Plan for the period October, 1928, to the end of 1932. There is no question but that the utilization of a state planning organization to draw up a nationwide plan was a new and ingenious innovation. Many Russians acknowledge that the concept of a plan derived from the practice of individual American firms that found it necessary to project their budget and production needs far in advance. Leon Smolinski of Boston College has found that in addition, early Russian planning relied heavily on the model proposed by Professor Karl Ballod of Germany. But whatever the un-Marxist origins of the state plan, and however fragile the data and the degree of control, nothing comparable to this comprehensive planning had ever been attempted before on a nationwide basis, nor had all the industries of a country ever been put under unified state rule.

It could be argued that the switch to planning was Marxist because it put control of the economy in the hands of the state for the first time. At the same time, however, the desire for economic development played as important and probably a more important role than Marxism in the decision to adopt a Five-Year Plan. This should not be interpreted to mean that the plan as a Marxist instrument and the plan as a means for economic development are necessarily mutually exclusive.

Clearly the plan could have served both purposes. However, given Stalin's mania for growth, it does seem fair to suggest that he was more concerned about expansion than doctrine.

Reality: *Even though some of the measures they took could be considered steps in the direction of ideological purity, for the most part the Bolsheviks were motivated primarily by practical considerations. The closest they came to following Marxist precepts was their nationalization of industry in the late 1920s and their adoption of a system of annual and Five-Year Plans. But, on balance, it is hard to deny that the institutional forms adopted by the Russians were dictated as much by the needs of economic development as ideological conformity.*

WALT ROSTOW (b. 1916), professor of economic history at Texas University and former adviser to Presidents Kennedy and Johnson, argues that the results of Soviet economic growth are not exceptionally impressive. Other economic systems, such as that of the United States, have done as well. Communism was not, therefore, the only way for Russia to achieve rapid economic development. The Communist regime was able to seize power in part because of "political and social confusion" created by the transition from a traditional to modern society. It was in this sense a "disease of transition."*

Walt Rostow

The Disease of Transition

When we think journalistically of Russian economic development a number of images may come to mind: an image of a nation surging, under Communism, into a long-delayed status as an industrial power of the first order—symbolized by the Russian success in launching the first earth and solar satellites; an image of a pace of industrial growth unique in modern experience, held at forced draught by a system of state controls that constrains consumption, maintains unexampled rates of investment, and avoids lapses from full employment; an image of a planned economy so different in its method and institutions as to require forms of analysis different from those applicable in the West. In short, the conventional image is of a story apart.

There are, of course, profound special elements in the story of the evolution of modern Russian society and of its economy; and, before we finish, we shall try to identify the nature of its uniqueness. But the first point to grasp is that Russian economic development over the past century is remarkably similar to that of the United States, with a lag of about thirty-five years in the level of industrial output and a lag of about a half-century in *per capita* output in industry. Moreover, the Russian case, linking the Czarist and Communist experiences, falls, like the case of the United States, well within the

*From Walt W. Rostow, *The Stages of Economic Growth: A Non-Communist Manifesto* (New York: Cambridge University Press, 1960), pp. 93–95, 98–99, 104, 160–161, 162–164. Footnote omitted.

broad framework of the stages-of-growth analysis.

Now, first, consider [the figure shown below], reproduced from the work of G. Warren Nutter, showing industrial production per head of population for Russia from 1880 to 1955 and for the United States from 1870 to 1955. Note, particularly, that Nutter's chart converts industrial output per head into an index, with 1913 equal to 100. It shows, therefore, comparative rates of growth in output per head, not absolute figures; and it should be read with an awareness that the median lag in 1955, for the thirty-seven industries involved, is fifty-six years of growth: in short the whole Soviet curve is set below the American by an amount that does not vary greatly, in terms of time-lag.

What emerges is that, between the 1880's and the First World War, Russia, relatively, came forward during its take-off;[1] it fell behind, in the 1920's, when the United States enjoyed a boom, and Russia reorganized slowly after war and revolution; it came forward relatively during the first Five Year Plans of the 1930's, when the United States was gripped in a slump; and in its post-1945 phase Russia again came forward relatively, at a time when Russian output was more heavily concentrated in industry and American output was shifting structurally to housing and non-manufactured services. . . .

All of this is, in a sense, a statistical way of stating that the Russian take-off was under way by the 1890's, whereas the American take-off was completed by 1860. After take-off both societies suffered severe vicissitudes: the United States in the Civil War and the protracted depression of the 1930's, Russia in two World Wars which brought devastation from which the United States was spared. But the progress of industry, after take-off, was remarkably similar in the two cases, in terms of output; and in terms of productivity per man, the initial American population-resource balance advantage[2] was, down to 1955, roughly maintained. And the similarities include the fact that Russian take-off was also a railway take-off, bringing to life new modern coal, iron, and heavy-engineering industries; and these railway

[1] Beginning of sustained economic growth in an industrializing economy.—Ed.

[2] High proportion of economic resources to total population.—Ed.

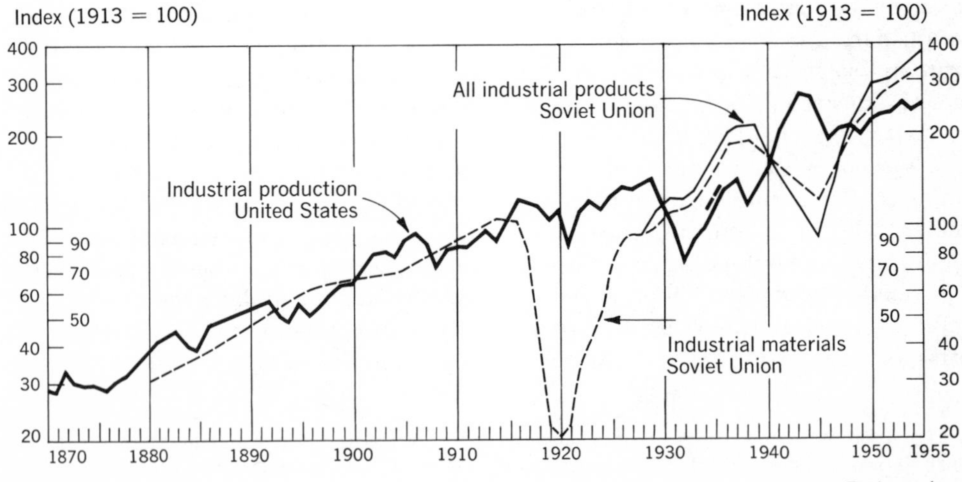

take-offs were also each followed by a stage dominated by the spread of technology to steel fabrication, chemicals and electricity. . . . Having established this rough but important framework of uniformity of experience now let us catalogue some of the major differences between Russia and the United States.

First, the creation of the preconditions for take-off[3] was, in its non-economic dimensions, a quite different process in Russia. Russia was deeply enmeshed in its own version of a traditional society, with well-installed institutions of Church and State as well as intractable problems of land tenure, an illiterate serfdom, overpopulation on the land, the lack of a free-wheeling commercial middle class, a culture which initially placed a low premium on modern productive economic activity. The United States, again to use Hartz' phrase, was "born free"—with vigorous, independent land-owning farmers, and an ample supply of enterprising men of commerce, as well as a social and political system that took easily to industrialization, outside the South. Thus, whereas Russia had to overcome a traditional society, the United States had only to overcome the high attractions of continuing to be a supplier of food-stuffs and raw materials—as well, if you like, as the damper of a milder colonialism.

Second, throughout this sequence, American consumption per head, at each stage of growth, was higher than in Russia. We have, as in other cases, a high degree of uniformity in the timing of the spread of technology, taking place within a considerable spread in income and consumption *per capita.* Basically, this is a matter of population-resource balances; but the tendency was reinforced in both Czarist and Soviet Russia by constraints imposed by the State on the level of mass consumption.

Third, the drive to maturity[4] took place in the United States, after the Civil War, in a setting of relative political freedom—outside the South—in a society tightly linked to the international economy, at a time of peace, and, generally, with rising standards of consumption per head. In Russia it occurred in the three decades after 1928, in a virtually closed economy, against a background of war and preparations for war, which did not slow the spread of technology, but which did limit the rise of consumption; and it occurred with something over 10 million members of the working force regularly in forced labour down to very recent years.

Fourth, the Soviet drive to maturity took place not only with constraints on consumption in general but severe restraints in two major sectors of the economy . . . : agriculture and housing. In housing the Soviet Union lived substantially off the Czarist capital stock down to recent years, minimizing housing outlays, letting space per family shrink; in agriculture it invested heavily, but within a framework of collectivization that kept productivity pathologically low, once Lenin's "New Economic Policy" was abandoned in 1929. In addition, Russia has invested very little indeed in a modern road-system, which has drawn so much American capital. . . .

The lesson of all this is, then, that there is nothing mysterious about the evolution of modern Russia. It is a great nation, well endowed by nature and history to create a modern economy and a modern society. In the course of its take-off it was struck by a major war, in which the precarious and

[3] Preparation of a society for sustained economic growth.—Ed.

[4] Period of sustained economic growth leading to application of advanced technology to all sectors of the economy.—Ed.

changing balance between traditional and democratic political elements collapsed in the face of defeat and disorder; and a particular form of modern societal organization took over control of a revolutionary situation it did not create. Its domestic imperatives and external ambitions have produced a version of the common growth experience, abnormally centered in heavy industry and military potential. . . .

What has emerged, then, is a system of modern state organization based not on economic determinism, but on political or power determinism. It is not the ownership of the means of production that decides everything, it is the control of the army, the police, the courts, and the means of communication. Lenin and his successors have, in effect, turned Hegel back on his feet; and they have inverted Marx.[5] Economic determinism did not work well for them; but power determinism has, quite well, filled the gap. They have operated on the perception that, under certain circumstances, a purposeful well-disciplined minority can seize political power in a confused ill-organized society; once power is seized, it can be held with economy of force, if the Communist élite maintains its unity; and with power held, the resources of a society may be organized in such a way as to make the economy grow along lines which consolidate and enlarge the power of the Communist élite.

The irony in this story even extends to the nature of political economy under Communism. In the history of modern Russia, and in post-1945 Eastern Europe and Communist China as well, one can find a quite good approximation to Marx's inaccurate description of how the capitalist economy would work: wages are held as near the iron minimum as the need for incentives permits; profits are ploughed back into investment and military outlays on a large scale; and the system is so structured that it would be fundamentally endangered if the vast capacity that results were to be turned wholeheartedly to the task of raising real wages. The difference between Marx's image of capitalism and Communist political economy is, of course, that the motive in the one case was to have been private profit; in the other it is the maintenance and extension of the élite's power. . . .

Communism as it is—a great fact of history—cannot be disposed of merely by revealing its nature, its deceptions, and its dilemmas. To identify the errors in Marxism and to demonstrate the un-Marxist character of Communism is not a very important achievement. The fact is that Communism as a technique of power is a formidable force. Although it was an un-Marxist insight, it was a correct insight of Lenin's that power could, under certain circumstances, be seized and held by a purposeful minority prepared to use a secret police. Although it was an un-Marxist insight, it was a correct insight that societies in the transition from traditional to modern status are peculiarly vulnerable to such a seizure of power.

It is here, in fact, that Communism is likely to find its place in history. Recall again . . . the preconditions period . . .: a situation in which the society has acquired a considerable stock of social overhead capital[6] and modern know-how, but is bedevilled not merely by the conflict between the residual traditional elements and those who would modernize its structure, but bedevilled as well by conflicts among those who would move forward,

[5] Referring to Marx's belief that economic forces determine political institutions and behavior.—Ed.

[6] The capital goods, such as ports, roads, and railroads, necessary for the take-off.—Ed.

but who cannot decide which of the three roads to take, and who lack the coherence and organization to move decisively forward in any sustained direction.

It is in such a setting of political and social confusion, before the take-off is achieved and consolidated politically and socially as well as economically, that the seizure of power by Communist conspiracy is easiest; and it is in such a setting that a centralized dictatorship may supply an essential technical precondition for take-off and a sustained drive to maturity: an effective modern state organization.

Remember, for example, what it was in Communism that attracted the Chinese intellectuals after the First World War. It was not its Marxist strain; for the Chinese Communists were—and have remained—indifferent Marxists. It was not the Communist economic performance; for the Russian economy was in poor shape in the early 1920's. The Chinese intellectuals were drawn by Lenin's technique of organization as a means to unify and control a vast, deeply divided country. Both the Kuomintang and the Chinese Communists set themselves up on the Leninist model; and this was understandable in a transitional nation without an effective central government, dominated, in fact, by regional warlords. (Incidentally, if the First World War had not occurred—or had occurred a decade later—Russia would almost certainly have made a successful transition to modernization and rendered itself invulnerable to Communism. Communism gripped Russia very nearly at the end of the phase when it was likely to be vulnerable to the kind of crisis which confronted it in 1917.)

Communism is by no means the only form of effective state organization that can consolidate the preconditions in the transition of a traditional society, launch a take-off, and drive a society to technological maturity. But it may be one way in which this difficult job can be done, if—and this still remains to be seen—if it can solve the problem of agricultural output in the take-off decades. Communism takes its place, then, beside the regime of the Meiji Restoration in Japan, and Ataturk's Turkey, for example, as one peculiarly inhumane form of political organization capable of launching and sustaining the growth process in societies where the preconditions period did not yield a substantial and enterprising commercial middle class and an adequate political consensus among the leaders of the society. It is a kind of disease which can befall a transitional society if it fails to organize effectively those elements within it which are prepared to get on with the job of modernization.

Looking at Soviet agricultural policy, CHARLES WILBER (b. 1935), professor of economics at The American University, Washington, D.C., finds the results satisfactory. His interest is in the Soviet economic model as an example of the development of a backward country. His criteria for judging agricultural performance are quite different, therefore, from those used by Rostow in the preceding selection. He evaluates the policies in terms of the needs and problems of underdeveloped countries. From this perspective, the Soviet experience in agriculture was worth the high price paid by the peasant population.*

Charles Wilber

The Success of an Economic Strategy

Contrary to the popular belief that agriculture hindered Soviet development, it can be shown that agriculture has successfully contributed to the economic development of the Soviet Union. The agricultural sector contributed both labor and capital to the development effort. It provided the food and raw materials (two forms of capital) necessary for an expanding industrial sector and the exports required to pay for imports of scarce capital goods. In addition, agriculture provided a large share of the industrial labor force.

Johnston and Mellor have listed five important ways in which agriculture can contribute to economic development. First, economic development expands the demand for food which, if unfulfilled, would impede further development. Second, exports of agricultural products can increase badly needed foreign exchange earnings. Third, agriculture must supply a significant part of the expanding labor needs of the industrial sector. Fourth, agriculture, as the dominant sector in a peasant economy, must provide capital for industry and social overhead investment; and fifth, rising cash incomes in agriculture can be an important source of demand.

In the Soviet model, however, the first requirement loses some of its urgency because of the large number of controls available in a socialist economy. The fifth requirement is relatively unimportant in a planned economy, since the plan deter-

*From Charles K. Wilber, *The Soviet Model and Underdeveloped Countries* (Chapel Hill, N.C.: The University of North Carolina Press, 1969), pp. 30–37, 47–48, 52. Reprinted by permission. Footnotes omitted.

mines the size and composition of demand. Thus, there remain essentially two major roles for the agricultural sector: the provision of capital in the form of food and raw materials for industry and for export, and the freeing of large numbers of rural workers to join the urban labor force. The key to these requirements is twofold: a growing marketed surplus of agricultural products and a freeing and utilization of surplus labor through structural reorganization, and increasing agricultural productivity per man. The collective farm system in the Soviet Union was designed to provide these solutions.

Soviet agriculture has gone through two stages since industrialization began. The first stage, during the Stalin period, lasted from 1928 to 1953. During this stage agricultural investment was held to the minimum necessary to provide industry with sufficient food, raw materials, and labor. Thus many agricultural problems, that did not immediately affect industry, were allowed to accumulate. By 1953, these accumulated problems had brought the economy to a crisis. Possibly a major achievement of this period was the successful deferral of these problems until the economy was better able to handle them. Beginning in 1954, the regime began a program of agricultural reform to alleviate these problems. Agricultural investment was increased, the new lands program was started, procurement prices were increased, etc. However, these reforms did not change the basic structure of Soviet agriculture.

In this chapter, agricultural growth will be measured for the two stages discussed above. Statistics for the period from 1928 to 1940 will be used for the first stage. This is done because more data are available for 1940 and because the war and reconstruction period of 1940–48 causes serious distortions. Agriculture was slow to recover from the effects of the war. In 1953, the 1940 output level had been barely regained.

Soviet agriculture is organized on the basis of state and collective farms. Because workers on state farms receive regular wages and collective farmers are only residual claimants to their output, the collective farm system was a more effective system to mobilize the agricultural surplus during the early period of industrialization. Because of its predominance during the industrialization period (90 per cent of output during the first stage and 70 per cent after the new lands program) only the collective farm system will be examined in detail.

There were several characteristics of the collective farm system that made it fit into the Soviet strategy of economic development. Collective farms were formed as co-operative associations, established on government owned land given to the farms on indefinite tenure. The farms were required to sell a major part of their output to the state at prices set well below the free market level.

The goal set for the collective farms was maximization of the marketed agricultural output. In addition, special emphasis was placed on the maximization of a particular product-mix of the marketed output. This goal was to be achieved by emphasizing increased output per man instead of increased yields per acre. At the same time this would release needed labor for industry.

The distribution of the collective farm output was regulated by a set of general priorities established by the collective farm charter. In descending order of priority these were: (1) deliveries of the share of output purchased by the state, (2) payment of direct taxes in kind to the state, (3) reimbursement for cost of seed and outside production costs such as services of the machine tractor stations, and (4) distribution of the residual (the wage fund) among collective farm members in accordance with their contribution of labor to production.

The collective farm members were required to render labor services for which they were paid in two forms. First was the assignment of a small plot of land for private use. The output could either be consumed by the collective farm family or sold on the free market. The second form of payment consisted of an unspecified volume of agricultural products in kind and an unspecified money payment out of the total wage fund, which reflected the member's relative share of each farm's total labor time expended in production.

The major decisions of the collective farms were subject to the administrative direction of the state and the actual execution of the decisions was under state control. The state constantly intervened in the internal affairs of the collective farms in order to assure compliance with its policy objectives.

Collection of the Agricultural Surplus. In providing a marketed surplus, agriculture was a source of savings and in the Soviet economy, where saving and investment decisions coincide, it was a source of capital accumulation. This put the Soviet agricultural problem back in the world of classical economics where capital accumulation is limited by the wages fund (conceived as a stock of food). It should be noted that this agricultural surplus was a function not only of surplus manpower, but also of increased total output, increased yields per man, and the level of the peasants' consumption.

The crux of economic development is the capture of this potential agricultural surplus. Ragnar Nurkse points out that "this crucial problem of collecting the food seems to be solved in Soviet Russia by the system of collective farms. The word "collective" has here a double meaning. The collective farm is not only a form of collective organization; it is above all an instrument of collection."

The collection of the marketable agricultural surplus was facilitated in two ways. First, the state, not the market, determined industrial and agricultural prices. The collective farm had to accept both the amount and the prices of the marketed output set by the state. Therefore, the planners could increase the amount of agricultural products needed to exchange for manufactured goods. This shift in the rural-urban "terms-of-trade" in effect forced the agricultural sector to "save."

Second, the collective farm organization enabled the marketed share of output to be determined independently of the size of total agricultural output. Any shortfall in total production was absorbed by a reduction in the residual received by peasant households. Thus, 25 million tons of grain were delivered to the state in 1937 and 24 million tons were delivered in 1939 out of a harvest 20 million tons smaller [than the 1937 harvest]. There were, of course, constraints in the form of minimum peasant health and morale (constraints that during 1932–34 Stalin either miscalulated or ignored).

The success of the collective farm system in capturing the marketable agricultural surplus can be seen from the following figures. The percentage of total agricultural output marketed was 20.3 per cent in 1913 and, during the crucial period of industrialization, it was 28.8 per cent in 1937, and 36.2 per cent in 1939. The marketed output of grain averaged 18.2 million tons per year over the period 1928–32, 27.5 million tons over 1933–37, 32.1 million tons over 1938–40, and 43.5

million tons over the period 1954–58. Marketings of all agricultural products were 65 per cent greater in 1940 and 300 per cent greater in 1961 than in 1913.

Limiting the size of the collective farm's wage fund facilitated Soviet economic growth in another way. The resulting low incomes of the peasants, coupled with high prices of manufactured consumer goods, repressed the effective demand for these goods. Thus, the Soviets were able to restrict investment in consumer goods industries and concentrate most of the investment in capital goods industries, which increased the growth rate of the strategic sectors of industry. It can be concluded therefore, that ". . . the socialization drive in agriculture achieved to a large extent its major economic purpose of serving as a basis for the industrialization drive."

Agricultural marketings not only provided a source of capital by feeding the rapidly expanding industrial labor force, but also by providing exportable products. The large imports of capital equipment in the 1930's were paid for with foreign exchange earned by food and raw material exports. The effectiveness of agricultural exports, however, was severely restricted by the decline of primary product prices on the world market in the 1930's. In addition, agriculture played an important role in a policy of import substitution. Industrial crops such as cotton and sugar beets were rapidly expanded to replace imports of these goods and thus free foreign exchange for the importation of capital goods.

The Release and Utilization of Agricultural Labor. Rapid industrialization ordinarily requires a large increase in the nonagricultural labor force. This demand for labor can be fulfilled either by utilizing available urban labor resources or by freeing a part of the labor force employed in agriculture. The urban labor sources, however, are usually small and quickly used up. Thus, agriculture must carry the main burden of providing the nonagricultural labor force.

In the Soviet Union, where the agricultural structure consisted of individual ownership with the land worked in small plots, potentially surplus labor existed mainly as seasonal unemployment or underemployment of self-employed farmers, tenants, and hired agricultural workers. Year-round disguised unemployment was probably less important because, given the existing technique (the essence of which was individual, small-scale cultivation), a significant proportion of agricultural labor could not be transferred without causing a fall in total farm output. There was little possibility of freeing labor for year-long, off-the-farm work or for seasonal work on capital formation projects without structural reorganization and mechanization. Both were important in the agricultural strategy adopted in the Soviet Union.

To release surplus labor for capital formation projects, seasonal underemployment had to be transformed into seasonal unemployment. Collectivization facilitated this process by converting agriculture from a small-scale unorganized operation into a large-scale planned activity. In the off seasons, farm operations were handled by just part of the farmers, each continuing to work full time, instaed of all the farmers working a few hours each. The labor of the released farmers was then utilized in capital formation. The average number of days worked per year was greatly increased by this method. Thus in the Soviet Union the work-year per person at work in agriculture was lengthened from around 120 days to approximately 185 days.

The Soviet collective farm system also served as a convenient organizational framework for the mobilization of this seasonal unemployment for capital formation. The Fergana irrigation canal was dug by 165 thousand collective farm members from Uzbekistan and Tadjikstan. The Uralo-Kushumskii canal in Kazakhstan and the Samur-Divichinskii canal in Azerbaidjan were each constructed by tens of thousands of collective farmers. In addition, the collective farms supervised the implementation of the statutory obligation of peasants to work six days a year on road construction. Since the collective farms supplied almost all of the labor and some of the equipment they made substantial contributions to capital formation. All together the collective farms contributed labor equal to an annual average of about one million yearly workers. Since this labor was rendered during the off season and without compensation by the state (the greater number of workdays earned divided into the unchanged total income would give each workday a lower value), there was a net gain for the economy. The Soviets did not, however, make use of all the available possibilities. For example, in October, 1938, a decree was issued discouraging industrial activity unconnected with agriculture on the farm.

Off-season employment of agricultural labor in construction, transportation, forestry, road and railroad construction, and even in mining and manufacturing existed under the traditional agrarian structures of Tsarist Russia and the Soviet New Economic Policy of the 1920's. The collective farm system, however, did more. It enabled the Soviets to organize and control the flow of temporary off-the-farm labor. The Soviet Union established *Organizovannyi Nabor* (organized recruitment) among the collective farms which, in turn, assigned certain members to work off the farms for various time periods. The total number recruited between 1931 and 1940 was 28.7 million workers. The average time worked off the farm per person was five to six months during 1933 to 1935 and eight to nine months in 1940. The demand for this type of seasonal labor declined over the period, however, for several reasons. There was a decrease in demand for unskilled labor in general, an increase in labor recruitment through vocational schools, and an increasing demand for permanent rather than seasonal labor in nonagricultural work.

While the organized use of seasonal farm labor on agricultural capital formation projects and temporary urban work was important, even more important was the release of agricultural labor for permanent relocation in the urban areas. This required that output per *man* be increased so that at least the same output could be produced with a smaller agricultural work force. Both reorganization of the agrarian structure and mechanization contributed to this needed increase in productivity per man.

Reorganization through consolidation of small peasant holdings increased the division of labor and the degree of specialization, thus raising productivity per man. Instead of each peasant performing all of the farm tasks, some specialized in plowing, some in weeding, some in animal husbandry, and so on. In addition, labor was saved through the consolidation of farm buildings, equipment, and the like. The labor required, for example, to maintain one set of farm buildings was less than that required to maintain fifty smaller but separate ones. Also idle machine time was reduced on pre-existing farm equipment, even small-scale hand tools, rakes, hammers, and the like. Instead of each farmer requiring a full set of tools with much duplication, gains were made by computing needs on an economic, not a legal, foundation.

More important, consolidation of land holdings made possible the widespread use of tractors, sheaf-binders, threshing machines, cultivators, seed selection apparatus, combine-harvesting machines, and other agricultural equipment, which improved cultivation of the soil, saved labor, and prevented harvesting losses. This mechanization, by increasing labor productivity, also released labor for permanent nonagricultural work.

Nonagricultural employment in the Soviet Union increased very rapidly after 1928. The number of workers employed outside of agriculture increased from 9.0 million in 1929 to 19.6 million in 1932, 28.2 million in 1940, and 61.8 million in 1963. The same trend is evident when data reflecting the transfer of the rural population to urban areas are examined. Between 1926 and 1939, 18.7 million people moved from rural to urban areas and between 1939 and 1959 another 24.6 million moved, for a total of 43.3 million as compared to a net increase in the urban population of 73 million between 1926 and 1959. . . .

Collectivization did have one major negative effect on Soviet agriculture. The attempt to go too far too fast led to resistance by the Russian peasant, particularly by the livestock owning kulaks, and resulted in a massive slaughter of livestock (not to mention people). Between 1928 and 1933 the number of horses fell from 33.4 to 14.9 million, of cattle from 70.4 to 33.7 million, and of sheep and goats from 145.9 to 41.8 million. Collectivization was carried out by urban activists who were ignorant of rural life and unsympathetic to the peasants. The process was a crude improvisation. Even the organizational pattern of a collective farm was unclear. The decision to collectivize all livestock, soon reversed, led to the mass slaughter of animals by the peasants. The decision to collectivize all livestock was a costly mistake. . . .

In spite of the many difficulties noted above, Soviet agricultural strategy succeeded in fulfilling its role in the development process and facilitated the construction of a modern industrial economy. Collectivization increased output per man, thus releasing labor for industry and rural capital formation projects. Collectivization also facilitated the collection of the agricultural surplus and its allocation to the industrial and export sectors. In this way, Soviet agriculture has been a success when evaluated in terms of its assigned development goals.

Social change has been central to the Soviet experience, but the results have often been different from expectations. ALEX INKELES (b. 1920), professor of sociology at Harvard University, emphasizes the disparity between old and new social institutions, and between planned and achieved social change. He points out the great transformation of formal institutions in Soviet society, along with a continuation of old patterns of behavior. The Soviet leaders sought to remake their society, but their efforts at "social engineering" had to be modified to allow greater order and stability in Soviet life.*

Alex Inkeles

The Great Social Experiment

The second major period of revolutionary development, the period of the consolidation of power, beginning in 1924, extends through the latter part of the New Economic Policy and the massive programs of industrialization and forced collectivization, down to the formal declaration of the establishment of socialism embodied in the so-called Stalin Constitution of 1936. The revolution had been fought to a successful issue. The old society was a bombed-out shell, with only here and there a torn wall still standing, although a certain subterranean structure or foundation stood relatively undamaged and firm, representing a phenomenon yet to be dealt with by the regime.

The task of revolution shifted to that of building the new society on the ruins of the old. Lenin was not unaware that the revolution was only a surface phenomenon so long as it was restricted to the formal destruction of the old social order. Many a revolution before had seen the rapid restoration of the old order despite the most sweeping formal legal changes. Indeed, Lenin was wont to speak of what he termed a peculiar "Bolshevik conceit" implicit in the assumption that revolution could be effected by decree rather than by the systematic construction of new institutional forms and patterns of social organization and human relationship. It is in this period, therefore, that we find the

*Reprinted by permission of the publishers from Alex Inkeles, *Social Change in Soviet Russia,* Cambridge, Mass.: Harvard University Press, Copyright 1968, by the President and Fellows of Harvard College, pp. 9–23. Footnotes omitted.

extensive social experimentation and innovation which produced the main institutional forms that we recognize today as the characteristic features of Soviet society. Indeed this period may be regarded as the second Soviet revolution—the first revolutionized the structure of formal power and authority, the second, the social revolution, revolutionized the forms and patterns of socio-economic organization.

By the late 1920's, in the agricultural realm, for example, the land was nationalized and the landowner gone from the countryside. But in most essential respects the forms of rural social and economic organization remained much as they had been before the Revolution. The old patterns of social differentiation were still much in evidence. In 1927, 8 per cent of the peasants were still landless, 20 per cent were classified as semi-proletarians, and over a third of the households were still obliged to hire their animal power and farm implements from the rich peasant, or "kulak." Only about 3 per cent of the peasant households were joined in state or cooperative farms. As Sir John Maynard has phrased it, ten years after the Revolution "the countryside was back in pre-war days, minus the landlord."

It was into this situation that the regime moved with its astounding program of forced collectivization on a scale unprecedented in history and with a ferocity and intensity such that even Stalin had to draw back, call a temporary halt, and cry "dizzy with success." Some 25 million farm families, constituting more than 100 million souls, were forced in the span of a few short years radically to change the whole pattern of their lives. Five million of these people, those in the families designated as "kulak," were dispossessed outright of their land and property, and a large proportion forcibly transplanted to other parts of the country. The Russian countryside glowed red, the sky with flames of burning peasant huts and government buildings, the ground with the blood of cattle slaughtered by the peasants and peasants slaughtered by the militia and by the flying squads of Communist workers and the agitated peasant "Committees of the Poor." Between 1928 and 1933, the cattle population fell from 70 to 38 million, sheep and goats from 147 to 50 million, and pigs from 26 to 12 million. Losses of this magnitude for a predominantly agricultural country are so staggering as to be very nearly beyond comprehension. They meant for the country at large a drastic and violent decline in the supply of animal food and industrial raw materials, and for the villages, in addition, a colossal loss of draught power and animal fertilizer. Once again famine stalked the land.

Yet out of this chaos and destruction there emerged a new form of social organization which constitutes one of the major institutional complexes of Soviet society, incorporating well over half the population. The *kolkhoz,* or collective farm system, is a distinctive form of social organization, with its *kolkhoz* chairman, general meeting, advisory council, and other administrative forms; its brigades and links for the organization of the work group; its labor day, piece rate, and bonus system of remuneration; its social insurance funds, communal buildings, peasant reading huts, radio loudspeaker nets, and other instrumentalities for the provision of social services and facilitation of communication by the regime; its complicated contracts with the machine tractor stations and state breeding farms, and with government agencies which control production and regulate delivery to the state of assigned quotas of produce; its *usadba,* or private garden plot, and other devices for relating the private economy of the peasant to the collectivized, state-oriented segment of the agricultural economy. All these are examples of the diverse institutional arrangements which had to be devised to convert the idea of collective farming into an adequate form of social organization capable of effecting agricultural production in accord with the interests of the regime, which would yet have an essential minimum of congruence with the needs and expectations of the peasants. Thus we see in the agricultural realm the characteristic pattern of the second phase of revolutionary development—to meet newly created or perceived needs, new forms of social organization are devised, tested, re-formed and reshaped, and finally woven into some viable system of social institutions for relating men to men, to the machinery of production, and to the larger society.

Certainly less violent, but perhaps no less spectacular, was the industrial transformation of Soviet society effected by the Five-Year Plans. In the course of the first Five-Year Plan more than 20 billion rubles were invested in industrialization, above 80 per cent of that sum going to heavy industry alone. The gross product of large-scale industry as evaluated in fixed prices was by Soviet report more than doubled, and although there is much doubt as to the accuracy of the figure it does reflect the magnitude of development, which is also apparent in the fact that the industrial labor force doubled in size from 11 to 22 million workers and employees.

In contrast to the situation in agricultural production, the regime was faced with the much less difficult task of creating institutional forms *de novo,* for there was at hand both the model of industrial organization in pre-revolutionary Russia and throughout the Western world as well as Soviet experience gained in the years of state industrial administration since 1917. At the same time, the leaders' experience was largely limited to restoring to its former level an already established industrial structure, whereas they were now faced with the rather different task of building a new industrial system. The problem was intensified not only by the greater magnitude and complexity of the new industrial order, but also by the fact that many of the industries now introduced were new to the Russian scene. Consequently, in this area as well, there arose imposing problems of evolving new forms of social organization, and of integrating the new molecular institutions with the molar social system.

The result was a vast amount of experimentation, invention, revision, and readjustment in the social and organizational forms which constituted the structure of Soviet industry. For example, to find the most efficient formula for relating the discrete industrial enterprises to each other the regime abolished the chief administrations, or *glavks,* and replaced them with combines in May 1929, only to abolish the combines in turn and replace them in 1934 with the previously abolished chief administrations, now reconstituted in revised form. As might be expected, the greatest uncertainty centered on problems of managerial responsibility, with a constant strain manifested between the demands of efficient, authoritative management on the one hand, and on the other the requirement for central control by higher economic organs and for supervision and political surveillance by the local Party and trade union organizations. There was, consequently, a long history of experimentation and halting development before there emerged the current (1954) Soviet variant on the common pattern of responsible plant management, which they termed *edinonachalie,* or one-man management. . . .

By the mid 1930's the process of tearing down the old social structure was complete in virtually all its phases, and the main foundations of the new social order laid down. The factories were built, and the peasants organized in collective farms under firm state control. The first process, that of tearing down the old social structure, was particularly facilitated by the release of revolutionary energies and by the natural destructive forces set in motion with the loosening of social bonds characterizing revolutionary periods. The second process, that of laying the foundations for the new social order, was greatly facilitated by the devotion and extra human effort of a small minority—even though a minority of several millions—pushing the rest of the population by example, persuasion, and, where necessary, by force. This was the "heroic" phase of the revolutionary process.

But neither revolutionary fervor nor extra human effort constitutes a firm basis for the persistent day-to-day operation of a large-scale social system. The political and economic development of the revolution had now run far ahead of the more narrowly "social." In the haste of revolutionary experiment, no systematic attention had been given to the congruence of the newly established institutional forms with the motivational systems, the patterns of expectation and habitual behavior, of the population. Furthermore, as the new institutions began to function they produced social consequences neither planned nor anticipated by the regime. The leaders found themselves somehow compelled to bring these elements into line. For they found that it was one thing to build large factories and form collective farms, but quite another matter to get those institutions to function persistently at reasonable levels of efficiency. They came slowly to realize that it was one matter to enroll the peasants in collectives and to mobilize millions of workers in industry, but yet another matter to induce them to labor discipline and high productivity. This realization was symbolized in Stalin's declaration in 1935 that, whereas in the first years of the plan it was technique that was decisive, in the new period "cadres [personnel] decide everything."

We enter therefore what we have termed the third phase of revolutionary development in the Soviet Union—the period of the stabilization of social relationships. It is this period that answers in large part the question, "What elements in the old social order tend to persist despite the revolution, and are changed, if at all, only in the long run?" It appears that despite the massive destruction of the main formal elements of the old social structure and the extensive elaboration of new social forms, a large number of basic attitudes, values, and sentiments, as well as traditional modes of orientation, expression, and reaction were markedly persistent. Although the revolution effected a radical shift in the locus of power, the traditional attitudes of the population to authority and authority figures cannot be assumed to have undergone a comparable transformation. The change in the formal pattern of property relationships was equally fundamental, yet there is little evidence that the common man's "sense" of property, his attitude toward its accumulation, possession, and disposition, was altered in significant degree. In brief, we come in contact here with national character, or better, the modal personality patterns of the population, which show a marked propensity to be relatively enduring despite sweeping changes in the formal structure of society.

Certain core or primary institutional forms, notably the kinship structure and the pattern of interpersonal relations within the family, show a comparable resistance and delayed reaction to change despite the revolutionary process.

Such persistent elements in the social system have a major impact on the revolutionary ideology and the new institutional patterns created under its imperative in the earlier phases of the revolution. The interaction of these forces of course changes both elements, but if we are to judge by Soviet experience, the accommodations and adjustments come sooner and are more extensive in the new institutional forms than in the traditional primary institutions and their associated behavioral patterns. The really massive attack on the problem, the large-scale conscious adjustments to meet this situation, appear to be delayed until the later stages of revolutionary development. This delay occurs in part because realization of the need for such adjustments comes but slowly to practical men in the habit of effecting social change by decree, and in part because the initial focus was so heavily on the destruction of the old society and the institution of the major formal structure of the new social order. In the case of a Marxist-oriented revolution, furthermore, there is the added influence of an ideology which predisposes the leaders to assume that fundamental changes in the patterns of human relations, seen by them as part of the *dependent* "superstructure" of society, must follow naturally and inevitably from changes in the formal political and economic system.

In any event, from the early 1930's there began, in regard to a large number of Soviet institutions, a series of fundamental policy changes which many saw as the restitution of the old social order, others as the betrayal of the revolution. The "great retreat," as Timasheff has labeled it, represented the regime's effort to place social relations on a stable basis adequate to the demands of a large-scale industrialized, hierarchic, authoritarian society. In the last analysis it was designed to produce disciplined, compliant, obedient individuals with respect for authority, who yet had a strong sense of individual responsibility and were active, goal-oriented, optimistic, stable.

Appropriately, basic changes came earliest in the realm of education, which witnessed rapid abandonment of progressive education and its replacement by traditional subjects organized in standard curricula, a formal system of examinations and grades, and perhaps most important, the restoration of the authority of the teacher. History was rewritten to reconstitute the role of the individual as a historical force, the great national leaders of the past were restored and now glorified, and the inculcation of patriotism became a prime responsibility of the school. The family, as already indicated, was restored to grace and defined as a pillar of the state, the authority of parents emphasized and their role defined as partner of the state in the upbringing of disciplined, loyal, patriotic citizens devoted to hard work and exemplary social behavior. The law was fetched out of the discard heap of the revolution and given an honored place as an essential ingredient of the new social order. Social stratification emerged in an elaborate and refined system of gradation of income and status which gave rise to a full-blown system of social stratification bearing significant resemblance to the classic model of Western industrial society. Accompanying these changes, and in a sense symbolizing the whole range of development, was the profound reorientation of Soviet psychology. The old determinist attitude toward human behavior was condemned and replaced wholesale by a psychology which emphasized individual responsibility and the ability of man to shape his own personality and behavior by the action of his will. The whole trend was perhaps climaxed by the startling accommodation with the Church which the regime made during the later years of the Second World War and in the postwar years.

Thus virtually all the novel and radical orientations of the regime to interpersonal relations and primary social groupings, which for many people were the distinguishing characteristics of the revolution, were replaced by traditional orientations of a distinctly conservative cast. There emerged by the time of World War II a definite and relatively stable social structure that was a distinctive mixture of the old social order and of the new institutional elements which had emerged out of the commitments of the revolutionary ideology. Both elements were, however, greatly transformed, adapted to the inherent demands of large-scale organization and the traditional motivational and behavioral patterns of the population. In significant degree the revolutionary process inside Russia had come to an end.

Although the pressure on the Soviet leaders to adapt the patterns of social relations better to suit them to the demands of the new industrial order is clearly evident, it is by no means equally clear why the course of action adopted involved so marked a restoration of previously scorned patterns of social organization. The availability of those traditional patterns may perhaps be attributed to the inherent resistance of primary relationship patterns to social change. Since the regime shifted its policies after little more than two decades of rule, during part of which time its preoccupation with merely staying in power drew off much of its energy, it is hardly to be expected that a radical transformation in popular values and attitudes should have occurred in anything but a small segment of the population. Furthermore, the widespread absence of enthusiasm—indeed the active hostility—of large segments of the population to the Bolsheviks and their program, undoubtedly heightened allegiance to old values and ways of life. This allegiance to old ways, which constituted a stubborn mute resistance to the regime, could be expressed with relative safety because it was so covert. Finally, one should not neglect the fact that in times of rapid change and general social disorganization there is a widespread tendency to find a modicum of security in ritualistic adherence to familiar values and patterns of life.

The resistance offered, and consequent strain posed, by these persistent orientations undoubtedly forced some direct compromises on the regime. The granting to the collective farm peasant of the right to a private plot, and later the right to sell his surplus more or less freely in the peasant market, exemplify such forced compromises. But the changes in policy toward the family, the restoration of law, the reorientation of the school system, the reintroduction of ranks and distinctive uniforms in the military services, can hardly be fully explained as the product of any inescapable compromise on the regime's part with the demands of the populace. The stimulus for most of the changes came directly from the central authorities; they were another manifestation of what Stalin has called "revolution from above." Indeed, in the case of the law making abortion illegal,[1] the mea-

[1] Declared illegal in 1936, restored in 1955.—Ed.

sure was forced through despite obvious widespread resistance on the part of major segments of at least the urban women.

The explanation of such changes must, therefore, be sought primarily in changed orientations of the Bolshevik leadership, changes in their conception of the nature of Soviet society and their role in it. Although Lenin was an exceedingly hard and ruthless politician, there were elements of radical "libertarian," indeed utopian, thought in his conception of the new society under socialism. These "libertarian" sentiments were given full expression by Lenin only during the brief period immediately preceding and following the Revolution, particularly in his *The State and Revolution.*[2] Yet we cannot dismiss them entirely. Although those thoughts represented a definitely minor mode in the total pattern of Lenin's thinking, they did constitute one facet of his intellectual make-up. Thus, alongside of Lenin's view of the mass man as inert, lacking in consciousness, and requiring stimulation and direction from without, another element of Lenin's view of human nature treated man as essentially spontaneously "good," and capable of tremendous works of creative social living once freed from the constraints, pressures, and distorting influences of capitalist society. He envisioned a relatively "free" society, in which the oppression of the state would be directed primarily against the former possessing classes, whereas the proletarian masses would enjoy a new birth of freedom. Lenin therefore assumed a high degree of direct mass participation in the processes of industry and government, epitomized in his statement that every toiler and cook could help run the government. He assumed that personal motivation would also undergo a transformation, and that men would work harder and better than ever before, because now they would be working "for themselves." Finally, the general problem of social control would diminish in importance, partly because of the new motivations of man under conditions of freedom, and partly because the community of men would take it directly into its own hands to deal with those who violated social norms. . . .

Lenin's successors, Stalin and his coterie, at no time revealed a philosophic orientation to the problems of man's role in society which was at all comparable to that revealed, however briefly, by Lenin in 1917. They were hardly social radicals in the sense that Lenin was. They came to power by means of their talent for controlling and manipulating the Party apparatus, wielding traditional instruments of power. They effected their program by force, and came through further experience to rely on the efficacy of organization and discipline, and to respect rules, order, training, and duty. Their approach to institutional forms was exceedingly pragmatic, their faith being largely in institutions that "worked"—that is, accomplished the functions assigned them in the social realm—so long as those institutions were consonant with the general goal of maintaining the Communist Party in power and facilitating the transformation of Soviet society into a large-scale industrial power, state-socialist in form.

This new leadership was faced, in the late 1920's and early 1930's, with a distinctive problem in Soviet development which heightened the probability that its basic propensities in the treatment of people would be maximally expressed. The rate of industrial expansion in the initial Plan period was much more intense than had been earlier expected or indeed planned. This rate of development, im-

[2] Written in 1917.—Ed.

posed as it was on a system already operating with a most meager margin of popular consumption, created enormous, seemingly insatiable and self-perpetuating demands for the sacrifice of individual comfort and freedom of choice. Unless the pace of industrialization were to be significantly relaxed—a possibility the Stalin leadership apparently rejected outright—continued functioning of the system required absolute control of every resource, and of human resources first of all. The problem of social control became central to the Stalin group, and the answer it posed to the problem was consistent with the patterns it had manifested in its own ascent to power with the Communist Party. Thus, however limited their chances for survival even under continued Leninist rule, the radical libertarian aspects of the earlier stages of the revolution fell a certain victim to the combination of circumstances represented by the propensities of the Stalinist group and the demands of the forced pace of industrialization which that group set.

The type of authority which the Stalinist leadership represented, and the pattern of institutional relations it had forged in Soviet society, required obedience, loyalty, reliability, unquestioning fulfillment of orders, adherence to norms and rules, willingness to subordinate oneself to higher authority, and other personal qualities suitable to an authoritarian system. In fact, however, the supply of such people was exceedingly limited.

The Stalinist faction was obliged, rather, to deal with two main types. First, more limited in number but widely present in positions of responsibility and trust within the elite, were the goal-oriented idealists, who found it difficult to compromise principle and to accept the apparent sacrifice of basic revolutionary goals for short-run intermediate objectives. Although these people were most prominent amongst the older generation of Bolsheviks, the Soviet school and the Young Communist League continued to attract and develop such individuals in substantial numbers. The second group, the great mass of the rank-and-file of the population, posed a related but different problem. Here, the widespread traditional Russian characteristics of evasion and suspicion of authority, avoidance of responsibility, lack of discipline and striving, were not being systematically countered by Soviet education, nor discouraged by Soviet law and custom through rigorous sanctions. Indeed, the system of progressive education probably seemed to the Stalin leadership to reinforce many of these basic orientations, and the beleaguered family was hardly a model of "proper" authority relations.

The problem posed by the core of goal-oriented idealists was of course summarily resolved by the ruthless method of the great purge in the mid 1930's, and by the reorientation of Party and Konsomol[3] selection and training. The problem posed by the rank-and-file of the population, and particularly by the growing generation of young people many of whom were expected to enter the Soviet elite, was not resolvable by such simple means. The Stalinist leaders recognized that marked changes would be required in both the initial training of young people and in the environment in which those individuals would live as adults. The restoration of law, the reintroduction of ideas of guilt and personal responsibility, the intensification of sanctions, the imposition of firmer discipline, were therefore largely rational selections of means for the given end.

The restitution of the family and the

[3] Young Communist League.—Ed.

changes in educational policy may be understood in much the same way. The leadership was concerned with developing disciplined, orderly, hard-working, responsible individuals who respected and feared authority. The restoration of the teacher's authority along with the reintroduction of regular curricula, examinations, school uniforms, student "passports," and the rest was apparently a product of careful calculation relative to the attainment of the goals indicated.

In seeking to achieve those goals it is not surprising that Soviet leaders should have looked to the past for models which had proved that they could "work" and which might be expected to take more "naturally" with the people. It is not at all necessary to assume, as some have, that this tendency arose because the Bolshevik leaders had "mellowed" as their stay in power extended itself, and that they consequently came to value traditional Russian forms as ends in themselves. Indeed, it is perfectly clear from the marked selectivity in the choice of elements from the past to be reconstituted, that only those were chosen which could serve the current objectives of the regime. The Bolsheviks restored many old forms, but they were not restorationists. Although the forms utilized were conservative, they were adopted to serve the radical end of remaking Soviet man in a new mold of subservience, and although tradition was emphasized the Soviet leaders sought to manipulate it and not to follow it.

There were, of course, other alternatives open. Particularly in the case of the family, the regime could conceivably have attempted to bring up all children in state institutions in an effort to develop precisely the type of human material it desired. Indeed, the development of such institutions on a limited scale in the postwar period, in the form of the Suvorov and Nakhimov military schools, reveals the probable attraction of this solution for the present Soviet leaders. But the cost and burden for the state would have been enormous, the alienation of the population extreme, and the effect on the birth rate severe. Since the family could therefore not easily be replaced, the leaders acted instead to convert it to their purpose of raising a work-loving, loyal, disciplined, authority-fearing generation. Again, although the solution adopted may have been conservative, it hardly derived from any desire to return to the old way of life. Rather, it was an adaptation of established and tested institutional forms to the purposes of the regime. Indeed, it may be said that a characteristic of the last fifteen years of Soviet rule has been the increasing precision with which the leadership has come to manipulate institutions and juggle situations in order to harness private motivation to its own ends.

Marx was much more concerned with elaborating the developmental "laws" of capitalism than he was in outlining the instutitional structure of socialist society. Indeed, he tended to regard such efforts in a class with utopianism. Lenin, in his turn, was much more concerned with developing a model of the revolutionary political party, and with the strategy and tactics for the revolutionary seizure of power, than with detailing the pattern of social relations that should exist in the new society. Yet they left a sufficiently large number of explicit prescriptions and prognostications about the institutional forms of socialist society to permit a meaningful comparison between their expectations and the reality of Soviet social organization. Barrington Moore, attempting such an assessment in his *Soviet Politics,* has concluded that, of all the aspects of Bolshevik doctrine, the transfer of the means of production to the community as a whole represents the main instance of close congruence between pre-revolutionary anticipations and post-revolutionary facts. Although many observers might produce a more extended list, there certainly is no doubt that the expectations concerning the school, the family, the organization of industry, mass political participation, social equality, and even religion, are hardly met by contemporary social reality in the Soviet Union.

In the light of this fact, what remains of the characterization of Soviet society as the product of planned social change? Certainly little, if anything, if our measure be the congruence between the current social structure of the U.S.S.R. and the specific institutional patterns called for in the social blueprint of Marxist-Leninist doctrine to which Soviet leaders ostensibly adhered. Long-range planning in this sense in the Soviet Union has been largely limited to the pursuit of very general goals, which were themselves frequently subject to change. It is perhaps more appropriate, therefore, to describe the pattern of social change in the Soviet Union as one in which the *forces* that produced change were centrally planned—or, better, set in motion—rather than to speak of the precise resultant *institutions* themselves as having been planned. Thus, Stalin decreed the forced collectivization, and in some degree he planned and controlled the stages of its execution. But apparently no one in the Soviet regime had a plan for the detailed, or even the broad, structure of human relations within the collective farm. The collective farm system as the complex of social organization which we know today was planned by no one. It grew out of a continuous process of accommodation and adjustment between the regime's interest in production and its control, the requirements of efficient organization within the structure of large-scale farm units, and the persistent desires, needs, interests, and expectations of the people who worked the farms.

The relatively unplanned development of the internal organization of the collective farm, however, represents only one aspect of advanced social planning in the U.S.S.R. In particular, this type of development was most characteristic of the middle period of Soviet history, which we have termed the period of the consolidation of power. In the more recent period, as the preceding discussion of the changes in family, education, law, and so on, sought to emphasize, there has been a marked tendency for the "revolution from above" to become ever more precise in effecting change rationally designed to achieve specific social ends. Furthermore, evidence from both published Soviet sources and interviews with former Soviet citizens strongly supports the premise that the regime has been surprisingly successful in its attempt to build "stability" in social relations.

The lower classes of the cities and countryside have experienced profound changes in their ways of life since 1917. ISAAC DEUTSCHER (1907–1969), author of many books on Soviet history, distinguishes between the progressive and backward groups in Soviet society. The workers, destined to become the largest single social group, had the most to contribute and the most to gain by the revolutionary changes. The peasantry, on the other hand, were doomed to decline in size and importance by the very dynamics of industrialization and urbanization. Their cruel fate under Stalin was in the broad perspective only a more dramatic form of the suffering of peasants in underdeveloped countries.*

Isaac Deutscher

The New Urban Society

Before we proceed any further we ought, perhaps, to remind ourselves that these fifty years [1917–1967] have not been a single uninterrupted period of growth and development. Seven or eight of the fifty years were taken up by armed hostilities which resulted in severe setbacks and widespread destruction, unparalleled in any other belligerent country. Another twelve or thirteen years were spent on replacing the losses. The actual periods of growth cover the years from 1928 to 1941 and from 1950 onwards, about thirty years in all. And in these years an unusually high proportion of Soviet resources, about one-quarter of the national income on the average, was absorbed in the arms races that preceded and followed the Second World War. If one could calculate the advance in ideal units of truly peaceful years, one would conclude that the Soviet Union achieved its progress within twenty or, at the most, twenty-five years. This has to be kept in mind when one tries to assess the performance. But, of course, present Soviet society is the product of the turmoil of this half-century so that in its development gain and loss, construction and destruction, have been inseparable; and the combination of productive effort, unproductive work, and waste has affected both the material life and the spiritual climate of the U.S.S.R.

The first and most striking feature of

*From *The Unfinished Revolution: Russia 1917–1967,* by Isaac Deutscher. © 1967 by Isaac Deutscher. Reprinted by permission of Oxford University Press, Inc. Pp. 42–46, 47–53.

the transformed scene is the massive urbanization of the U.S.S.R. Since the revolution the town population has grown by over 100 million people. Here again a corrective in the time scale is needed. The first decade after 1917 was marked by a depopulation of the cities and a slow reverse movement. The effect of the Second World War was the same, at least in European Russia. The periods of intensive urbanization were between the years 1930 and 1940 and between 1950 and 1965. About 800 big and medium-sized towns and over 2000 small urban settlements were built. In 1926 there were only 26 million town dwellers. In 1966 their number was about 125 million. In the last fifteen years alone the urban population has increased by 53 or 54 million people, that is by as much as the entire population of the British Isles. Within the lifetime of a generation the percentage of the town dwellers in the total population has risen from 15 to about 55 per cent; and it is fast climbing up to 60 per cent. In the United States—to take the previous record in this field—it took over 160 years for the urban population to increase by 100 million people; or, if the more relevant percentual comparison is made, it took a full century, from 1850 to 1950, for the proportion of the town dwellers to rise from 15 to 60 per cent. Throughout those hundred years the phenomenal growth of the American cities and towns was stimulated and facilitated by mass immigration, influx of foreign capital and skill, and immunity from foreign invasion and wartime destruction, not to speak of the inducements of climate. Soviet urbanization, in tempo and scale, is without parallel in history. Such a change in social structure, even if it had taken place in more favourable circumstances, would have created huge and baffling problems in housing, settlement, health, and education; and Soviet circumstances were as if designed to intensify and magnify beyond measure the turmoil and the shocks.

Only a small proportion of the expansion was due to natural growth or to the migration of townspeople. The mass of the new town dwellers were peasants, shifted from the villages, year after year, and directed to industrial labour. Like the old advanced nations of the West, the Soviet Union found the main reserve of industrial manpower in the peasantry. In the early stages the growth of capitalist enterprise in the West was often accompanied by the forcible expropriation of farmers—in Britain by the "enclosures"—and by draconic labour legislation. Later the West relied in the main on the spontaneous work of the labour market, with its laws of supply and demand, to bring the required manpower to industry. This euphemism means that in the course of many decades, if not of centuries, rural overpopulation, and sometimes famine, threw great masses of redundant hands onto the labour market. In the Soviet Union the State secured the supply of labour by means of planning and direction. Its dominant economic position was the decisive factor; without it, it would hardly have been possible to carry out so gigantic a transformation within so short a time.

The transfer of the rural population began in earnest in the early 1930s, and it was closely connected with the collectivization of farming, which enabled the government's agencies to lay hands on the surplus of manpower on the farms and to move it to industry. The beginnings of the process were extremely difficult and involved the use of much force and violence. The habits of settled industrial life, regulated by the factory siren, which had in other countries been inculcated into the workers, from generation to generation, by economic necessity and legislation, were lacking in Russia. The peasants had been accustomed to work in their fields according to the rhythm of Russia's severe nature, to toil from sunrise to sunset in the summer and to drowse on the tops of their stoves most of the winter. They had now to be forced and conditioned into an entirely new routine of work. They resisted, worked sluggishly, broke or damaged tools, and shifted restlessly from factory to factory and from mine to mine. The government imposed discipline by means of harsh labour codes, threats of deportation, and actual deportation to forced labour camps. Lack of housing and acute shortages of consumer goods, due in large measure to deliberate acts of an anti-consumptionist policy—the government was bent on obtaining the maximum output of producer goods and munitions—aggravated the hardships and the turbulence. It was common in the cities, even quite recently, for several families to share a single room and a kitchen; and in the industrial settlements, masses of workers were herded in barracks for many years. Crime was rampant. At the same time, however, many millions of men and women received primary or even secondary education, were trained in industrial skills, and settled down to the new way of life.

As time went on, social friction and conflicts engendered by the upheaval lessened. Since the Second World War the feats of Soviet industry and arms have appeared to justify retrospectively even the violence, the suffering, the blood, and the tears. But it may be held, as I have held through all these decades, that without the violence, the blood, and the tears, the great work of construction might have been done far more efficiently and with healthier social, political, and moral after-effects. Whatever the truth of the matter, the transformation of the social structure continues; and continues without such forcible stimulation. Year after year the urban population is expanding on the same scale as before; and the process, though planned and regulated, obeys its own rhythm. In the 1930s the government had to drag a sullen mass of peasants into the towns; in this last decade or so it has been confronted by a spontaneous rush of people from the country to towns; and it has had to exert itself and make rural life a little more attractive in order to keep young labour on the farms. But the present population trend will probably continue; and in another ten or fifteen years, three-quarters of the population may well live in towns.

The industrial workers, the small minority of 1917, now form the largest social class. The State employs about 78 million people in workshops and offices—it employed 27 million after the end of the Second World War. Well over 50 million people work in primary and manufacturing industries, in building, transport, communications, and on State-owned farms. The rest earn their livelihood in various services—13 million of them in health, education, and scientific research. It is not easy to distinguish with any precision the numbers of manual workers and technicians from those of office workers, because Soviet statistics lump them together. . . . The number of the workers proper may be put at between 50 and 55 million.

The working class is highly stratified. Stalin's labour policy centred on differential scales of salaries and wages and raised the labour aristocracy high above the mass of the underpaid semiskilled and unskilled, workers. To some extent this was justified by the need to offer incentives to skill and efficiency; but the discrepancies in wages went far beyond. Their actual extent was and still is surrounded by extraordinary secrecy. Since the 1930s the government has not published the relevant data about the national wage structure, and students have had to content themselves with fragmentary information. Throughout the Stalin era a ferocious witch-hunt against the levellers —or the "petty bourgeois egalitarians" —was in progress; but it was less effective than it appeared to be, and certainly less so than the political witch-hunts. . . .

The social and cultural stratification of the working class is sometimes even more important than the economic one. This is a subject which does not lend itself to a clear-cut sociological description or analysis; all I can do here is to try to convey a general idea of it and to indicate its complexity. The prodigious growth of the working class has resulted in many social and cultural discrepancies and incongruities, reflecting the successive phases of industrialization and their overlapping. Each phase brought into being a different layer of the working class and produced significant cleavages. The bulk of the working class is strongly marked by its peasant origins. There are only very few working-class families who have been settled in town since before the revolution and have any sort of industrial tradition and memories of pre-revolutionary class struggle. In effect, the oldest layer of workers is the one which formed itself during the reconstruction period of the 1920s. Its adaptation to the rhythm of industrial life was relatively easy—these workers came to the factory of their own accord and were not yet subjected to strict regimentation. Their children are the most settled and the most distinctly urban element of the industrial population. From their ranks came the *vydvizhentsy,*[1] the managerial elements and the labour aristocracy of the 1930s and 1940s. Those who remained in the ranks were the last Soviet workers to engage freely, under the New Economic Policy, in trade union activities, even in strikes, and to enjoy a certain freedom of political expression.

The contrast between this and the next layer is extremely sharp. Twenty-odd million peasants were shifted to the towns during the 1930s. Their adaptation was painful and jerky. For a long time they remained uprooted villagers, town dwellers against their will, desperate, anarchic, and helpless. They were broken to the habits of factory work and kept under control by ruthless drill and discipline. It was they who gave the Soviet towns the grey, miserable, semi-barbarous look that so often astonished foreign visitors. They brought into industry the *muzhiks'*[2] crude individualism. Official policy played on it, prodding the industrial recruits to compete with one another for bonuses, premiums, and multiple piece rates. Worker was thus turned against worker at the factory bench; and pretexts of "socialist competition" were used to prevent the formation and manifestation of any class solidarity. The terror of the 1930s left an indelible imprint on the men of this category. Most of them, now in their fifties, are probably—through no fault of theirs—the most backward element among Soviet workers—uneducated, acquisitive, servile. Only in its second generation could this layer of the working class live down the initial shocks of urbanization.

The peasants who came to the factories

[1] Professional and administrative elite promoted from lower classes with no previous experience—Ed.

[2] Russian for "peasant."—Ed.

in the aftermath of the Second World War still experienced the trying living conditions, virtual homelessness, severe labour discipline, and the terror. But most had come to town voluntarily, eager to escape from devastated and famished villages. They had been prepeared for industrial discipline by years of army life and found in their new places an environment better able to absorb and assimilate newcomers than were the towns and factory settlements of the 1930s. The process of adaptation was less painful. It became easier still for the next batches of trainees who arrived in the factories during the post-Stalin years, when the old labour codes were abolished, and who settled down to their occupations in relative freedom from want and fear. The youngest age groups, the latest immigrants, and the town-bred children of the earlier ones have arrived in the workshops with a self-confidence which was altogether lacking in their elders and have played a big part in reforming outdated labour routines and in changing the climate of Soviet factory life. Nearly all of them have ("complete or incomplete") secondary education, and many take extra-mural academic courses. They have often clashed with their less efficient and less civilized foremen and managers. This is probably the most progressive group of the Soviet working class, comprising the builders of nuclear plants, computers, and space ships, workers as productive as their American counterparts, even though the average Soviet productivity per man-hour is still only 40 per cent of American productivity or even less. The low average is, of course, due to the great diversity of Soviet industrial manpower, to the many different and uneven levels of culture and efficiency, which I have just tried to trace. Even so, the average Soviet productivity is somewhat ahead of the West European; and it is worth recalling that in the 1920s, when American productivity was about one-third of what it is at present, Soviet production per man-hour was only one-tenth of the American.

This all too sketchy description gives us only a general idea of the extraordinary social and cultural heterogeneity of the Soviet working class. The process of transplantation and expansion was too rapid and stormy to allow for the mutual assimilation of the diverse layers, the formation of a common outlook, and the growth of class solidarity. We have seen how a few years after the revolution the shrinkage and disintegration of the working class had permitted the bureaucracy to establish itself as the dominant social force. What came after that allowed it to consolidate this position. The manner in which the new factory hands were recruited and the furious pace of growth kept the working class in a state of permanent disarray and fragmentation, unable to gain cohesion, balance, unity, and to find a sociopolitical identity. The workers were incapacitated by the very swelling of their numbers. The bureaucracy did what it could to keep them in this state. Not only did it play them against one another at the factory bench; it fanned all their mutual dislikes and antagonisms. It denied them the right to raise demands and to defend themselves through the trade unions. But these devices and the terror would not have been as effective as they were, if the working class had not been torn by its own centrifugal forces. What made matters worse was that the constant promotion of bright and energetic workers to managerial posts deprived the rank and file of potential mouthpieces and leaders. While education was scarce among the toilers, this brain drain had important consequences: the social mobility which benefited some of the workers, condemned the rest to social and political debility.

If this analysis is correct then the prospect for the future may be more hopeful. An objective process of consolidation and integration is taking place in the working class, and it is accompanied by a growth of social awareness. This—as well as the requirements of technological progress—has compelled the ruling group to sweep away the old factory discipline and to concede to the workers much more elbow room than they had in the Stalin era. There is still a long way from this to freedom of expression and to workers' genuine participation in control over industry. Yet as the working class grows more educated, homogeneous, and self-confident, its aspirations are likely to focus on these demands. And if this happens the workers may re-enter the political stage as an independent factor, ready to challenge the bureaucracy, and ready to resume the struggle for emancipation in which they scored so stupendous a victory in 1917, but which for so long they have not been able to follow up.

The obverse side of the expansion of the working class is the shrinkage of the peasantry. Forty years ago rural smallholders made up more than three-quarters of the nation; at present the collectivized farmers constitute only one-quarter. How desperately the peasants resisted this trend, what furious violence was let loose against them, how they were forced to contribute to the sinews of industrialization, and how resentfully and sluggishly they have tilled the land under the collectivist dispensation—all this is now common knowledge. But, as Professor Butterfield says in a somewhat different context: "It is the tendency of contemporaries to estimate the revolution too exclusively by its atrocities, while posterity always seems to err through its inability to take these into account or vividly appreciate them." As one who witnessed the collectivization in the early 1930s and severely criticized its forcible methods, I would like to reflect here on the tragic fate of the Russian peasantry. Under the *ancien régime* the Russian countryside was periodically swept by famine, as China's countryside was and as India's still is. In the intervals between the famines, uncounted (statistically unnoticed) millions of peasants and peasant children died of malnutrition and disease, as they still do in so many underdeveloped countries. The old system was hardly less cruel towards the peasantry than Stalin's government, only its cruelty appeared to be part of the natural order of things, which even the moralist's sensitive conscience is inclined to take for granted. This cannot excuse or mitigate the crimes of Stalinist policy; but it may put the problem into proper perspective. Those who argue that all would have been well if only the *muzhiks* had been left alone, the idealizers of the old rural way of life and of the peasantry's individualism, are purveying an idyll which is a figment of their imagination. The old primitive smallholding was, in any case, too archaic to survive into the epoch of industrialization. It has not survived either in this country or in the United States; and even in France, its classical homeland, we have witnessed a dramatic shrinkage of the peasantry in recent years. In Russia the smallholding was a formidable obstacle to the nation's progress: it was unable to provide food for the growing urban population; it could not even feed the children of the over-populated countryside. The only reasonable alternative to forcible collectivization lay in some form of collectivization or co-operation based on the consent of the peasantry. Just how realistic this alternative was for the U.S.S.R. no one can now say with any certainty. What is certain is that forcible collectivization has left a legacy of agricultural inefficiency and antagonism between town and country which the Soviet Union has not yet lived down.

These calamities have been aggravated by yet another blow the peasantry has suffered, a blow surpassing all the atrocities of the collectivization. Most of the 20 million men that the Soviet Union lost on the battlefields of the Second World War were peasants. So huge was the gap in rural manpower that during the late 1940s and in the 1950s in most villages only women, children, cripples, and old men were seen working in the fields. This accounted in some measure for the stagnant condition of farming, and for much else besides: for dreadful strains on family relations, sexual life, and rural education; and for more than the normal amount of apathy and inertia in the countryside.

The peasantry's weight in the nation's social and political life has, in consequence of all these events, steeply declined. The condition of farming remains a matter of grave concern, for it affects the standard of living and the morale of the urban population. A poor harvest is still a critical event, politically; and a succession of bad harvests contributed to Khrushchev's downfall in 1964. Nor has the peasantry been truly integrated into the new industrial structure of society. Much of the old individualistic farming, of the pettiest and most archaic kind, is still going on behind the façade of the *kolkhoz.*[3] Within a stone's throw of automated computer-run concerns there are still shabby and Oriental bazaars crowded with rural traders. Yet the time when the Bolsheviks were afraid that the peasantry might be the agent of a capitalist restoration has long passed. True, there are rich *kolkhozes* and poor ones; and here and there a crafty *muzhik* manages to by-pass all rules and regulations and to rent land, employ hired labour surreptitiously, and make a lot of money. However, these survivals of primitive capitalism are hardly more than a marginal phenomenon. If the present population trend—the migration from country to town—continues, the peasantry will go on shrinking; and there will probably be a massive shift from the collectively owned to the State-owned farms. Eventually, farming may be expected to be "Americanized" and to employ only a small fraction of the nation's manpower.

Meanwhile, even though the peasantry is dwindling, the *muzhik* tradition still looms very large in Russian life, in custom and manners, in language; literature, and the arts. Although a majority of Russians are already living in town, most Russian novels, perhaps four out of five, still take village-life as their theme and the *muzhik* as their chief character. Even in his exit he casts a long melancholy shadow on the new Russia.

[3] Collective farm.—Ed.

The experience of the non-Russian nationalities under Soviet rule reveals a unique aspect to Soviet history. These peoples were not the makers of the Revolution, but felt directly its consequences. For those in the eastern regions of the new state the Bolshevik regime promised modernization and emancipation from colonial oppression. The British economists ALEC NOVE (b. 1915) and J. NEWTH (b. 1921) examine the case for and against Soviet treatment of these nationalities. Their attention is directed specifically to the three Transcaucasian Soviet republics of Georgia, Armenia, and Azerbaijan and the five Central Asian republics of Kazakhstan, Uzbekistan, Tadzhikistan, Turkmenistan, and Kirgizia.*

Alec Nove and J. Newth

Modernization of the Soviet Middle East

In assessing the progress of the eastern and southern national republics of the USSR, the fact that the Russian contribution has been very considerable may be taken as proved. But many pertinent questions remain. Has the Soviet Union, or Russia, acted as a colonialist Power, in the pre-1947 sense of the term? Or as a neocolonialist Power, in the sense of ruling through "tame" local appointees? Or is there any valid comparison with the French "assimilationist" approach? Does the Soviet experience have any relevance to the problem of agriculture, of land reform and its relationship with economic development? Could such concepts as foreign aid, or technical assistance, be usefully applied to the recent economic history of the eight republics? We will try to answer such questions, concentrating particularly on the "colonialism" issue, which is not only of great interest and importance, but also bears directly on any interpretation of the economic and social progress that has been achieved. We will end with some tentative views concerning relations between the nationalities involved.

(a) Colonies? The case against

Let us imagine a debate in which the first speaker is seeking to disprove the validity of the charge of colonialism.

It is a characteristic of colonial status

*From Alec Nove and J. A. Newth, *The Soviet Middle East: A Communist Model for Development* (New York: Frederick A. Praeger, 1966), pp. 113–122, 132. Reprinted by permission of Frederick A. Praeger, Inc., and George Allen & Unwin, Ltd. Footnotes omitted.

(so he would argue) that the dominant Power uses the economy of the colony for its own benefit, keeping it industrially relatively under-developed, extracting profit from investments, underpaying colonial labour, neglecting education and so on. None of these features of traditional colonialism can be discerned in an impartial analysis of Soviet policy in the republics. Far from there being any economic exploitation, it is reasonable on the evidence to assert that industrialization, especially in Central Asia, has been financed with money raised in Russia proper. In other words, capital has tended to move to those outlying under-developed areas and there has been virtually no counterbalancing move of remittances of profit or interest, because in the Soviet Union capital grants are not repayable and do not bear interest. It is true that a part of the profits of enterprises located in these republics can find its way to the all-Union Budget,[1] but the sums are small, since the major part of profits taxes are retained for republican use. This may be contrasted with the very substantial remittances of profits to capitalist companies from Latin-America. No reasonable person can doubt that industrial growth would have been less rapid without Russian capital and Russian skills.

One of the main ways in which capital was accumulated in the Soviet Union was through the imposition on the peasants of compulsory deliveries at low prices. The areas which have been analysed here have suffered least from these impositions. Already, in 1935, prices paid for raw cotton were relatively high, and this applied broadly to most of the products in which these republics specialize. Consequently the average income of peasants in these republics has tended to be significantly above that, for instance, of Central Russia. It does not matter for our purpose whether the reason for this was political (to build up these countries as show places to impress the Asians) or economic. The economic reason would be connected with the scarcity value of semi-tropical products in the Soviet Union with the consequent tendency, even under Stalin, to pay higher prices to stimulate production. It could also be that Stalin had a personal soft spot for Georgia,[2] which had the effect of benefiting other republics which produced the kind of things which Georgia produces. Anyhow, whatever the reasons, it cannot possibly be said that sacrifices imposed on the peasants in the republics which we are considering match those borne by the Russians or the Ukrainians.

The workers in these republics benefited from wage scales designed for the USSR as a whole, i.e. from a level of wages related primarily to the more developed parts of the Soviet Union. Therefore any Central Asian native who became an industrial worker received pay equal to a Russian. He is entitled to the same social welfare payments. There is certainly no evidence of wage discrimination, and if the average wages received by Uzbeks were probably lower than those of Russians, the explanation could only be that relatively fewer Uzbeks were skilled workers. In the case of the much more advanced Georgians and Armenians, in all probability the average was higher than in Russia.

So far as educational policies are concerned, there has been a prolonged effort to bring forward to responsible positions a native intelligentsia in these republics where educational levels had been very

[1] Budget of the Soviet government, as opposed to those of the individual republics.—Ed.

[2] Birthplace of Stalin.—Ed.

low. No one who is not blinded by prejudice could fail to be impressed by the statistics quoted here concerning educational advance. The more highly developed republics, i.e. once again Georgia and Armenia, are far ahead of the Russians in the numbers of graduates relative to their population. While it is true that many Russians hold high positions in Central Asia, this is explicable primarily by the continued relative shortage of native cadres and should not be regarded as a form of deliberate Russian penetration. This can be seen from the extremely small percentage of such Russians in Georgia and Armenia. Cultural development, and in some cases a consciousness of the very existence of a national culture, should also be placed to the credit of the Soviet régime. There have been notorious instances of cultural oppression, but it can be claimed that the Russians as a people suffered at least as much as anybody else, and the tyranny of the *Georgian* dictator does not seem relevant to the issue of colonialism. The spectacular improvements in health, proportionately greatest in rural areas, speak for themselves.

Some critics have made much of the destruction of the traditional Muslim way of life. Such a destruction has indeed occurred, but it is at least arguable that this is part of the price one has to pay, inside and outside Soviet borders, for modernization and development. One has only to examine the policy of Ataturk. It is surely important not to confuse such policies with specifically Soviet methods.

Finally, it is not a mere verbal quibble that multi-racial States, even when one of the races is predominant, do not fit into the "colonial" category. There are several States in Eurasia where this can be observed. If the Azerbaijanis in the Soviet Union are subject to "colonial" rule, does this apply also to the Azerbaijanis in Iran? Are the Albanians and Macedonians in Yugoslavia victims of colonial oppression? What is the position of the Chinese minorities in South-east Asia? Or Bengalis in India? And what about Scotland? Obviously one must be careful about the use of such words as colonialism.

(b) Colonies? The case for

A case for the other side could be made as follows: Undeniably there are certain special features in the Soviet situation. It would certainly be wrong to regard all the non-Russian nationalities within the Soviet borders as being under "Russian colonial rule." Some of the nationalities, for instance the Belorussians, do not seem to feel this way at all, and oppression, including colonial oppression, is partly a matter of what people think about their own position. In some other cases, as, for example, the smaller nationalities in Siberia, it is futile to argue as if they could conceivably be independent States. However, when one is dealing with a relatively compact and self-conscious nationality, perhaps the most relevant factor of all is *control,* i.e. who decides how these people should live. The Soviet constitution itself asserts the right of the federal republics to run their own affairs, and even to secede from the Soviet Union. Yet, in practice, decisions on virtually every subject of importance are taken in Moscow. The first secretaries of the Communist Parties of these republics are almost always natives, but they can be and have been dismissed on the instructions of the all-Union party leadership. The second secretaries and "cadres" secretaries are usually Russians. The Communist Party is a highly centralized organization, which takes all significant decisions on economic, cultural, political and organizational matters. It so happens that the central organs of the Communist Party have become increasingly more Russian. While Stalin was in power, several Georgians had great influence, and it is still true that Armenians play a disproportionately large role in Soviet life. However, since the fall of Mukhitdinov, there has been no citizen of any of the Central Asian republics at the highest level of the Communist Party or the Central Government, although the first secretaries of Uzbekistan and Georgia (Rashidov and Mzhavanadze) are at present candidate members of the Praesidium of the CPSU. A dramatic example of the power of Moscow over the very existence of the republics was the creation, in March 1963, of the Central Asian bureau of the Communist Party and of a Central Asian economic council, which greatly reduced the status of each of the separate republics. This was undone after Krushchev's fall, as already noted. No doubt some of the Moscow decisions have been wise, but they have been taken in Moscow and often for reasons which have nothing to do with the specifically local situation.

Examples of central interference in comparatively minor matters include orders about the methods which should be used in cotton picking, and, in a vigorous speech by Krushchev, the breed of sheep on which the Uzbeks should specialize (the First Secretary maintained that sheep bred for wool ought to be preferred, although the meat would be of lower quality; he claimed to have learned from his female forebears that what matters is the quality of the cook).

Control over foreign trade by Moscow, and the exclusion of almost all imports of consumers' goods for long periods, made of the eight republics a captive market for Russian textiles, and vehicles, refrigerators, etc. This fact must be set against the relatively favourable "terms of trade" at which raw cotton and other semitropical products exchanged for manufactures. In recent years a range of imports of consumers' goods from Czechoslovakia, North Korea, etc., have been available, but the citizens of the eight republics are not able to buy such goods from "capitalist" countries. True, they are in no worse position in this respect than any other Soviet republics, but they are given no choice in the matter, since foreign trade is controlled very strictly by the centre.

It would not matter so much that orders come from Moscow if the Soviet Union were truly a multi-racial State. However, Soviet Communism has become increasingly associated with Russian nationalism. This tendency was most highly developed under Stalin's rule, despite the fact that Stalin himself was a Georgian. One recalls Lenin's warning that the worst Russian chauvinists were sometimes non-Russians (as Napoleon was not French). Since Stalin's death there has been some reduction in russification pressures, but it remains true that, in literature and historiography alike, the glorification of the historical past of Russia is encouraged, while any similar tendency in respect of other nationalities would be characterized as *bourgeois* nationalism. Therefore, especially as so few central Asians are in a position to influence the decisions of Moscow, there is an important sense in which they are subject to alien rule. It is this which constitutes the principal argument in favour of relevance of the word "colonialism." The situation would be different if there were a tendency towards assimilation, through inter-marriage. This is still rare, especially in Central Asia. There is still the tendency for Russians to congregate in a few cities, or in compact Russian villages, while the bulk of the rural area is inhabited by the natives. The flow of Russian immigrants may be explained by the lack of special skills on the part of the native population, and for the same reason many Russians in Central Asia hold positions of manager or foreman. But, whatever the reason, the fact remains that in several Central Asian republics there is a *de facto* Russian dominance while the subordinate positions are held by the natives. It would be surprising if there were not some resentment of this state of affairs, especially as the Russians have not as a rule shown much sympathy and understanding for the local way of life. It is certainly true, however, that some of the republics we have been analysing are in a very different situation. Any generalization which deals with Kirgizia is unlikely to apply also to Georgia, but both these republics have one thing in common; decisions concerning any and every aspect of the life of their peoples are frequently taken in Moscow, and such autonomy as they possess is a matter which is also decided by Moscow and can change in either direction for reasons totally unconnected with the situation, needs and wishes of the republics concerned.

(c) Colonies? Yes and no

It may indeed by argued that the Soviet régime, unlike its Tsarist predecessor—for reasons which we shall examine in outline—has imposed a form of ideology which has led to the suppression of social developments which were not necessarily incompatible with membership of the USSR or at least of a polycentric socialist community of nations. We must distinguish between the relatively sophisticated nationalism of Transcaucasia and the part-panIslamic, part pan-Turkistic, part-"pure" nationalisms of Central Asia (as at, say, 1912). It was to some extent a historical accident that permitted the Baltic States to dissociate themselves from the first two decades of Soviet development,[3] while Transcaucasia and Turkestan were rapidly incorporated in the USSR with virtually the same frontiers as the Tsarist Empire. The provocation of revolution in Bukhara and Khiva in the early 'twenties[4] was a logical continuation of Tsarist policy (as was, at a different point of the frontier, the ultimate absorption of Tuva), and the motivation of the Soviet Government in rounding off its frontiers in Central Asia and Transcaucasia was a combination of three principal factors—the vital necessity of procuring raw materials, the equally vital necessity of eliminating potential bridgeheads for an enemy attack combined with a desire (so noticeable in the behaviour of Chinese Communists today) to restore the traditional imperial border wherever possible. One may criticize these actions of the infant Soviet Government on moral grounds, but this is the way in which governments do in fact behave. Further, having imposed political control for reasons of its own security, the Soviet Government was faced with the task of promoting the rapid economic development of the two regions, and given the necessary condition of speed, the Government had to employ these resources of manpower, both local and immigrant, which were available at the time. As indicated elsewhere in this study, the existence of political groups at the local level which were prepared to accept modernization as an ideal was a considerable asset to the Soviet authorities in this early phase; the conflict arose over the speed of modernization—the rate at which society was to be transformed, and the ideas and institutions which were to be

[3] Until 1940 the Baltic republics of Estonia, Latvia, and Lithuania were independent.—Ed.

[4] Incorporated into the Union of Soviet Socialist Republics in 1924.—Ed.

jettisoned—rather than the direction in which society was to be moved.

In one sense, therefore the transformation of Transcaucasian and Central Asian society is only a special case of the transformation of society throughout the Union. In each case, elements of the old outlook and the old society have survived—after all, the Revolution took place only forty-nine years ago[5]—which continue to affect the new synthetic society which is being built today. The authorities are, of course, reluctant to permit any revivals which may tend to undermine the synthesis, so that a continuous process of guidance is required. Those natives who accepted the need for a transformation of society under Communist leadership were often those who played a leading part in coercing their less enlightened fellow-citizens. From this point of view, the central control of the development of society, permitting only limited expression of local peculiarities, may be regarded as a constraint which denies to groups of the Soviet population a right to which they are inherently entitled. Had the development of Soviet history as a whole proceeded along more liberal lines, the balance between central control and local traditionalism might well have been different, but we must take history as we find it, and it is difficult to maintain that the kind of pressures exerted at the periphery were essentially different from those exerted in the heart of Russia proper.

Turning to the question of centralization of economic decision-making in Moscow, it could be said that economic controls in any large area tend to be centralized also under capitalism. For example, monopolists and giant firms control great numbers of enterprises from a central office, thus affecting the lives of many people within and also outside the borders of a given country. There are clear advantages in the case of modern industry in organizing planning over a wide area. The key problem is—so it could be argued—"For whose benefit is the economy run?" It may also be said that republican political organs, including the republican Communist Party leadership, do exercise informal influence over decision-making at the centre, apart from the constitutional functions of the Soviet of Nationalities and its committees.

However, on the evidence, we must surely conclude that each of the republics has very little political power and that this is particularly significant in a country in which politicians claim the right to decide far more than is considered "political" in a Western country. For example, the boundaries between republics (as indeed between administrative areas in purely Slavonic districts of the USSR) are subject to constant flux, and although the local people may in practice have some voice in such decisions, the ultimate right remains in the centre, and local politicians who are too vocal in their objections to the arbitrary transfer of land to other republics (e.g. parts of southern Kazakhstan to Uzbekistan) are liable to be dismissed for carrying their legitimate nationalism too far. Therefore the republics are to a great extent ruled from the outside. Yet we still face some genuine difficulty. It is perfectly true that power was exercised in such a way that the republics of Central Asia and Transcaucasia registered some notable economic and social gains and that these gains were partly paid for by the Russians.

If one's picture of colonialism is associated with exploitation, with grinding the faces of the poor, then clearly the word does not fit the circumstances of the

[5] Written in 1966.—Ed.

case. It must also be admitted that some of the accusations which are sometimes levelled against Soviet policy in these areas are wide of the mark. Living standards do compare favourably not only with neighbouring Asian countries but also with Russia itself. The use of the Russian language in schools and universities is in some respects a mere convenience rather than a means of russification. It is easier for Uzbek students to learn physics and other sciences from Russian textbooks and it helps them in their subsequent career to know Russian. It is quite likely that this feeling is shared by the Uzbeks (it is noteworthy that the worship of the ancient Irish tongue by English-speaking Irish nationalists is hardly ever shared by those who actually speak Irish!). Some of the critics do seem to adopt an attitude which could be characterized as: "Whatever they do must be wrong because they do it." Thus, if a large deposit of valuable minerals was discovered in an under-developed region of a national republic, the critics would accuse Moscow as follows. If the mines are not worked, the object is to keep the region under-developed, an agricultural appendage of Great Russia. If the mines were worked with native labour, the object would be to disrupt the traditional way of life of the given nationality. If the mines were worked with imported Russian labour, then this would be colonialist settlement designed to swamp the local nationality. We should certainly not adopt criteria of this kind. Yet, experience in other parts of the world suggests that an essential factor in the situation is the *attitude of people* to their neighbours and to their own national status. One has but to contrast the relationship between England and Ireland on the one hand and England and Scotland on the other. Until 1921 they shared common membership of a constitutional multinational State, the United Kingdom. The differences did not lie in institutions but essentially in history and national and religious consciousness.

In the Soviet case, it is generally admitted that in Georgia one finds widespread and deeply-felt anti-Russian nationalism. This is so despite the fact that from the standpoint of material and cultural advances they might seem to have little to complain about. The Georgians happen to be particularly open in telling foreign visitors just what they think about Russia and Muscovite rule. It is rarer to hear such things from the Uzbeks and Tajiks. Since the police system is much the same throughout the Soviet Union and since the Georgians appear to have no special difficulty in conveying their views to others, the fact that one hears much less of anti-Russian nationalism in Central Asia cannot be attributed merely to fear. It may be a matter of communication. Quite possibly, as a local intellectual once did say to a visiting foreigner, "we still need the Russians," i.e. the local intellectuals are aware that they are still culturally far behind and that the Russians provide a still essential degree of assistance in bringing them forward to the twentieth century. For example, every Uzbek scientist must know that he would not have the chance of working in advanced and modern laboratories unless these were provided by the Russians. It may therefore be that Central Asian nationalism is still in a somewhat dormant state, but that it will manifest itself in future years, especially if the Russians are tactless or oppressive.

The economic development of these areas, which are in the main lacking in industrial raw materials, have plainly benefited from the Russian connection. The Soviet ideological commitment to creating a native proletariat and combating backwardness in the national republics caused a diversion of capital to those areas which, on strictly economic grounds, would have provided a higher return elsewhere. To that extent it could be argued with justice that development in these republics was more rapid than would have been the case in a Russian Empire run on the principles of the free market. However, we would have called such an empire a colonialist Power, not because of the way it used its material resources but because a bureaucracy, based on a Russian monarchy, in a Russian city, ran the affairs of other nationalities. In this respect the USSR shares certain characteristics with its imperial predecessors, though it can claim that the territories inhabited by its nationalities were acquired by the Tsars. Is this colonialism? The conception of a multi-national union of Soviet republics is plainly designed to exclude colonial relationships. Yet the centralizing practice of the Soviet Government, and the dominant role of Russian nationalism suggests that there is a large gap between theory and practice. Therefore, if we do not call the present relationship colonialism, we ought to invent a new name to describe something which represents subordination and yet is genuinely different from the imperialism of the past. . . .

If, in the next generation or so, opinion throughout the world polarizes along lines of colour, with the Whites against the Rest—which will also mean the rich nations against the poor, the advanced against the primitive, the peripheral minorities of the USSR seem more likely to take their stand on the side of the North and West—which includes for this purpose the advanced regions of the USSR—than on the side of the East and South. However, this is unavoidably an interpretation which may well be wide of the mark. Certainly it is hard to discern any tendency to pro-Chinese sentiments in Central Asia, especially after Kazakhs resident in Sinkiang have fled into the Soviet Union with stories of Chinese oppression.[6] None the less, the local intelligentsia may turn strongly anti-Russian, unless the Soviet leadership is tactful and skilful in handling the tensions which must arise as the increasingly well qualified natives lay claim to more positions of responsibility and question the right of Moscow to issue orders to the republics. The less educated, especially the peasants, cling to the old ways, and their resentment at modernizing reforms extend impartially to both native and Russian Communists. Already now, as is clear from travellers' reports, *some* natives deeply resent the existing situation and are willing to say so. The problem, as already pointed out in the section on "colonialism," is how to assess public opinion in the absence of reliable information, and how to distinguish grumbles and grievances from real disloyalty. It is therefore right to end with a question mark, and with the assurance that a clear and unambiguous answer to so complex and varied a set of problems is bound to be wrong.

[6] A large-scale move of Kazakh nomads occurring in 1962–1963.—Ed.

The Jewish population has always represented a special group in Russia. Their religion and traditions marked them as a people apart, and the virulent anti-Semitism of much of the Christian population further heightened their isolation. Their status as a nationality under the Soviets promised protection of cultural traditions, but they had no central territory, as did the nationalities of Central Asia, around which they could form their own government. They were also vulnerable as a religious group, against which the Soviet antireligious policies were naturally directed. The history of their tormented experience under the Soviet regime is described by PETER GROSE (b. 1934), *New York Times* correspondent and Moscow bureau chief from 1965 to 1967. He begins with a description of a special place in Kiev, capital of the Ukraine, where anti-Semitism had a long and bloody history.*

Peter Grose

The Tradition of Anti-Semitism

I went to see Babi Yar one evening in the summer of 1966. The bus drivers in downtown Kiev were most helpful in giving instructions, though I knew only the ominous name of the ravine, not the new names for the streets and residential districts that sprang up after the war in the fresh air of the suburbs. It was the rush hour for homeward-bound office workers, and for this new generation of Kievites the thirty-minute bus ride to Babi Yar was everyday routine. Tired clerks dozed on their feet or read novels taken from battered briefcases, a secretary patted her uneasy hairdo, a young man had eyes only for his date. The rattling bus turned onto Demyan Bedny Street. On the right were modern five-story apartment houses with grocery stores and little repair shops on the ground floors. On the left was Babi Yar. Anatoly Kuznetsov[1] wrote of a different journey to this wild ravine: "With their wailing children, their old and their sick, the Jewish tenants of the kitchen garden spilled out into the street, weeping and quarreling among themselves. They carried rope-tied bundles, battered wooden suitcases, patched carpetbags and carpentry toolboxes. A great crowd of them ascended toward Lukyanovka, just

[1] Author of novel entitled *Babi Yar,* published in 1966, describing wartime Kiev and the German mass executions of its Jewish population.—Ed.

*From Peter Grose, "The Kremlin and the Jews," in *The Soviet Union: The Fifty Years,* edited by Harrison Salisbury, copyright © 1967 by The New York Times Company. Reprinted by permission of Harcourt Brace Jovanovich, Inc., and *The New York Times.* Pp. 483–492.

across the ravine. . . . I hear it distinctly now: the even ra-ta-ta of a machine gun from Babi Yar."

That took place in 1941. In the autumn of 1966 the Soviet Union permitted the true story of Babi Yar to be told at last through Kuznetsov's documentary novel. The publication of this shattering account marked an epic moment for Jews and for humanity.

It is characteristic of modern Soviet society that an event of such magnitude and horror could go publicly unacknowledged for over two decades because it was politically inconvenient for the regime. The poet Yevgeny Yevtushenko wrote of the slaughter in that ravine outside Kiev in a bold poem that was published in 1961, for which he was roundly condemned by officialdom. But until last year, the awesome German massacre at Babi Yar was still shrouded in rumor and obfuscation in the U.S.S.R., and the tens of thousands of Jews who died there went without the tributes and commemorations accorded to those who perished at Auschwitz, Buchenwald, or Dachau. . . .

Why was the story of Babi Yar suppressed? In the first place, as Kuznetsov describes so vividly, there were Ukrainian collaborators alongside the German executioners of Babi Yar. Though renegades, they were Soviet citizens and they shared responsibility for the atrocity. Then, more fundamentally, any tribute to the victims of this ghastly episode was inconvenient to Soviet officialdom simply because the vast majority of the victims were Jews.

The Jew in Soviet society poses a special problem for the U.S.S.R. today. So much has been written in the West with deep emotion and high drama about the sad plight of Soviet Jews that one could assume, wrongly, that the Jews are the only religious, national, or social group with a deep grievance against Soviet power. There are more Jews in the U.S.S.R. than in Israel; only the United States has a larger Jewish population. But there are surely more people outside Soviet frontiers who are deeply concerned about the status of Soviet Jews than there are Jews in the Soviet Union. An international campaign in their defense brings together such strange colleagues as senators from New York State and Bertrand Russell, large American corporations and the British Communist party.

All organized religion in the Soviet Union operates under difficulties—administrative attempts to discourage believers, police penetration, the widening gap between the faith of an older generation and the interests of the young. If this were all there was to the Jewish problem there would be no Jewish problem; it would be the more general question of the dilemmas of all religious faiths under Communism. But Jewry is more than a religion, and the status of Soviet Jews reaches into other problem areas in Soviet society: the status of minorities, the fate of exclusive cultures in a unitary society, the fact of international connections independent of the world Communist cause. There are countless Jewish stories with the theme that whatever happens to a gentile happens more so to a Jew—a gentile sneezes and the Jew catches pneumonia, a gentile makes money and a Jew makes more money, a gentile is reprimanded and a Jew is punished—all of which can be applied to the Soviet Jew today.

It is difficult to form conclusions about the status of Soviet Jewry. There are countless case studies and individual stories on which to base generalizations, but too many of these can be contradicted by the experiences of other Jews. Broad and general information on the Jewish population is sparse—largely because of deliberate efforts by Soviet officials to cloud the issue. The Soviet Communists are on the defensive in this area, and they have much to be defensive about.

Yet some of the world-wide concern is misplaced, for a picture has been created of a community of almost 3,000,000 Jews under persecution, living in daily misery and fearing for their lives. This picture is wrong. One can meet Soviet Jews every day whose reactions to the campaigns in their defense range from total bewilderment to sincere anger. Individuals in the Soviet Union, by and large, are not fearful of being persecuted because they are Jews, though many of them, in common with those in other countries, know well the meaning of discrimination.

What has been persecuted throughout half a century of the Soviet system, persecuted almost unto death, is the Jewish heritage: the religious practices and the culture through which Jews come together to acknowledge a common bond. Soviet pressures for assimilation, general strictures on worship and specific limitations on teaching children about God, geographical dispersion and the traditional, if frowned upon, sentiments of anti-Semitism—all these have dealt a savage blow to the Jewish community in the U.S.S.R.

In 1967 Soviet Jewry has all but ceased to exist as a unity, and in the years to come any hopes for a rebirth of a viable community of Jews must be grounded more on faith than on present reality. Many of those outside the country who express their concern about this situation condemn the present government. However, the breakup of the Jewish community has been a consistent trend throughout the Soviet era, and, against a background of the long, dark decades through which Soviet Jews have lived, the present leadership often seems to offer a fresh breath by its moderation. The story of these decades needs to be retold.

From the start of the Soviet era, the Bolshevik leaders found that there could be no simple "Jewish policy"—the problem cut across too many spheres the revolutionaries were trying to remold. Their underlying purpose was the construction of a unitary state, in which local interests and parochial allegiances were to be surrendered to the primacy of Communism, the society of all the people. The Jewish community, thus, did not fit in from the beginning. It constituted an exclusive society inside what was designed to be a hegemony.

In the first years after the revolution, however, there was no hint of anti-Semitism in the official attitudes of the Bolsheviks. Many of Lenin's closest associates were of Jewish origin, among them Trotsky, Kamenev, and Zinoviev. They had turned their backs on the religious faith of Judaism but they were staunch in their hatred for anti-Semitism, which had been one of the prime weapons of the czarist regime in its policy of dividing and ruling the minorities of the vast Russian empire. The czarist policies had left endemic in the country strong veins of anti-Semitic feeling. This was particularly common in the Ukraine, where it had been encouraged by the czarist police. Indeed, it was in this milieu that the infamous anti-Semitic propaganda pamphlet called *Protocols of the Wise Men of Zion*[2] had its origin.

Middle-aged Soviet citizens of Jewish origin say today that growing up in the early 1920's they were almost literally unaware of anti-Semitism. If their Jewish parents chanced to be staunch Communists, the children could even be completely unaware of their Jewish heritage.

---

[2] Forgery written in 1905 purporting to relate a meeting of Zionist leaders conspiring to seize political power in the Western world.—Ed.

Lenin warned of the danger of anti-Semitism, and the Communist party conducted an intensive campaign against any manifestations of it in factories and universities. Stalin was quoted in 1931, in an interview for publication outside the Soviet Union, as saying: "Communists, as consistent internationalists, cannot help being the implacable and sworn enemies of anti-Semitism." Vyacheslav M. Molotov[3] was more detailed when he spoke in praise of Jewish culture in November, 1936—almost the last date on which such a statement could be made by a Soviet leader. He said: "Whatever the contemporary cannibals from among the Fascist anti-Semites may say, our fraternal feelings toward the Jewish people are determined by the fact that this people gave birth to Karl Marx, numerous great scientists, technicians and artists, many heroes in the revolutionary struggle."

Less than three years later, Molotov signed a pact of friendship with Hitler's "contemporary cannibals."[4] And in those years the Soviet Union had been scoured by the Great Purge, which numbered among its victims most of Lenin's Jewish associates. Jewish newspapers were suspended, and Yiddish cultural life was sharply restricted.

While the Communist party was resisting outcroppings of anti-Semitism in the first Soviet decades, the authorities were at the same time busy with another aspect of the Jewish problem—the survival of religious practice. Here Bolshevik policy was clear and unequivocal: the Jewish faith, like any other religion, had no place in a Communist society. Judaism held doctrinal beliefs that were particularly hateful to Marxists, notably a belief in the advent of the Messiah, which, according to the Great Soviet Encyclopedia, "was aimed only at breaking the revolutionary activity of the exploited lower classes."

In the heyday of organized atheism, the late 1920's and 1930's, the League of Militant Godless[5] was as active against the Jewish religion as against the Christian. Soviet Jews were harassed if they refused to work on the Sabbath, young Jewish Communists who had already broken with the religious life of their parents made a show of doing menial work—sweeping streets, lugging coal—on Saturdays and Holy Days. Special entertainments, concerts, and other cultural attractions were scheduled by the authorities to attract Jews away from observance of the Passover. Communal meals were provided on the fasting Day of Atonement. Jewish religious schools were closed starting in 1922 in accordance with the general ban on any religious education for children, though an educational network with Yiddish as the language of instruction continued well into the 1930's. A vast campaign to close down synagogues and harass rabbis coincided with similar campaigns during the early Soviet decades against Christian churches. The economic propensities of the Jews gave added sting to the drive after 1928, when the private enterprise of the New Economic Policy (NEP) was halted. Synagogues were branded "clubs of profiteers, of Nepmen," and were categorized as distasteful to loyal Communists not only as places of worship, but also as centers of exploitation and speculation.

At this time, when the Communist party

[3] Molotov's wife, of Jewish origin, was imprisoned between 1948 and 1953 during the anti-Jewish purges.—Ed.

[4] Soviet-German Nonaggression Pact signed in August 1939.—Ed.

[5] Movement sponsored by the Communist party directed against organized religion and religious beliefs.—Ed.

was declaring its "implacable" hostility to anti-Semitism, the following poem was published in a Soviet journal. This translation is quoted by Walter Kolarz in the book *Religion in the Soviet Union,* published in 1962:

The synagogue: house of the living God . . .
Gleam, oily eye! Cheek, be suffused with red!
The pathway to its portals is well trod
By all the dealers that devoutly treat.
Within its walls you may with unbowed head
Glorify God, while joy your being fills;
Push out your belly, sleek and nobly fed,
And handsomely discount your notes and bills.
But for the synagogue, what would avail?
Elsewhere you'll feel disconsolate, depressed!
Let ancient talith from your shoulders trail,
And here, but only here, your soul will rest.
The synagogue's the place—to get the best
Of prices, for a coat, a ring, a fake;
The synagogue is, soberly assessed,
The best of clubs for nepmen on the make.

The author of this verse, Nikolai Aseyev, was later awarded the Stalin Prize.

The concept of Zionism and of a special Jewish state has always been anathema to the Communists. Lenin opposed it from the beginning. As far back as 1903 he branded the Zionist concept as "politically reactionary." Later on he called demands for a national Jewish culture the "slogan of rabbis and bourgeois." The Communist opposition to Zionism was twofold: the cause of Zionism took the energies of many Jews who otherwise might have devoted themselves to Communism, and the Zionists, although embracing many socialist concepts, were firm supporters of capitalism and bourgeois society.

The antagonism to Zionism and to a political Jewish state has constantly colored the Soviet attitude toward Jews in Russia. Stalin, for example, considered himself a specialist on "minority" questions. He assigned to the Jews the status of a minority nationality. But this posed problems. Whereas the Ukrainian or the Georgian national minority had language, culture, tradition, and a territorial base, the Jews had no territory. They were scattered through the country. In the late 1920's a tentative, but never very successful, effort was made by Soviet authority to give the Jews of Russia a territorial base. An area on the Amur River, in eastern Siberia, just west of Khabarovsk, was set aside for settlement, the beginning of what became Birobidzhan, or the Jewish Autonomous Region.

The experiment tied in with the continuing attraction the Zionist campaign to establish a Jewish homeland in Palestine had for Jews both inside and outside the Soviet Union, including some who sympathized with the Communist cause. With the creation of Birobidzhan, the Soviet authorities felt they had a competing attraction for Jewish sentiment. The project was launched with great fanfare. Extensive propaganda campaigns were conducted in the 1930's. Much sentiment was generated for it, but, in fact, no great movement of Jewish population to the remote agricultural region ever developed. The purges of the late 1930's hit the Jewish authorities of Birobidzhan as they did all Jews. By 1940 many Jewish cultural institutions had been closed down, including the daily Yiddish papers in Moscow, Kharkov, and Minsk. The Yiddish publishing press had been sharply curtailed, though the twice-a-week *Birobidzhaner Shtern* continued to circulate in Yiddish to about 2,000 subscribers and the Yiddish libraries and theaters of Birobidzhan remained open.

World War II brought new crises to the Jewish community. Stalin had employed harsh measures in the late 1930's to curtail Jewish religious life. His police had charged rabbis with espionage (in behalf of the Nazis!) and had carried out harsh repressive measures against Moscow's Central Synagogue. The Nazis brought into Russia the most virulent kind of anti-Semitism, spreading their propaganda on soil that had by no means been freed of the prejudices encouraged by the czarist regime. Notably in the Ukraine, the arrival of Nazi troops often was a signal for anti-Semitic outrages in which local populations joined the German invaders. In Moscow, anti-Semitism burst out violently, particularly in the autumn of 1941, when the Germans approached the capital. It persisted for months thereafter, encouraged by the complaisant or even approving attitude of Communist party officials. Many believed that anti-Semitic propaganda was deliberately encouraged by Moscow officials to provide a scapegoat for the tragic losses the Red Army was suffering. Anti-Semitism raged in Moscow until high party officials called in their underlings and rebuked them for permitting it to continue, saying in ostentatious indignation that anti-Semitism was not officially sanctioned.

The Jewish Anti-Fascist Committee was then organized by Soviet authorities to carry on pro-Soviet propaganda in Jewish committees of the West, particularly in the United States. The prominent Jewish actor Solomon Mikhoels, a leader in the Jewish Theater, and the Yiddish poet Itzik Fefer traveled from coast to coast in this country enlisting the support and sympathy of the American Jewish community. Paralleling this, there was a relaxation of anti-Jewish activity. Yiddish newspapers, cultural institutions, and publishing activities resumed. The Jewish Anti-Fascist Committee counted in its membership leading writers, including Ilya Ehrenburg, scientists, and Red Army generals.

The committee continued its activity after the war. It issued some reports telling of the anti-Jewish atrocities of the Nazis in the Soviet Union. But in 1948 Stalin cracked down with a savage purge. Almost all members of the committee were executed, as was Deputy Commissar for Foreign Affairs Solomon Lozovsky. They were charged with conspiring to "detach" the Crimea and set up a separate Jewish state. The paranoid origin of this Stalinist suppression apparently lay in a suggestion by Lozovsky that the western Ukraine and Byelorussia might be provided with resettlement areas in the Crimea, from which Stalin had forcibly removed the Tatar inhabitants on charges of disloyalty during the Nazi occupation.

From 1948 to 1953 over four hundred Jewish writers, poets, journalists, scholars, and artists were arrested, exiled, or executed. Anti-Semitism became an official but unacknowledged policy. Quota systems were introduced for the admission of Jews to educational and other institutions. Jews were banned from the top echelons of the Soviet army, the Foreign Ministry, the Communist party. Only in the secret police were they permitted.

The anti-Semitic inclinations of Stalin became clearer and clearer as his life neared its end. In January, 1953, it was announced that a group of Kremlin physicians, most of them Jews, had conspired through the instigation of Zionist organizations—and British and American intelligence agencies—in a plot against Kremlin leadership. Stalin, it was later learned from his heirs, talked wildly of exiling the whole Jewish community in Russia to Siberia.

When Stalin died in 1953, his successors announced that the doctors' plot was a frame-up and called an abrupt halt to the spread of officially encouraged anti-Semitism.

Tension eased in the immediate post-Stalin years, and the old rabbinical dream of a Yeshiva, a seminary for future rabbis, was realized in 1956 when the Moscow Synagogue was authorized to open a small school for higher religious education. A Hebrew prayer book was cleared for publication in an edition of 4,000 copies.

Religious Jews were emboldened by the apparent thaw, and there were reports of new synagogues under construction, new assertions of Jewish community interests. But in 1957 the situation began to revert to what new generations of Jews under Communism had come to accept as normal. Local government authorities were told to adopt a stern attitude toward their Jewish communities, and the administrative measures enacted against the Orthodox Church hit the synagogues with special vigor. Some were closed down by atheist agitators; private prayer meetings were prohibited and propagandists stepped up their "analyses" of the Jewish religion as a particularly reactionary force for exploiting the working people.

A special political factor may have been at work behind this particular suppression of Jewish community life, which coincided with the years of Nikita S. Khrushchev's dominance. Khrushchev's main effort was de-Stalinization, and in his campaign he took serious political risks in riding roughshod over the perpetuators of the Stalinist mentality in the Communist party. Sanctions against the Jewish community were the one aspect of Stalinism that he did not suppress; foreign analysts have speculated that this may have been an attempt by Khrushchev to go at least part way toward pacifying the neo-Stalinists in the party so he could carry on with de-Stalinization in other fields.

Whatever the reason, Jewish religious practice was stultified as effectively as the living cultural heritage had been snuffed out under Stalin. The Yeshiva found itself devoid of students, a new prayer book lay in ineffective manuscript form in a drawer of the Moscow Chief Rabbi's desk, and, as in the 1930's, the ritual requirements for the use of unleavened bread, matzoth, had to be relaxed—there was none to be had.

Through this historical survey one can see the varied pressures against which the world-wide campaign in defense of Soviet Jewry is now mobilized, and the particular sensitivities of Soviet officials in the face of it. If it were simply a matter of religious hostility, that could be explained away in the context of the general policy of atheism. But reinforcing the antireligious moves was the Stalinist policy of cultural suppression, guided by the fear that the Jewish community somehow constituted a more dangerous threat to Soviet power than any other culture. Doubly tainted, the Jews were suspect for their potential sympathies to the "bourgeois" movement of Zionism and its incarnation in the state of Israel—originally welcomed by the Kremlin as an anticolonial development, then gradually blackened with "imperialist" motives as Moscow bid for friendship in the Arab world.

The delicacy of the Jewish question for Communist leaders reverts to the original problem of anti-Semitism. For ideological reasons, and with Lenin's own warnings in hand, the Communist party cannot appear to be authorizing any manifestation of a durable old czarist scourge which then became a Stalinist scourge. The publication of a vicious anti-Semitic book in 1963, *Judaism Without Embellishment,* by T. K. Kichko, was widely noted and condemned abroad. Less noted was the official condemnation of this book as "offensive" by the Ideological Commission of the Communist party.

Politically, there seems to be no room in Communism for a strong Jewish community; ideologically, there is no room for anti-Semitism. The status of the Jew in Soviet society is as much a dilemma for U.S.S.R.'s Communist leaders as it is a concern for the outside world.

The Soviet ideal for the future called for the creation of a new man in a new society. Reliable measures of the actual progress toward that new man are difficult to define. FEDOR KOROLEV (b. 1898), a leading Soviet educator, seeks his evidence primarily in outstanding Soviet heroes of war and socialist labor, and in Soviet literature, which he presents as mirror of real life. He points also to the advances of Soviet schooling as proof of the "education of the new man." In his view, the Soviet experience marks a dramatic new stage in the cultural development of the peoples of the Soviet Union.*

Fedor Korolev

The New Soviet Man

From the point of view of history, fifty Soviet years is an instant, an extremely small period of time; but in terms of its wealth and the historical significance of its content, it is an entire era, the most remarkable era in the formation of the new man. The new man is not an abstract aggregate of the best qualities and traits. He is a concrete person, the bearer of the most progressive ideas of his century. He marches in the front rank of discoverers and builders of the new world. Such people are outstanding factory and collective farm workers, scientists and writers, engineers and physicians, artists and teachers. They are the best representatives of all generations and of those who laid the cornerstone in the building of socialism, and of those who are completing the transition from socialism to communism. They represent the leading segment of our people. . . .

The new person matured and developed in the unforgettable years of the first five-year plans, during the industrialization of the nation and the collectivization of agriculture at a time when the cultural revolution gathered full momentum. In the words of A. V. Lunacharskii,[1] this was a colossal pedagogical process. During these years, heroes of labor blazing a trail to the communist

[1] First Commissar of Education in the Soviet state. —Ed.

*From Fedor Korolev, "The October Revolution and the Education of the New Man," *Sovetskaia pedagogika* (November, 1967). Reprinted in translation in *Soviet Education,* October 1968, pp. 40, 41–46. Permission to reprint by International Arts and Sciences Press, Inc., White Plains, New York. Footnotes omitted.

future came into being. In industry and agriculture, in the field of culture and science, people of a new type developed. Who does not remember such innovators of socialist labor as Nikita Izotov, Mariia and Evdokiia Vinogradova—the renowned textile workers; Pasha Angelina—the heroine of collective farm work, and many others? What remarkable new people headed the collective farm movement!

During these years, the new qualities of man were shaped. In the article "On Communist Ethics," A. S. Makarenko wrote: "And man among us is a new man, even though he frequently does not know this himself as a result of his new modesty. Several new special features have taken shape in our man which not only were absent in him previously but which it seemed could not be born in him. . . ." Just what "new features" did this remarkable pedagogue have in mind? In the words of Makarenko, the new man had finally lost, for all time, his infamous penchant for "isolation." He was interested in the entire world. He had a capacity for joy and sorrow on a broad human scale; he could think in worldwide dimensions.

A poverty-stricken farmer in the recent past, he now mastered modern technology. "Millions upon millions," Makarenko wrote, "of them began to man the most complex machine tools and assemblies, to take over the controls of machines, and to work with the retorts and test tubes in the laboratory. Not only do they perform wonderfully in these places, but they also know how to animate metal and to give it new expression, norms, and functions. They have become technician-managers, inventors, Stakhanovites, creative engineers."

Imperceptibly, the new man's slavish customs vanished as if these customs had never existed. He displayed the talents of the master, the organizer, the director. He also showed himself to be a remarkable reader. We have produced more books than were printed in old Russia through all its history, but he never has enough. "Despite the large number of nationalities and the distribution of people speaking a hundred languages over an enormous territory, the new man has become part of a single people, the monolithic will of which is almost miraculous. History has not seen, nor could it see, anything like this in any era or in any place. . . .

"All these things represent history, an incomprehensible story, a living part of our biographies; and all this has been created by our efforts, our will, and our hands," wrote A. S. Makarenko.

These profound social changes have been brilliantly portrayed in Soviet literature. *Virgin Soil Upturned* by M. Sholokhov, *Cement* and *Energy* by F. Gladkov, . . . and other artistic works reveal the formation of new relations, new kinds of thoughts and feelings, new traits and qualities in people, and deep-seated processes that underlie changes in psychology, ideology, and habits. Collectivist man is born in life and reflected in literature. He wages the struggle against proprietary psychology and morals, against egotism and individualism, and for the new thought, new views, and morals of socialism. Soviet literature has extensively reflected the contradictions and conflicts in life, the contradictory, dialectical formation of the new man. Soviet literature has far from espoused the idea that people change instantaneously—that the new man is born without storm and tempest. It has clearly shown that the reshaping of people is a complex historical process.

The Great Patriotic War gave rise to

mass heroism and gave life to such human traits as ultimate courage and self-sacrifice, the ability to endure severe deprivation in the name of the highest goals, and unshakable faith in the correctness of the chosen socialist path, in the firmness of ideological principles, the wealth and generosity of spirit, and comradely loyalty. The war was the severest test of the stability of the Soviet system and the "strength" of Soviet people, and of their devotion to communist ideals.

Throughout the centuries, the undying feats of Soviet soldiers will be remembered, and the names of Panfilovites, Young Guards, and A. Matrosov, of the defenders of the Brest Fortress, Captain N. Gastello, N. V. Fil'chenkov, and many others, will be immortal. And how many heroes did the people's volunteer corps produce! What great feats the partisans and scouts performed in the enemy rear! By the end of 1943, over a million armed partisans were battling the German-fascist occupying forces. With the slogan "In labor as in battle," tens of thousands of labor heroes won renown. We recall the labor feats of milling machine operator D. F. Bosykh, drillers A. I. Semivolos and I. P. Iankin, and locomotive machinist N. A. Lunin.

All these very complex processes in forming new people found embodiment in the literature of the war and of the postwar years. Works created at that time reproduce the magnificence of Soviet man, his unprecedented bravery and courage in battle against the most vicious foe of mankind—fascism. We recall the works of M. Sholokhov, A. Tvardovskii, K. Simonov, A. Fadeev, I. Ehrenburg, . . . and others. The names of the works themselves—*The Unsubdued, An Immortal People, They Fought for the Homeland,* and *Russian People*—reflect their main content. The heroism of creation is the main, characteristic feature of the postwar years and of the present period in the building of communism. Workers and engineers, collective farm workers and agronomists, teachers, physicians and scientists, cosmonauts and Soviet servicemen, fighters for peace and social progress—they are in literature's field of vision. The man of labor, the conscious transformer of life, is the hero of this literature. This makes it possible to reflect his spiritual growth, to reveal his character, his spiritual and moral beauty. In many works of recent times, the growing feeling of citizenship, of the intellectual and moral enrichment of man, has been extensively reflected. We recall *I Walk into the Storm* by D. Granin, *Hello, My Name Is Baluev!* by V. Kozhevnikov, *Tronku* by O. Gonchar, *Light from a Distant Star* by A. Chakovskii, and others. . . .

The formation of the new man in all stages of development of Soviet society is inseparably bound up with the diversified organizational and educational activities of the Communist Party. In directly carrying out the immense work of educating the new man, the party has guided the activity of all social and state education institutions and has directed their work with respect to ideology. The purposeful educational work of the Communist Party, of the Soviet state, and of public organizations; the extensive development of cultural-educational institutions—kindergartens, schools, institutions of higher education, clubs, theaters; and the use of such a great force as the press, literature, art, and such modern means of communication as movies, radio, and television for educational purposes—these things are mighty subjective factors in forming the new man. In conjunction with the objective factors of the new social way of life, they have produced an unprecedented upsurge and qualitative change in the spiritual life of the people, an unprecedented elevation of the cultural level of the broad masses, and deep-seated changes in their social and moral makeup.

It is difficult to exaggerate the enormous role played in the education of the new man by the school, the entire system of public education, the broad network of all kinds of cultural and educational institutions and children's out-of-school institutions created after the Revolution, and, finally, children's and youth communist organizations.

In the course of its glorious fifty-year history, the Soviet school—general education and specialized schools, secondary and higher schools—has served the great cause of transforming society on a socialist basis. From the first days of the October Revolution, it has carried out the truly great historic missions put before it by the Communist Party: education of roundly developed members of the new society. In all stages of development, the Soviet school has played an outstanding part in educating the younger generations in the spirit of the great ideals of the October Revolution, in the cultural revolution, in the formation of a new intelligentsia that emerged from the people, and in the training of numerous cadres of specialists. It stubbornly and persistently developed and cultivated qualities of the new person in children and youth. It was the means by which communist ideas were introduced into the minds and lives of the young generation. The Soviet school developed a scientific world view and communist morals in the young generation and forged its will and character. The Soviet school imparted the treasures of socialist culture to children and the youth, and it taught them to prize and multiply spiritual values. Its greatest service lies in the fact that from the moment of its origin as a labor school, it did much to change the attitudes of children toward work, toward laboring people, toward the creators of all material and spiritual wealth of society. In each new stage of development of our society, the school has taken on more and more significance as the largest and most essential social institution for educating and training the younger generations. Its role has constantly risen, and therefore the scope and depth of its influence have grown from year to year.

This is the road that has been traveled. Illiteracy has been eliminated. Century-old cultural backwardness, savagery, and ignorance have been overcome. Adults and children have been educated. Compulsory universal elementary education has been introduced. In its day, this was a decisive step in the cultural revolution, an initial prerequisite to the further rapid spread of education and the development of Soviet socialist culture. Public education began to improve at all levels. In a historically brief period, the transition to universal 7th grade, and then to 8th grade, compulsory education was made; secondary education was expanded. Today, the introduction of universal secondary education is not far away. Specialized secondary and higher education have attained an unprecedented scale.

In the collection of the Central Statistical Administration of the Council of Ministers of the USSR entitled *Fifty Years of the Land of Soviets*, data reflecting astonishing successes in the field of public education and culture are cited. We shall present the most impressive figures.

Every third person in the Soviet Union (not counting preschool children), i.e., 73.6 million persons, is studying. While in tsarist Russia only 1 out of 5 children of school age was in school, today we are close to realizing universal secondary education. Forty-eight million persons are studying in general education schools; before the Revolution there were a little over 9 million. Over 4 million students are studying in USSR institutions of higher learning—3.5 times more than in England, France, the Federal Republic of Germany, and Italy combined. There has been an enormous increase in the cultural level of the populace. At the present time, 84.5 million persons in the USSR have secondary (complete and incomplete) or higher education; of this number, 21.1 million persons have higher, incomplete higher, and secondary specialized education. Of those who are working, 56% have higher and secondary (complete and incomplete) education. This number includes 50% of the factory workers and 33% of the collective farmers.

All these facts show that our country has achieved genuine democratization of education at all levels. The principle of socialist democracy finds expression principally in the fact that the entire system of public education—from the kindergarten to the higher school—serves the interests of all the people rather than individual classes and groups, as occurred under the capitalist system. In our country, everyone enjoys equal rights to study and training. But the principle of socialist democracy is not limited to this; it is also manifested in the entire structure of our training and cultural-educational institutions, in the relationships between the teachers and the taught, in the general orientation of educational work. . . .

Random sampling research, which has become widespread in recent years (the Institute of Public Opinion of *Komsomol'skaia pravda;*[2] the data of sociological research in Leningrad, Sverdlovsk, and elsewhere), makes it possible to draw certain very important conclusions as to the moral countenance of our youth. A chief and leading trend is that the majority of the youth recognize and actively support communist social ideals as the most just and humane. From this stems the striving to join the ranks of communist organizations for children and youth (the Pioneer organization, Komsomol) and the striving for the leading part of the youth to join the ranks of the CPSU. Children and youth take an active part (in an accessible form) in the nation's public life. Their interest in international life is increasing; a deep feeling of solidarity is growing in their hearts and minds with the workers of countries waging the battle against colonialism, against the imperialist aggressors who are fanning the flames of war and are prepared to plunge mankind into a new world war.

By the time of the 15th Komsomol Congress,[3] sociologists had interviewed 15,000 young boys and girls in 15 oblasts, krais, and republics. Of this number, 84.5% put the social usefulness of their work in first place and only 2.6% answered: "Any job is fine as long as it pays well." This research confirms typical factors characterizing the attraction of youth for creative work. There is an unprecedented increase in the interest of children and youth in the new advances in science and technology that help to transform life on a new basis, on the basis of justice and humanity.

The basic moral requirements of our society—a communist attitude toward work, collectivism, patriotism, and internationalism—are perceived by our youth as necessary traits for a Soviet person. The youth passionately support the de-

[2] Major newspaper of the Young Communist League.—Ed.

[3] Held in 1966.—Ed.

mands for sensitivity and humaneness in relations with people. Only a very small number of young people feel a nihilist, negative attitude toward public ideals, toward the revolutionary traditions of the people, a disrespectful attitude toward the norms of socialist communal living, and the lack of desire to combine their personal wants and personal interests with the interests of those around them. By the very nature of Soviet society, there is not and cannot be suitable soil for such negative phenomena. By virtue of its social nature, socialism does not create ground for skepticism, nihilism, social passivity, or ideological emptiness. But our Soviet society has not yet freed itself from the remnants and survivals of the old system and, to a certain extent, this engenders the phenomena mentioned above. To a large extent, these phenomena are the result of poor rearing practices in the family, the school, and other social institutions of education.

The new Soviet man may be a figment of the imagination. The literature of the Soviet Union portrays a life closer perhaps to the communist ideal than to Soviet reality. ANDREI SINIAVSKY (b. 1925), Soviet literary critic writing under the pseudonym of Abram Tertz, presents a sardonic judgment of the value of Soviet literature, written since the 1930s in the style of "socialist realism" and offering the literary version of the new man, the "positive hero." He was actually one of those "suffering from superfluous differences of thought." For having sent abroad for publication such clandestine writings as *On Socialist Realism,* he was sentenced in 1966 to seven years in a Soviet prison camp.*

Andrei Siniavsky

The Literature of Irreality

What is socialist realism? What is the meaning of this strange and jarring phrase? Can there be a socialist, capitalist, Christian, or Mohammedan realism? Does this irrational concept have a natural existence? Perhaps it does not exist at all; perhaps it is only the nightmare of a terrified intellectual during the dark and magical night of Stalin's dictatorship? Perhaps a crude propaganda trick of Zhdanov's or a senile fancy of Gorki's?[1] Is it fiction, myth, or propaganda?

Such questions, we are told, are often asked in the West. They are hotly debated in Poland. They are also current among us, where they arouse eager minds, tempting them into the heresies of doubt and criticism.

Meanwhile, the productions of socialist realism are measured in billions of printed sheets, kilometers of canvas and film, centuries of hours. A thousand critics, theoreticians, art experts, pedagogues are beating their heads and straining their voices to justify, explain, and interpret its material existence and dialectical character. The head of the state himself, the First Secretary of the Central Committee, tears himself away from pressing economic tasks to pronounce some weighty

[1] Famous Russian author and supporter of the Soviet Union in the last years of his life.—Ed.

*From *On Socialist Realism,* by Abram Tertz, trans. by George Dennis. Pp. 23–25, 43–52. Footnotes omitted.

words on the country's aesthetic problems.[2]

The most exact definition of socialist realism is given in a statute of the Union of Soviet Writers: "Socialist realism is the basic method of Soviet literature and literary criticism. It demands of the artist the truthful, historically concrete representation of reality in its revolutionary development. Moreover, the truthfulness and historical concreteness of the artistic representation of reality must be linked with the task of ideological transformation and education of workers in the spirit of socialism." (First All-Union Congress of Soviet Writers, 1934, p. 716.)

This innocent formula is the foundation on which the entire edifice of socialist realism was erected. It includes the link between socialist realism and the realism of the past, as well as its new and distinguishing quality. The link lies in the *truthfulness* of the representation; the difference, in the ability to seize the *revolutionary development* and to educate readers in accordance with that development, *in the spirit of socialism.* The old realists, or, as they are sometimes called, critical realists (because they criticized bourgeois society), men like Balzac, Tolstoi, and Chekhov, truthfully represented life as it is. But not having been instructed in the genius and teachings of Marx, they could not foresee the future victories of socialism, and they certainly did not know the real and concrete roads to these victories.

The socialist realist, armed with the doctrine of Marx and enriched by the experience of struggles and victories, is inspired by the vigilant attention of his friend and teacher, the Communist Party. While representing the present, he listens to the march of history and looks toward the future. He sees the "visible traits of Communism," invisible to the ordinary eye. His creative work is a step forward from the art of the past, the highest peak of the artistic development of mankind and the most realistic of realisms. . . .

Works produced by socialist realists vary in style and content. But in all of them the purpose is present, whether directly or indirectly, open or veiled. They are panegyrics on Communism, satires on some of its many enemies, or descriptions of life "in its revolutionary development," i.e., life moving toward Communism.

Having chosen his subject, the Soviet writer views it from a definite angle. He wants to discover what potentialities it contains that point to the splendid Purpose. Most subjects of Soviet literature have in common a remarkable purposefulness. They all develop in one direction, and a direction well known in advance. This direction may exhibit variations in accordance with time, place, conditions, etc., but it is invariable in its course and its destiny: to remind the reader once more of the triumph of Communism.

Each work of socialist realism, even before it appears, is thus assured of a happy ending. The ending may be sad for the hero, who runs every possible risk in his fight for Communism; but it is happy from the point of view of the superior Purpose; and the author never neglects to proclaim his firm belief in our final victory, either directly or through a speech of his dying hero. Lost illusions, broken hopes, unfulfilled dreams, so characteristic of literature of other eras and systems, are contrary to socialist realism. Even when it produces a tragedy, it is an *Optimistic Tragedy,* the title of Vishnevski's play in which the heroine dies at the end but Communism triumphs.

---

[2] This refers to Khrushchev's speeches to Soviet intellectuals, collected and published in 1957 under the title *For a Close Link Between Literature and Art and the Life of the People.*—Translator.

A comparison between some representative titles of Soviet and Western literature is revealing. *Journey to the End of the Night* (Céline); *Death in the Afternoon* and *For Whom the Bell Tolls* (Hemingway); *Everyone Dies Alone* (Fallada); *A Time to Live and a Time to Die* (Remarque); *Death of a Hero* (Aldington) are all in minor key. *Happiness* (Pavlenko); *First Joys* (Fedin); *It is Well!* (Mayakovski); *Fulfilled Wishes* (Kaverin); *Light over the Earth* (Babaevski); *The Victors* (Bagritski); *The Victor* (Simonov); *The Victor* (Chirikov); *Spring in the Victory Collective Farm* (Gribachev), and so on, are all in a major key.

The splendid aim toward which the action develops is sometimes presented directly at the end of the work. This method was brilliantly used by Mayakovski.[3] All his major works after the Revolution end with passages about Communism or with fantastic scenes describing life in the future Communist state (*Mystery Bouffe; 150,000,000; About This; Vladimir Il'ich Lenin; It is Well!; With a Full Voice*). Gorki, who during the Soviet era wrote mainly about the days before the Revolution, ended most of his novels and plays—*The Artamonov Affair; The Life of Klim Samgin; Egor Bulichev; Dostigaev*—with a vision of the victorious Revolution, which was a stage on the way to Communism, and the concluding gesture of the old world.

Even when the book does not end with such a grandiose denouement, it still exists implicitly and symbolically, commanding the development of characters and events. For example, many of our novels and stories deal with the work of a factory, the building of a power plant, the application of an agricultural decree, and so on. An economic task is carried out in the course of the action (e.g., the start of building introduces the plot, the end of building, the denouement). But the task is presented as an indispensable stage on the way toward a higher purpose. In such a purposeful view, even technical processes acquire dramatic tension and can be followed with great interest. The reader finds out step by step how, against all kinds of obstacles, the plant was put to work, the "Victory" collective farm gathered a good crop of corn, and so on. He closes the book with a sigh of relief and realizes that we have made yet another step toward Communism. . . .

Another subject is offered to our literature by the internal world of man's psychological life. This internal world moves toward the Purpose by dynamics of its own, fights against "the traces of the bourgeois past in its conscience," and re-educates itself under the influence of the Party and of surrounding life. A large part of Soviet literature is an "educational novel" which shows the Communist metamorphosis of individuals and entire communities. Many of our books turn around the representation of these moral and psychological processes, which aim at producing the ideal man of the future. One such is Gorki's *Mother,* where an ignorant woman, defeated by life, is transformed into a conscious revolutionary. Written in 1906, this book is generally considered the first example of socialist realism. Or there is Makarenko's *Pedagogical Poem* about the young criminals who take the road to honest work, or Ostrovski's novel *How the Steel Was Tempered,* i.e., how the steel of our youth was tempered in the fire of the Civil War and the cold of early Communist construction.

As soon as the literary character becomes fully purposeful and conscious of his purposefulness, he can enter that privileged caste which is universally re-

[3] Soviet poet and playwright.—Ed.

spected and called "positive heroes." This is the Holy of Holies of socialist realism, its cornerstone and main achievement.

The positive hero is not simply a good man. He is a hero illuminated by the light of the most ideal of all ideals. Leonid Leonov[4] called his positive hero "a peak of humanity from whose height the future can be seen." He has either no faults at all or else but a few of them—for example, he sometimes loses his temper a little. These faults have a twofold function. They help the hero to preserve a certain likeness to real men, and they provide something to overcome as he raises himself ever higher and higher on the ladder of political morality. However, these faults must be slight or else they would run counter to his basic qualities. It is not easy to enumerate these basic qualities of the positive hero: ideological conviction, courage, intelligence, will power, patriotism, respect for women, self-sacrifice, etc., etc. The most important, of course, are the clarity and directness with which he sees the Purpose and strives toward it. Hence the amazing precision of all his actions, thoughts, tastes, feelings, and judgments. He firmly knows what is right and what is wrong; he says plainly "yes" or "no" and does not confuse black with white. For him there are no inner doubts and hesitations, no unanswerable questions, and no impenetrable secrets. Faced with the most complex of tasks, he easily finds the solution—by taking the shortest and most direct route to the Purpose.

The positive hero first appeared in some books of Gorki's written in the first decade of the twentieth century. . . . Since then the positive hero has gone through many changes and presented himself in many guises. He unrolled his positive qualities in many ways, grew big and sturdy, and finally drew himself up to his full stature. This happened as early as the 1930s, when the Soviet writers dropped their little cliques and their literary tendencies, and accepted, almost unanimously, the best and most advanced trend of all: socialist realism.

To read the books of the last twenty or thirty years is to feel the great power of the positive hero. First he spread in every direction, until he filled all our literature. There are books in which *all* the heroes are positive. This is but natural, since we are coming ever closer to the Purpose. So that if a book about the present deals not with the fight against the enemies but with, say, a model collective farm, then all its characters can and must be positive. To put negative characters in such a situation would, to say the least, be strange. And so we get dramas and novels where all moves smoothly and peacefully. If there is a conflict between the heroes, it is a conflict between good and better, model and supermodel. When these books appeared, their authors—men like Babaevski, Surkov, Sofronov, Virta, Gribachev, etc.—were highly praised and set up as examples for others. True, since the Twentieth Congress—one hardly knows why—our attitude toward them has changed somewhat and we apply to them the contemptuous adjective "conflictless." Once Khrushchev came out in defense of these writers, such reproaches were stilled somewhat, but they are still voiced here and there by intellectuals. They are unjust.

Since we don't want to lose face before the West, we occasionally cease to be consistent and declare that our society is rich in individualities and embraces many interests; and that it has differences of opinion, conflicts, and contradictions, and that literature is supposed to reflect all that.

[4] Soviet novelist.—Ed.

True, we differ from each other in age, sex, nationality, and even intelligence. But whoever follows the Party line knows that these are heterogeneities within a homogeneity, differences of opinion within a single opinion, conflicts within a basic absence of conflict. We have one aim—Communism; one philosophy—Marxism; one art—socialist realism. This was well put by a Soviet writer of no great literary gifts but politically irreproachable: "Russia took its own road—that of unanimity. . . . For thousands of years men suffered from differences of opinion. But now we, Soviet men and women, for the first time agree with each other, talk one language that we all understand, and think identically about the main things in life. It is this unanimity that makes us strong and superior to all other people in the world, who are internally torn and socially isolated through their differences of opinion." (V. Il'enkov, *The Great Highway,* a novel which appeared in 1949 and was awarded the Stalin Prize.)

Beautifully put! Yes, we really are all alike and we are not ashamed of it. Those of us who suffer from superfluous differences of thought we punish severely by excluding them from life and literature. There can be no substantial differences of opinion in a country where even the anti-Party elements confess their errors and wish to rectify them as soon as possible, and incorrigible enemies of the people ask to be shot. Still less can there be such differences among honest Soviet people and least of all among positive heroes who think only of spreading their virtues all over the world and of re-educating the few remaining dissidents into unanimity.

The events of the Soviet period had a strong impact on the character of the Russian people, in the view of LEWIS FEUER (b. 1912), professor of sociology at the University of Toronto. Using the techniques of psychoanalysis, he explores the character types as defined by the Soviet party elite. The changes which these types went through seem to him indicative of changes in the Russian people as a whole. He finds the first period of Soviet history one of "liberation of energies and creativity." But the Stalin years saw the rise of a new sadistic personality model accompanied by "massive self-repression." The traumatic experiences of these years left, in his opinion, profoundly disturbing psychological effects on the Russian population.*

Lewis Feuer

The Bolshevization of the Personality

The Bolsheviks of 1917 certainly believed that the new society, conceived in the October Revolution, would bring forth a wonderful new human being. Leon Trotsky believed the future would see men with noble gait and bearing, with beautiful speech and high intelligence. "Man will become immeasurably stronger, wiser and subtler; his body will become more harmonized . . . his voice more musical . . . The average human type will rise to the heights of an Aristotle, a Goethe, a Marx." Lenin foresaw a blending of mental and physical labor which would make the workingman-ruler the realization of a philosopher-king. Alexandra Kollontai[1] foretold a love of the sexes ennobled, free from cruelty and selfishness. Such were the dreams. What then were the realities of Soviet psychological evolution? Lenin insisted that every creative idea must have an element of the dream in it. If so, what was achieved, and in what ways did the dream's superimposition do violence to human nature?

If there is one great achievement of the Soviet society, it is that during its first twelve years or so, it carried through a psychological revolution against the tra-

[1] One of the most active of Bolshevik intellectuals and defender of women's liberation in the Soviet Union.—Ed.

* From Lewis Feuer, "The Social-Psychological Transformations," in *Fifty Years of Communism in Russia,* ed. Milorad Drachkovitch (University Park, Penn.: The Pennsylvania State University Press, 1968), pp. 100–104, 106–107, 108, 109–110. Reprinted by permission. Footnotes omitted.

ditional masochist psyche of the Russian people. This first era might well be called the anti-masochist period of the Soviet evolution. Paul Miliukov[2] once said that he regarded E. J. Dillon's *Russian Characteristics* as the best portrayal of prerevolutionary Russia; it gave a picture of a flagellant people, fatalistic, immoral, dishonest, lying, superstitious, and given to alternate brutality and self-castigation; its passive perspective, its acceptance of its own sinful character, was summed up in the proverb: "What is to be, cannot be avoided." When this same observer visited the Soviet Union in 1928, he was astonished by the transformation. The obsequious muzhik had changed, he wrote, into "a full-blown citizen, conscious that he has a country with whose interests he identifies his own, and a government which is largely of his own making." Dillon went to the bookstores of Moscow. "I never anticipated anything like this," he wrote. "The notion that a large percentage of mooshiks were smitten with a mania for enlightenment . . . seemed hardly admissible . . . But the fact was undeniable. The stores were crowded, . . . and millions of volumes were circulating in the various Republics." The sight of these book-seeking peasants, he said, "opened my eyes to the completeness of the change that had come over the population." Scientific, technical, and medical films were being shown everywhere, *The Mechanism of the Human Brain, The Choice of a Profession.* The most popular medical film was entitled *Abortion;* produced five or six years earlier, it was still drawing well. This was not the Russian man whom Saltykov had satirized—the suffering-deadened, consciousness-blunted Russian man, who looked at his hunger, misery, and humiliation as predestined.

The Bolshevik personality-structure refused to take physical suffering as the law of existence. Insofar as man was beset by technical problems, there were technical answers, and the Marxist was at one with the Comtist in asserting confidently the power of science. "We shall win over all the Russian and European Archimedes, and then the world will have to change whether it wants to or not!" said Lenin.

This hatred for masochism, for "self-castigation" as he called it, was a primary component in Lenin, and a dominant element in the ego-ideal which he transmitted to the first decade of Soviet history. This was the Lenin who ridiculed the Tolstoyan, "the exhausted hysterical, misery-mongering Russian intellectual, who, publicly beating his breast, cries: 'I am bad, I am vile, but I am striving for moral self-perfection; I no longer eat meat but live on rice cutlets.'" He mocked at even the Jamesian religious philosophy to which Gorky was attracted; its adherent, he wrote, "castigates himself in the worst possible way, because instead of occupying himself with 'deeds' he indulges in self-contemplation." Lenin as an ego-ideal stood for a categorical rejection of the Russian wallowing in suffering. As Gorky defined Lenin's role: "I have never met in Russia, the country where the inevitability of suffering is preached as the general road to salvation, nor do I know of any man who hated, loathed and despised so deeply and strongly as Lenin, all . . . suffering."

The anti-masochist vector in the Soviet psychology brought a liberation of energies and creativity; something like a Soviet Renaissance seemed to be in the making, an experimentation in art forms, an

[2] Leader of the Russian liberal movement under Nicholas II and Russian historian.—Ed.

enthusiasm for progressive education, a popular cultural revolution. This liberation of energies was the phenomenon which enthralled the Western intellectuals who visited the Soviet Union during this era and touched them with its infectious hopes. Isadora Duncan, the votary of the new dance with its free bodily expression, spent three years in Russia from 1921 to 1924, "to dance for the people," and she regarded that time as the happiest in her life. John Dewey, America's foremost philosopher, came to the Soviet Union in 1928, and was stirred by its teachers, "some of the wisest and most devoted men and women it has been my fortune to meet." Never had he seen in the world, he wrote, "such a large proportion of intelligent, happy, and intelligently occupied children." He found the Soviet effort "nobly heroic, evincing a faith in human nature which is democratic beyond the ambitions of the democracies of the past," while the Russian intellectuals seemed to him "organic members of an organic going movement." His colleagues from the Teachers' College at Columbia University, William Heard Kilpatrick and George S. Counts, joined with him in these judgments. The noted social worker, Lillian D. Wald, found the Soviet achievement in public health "extraordinary" and admired the campaigns to teach the people the rules of hygiene. The economist Professor Paul Douglas sensed "the big, the spiritual fact" behind the Soviet material construction, and his faith in socialism was strengthened. The distinguished liberal thinker, Horace M. Kallen, saw the realization of a cultural pluralism in the Soviet setting; he found a thriving culture among his fellow-Jews; for them, he wrote, "more truly than for any people under the Soviets, a new life is beginning." The American travellers, to be sure, were all affected by a social will to believe as far as Soviet society was concerned. Nevertheless, there was a large counterpart in Soviet realities to their observations. The revolt against traditional masochism was releasing hitherto suppressed or dissipated human energies.

The anti-masochist period in the Soviet psychological evolution gave way in the early thirties to a new stage which might be called that of the Bolshevization of the personality, from an anti-masochist to a sadistic elitist personality-structure. Stalin's famous speech in February 1931 to the First All-Union Conference of Managers, the most eloquent he ever gave, placed the motive for industrialization primarily in overcoming the Russian masochist tradition:

> The history of old Russia is the history of defeats due to backwardness. She was beaten by the Mongol Khans. She was beaten by the Swedish feudal barons. She was beaten by the Polish-Lithuanian squires. She was beaten by the Anglo-French capitalists. She was beaten by the Japanese barons. All beat her for her backwardness . . . She was beaten because to beat her was profitable and could be done with impunity. Do you remember the words of the prerevolutionary poet: "You are both poor and abundant, you are both powerful and helpless, mother Russia" . . . They beat her saying: "You are poor and helpless," . . . Such is the law of capitalism—to beat the backward and the weak. The jungle law of capitalism.

Here was a version of Russian history not as class struggle but as repeated submission to beating by foreigners. The memorable iteration of "beaten" indicated above all the psychological motive power for industrialization. But then the sadistic component, emerging to dominance, chose of all the possible ways to industrialization that one which would enforce the government's will most harshly on the people.

The Russian ego-ideal in its fluctuation

from masochism in effect now swung to sadism—from an exaltation of suffering to one of cruelty. There took place a remarkable psychological change in the Soviet ego-ideal structure. Already in the twenties, observers had often spoken of "Communist Puritans," of those who like Marxist Calvinists renounced the goods and joys of life, and lived with frugality, industry, and thrift. Thus Louis Fischer, writing from Moscow in 1924, in an article entitled "Communist Puritans," expounded their psychological similarity: "The Bolsheviks presume to tell the individual how to act and how to live. This is the 'superiority complex' which is one of the most essential characteristics of puritanism. 'I am perfect. Watch me. Go thou and do likewise.' The Russian Communists are puritans without religion." Cotton Mather, wrote *The Nation*'s Moscow correspondent, would have approved of Trotsky; also Lenin lived as an ascetic, and there was "something reminiscent of Christian self-abnegation in Chicherin's, Bukharin's, Radek's disdain for good clothes.". . .

The Puritan virtues were appropriate to a revolutionary period in which pleasures were associated with the upper classes; to live like a proletarian was to live frugally. Moreover, these Marxist Calvinist virtues were validated by the needs of an era of industrialization; the people were being called upon to consume less and to accumulate more. It was also true that side-by-side with the liberating, anti-masochist component of the Soviet Revolution there had been copresent a strong, harsh, sadistic vector. Bertrand Russell, a keen psychological observer, perceived the sadistic component which moved Lenin's asceticism. The Bolshevik Revolution, as William H. Chamberlin wrote in his history, opened the gates to a tremendous mass release of hatred. Under these circumstances, men whose personalities were dominated by sadistic motives moved ahead into the highest positions of leadership. The conditions of the civil war, the frustrations of material existence, the accumulated personal envies of class existence, the bitterness of life where survival had become the primary end, while emotions and thinking became survival-emotions and survival-thinking, all this filled the interstices of social life with a free-floating aggression. Political leaders who came from the most extreme sadistic segment of the spectrum of personality-types fond a psychological climate in which they could forge to the top. The Bolsheviks of this time, to use Max Eastman's classification, were divided into the "softs" and the "hards." The "hards," the sadists, began to displace the "softs." Leon Trotsky was aware that one psychological type was gradually displacing another. He tried to explain the phenomenon of the rise of Stalin and his henchmen by reference to a psychological law—that there is a reaction of exhaustion on the part of the people to the great social and psychological strain of revolution, and that in this situation, the mediocrities push ahead, displacing the men of talent and genius. Stalin, in Trotsky's eyes, was "the outstanding mediocrity of the party." But something more was involved than the rise of mediocrities. Even a mediocracy can take either malevolent or benevolent forms. John Stuart Mill wrote in *On Liberty* that "the general tendency of things throughout the world is to render mediocrity the ascendant power among mankind." A distinguished president of the United States, Harry Truman, did not regard himself as an exceptional man; Trotsky would have called him a mediocrity. The psychological character of the Stalinist era, however, derived not from the intellectual mediocrity of its leaders but rather from their qualities of emotion —their sadistic vectors. Whatever the social causes for the elevation of such a psychological type to the Soviet leadership, it expressed itself in the Bolshevization of the ego-ideal for the character-structure of the Soviet people. . . .

"Spontaneous" processes were taken to be the road to "leftist" deviations. The kind of personality a man should train himself to have was dictated by the needs of the Five-Year Plan. It was as if each citizen was being assigned a personality quota to fulfill. He must repress troublesome questions, suppress his inner discontent, identify with the Party, and regard its edicts as his own. The Bolshevization of the personality on a collective scale thus involved a massive self-repression.

It was this massive self-repression which made possible the acquiescence of the Soviet people to the large-scale purges and liquidations of the thirties. The questioning intellectual, the recalcitrant worker, the writer insisting on his freedom, the obstinate peasant, each externalized motivations which the majority of the Soviet citizenry felt and expressed within themselves. Soviet citizens struggled to talk and behave as the official policy demanded. There developed that separation into two selves which Soviet thinkers now describe as the separation between the "official self" and the "real self." Every society has some degree of such a separation but in Soviet society it reached extremes. People found themselves intoning public speeches which they didn't believe; parents curbed their comments to their children lest they be quoted or reported for counter-revolutionary utterances. The atmosphere resembled that which the historian Ammianus Marcellinus described as existing in the Rome of the fourth century A.D. when things reached the point that people denied they even had dreams for fear that they would be held accountable for what they had dreamed. It was the depth and extent of the division between the "real" and the "official" self which became the primary characteristic in the latter thirties of the Soviet personality structure. It was a harsh, disharmonious self rather than the harmonious self which Trotsky had foreseen. The decrees against abortion and divorce, the official notation of illegitimacy, were all aspects of the attempt to Bolshevize personality. The "spontaneous" individualistic concern with private happiness was out of keeping with the repressive temper.

Such a laceration and duality of selves was always in an unstable equilibrium, the maintenance of which required all the resources of social controls and threats to assure the individual's collaboration. For almost every person felt guilty, almost everyone repressed some discontent, some frustration, some clear insight into the workings of the regime. Every person knew he was guilty of sins, original and unoriginal, against the regime. The price of survival was successful repression. Every deviationist who was tried and condemned externalized one's own inner repressed deviation, and joining in condemning them was a collective easement of the aggressions which had accumulated in one's self. Every totalitarian system from the Spanish Inquisition on has seen the complicity of its people in the extirpation of heretics, for the simple reason that the modal personality structure which such systems require is based on every individual's repressing his angers and doubts into his unconscious; hence, every totalitarian system must cope with the accumulated aggressions issuing from the histories of individual repression and frustrations. To engage in any causal psychological analysis which might uncover the contents of the unconscious was *prima facie* evidence of a leftist deviation; the unconscious indeed was presumed by the Soviet regime to be a Trotskyist. Thus the popular play *Fear* produced in 1931 depicted the counter-revolutionary activities of an "Institute for Physiological Stimuli"; they consisted in the administering of questionnaires among the people which supported the conclusion that eighty percent were cowed into social submission by an "unconditioned response of fear." The play showed how the institute's director was unmasked and removed, and then repented. . . .

A kind of hatred and suspicion of one's fellow-man came to pervade the emotions of Soviet people during the latter thirties. The goals of upward mobility were more available if one's bureaucratic superiors or rivals were "physically liquidated"; denunciation became a technique for rising in the bureaucratic hierarchy or for venting one's grudges; at the same time, one could claim the warrant of one's Socialist conscience. The unethical, the envious mediocrity, the ambitious gifted, the time server profited from the removal of the ethical, the talented, the sincere. The insincere could Bolshevize their personalities most easily. Participant-observers, as the phrase goes, described the time as Machiavellian. Lev Kamenev,[3] shortly before the shadow of the purges fell upon him, wrote about Machiavelli in the language of Soviet indirect discourse. "This servant of the Florentine oligarchy," he said, had not been afraid "to look at the political reality of his time and to reveal behind the broad banner and paltry finery its true countenance: an oppressive class of masters struggling amongst themselves for power over the laboring masses." And Ilya Ehrenburg,[4] recalling the character of the Stalinist era in later years, said it evoked Machiavelli and the chieftains of the Renaissance, when any means were regarded as justified in creating a strong state—poison, informing, stabbing in the back. . . .

The war years from 1941 to 1945, for all their untold physical hardship, brought an easement of the psychological strains under which the Soviet personality lived. Ehrenburg has described the prewar years: "In March, 1938, I had listened to the elevator with alarm; at that time I wanted to live, and like many others I had a small suitcase in readiness with two changes of linen." The internal enemy receded during the war years; the enemy became real and external, and every person felt needed in the struggle. From a psychological standpoint, the war helped the Soviet equilibrium by providing a target for the accumulated aggressive resentments. The aftermath, however, brought the renewed anxieties of Bolshevization. Exhausted and indifferent, people submitted. The second Bolshevization had an aspect of the *déjà vu.* "In March, 1949," writes Ehrenburg, "I did not think about linen, and I awaited the outcome almost with indifference . . . I had had time to grow tired, old age was setting in. Or perhaps because this was a repetition, and after the war, what was taking place was particularly unbearable. We would go to bed late—just before morning; the thought of their coming was particularly unbearable."

The Stalinist era ended in 1953, but it left the deepest imprint on the Soviet personality structure. The Soviet intelli-

[3] One of the original members of the Communist party leadership, arrested and shot in 1936.—Ed.

[4] Soviet writer of Jewish origin, author of famous post-Stalin novel *The Thaw* (1954).—Ed.

gentsia had sustained the worst psychological trauma—the blow to the sense of their own sincerity. For sincerity was what the pre-revolutionary intellectuals proudly felt to be their most distinct trait. As Kropotkin[5] wrote, it was nihilism which had "impressed its stamp upon the whole of the life of the educated classes of Russia" and which would be "retained for many years to come." It gave to them, he said, "a certain peculiar character which we Russians regret not to find in the life of Western Europe . . . that remarkable sincerity, that habit of thinking aloud, which astounds Western European readers." This sincerity made the Russian intellectual refuse "to bend before any authority except that of reason, and in the analysis of every social institution or habit he revolted against any sort of more or less marked sophism." The traumatic surrender of this sincerity remained in their memory for the Soviet intelligentsia to abreact. As Pasternak put it in Dr. Zhivago: "To conceal the failure [of collectivization] people had to be cured, by every means of terrorism of the habit of thinking and judging for themselves, and forced to see what didn't exist, to assert the very opposite of what their eyes told them. This accounts for the unexampled cruelty of the Yezhov period."[6]

Second, there came to pervade Soviet society what we might best call a "Cain-Abel complex." The new society, the new elect of activists and Marxists, the new working class, had shown itself like Cain unable to guard its brothers; they had allowed the Abels to be destroyed. Each person had to come to terms with his share in the collective guilt. Some intellectuals said later with Ehrenburg: "Yes, I did know about many crimes; but it was not within my power to stop them." They were met with the query: Why hadn't they spoken out as Tolstoi had spoken out against the crimes of tsarist Russia? They answered: the Soviet society was different, and in any case, who would have believed the protesting voice? But the Cain-Abel complex imposed an especial burden of guilt on a people professing a higher historical mission. That is why Khrushchev's speech at the Twentieth Party-Congress was the single most politically and psychologically therapeutic act in the twentieth century: "Like millions of my countrymen," recalled Ehrenburg, "when I read the materials of the 20th Congress I felt that a weight had been lifted from my heart."

The phenomenon itself and its psychological effects were not easily exorcised; on a less grandiose scale, they persisted. The meaning of the Cain-Abel complex was a reiterated statement: "We killed our comrades, we still destroy them." Revolutionary France got rid of its guilt by using the Directory and Napoleon to eradicate all the Jacobin Clubs. Napoleon, we must remember, was the first great anti-ideologist. In the Soviet Union, however, the Communist Party, unlike the Jacobin Clubs, pervaded every domain of social and economic existence. The Jacobin Clubs, in contrast, led ephemeral lives for a few years. The Communist Party was the primary social institution, and of forty years' standing. Naturally an effort was made to keep unsullied its collective image, and to make of Stalin an almost sole bearer and scapegoat of the collective guilt.

[5] Russian anarchist.—Ed.

[6] Period between 1936 and 1938 of bloodiest purges under Nicholas Yezhov, head in those years of the secret police.—Ed.

No one can doubt the extensive transformation of Russia under the Soviet regime. But what type of society have these changes produced? One theory is that the Soviet Union is becoming more like the West. But another stresses the uniqueness of the Soviet experience. SIDNEY and BEATRICE WEBB (1859–1947 and 1858–1943, respectively), Fabian socialists active in the British Labor party, believe that the ideals of Soviet ideology accurately define a new way of life in Russia. So different is the Soviet way that it represents a new civilization.*

Sidney and Beatrice Webb

A New Civilization

As we have seen, the Bolsheviks consider that what they are doing among the 170 millions of people of the USSR[1] is much more than introducing them to newspapers and books, the theatre and the opera; or improving their health, and increasing their wealth production. What they believe themselves to be establishing in the world is nothing less than a new civilisation. . . .

It is plain that many different factors may enter into the making of a distinctive civilisation. To some the most important seems the nature and character of its particular religion. Those communities in which Christianity has been dominant stand out from the rest. In other instances, as in China, racial characteristics afford the most noticeable difference. What may be called the political organisation of a community has sometimes—for instance, in feudalism—served as the mark of a distinct civilisation. Even more distinctive of different manners of life may be the economic organisation, as in the contrast between communities living mainly by hunting or fishing, or by rearing cattle, or by cultivating the soil; and those engaging extensively in commerce, or, with the constantly increasing use of power-driven machinery, in mining and manufacturing. Or we may notice whether the several

[1] Population in 1937 when this was written.—Ed.

*From Sidney and Beatrice Webb, *Soviet Communism: A New Civilization,* third edition (New York: Longmans, Green and Company, 1944), pp. 898–901, 903–906, 908–909, 912–913. Published in Great Britain by Longmans, Green and Company Limited, copyright by the London School of Economics and Political Science. Footnotes omitted.

families of a community habitually work for themselves; or whether, as slaves, serfs or wage-labourers, the majority serve the owners of the means of production.

For our present purpose there is no need to discuss all known or possible civilisations. It will suffice to start from the common division of the three thousand years' history of Europe since the days of Homer into the three successive civilisations that are covered respectively by the story of Greece and Rome; by the widespread adoption of Christianity and feudalism; and by the modern world from 1492 down to our own day. Everyone is familiar with the characteristics of contemporary civilisation of this specifically European kind, which has undoubtedly resulted in great progress and has been carried by white settlers, traders or travellers all over the world. It will suffice to emphasise its four main features. First in date stands the Christian religion, with the code of conduct that it inculcates. Then, increasingly after the fifteenth century, comes the so-called capitalist system of the private ownership of property, notably in the means of production, to be utilised, under the direction of the owners, upon the incentive of the making of profit either by the employment of workers at wages or by trading in goods; or latterly, by the manipulation of money and credit by the financiers. Further we notice, continuously during the past two centuries, even if apparently momentarily arrested, a widespread trend towards government on the system of parliamentary democracy. Finally we have to note during the past hundred years, as peculiar to this particular civilisation, an unprecedented increase, through knowledge, of man's command over Nature, along with an increasing application of science, under the influence of humane feeling, to the amelioration of the lot of some sections of the poor. Such being the starting point, the question that is asked is whether what is developing in the USSR since 1917 is so markedly different from the manner of life in the England or the France or the United States of the past three or four centuries as to justify calling it a new civilisation. Let us try to set out the features in which Soviet Communism differs essentially from the characteristic civilisation of the western world of to-day.

The Abolition of Profit-making

We place first in far-reaching importance the complete discarding, as the incentive to production, of the very mainspring of the western social order, the motive of profit-making. Instead of admiring those who successfully purchase commodities in order to sell them again at a higher price (whether as merchant or trader, wholesale dealer or retailer), Soviet Communism punishes such persons as criminals, guilty of the crime of "speculation." Instead of rewarding or honouring those (the capitalist employers or entrepreneurs) who engage others at wages in order to make a profit out of the product of their labour, Soviet Communism punishes them as criminals, guilty, irrespective of the amount of the wages that they pay, of the crime of "exploitation." It would be difficult to exaggerate the difference that this one change in ideology (in current views of morality as well as in criminal law) has made in the manner of life within the USSR. No one can adequately realise, without a wide study of the facts of soviet life, what this fundamental transformation of economic relationships has meant, alike to the vast majority of the poor and to the relatively small minority who formerly "lived by owning," or by employing others for profit.

The change has not had the particular results anticipated by our capitalist reasoning. It has not meant compulsion to take service under the government as the only employer. It has not prevented millions of individuals from working independently, or in voluntary partnerships, for their own or their family's subsistence. It does not forbid either the independent producers or the producing partnerships to sell the product of their own labour in the public market, or by contract, for any price they can get. It has not involved the abolition of personal property, or any compulsion to have all things in common. It has not prevented inequality of possessions, or of incomes, or even difference of earnings. The payment of interest on government loans, and the receipt of interest on deposits in the savings bank, have not ceased. But the habit of able-bodied persons living without work has become disgraceful, however great may be their savings or their other possessions; and the class of wealthy families, whether as owners of land, employers of labour or rentiers and financiers, has ceased to exist. More important still is that the control of the instruments of wealth production by individuals seeking to enrich themsleves, and the power of the landlord and the capitalist over those whom they can employ at wages, or from whom they can exact rent, has passed away. . . .

Social Equality and Universalism

It is claimed that the whole social organisation of Soviet Communism is based upon a social equality that is more genuine and more universal than has existed in any other community. To engage in socially useful work, acccrding to capacity, is a universal duty. It is a distinct novelty in social life that there should be no exemption from this duty in favour of the possessors of wealth or the owners of land, the holders of high offices, or those having exceptional intellectual or artistic gifts or attainments, the geniuses or the popular favourites. Work, like leisure, has to be shared by all able to join in social service. There is only a single social grade in the USSR, that of a producer by hand or by brain; including, however, those so young that they can only prepare themselves for becoming producers, and those so aged or so infirm as only to be able to look back on the work they did in their strength. This is what is meant by the "classless society," in which each serves in accordance with his ability, and is provided for appropriately to his needs.

The depth of the difference between this manner of living and that of capitalist states is scarcely to be fathomed. But it involves the very opposite of uniformity or identity among all men. It not only allows, but even actively encourages and promotes, the utmost development of individuality in social service. Nor does it produce an exact equality of earnings or other income; although the prohibition of profit-making by "speculation," or "exploitation," and the collective ownership of all the principal means of production, coupled with drastically progressive income taxes and death duties on exceptional individual fortunes, effectively prevent the gross inequalities which threaten the stability of states in which millionairism is not only tolerated but allowed to become a plutocracy.

But the principle of social equality goes much further than community in work and leisure, common schooling and games, with a constant approximation to substantial equality of standards of income and expenditure. It extends, in a manner and to a degree unknown elsewhere, to the relations between the sexes, and within the family group. Husbands and wives, parents and children, teachers and scholars, like friends of different sexes, or of not too unequal incomes, like managers and factory operatives, administrators and typists, and even army officers and the rank and file, live in an atmosphere of social equality and of freedom from servility or "inferiority complex" that is unknown elsewhere. What is still more unique is the absence of prejudice as to colour or race. The hundred or more different races and language groups of the USSR of nearly all shades of colour, including the wildest nomads and the most rooted townsmen, the most urbane diplomatists and the most primitive barbarians, enjoy not only complete identity of legal and political rights, but also the fullest equality of freedom in economic and social relations. Wherever schools exist at all, those living within reach are educated in common; they work together at wage-rates differentiated only by differences in the tasks; they use the same public conveyances, the same hotels and holiday homes, the same public utilities; they join the same trade unions and other voluntary associations; they sit side by side in the lecture-rooms, libraries, theatres and cinemas. They form mutual friendships irrespective of race or colour, and intermarry freely. Again, there is no imposition of a central pattern. On the contrary, the cardinal bond of the Soviet Union is the guarantee to each "national minority" of its own "cultural autonomy." Each maintains its own vernacular, its own schools, its own newspapers, its own publishing houses, its own theatres; and they are all specially assisted to do so out of federal funds. What is more, each of the dozens of constituent or autonomous republics making up the USSR freely elects or appoints, if it chooses, its own people to the local representative bodies and to the local offices, and is vigorously incited and encouraged to do so by the Government at Moscow. It would be hard to over-estimate the sense of freedom and equality—far exceeding that of the corresponding arrangements as to "natives" in analogous dependencies of other states—produced by this effective cultural autonomy and local government by officials of one's own race.

There is yet another feature in the social equality of the civilisation of the Soviet Union which we term "universalism." Other communities have willingly acquiesced in the fact that the advantages and amenities which their civilisation provides, including most of the luxuries of life, do not reach the poorest or weakest, or least developed, or least thrifty or least well-conducted members of the community. The current economic and social arrangements do not enable these unfortunates to reach the same standard of health and education, or to attain the same longevity or intellectual development, or even to procure the amount of food, clothing and shelter that is deemed necessary and normal among the more favoured classes. A few such communities are, in the twentieth century, just beginning to realise these features of the inequality in which their social life is rooted. It is a distinctive feature of the social arrangements of the Soviet Union that, to a degree unparalleled elsewhere, they provide for every person, irrespective of wealth or position, sex or race, the poorest and weakest as well as those who are "better off," in all cases equality of opportunity for the children and adolescents, and, increasingly, also a common and ever-rising standard of living for the whole population. This is well seen in the sphere of education. Other communities, especially during the past century or two, have striven to create educated, and even cultivated classes within the nation. The Soviet Union is the first to strive, without discrimination of sex or race, affluence or position, to produce not merely an intelligentsia but a cultivated nation.

A Novel Representative System

In every community of any magnitude, social organisation has to include a system by means of which the desires and the common will of the population can be expressed. In contrast with every other community, the USSR has evolved a complex and multiform representative system of complete originality, based upon the principle of universal participation in public affairs, under the guidance of a highly organised leadership of a unique kind. As we have described, man is represented in three separate capacities, as a citizen, as a producer and as a consumer. In each case the franchise is the widest in the world, though with peculiar and steadily dwindling disqualifications, whilst the extent to which the entire population actually participates in elections is without parallel. The representative system has hitherto been, above the 70,000 village or city soviets, one of indirect election; but it was in 1935 decided to replace this by direct election upon a franchise uniform among both sexes, all races, and every kind of occupation, throughout the USSR.

It is impossible to enumerate all the channels, and it would be difficult to exaggerate the extent, of the participation in the public affairs of the Soviet electorate of over 90 millions of men and women. The characteristic multiformity of every kind of soviet organisation, economic or political, together with its threefold system of representation, and the omnicompetence, as regards powers and functions, of each tier of councils in its ubiquitous local government, are in vivid contrast with the dominance of the parliamentary systems of the western world. To begin with, the universal electorate in the USSR does a great deal more than elect. At its incessant meetings it debates and passes resolutions by the hundred thousand, in which it expresses its desires on great matters and on small; by way of instructions or suggestions to the "deputies" whom it chooses and can at any time withdraw by a vote of "recall," and who habitually take notice of these popular requirements, even when it is not found immediately practicable to carry them into effect. Nor does the participation in public affairs end with the perpetual discussions in which the Russian delights. In every village, as in every city, a large part of the detailed work of public administration is actually performed, not as in France or Great Britain or the United States, by paid officials, and not even, as in small or primitive communities, by the elected deputies or councillors, but by a far larger number of the adult inhabitants themselves, as part of the universally expected voluntary social service.

The same characteristic multiformity and popular participation prevails also in the extensive and highly organised trade unionism, in which are voluntarily included five-sixths of all the persons employed at wages or salaries, whatever their occupations or grade or remuneration. The trade unions by no means confine themselves to their extensive collective bargaining over wages and hours, and other conditions of employment, which far exceeds that of the trade unions elsewhere, together with their active share in the administration of the factory or the mine. For instance, it is to the trade union organisation that is now committed not only the control but also the actual administration of the colossal services of social insurance, which are more extensive and costly than those in any other country, and to which the workers make no individual contribution. This huge administration is carried on, not wholly or even mainly by the paid officials whom the trade unions appoint, or by the committees which they elect, but personally, without remuneration, by something like 100,000 "activists" among the trade unionists themselves as part of their social service.

The Consumers' Cooperative Movement, which numbers over 70 million members, displays a like multiformity of organisation, and a similar personal participation by its vast membership, in the complicated business of distributing over the huge area of the USSR the greater part of its food and other commodities.

Yet another variety is exhibited by the immense and highly differentiated voluntary associations, sometimes numbering even millions of members apiece. These multifarious self-governing associations, which often enjoy financial subventions, undertake public service of one or other kind; partly educational, partly propagandist, including also sports and games of every description, along with music, painting, dancing and acting, as well as active cooperation with various branches of government service, from the promotion of science and art up to the assistance of the defense forces. . . .

The Cult of Science

One of the differences between the soviet civilisation and that of other countries is the way in which science is regarded. Unlike the groups of landed proprietors, lawyers, merchants, bureaucrats, soldiers and journalists in command of most other states, the administrators in the Moscow Kremlin genuinely believe in their professed faith. And their professed faith is in science. No vested interests hinder them from basing their decisions and their policy upon the best science they can obtain. Moreover, under the guidance of the Communist Party, public opinion in the Soviet Union has come, to an extent unparalleled elsewhere, to be overwhelmingly in favour of making the utmost use of science as manifested in labour-saving and wealth-producing machines and invention. The whole community is eager for new knowledge. There is no country, we imagine, in which so large and so varied an amount of scientific research is being carried on at the public expense, alike in the realm of abstract theory and in that of technology. There is certainly none in which there is so little chance of that frustration of science by the profit-making instinct of which the British and American scientists are now complaining.

This intense preoccupation, and even obsession, with science in the USSR has steadily increased during the past six years of the successive Five-Year Plans—significantly enough, just at the time when even the United States has shut down much of its scientific activity. Nor is this contrast surprising. In the USSR the dominant purpose of everyone who takes part in public affairs is concentrated on increasing the aggregate wealth production, as the first condition of raising the cultural level of all the 170 millions of people. The instrument by which this universal levelling-up can be effected is, as is widely believed, science itself. As we have described in a previous chapter, science is more and more dominating the schooling and the college training, and more and more enrolling in its service the most energetic and capable of the young. The continuous application of science to agriculture as well as to manufacture; to the discovery and utilisation of new substances, plants or animals, as well as to the improvement of those already known; to the development without limit of electric power and its use, not only in the various forms of communication and transport, but also in altogether novel transformations of the processes of mining and metallurgy, opens up a bright vista of what may amount to a new "Industrial Revolution" in which, if only a parallel development in sociology and ethics enables it to avoid the mistakes of the previous centuries, the population of the USSR may give a practical example of what was meant by the old stipulation "unless you be born again.". . .

The foregoing summaries of the principal features of Soviet Communism demonstrate at least its contrast with western civilisation. But do these separate characteristics constitute a synthesis which can properly be considered a new way of living, distinct from that pursued by other civilised societies? We suggest that they do.

The characteristics of Soviet Communism, which we have summarised one by one, exhibit, when we take them together, a distinct unity, itself in striking contrast with the disunity of western civilisation. The code of conduct based on service to the community in social equality, and on the maximum development of health and capacity in every individual, is in harmony with the exclusion of exploitation and the profit-making motive, and with the deliberate planning of production for community consumption; whilst both are in full accord with that universal participation in a multiform administration which characterises the soviet system. The economic and the political organisations, and with them the ethical code, are alike staked on a whole-hearted reliance on the beneficial effect of making known to every citizen all that is known of the facts of the universe, including human nature itself; that is to say, on science as interpreted dialectically, to the exclusion of any miraculous supernaturalism or mystical faith in the persistence of personal life after death. The Worship of God is replaced by the Service of Man.

We may note in passing that the synthetic unity of the new civilisation of the USSR, whether or not it can be said to be in any degree due to geographical or racial factors, is at least in harmony with them. The vast monotonous and apparently boundless steppe, sparsely peopled and only patchily brought under cultivation, with its prolonged winter cold and darkness, certainly influences its various inhabitants towards a common unity; to this or that form of collectivism; to mutual help in voluntary cooperation. . . .

Suggestions for Further Reading

The literature on the history of the Soviet Union is extensive, but of very uneven quality. A bibliography of great assistance in locating English-language works is *Russia and the Soviet Union: A Bibliographic Guide to Western-Language Publications,* ed. Paul Horecky (Chicago, 1965). Also helpful is the section on Russian and Soviet history in *The American Historical Association's Guide to Historical Literature,* ed George F. Howe and others (New York, 1961), pp. 621–645.

General surveys of Soviet history concentrate on the political development of the country. Among these, the most complete is Donald Treadgold, *Twentieth Century Russia* (Chicago, 1964),. A useful reference source is the *McGraw-Hill Encyclopedia of Russia and the Soviet Union,* ed. Michael Florinsky (New York, 1961).

The historical approach to the Soviet experience has to take into account the influence of the prerevolutionary history of the country. The most ambitious study of this nature is *The Transformation of Russian Society,* ed. Cyril Black (Cambridge, Mass., 1960). A work which lays great stress on the role of Russian traditions in shaping Soviet history is Wladimir Weidlé, *Russia Past and Present* (New York, 1961). Russia's situation as an underdeveloped country on the borderlands of the West sets the context for Tsarist and Soviet history in Theodore Von Laue, *Why Lenin? Why Stalin?* (New York, 1964).

Another major factor in the background of the Soviet experience is the Marxist revolutionary movement. A good introduction to the Marxist ideology is Henry Mayo, *Introduction to Marxist Theory* (New York, 1960). One author who presents the Bolshevik Revolution as a continuation of the Marxist revolutionary movement is Robert Tucker, *The Marxian Revolutionary Idea* (New York, 1969). Robert Daniels in his *The Nature of Communism* (New York, 1962) argues on the other hand that Soviet communism was really a new method for forced modernization of a backward country. Even Marxism can best be seen as an "ideology of underdeveloped societies" in the opinion of Adam Ulam, *The Unfinished Revolution: An Essay on the Sources and Influence of Marxism and Communism* (New York, 1960). The early Soviet view of Marxism and Russia's communist future is spelled out in Nikolai Bukharin, *The ABC of Communism* (Ann Arbor, Michigan, 1966).

In the political history of the Soviet Union the formation of the new political regime and the struggle for political power among Communist leaders in the 1920s occupy a particularly prominent place. The standard work on these years is Edward H. Carr, *A History of the Soviet Union,* seven volumes to date (London, 1950–   ), covering the Civil War years and the New Economic Policy up to 1926. Leonard Schapiro discusses the establishment of the party dictatorship between 1918 and 1922 in *The Origin of the Communist Autocracy* (Cambridge, Mass., 1955). Barrington Moore looks at the circumstances which shaped the structure and policies of the new state in *Soviet Politics: The Dilemma of Power* (Cambridge, Mass., 1950). The activities and programs of the opponents to Stalin in the 1920s and early 1930s are the subject of another work by Robert Daniels, *The Conscience of the Revolution: Communist Opposition in Soviet Russia* (Cambridge, Mass., 1960).

The lives of the three prominent leaders of the first decades of Soviet rule—Lenin, Trotsky, and Stalin—have all been explored in detail. The best studies of Lenin are David Shub, *Lenin: A Biography* (Baltimore, Md., 1966), and Louis Fischer, *The Life of Lenin* (New York, 1964). Isaac Deutscher is an admiring but still critical biographer in his three-volume study of Leon Trotsky, *The Prophet Armed* (New York, 1954), *The Prophet Unarmed* (New York, 1959), and *The Prophet Outcast* (New York, 1963). The man who inherited Lenin's mantle, Joseph Stalin, has also been studied by Deutscher, *Stalin: A Political Biography,* second edition (New York, 1967). A fascinating account of life in the Stalin family has been written by Stalin's daughter, Svetlana Alliluyeva, *Twenty Letters to a Friend* (New York, 1967).

The organization and activities of the Soviet Communist party have received a great deal of attention. Joseph Stalin took a direct hand in preparing a "reliable" history of the party, officially brought out as a collective work in 1938, translated later into English as *The History of the Communist Party of the Soviet Union* (Moscow, 1943). Recently a new version was prepared by B. N. Ponomarev and others, *The History of the Communist Party of the Soviet Union* (Moscow, 1960). The most complete history of the party written in the West is Leonard Schapiro, *The Communist Party of the Soviet Union* (New York, 1960). The real life of the party at the provincial level is revealed in a book by Merle Fainsod, *Smolensk under Soviet Rule* (Cambridge, Mass., 1958), the material for which came from the Smolensk provincial party archives, seized by the Germans in 1941 and then by the American Army in 1945.

Stalin's impact on Soviet political institutions and behavior is the subject of many works. The concept of totalitarianism has been applied frequently to his regime, notably in Carl Friedrich and Zbigniew Brzezinski, *Totalitarian Dictatorship and Autocracy* (Cambridge, Mass., 1956). For Nicholas Vakar, *The Taproot of Soviet Society* (New York, 1962), Stalinism represented the triumph of the primitive "peasant element" in Russia. The grim details of the secret police terror are spelled out in Robert Conquest, *The Great Terror: Stalin's Purge of the 1930's* (New York, 1968). The operations of the secret police are discussed in *The Soviet Secret Police,* ed. Simon Wolin and Robert Slusser (New York, 1957). The experience of the victims of the secret police can be appreciated best by reading Alexander Solzhenitsyn's novels, *One Day in the Life of Ivan Denisovich* (New York, 1963) and *The First Circle* (New York, 1968).

Nowhere do we have a systematic discussion of the machinery of Stalin's government. The history of the Red Army is best known. The relations of the army with the Soviet political leadership is the subject of a book by John Erickson, *The Soviet High Command: A Military-Political History, 1918–1941* (New York, 1962). Stalin's conduct of the war with Germany is revealed in a collection of Soviet military memoirs recently brought out in English, *Stalin and His Generals,* ed. Seweryn Bialer (New York, 1969). The war itself is traced in Alexander Werth, *Russia at War, 1941–1945* (New York, 1964), while the terrible Leningrad siege unfolds in the pages of Harrison Salisbury, *The 900 Days* (New York, 1969). The activities of Stalin and his advisers after the war are brought to life in the memoirs of Milovan Djilas, *Conversations with Stalin* (New York, 1962).

The post-Stalin developments have been clarified by several good studies. A systematic treatment of the institutional distribution of power, formal and informal, is found in Wolfgang Leonhard, *The Kremlin since Stalin* (New York, 1962). Richard Lowenthal's article, "The Waning of the Revolution," *Problems of Communism* (January–February, 1965), pp. 10–17, is a brief but penetrating study of the significance of the fall of Khrushchev. The French journalist Michel Tatu has written a detailed analysis of the factional struggles within the Soviet leadership in the late 1950s and early 1960s in *Power in the Kremlin: From Khrushchev to Kosygin* (New York, 1969). The best institutional study of the political life of the Soviet Union is Alfred Meyer, *The Soviet Political System* (New York, 1966).

Works devoted exclusively to the economic history of the Soviet Union are relatively scarce by comparison with the wealth of material on Soviet political developments. The most readable survey of Soviet economics to the mid-1950s is Maurice Dobb, *Soviet Economic Development since 1917,* fifth edition (London, 1960). The complex economic problems which confronted Soviet leaders in the 1920s are examined in Alexander Erlich, *The Soviet Industrialization Debate, 1924–1928* (Cambridge, Mass., 1960). The industrialization process itself is treated in Naum Jasny, *Soviet Industrialization, 1928–1952* (New York, 1961). The agricultural revolution in the countryside is studied from the point of view of Soviet economic policy in Moshe Lewin, *Russian Peasants and Soviet Power: A Study of Collectivization* (Evanston, Ill., 1968). The rural famine which followed collectivization is discussed in Dana Dalrymple, "The Soviet Famine of 1932–1934," *Soviet Studies* (January, 1964), pp. 250–284. Alec Nove, *The Soviet Economy,* second edition (New York, 1969), provides an up-to-date picture of the current economic system. A new but significant development in Soviet economic life, the growth of consumer demand, is discussed in Margaret Miller, *The Rise of the Russian Consumer* (London, 1965).

There is no detailed study of the social transformation which has taken place in the Soviet Union in the past half century. The social upheaval of the 1930s is discussed in Nicholas Timasheff, *The Great Retreat* (New York, 1946). The rise of the working class is the subject of Arvid Broderson, *The Soviet Worker* (New York, 1966). A dramatic, first-hand account of what it was like to be a worker during the first five-year plan can be found in John Scott, *Behind the Urals* (Boston, 1942). A very good description of the difficult conditions of the Soviet peasantry is a book by a former collective-farm chairman, Fedor Belov, *The History of a Soviet Collective Farm* (New York, 1955). A brief historical discussion of the new managerial class in Soviet industry is found in Jeremy Azrael, *Managerial Power and Soviet Politics* (Cambridge, Mass., 1966). Several chapters of *The Russian Intelligentsia,* ed. Richard Pipes (New York, 1960), are devoted to Soviet intellectuals, professionals, and students. The emancipation of Soviet women can be studied in Norton Dodge, *Women in the Soviet Economy* (Baltimore, Md., 1966). Two very perceptive accounts of Soviet life in general are Klaus Mehnert, *Soviet Man and His World* (New York, 1962), and Wright Miller, *Russians as People* (New York, 1961).

The history of the minority nationalities of the Soviet Union constitutes a special and complex problem. The formation of the multinational Soviet state is traced in Richard Pipes, *The Formation of the Soviet Union,* revised edition (New York, 1964). A critical study of the nationalities policy of the Soviet government is Robert Conquest, *Soviet Nationalities Policy in Practice* (New York, 1967). The peoples of Central Asia have been the subject of several recent works, most comprehensive of which is *Central Asia: A Century of Russian Rule,* ed. Edward Allworth (New York, 1967). The Western nationalities have been studied as individual groups, with little effort to see their common developments and problems. On the Ukrainians one can read Robert Sullivant, *Soviet Politics and the Ukraine, 1917–1957* (New York, 1962). The history of Soviet Lithuania is traced in *Lithuania under the Soviets,* ed. V. Stanley Vardys (New York, 1965). On the controversial issue of the history of the Jews in the Soviet Union, Solomon Schwartz, *The Jews in the Soviet Union* (Syracuse, N.Y., 1951) presents both the role of the Jews themselves and the various forms of anti-Semitism which Soviet Jews have encountered.

The cultural history of the Soviet Union is another field lacking any good, comprehensive studies. The history of the Orthodox religion in the Soviet period is covered in John Curtiss, *The Russian Church and the Soviet State, 1917–1950* (Boston, 1953). A survey of education is *The Changing Soviet School,* ed. George Bereday (New York, 1960). The problems of scientific work in the early Soviet state are studied in David Joravsky, *Soviet Marxism and Natural Science, 1917–1932* (New York, 1961) and Loren Graham, *The Soviet Academy of Sciences and the Communist Party, 1927–1932* (Princeton, N.J., 1968). One of the most bizarre episodes in Soviet science, the perversion of biology by Trofim Lysenko, is examined by Zhores Medvedev, *The Rise and Fall of Lysenko* (New York, 1969). Soviet literature is surveyed in Marc Slonim, *Soviet Russian Literature: Writers and Problems* (New York, 1964). A collection of interpretive essays on the peculiar problems of Soviet literature are presented in *Literature and Revolution in Soviet Russia, 1917–1962,* ed. Max Hayward and Leopold Labedz (New York, 1963). The achievements and difficulties of the Soviet cinema are discussed by Jay Leyda, *Kino: A History of the Russian and Soviet Film* (New York, 1960).

The Soviet experience has attracted outside comment and criticism in great qualtity. A good survey of the wide range of American opinion on Soviet Russia between 1917 and 1933 is Peter Filene, *Americans and the Soviet Experiment, 1917–1933* (Cambridge, Mass., 1967).

TUNC

books by Lawrence Durrell

novels

The Avignon Quintet

MONSIEUR

LIVIA

CONSTANCE

SEBASTIAN

QUINX

The Alexandria Quartet

JUSTINE

BALTHAZAR

MOUNTOLIVE

CLEA

The Revolt of Aphrodite

TUNC

NUNQUAM

THE BLACK BOOK

THE DARK LABYRINTH

travel

BITTER LEMONS

REFLECTIONS ON A MARINE VENUS

PROSPERO'S CELL

SICILIAN CAROUSEL

THE GREEK ISLANDS

Poetry

COLLECTED POEMS

SELECTED POEMS

Drama

SAPPHO

Letters and Essays

SPIRIT OF PLACE EDITED BY

ALAN G. THOMAS

Humour

STIFF UPPER LIP

ESPRIT DE CORPS

SAUVE QUI PEUT

ANTROBUS COMPLETE

For Young People

WHITE EAGLES OVER SERBIA

ff

LAWRENCE DURRELL

Tunc

faber and faber
LONDON · BOSTON

First published in 1968
by Faber and Faber Limited
3 Queen Square London WC1N 3AU
First published in this edition 1969
Reprinted 1975, 1980 and 1986

Printed in Great Britain by
Whitstable Litho Ltd., Whitstable, Kent

ISBN 0 571 09220 9

For

CLAUDE-MARIE VINCENDON

deux fois deux quatre, c'est un mur

Dostoievsky. *Voix Souterraine*

I

Of the three men at the table, all dressed in black business suits, two must have been stone drunk. Not Nash, the reproachful, of course not. But Vibart the publisher (of late all too frequently): and then Your Humble, Charlock, the thinking weed: on the run again. Felix Charlock, at your service. Your humble, Ma'am.

A pheasant stuffed with nominal chestnuts, a fatty wine disbursed among fake barrels in a London cellar—Poggio's, where people go to watch each other watch each other. I had been trying to explain the workings of Abel—no, you cannot have a computer with balls: but the illusion of a proximate intuition is startling. Like a buggerish astrology only more real, more concrete; better than crystal ball or divining rod. "Here we have lying about us in our infancy" (they clear their throats loudly) "a whole culture tied to a stake, whipped blind, torn apart by mastiffs. Grrr! And here we are, three men in black overcoats, ravens of ill-omen in an oak-tree." I gave a couple of tremendous growls. Heads turned towards us in meek but startled fashion. "You are still drunk Felix" (This is Nash). "No, but people as destinies are by now almost mathematically predictable. Ask Abel."

"Almost"

"Almost"

"You interest me strangely" said Vibart dozing off for a second. Emboldened Charlock continued: "I call it pogonometry. It is deduction based on the pogon (πόγον) a word which does not exist. It is the smallest conceivable unit of meaning in speech; a million pogons make up the millionth part of a phoneme. Give Abel a sigh or the birthcry of a baby and he can tell you everything."

Vibart dropped his fork on the floor, I my napkin. Leaning down simultaneously we banged our heads smartly together. (Reality is what is most conspicuous by its absence.) But it hurt, we were dazed.

"I could explain what is wrong with you" said Nash all pious, all sententious "but in psychology an explanation does not constitute a cure."

* * * * *

I was brought up by women—two old aunts in lax unmanning Eastbourne. My parents I hardly remember. They hid themselves in foreign continents behind lovely coloured stamps. Most holidays I spent silently in hotels (when the aunts went to Baden). I brought introspection to a fine art. A cid I fell into milk; a ribonuclear cid. Where was she? How would she look if she came? Abel could have told me, but he wasn't born then. Eheu!

"And what" says Nash, all perk and arrogance "could Abel tell *me*, eh?"

"A lot, Nash, quite a lot. I had you in frame not a fortnight ago. I've recorded you frequently on the telephone. Something about a woman who lay on your horsehair couch, eyes shut, exciting you so much by a recital of her sins that you found you were masturbating. A real psi experience. Like religious confessors knee deep in sperm leaning forward in the confessional so as not to miss the smallest excuse for absolution. I didn't bother to find out her name. But Abel knows. Now where is your Hippocratic oath? You let her smash up the transference because she wanted to do it with you there and then. Daddy! I have your squeaks and gasps; afterwards to do you justice you swore and shed tears and walked up and down."

Nash lets off a screech like a parrot; he is on his feet, scarlet, his mouth fallen open on its hinges. "Lies" he shouts.

"Very well, lies; but Abel cannot lie. You must try and imagine it this way—as Abel sees it, with that infallible inner photoelectric eye of his. He X-rays time itself, photographing a personality upon the gelatine surface of flux. Look, I press a button, and your name and voice rise together like toast in a toast-rack. The fascia blaze blue, topaz, green, white. I spin the needles and they pass through the fixed points of a sort of curriculum vitae. The basic three points are birth-love-death."

Vibart gives a burst of hysterical laughter; tears crowd his eyes. We are going to be asked to leave at any moment now.

"Now if you take a simple geometrical progression, a scale, you can elaborate your graph until the needle passes through an infinity of points: whatever you choose to set up—say, jobs, skills, size, pigmentation, I.Q., temperament repressions, beliefs. . . . You see the game? No, there's nothing wrong with cogito or with sum; it's poor bloody ergo that's been such a curse. The serial world of Tunc whose God is Mobego. But come, we mustn't be cry-babies, mustn't pout."

I suddenly felt the need to vomit. Leaning my cold head against the colder glass wall of the urinal I continued. "As for me, scientifically speaking the full terror of death has not informed my loving. Ah Nash, my boy. I was a gland short." Ah Benedicta, I might have added under my breath. He holds my head while I am sick: but he is still trembling with rage at this astonishing exposure of his professional shortcomings.

I am forced to laugh. This carefully prepared hoax, I mean, about Abel. Actually I got the facts from the girl herself. At last my stomach comes to rest again. "The firm has given and the firm has taken away, blessed be the name of the firm" I intoned.

"Listen" says Nash urgently. "For godsake don't develop a delusional system like so many have. I implore you."

"Pish! Abel has coordinated all the psi-factors. A computer which can see round corners, think of it! On the prospectus it says distinctly 'All delusional systems resolved'; now what is our civilisation but a . . . ribonucleic hangover, eh? Why, Abel could even give you a valency notion for literature. Jerk, jerk, jerk, you in your swivel chair, she on her couch."

"I've told you it's a lie" he shouts.

"Very well."

Myself I much needed to be loved—and look what happens. At full moon in Polis, when cats conjugate the verb "to be", I held the thousandth and second night in incompetent arms watching the silver climb the cold thermometers of the minarets. Ach! I yark all this gibberish up for little dactyl my famulus; faithfully the little machine compiles it. To what end? I want the firm to have it, I want Julian to have to wade through it. When I am dead, of course, not before.

Iolanthe, in this very room, once removed the spectacles from my nose—like one lifts the lid from a jar of olives—in order to kiss me. Years later she starts to have a shadowy meaning for me, years later. While I had her, possession of her, I was quite unaware that she loved me. I had eyes for nobody but Benedicta. With her things were different, floating between rauwolfia-induced calms. Something had jumbled up her inner economy, she had never had a period: would the brain poisoning have started from this? I don't know. But I started things off. "Now" she says "I am bleeding at last, profusely bleeding: thanks to you, my darling Felix, thanks to you. Now I know I shall have a child." Well, and what came of all that? Answer me that, gentlemen of the jury. Rolling back to the alcove table to join Vibart my mind oscillates between the two women once more. Iolanthe talking of her film husband: "Always accusing me of not loving him, of not *trying*; but just when you're trying your best to come off an irrational thought crosses your mind and freezes you: if I forgot to turn off the stove those pigeons will be cinders."

Nash trots along beside me holding my sleeve. "I have an awful feeling you are going to try and break away, make a run for it. Tell me Felix? For goodness sake don't. The firm would always find you, you know." I gave him an owlish glance. "I have been granted leave by the firm" said firmly. "Up to two years' sick leave."

"Ah well. That's better." Nash was vastly relieved.

"I am going to the South Seas on legitimate leave."

"Why there?"

"Because it's like everywhere else nowadays. Why not?"

Is that why I am in Athens? Yes, just to make things a little difficult for them. Vindictive Felix. Partly that, but also partly because I had a sudden desire to come back to the point from which all the lines sprang out—the point of convergence being little Number Seven in this flyblown hotel. One candle and by God, the little wooden pattens which recently turned up in a suitcase full of junk—the very pattens of Iolanthe. The survival value of objects never ceases to puzzle and enthral me. People, yes, they turn up again and again, but for a limited time. But things can go on for centuries, quietly changing their owners when they tire of them: or quietly changing their owners *tout court*. I am terribly tired. Most of the pre-recorded and digested stuff I have fed into Abel—for the computer is simply a huge lending library of the mind—most of it has passed through these little dactyls, as I call them. Do you think it would be possible to resume a whole life in terms of predestination? I have imagined my own so thoroughly that you can switch it on like an obituary. The two women, one dark and one graven fair; two brothers, one darkness one light. Then the rest of the playing cards, catalogues of events, humble contingencies. A sable history! Well I've brought it up to this point. Abel must be carrying it on. Just pull the lever on the sign manual and traverse across the fascia marked "contingent data". Every sensible man should make a will. . . . But only after a long, wasteful and harmful detour across the parching watersheds of celebrity, financial success. I, Felix Charlock, being sound in mind and body ha ha do hereby etc etc. Not that I have anything much to leave; the firm has got its hands upon everything except for a few small private treasures like the dactyls here, my latest invention. I found a way to get the prototypes built without them finding out. Hardly larger than a lady's dressing case, she is a masterpiece of compression, as light as a feather. What is it?

Come closer, I will tell you. The dactyl was designed for those who talk endlessly to themselves, for Everyman that is. Also for a lazy man, such a one as myself who has an abhorrence for ink and paper. You speak and she records: more than that, she transcribes. The low feminine voice (the frequency dictated my choice) encodes the words and a tiny phonetic alphabet, no larger than a lama's prayer wheel, begins to purr. From the snout marked A the tip of the foolscap protrudes, and goes on slowly extending until with a sniff the whole page is evacuated, faultlessly typed. How is that done? Ah, that is what any firm would like to know. Nor is there any limit to the amount of dactyl's work, save lack of paper or a failing torch battery. But it is easy to see why the toy is so valuable—it could put all the stenographers in theworld out of business in a matter of weeks. Moreover the machine will sensitise to an individual voice to such a degree that she accepts a code-tone instead of a switch. This is arbitrary, of course. But in my case "*Konx*" will set her off, while "*Om*" will cut her out. She has made a joke of the laborious anachronism of typing. Yet I did not dare to try and take out a patent in my name, for the firm keeps a watchful eye on the Patents Office. They are at once informed when something new is in the wind . . . Julian anyway.

The reasons I have for wanting to get away are various and complex; the more superficial being self-evident, but the more profoundly buried inexpressibly difficult to expose, despite my relative experience with words. After all, the books are decently written, even though they deal with mechanics, electronics and that sort of thing. But if I were to apply a little archaeology to my case I would come upon the buried cultures of deeper predispositions I suppose which determined what I was to become? On the one hand, purely superficially, I could date my existence from the moment when, with a ball of thin twine and two empty cigarette tins, I managed to make an imitation of the telephone. Ting a ling! Nothing very strange about that, you will say; the old Bell system was clear as daylight even to a schoolboy. But then let me take a plunge in another direction. I gradually came to equate invention with creation—perhaps too presumptuously? Yet the symptoms are much the same, are they not? Anxiety, fever, migraine, anorexia nervosa, cyclothymia, (The Mother!) . . . yes, all the happy heralds of the epileptic fit. An intense strain, sense of dispersal. Then, quite suddenly the new idea breaking free from the tangle of dreams and fevers—Bang! That's how it is with me. The pain was in allowing the damned thing to ferment, to form in the imagination. In my youth I had not learned to recognise the signs. When my teeth began to chatter I suspected an attack of malaria. I had not learned to luxuriate in the convenience of a nervous breakdown. What rubbish!

Well, I have been off the map for some days now, alone in Athens with my famulus, doing a little occupational therapy every day in the form of these autobiographical notes! I have been delayed in my quest for Koepgen; the one man who could tell me where he is is out of Athens and nobody knows for how long. *Om.*

* * * * *

I went to see Nash in a purely formal way: I have always got on with him. He can rise to a joke on occasions, plonk! Like all analysts he is highly neurotic, leashing his hysteria with little grins and yawns and airs of omniscience. Take off glasses, cough, tap thumb, adjust paper flower in button-hole. I make him, I think, feel a little uncomfortable; he wonders no doubt how much I know about everything, for is not Benedicta his patient? We sparred gracefully in the fashion of well-educated Englishmen overcompensating. He was not surprised to hear I was going away for a rest. I did not mention the firm but I could see the thought flicker across his mind. Did the firm know where? Yes, the firm knew where—I took care to tell all my friends where: Tahiti. Already no doubt a message had flashed out to our agent there. I would find a large pink blotchy man in a Panama hat waiting shyly on the dock for me. Quietly, tactfully, unobtrusively my arrival would be recorded, reported upon. "I suppose you are just tired" he said. "Yet I see no cause for it. You've done nothing for months now, locked up down in Wiltshire. You are a lucky man Charlock. Except for Benedicta's illness. You have everything." I watched him quizzically and he had the grace to blush. Then he burst out laughing with a false heartiness. We understood each other only too well, Nash and I. Wait till I tell him about Abel, just wait.

"Shall we talk syllogistically, Nash, or just talk? Causality is an attempt to mesmerise the world into some sort of significance. We cannot bear its indifference." Tears came into his eyes, comico-pathetic tears, left over from laughter turned sour. "I know you are sick of your job, and just about as ill as I am, if I *am* ill." He blew out a windy lip and gave me a cunning sidelong glance. "You sound as if you have been playing with R.N.A. It's dangerous, Charlock. You will miss a step and go sprawling among the archetypal symbols.

We'll have to reserve you a room in Paulhaus." That was the firm's private mental asylum. "It is true" I said "that I wake up with tears pouring down my face, sometimes of laughter, sometimes of plain tears."

"There, you see?" he said triumphantly. He crossed and uncrossed his legs. "You had better take some action smartly, go on a rest cure, write another scientific book."

"I am off to Tahiti. Gauguin was here."

"Good."

"Inventors are a happy laughing breed." I stifled a sob and yawned instead. "Nash, is your laughter a cry for help?"

"Everyone's is. When do you go?"

"Tonight. Let me give you lunch."

"Very well."

"The glands all down one side are swollen—the sense of humour is grossly inflamed. Let us go to Poggio's."

He was pouring out Chianti when Vibart put in an appearance—my publisher, purple with good living: a kind of tentative affability about him whenever he spoke about the book he wanted me to write for him. "The age of autobiography." He solicited Nash's good offices in the matter. He knew too that over all these years I had been dribbling into recorders of one sort or another. A friend of twenty years' standing I first encountered here, yes, in Athens: dear old slowcoach of a horse-tramway buried in some minor proconsular role with his cabinets of birds' eggs. And here was Vibart persuading poor Felix to quit quasars and debouch into memoirs. I drank deeply of the wine and smiled upon my two friends in clownish gag. What was to be done with them?

"Please Charlock" he was fearfully drunk.

"Let those who have a good bedside manner with a work of art throw the first stone."

"Nash, can't you convince him?"

"Flippancy is a form of alienation" said Nash rather to my surprise; nevertheless I could not resist making dear Vibart sing once more "The Publisher's Boating Song". We were always asked to leave when he did this. I beat time with my fork.

Lord, you may cancel all my gifts,
I feel they can be spared
So long as one thing still remains,
My pompe à merde

My books will stand the test of slime
My fame be unimpaired
So long as you will leave me, Lord,
My pompe à merde.

To my surprise, despite angry glances, we survive this outburst. Vibart has just been acclaimed Publisher of the Year by the Arts Guild; he owes his celebrity to an idea of breathtaking simplicity. Who else would have thought of getting Bradshaw translated into French? The effect on the French novel has been instantaneous. As one man they have rallied to this neglected English genius. Vibart bangs the table and says in a sort of ecstasy: "It's wonderful! They have reduced *events to incidents*. It's truthful to your bloody science, Felix. Non-deterministic. In Nash's terms it would be pure catatonia. Hurrah. We don't want to get well. No more novels of the castration complex. Do you like the idea of the God of Abraham advancing on you with his golden sickle to cut off your little—your all too little bit of mistletoe?" He points a ghastly finger at Nash, who recoils with a shudder. "Nevermore" continues my friend thickly. "No more goulash-prone Hungarian writers for me, no more *vieux jew*, I spit on all your frightened freckled little minds. I'm rich! Hurrah. Bookstalls display me which heretofore were loaded with nothing but blood-coooling sex-trash. No more about sex, it's too boring. Everyone's got one. Nastiness is a real stimulant though—but poor honest sex, like dying, should be a private matter."

His voice failed and faltered; I noticed the huge circles under his eyes. His wife committed suicide last month; it must do something to a man's pride. One says one is not to blame and one isn't. Still. Quickly change the subject.

We could see that he was rippling with anxiety, like wet washing on the line. Said Nash unkindly, "He needs a rest, does Felix, O yes."

Yes, this was true.

Yes, this was true.

I remember Koepgen talking of what he called the direct vision, the Autopsia. In a poem called "The relevance of thunder". In the Russian lingo. "Futility may well be axiomatic: but to surprise oneself in the act of dying might be one way to come thoroughly awake, no?" I let out another savage growl. The waiters jumped. Ah! They are converging on us at last.

Later, leaning out of the taxi window I say in a deep impressive voice. "I have left you a message written on the wall of the Gents at Claridges. Please go there and read it." My two friends exchange a glance. Some hours earlier, a bag-fox drunk on aniseed, I had written in my careful cursive, "I think the control of human memory is essential for any kind of future advance of the species. The refining of false time is the issue." I did not leave any instructions about how to deal with the piggybank. It was enough to go on with for people like Nash. I waved them goodbye in a fever of health.

In the southbound train I read (aloud) the Market Report in *The Times*, intoning it like a psalm, my breast filled with patriotism for Merlins.

MILAN

The bourse opened quiet yesterday but increased buying interest spread to a number of sectors including quicksilvers, properties, textiles, and insurances, giving way to a generally firmer trend. Towards the close there was brisk buying of leaders with Viscosa and Merlin prominent.

AMSTERDAM

Philips, Unilever and Royal Dutch opened lower but later met some demand on some local and Swiss demand.

BRUSSELS

The forward market was quiet and prices showed little change.

FRANKFURT

Reversed the recent weaker trend in initial dealings and showed a majority of gains later: the close was friendly with gains generally up to seven points.

PARIS

Sentiment improved slightly under the lead of metallurgical shares, notably Merlin, which were firm.

SYDNEY

Quiet but easier.

TOKYO

Prices moved higher. All major industrial groups, along with rails, participated in the upturn. Market quarters looking for a significant summer rally found much to bolster their hopes. Among companies reporting improved net income were: Bethlehem Steel, Phelps Dodge, Standard Oil, Merlin Group.

On the blackboard in the senior boardroom of Merlin House I had left them some cryptic memoranda for their maturer deliberations like

motor cars made from compressed paper
paper made from compressed motor cars
flesh made from compressed ideals
ideas made from compressed impulses.

They will take it all seriously. So it is. So it is. Really it is.

Watching the trees go by and the poles leap and fall, leap and fall, I reflected on Merlin and on the F. of F. The Fund of Funds, the Holy Grail of all we stood for. Nash had said so often recently: "I hope you are not thinking about trying to escape from the firm, Charlock. It wouldn't work, you know?" Why? Because I had married into it? *Vagina Vinctrix!* At what point does a man decide that life must be lived *unhesitatingly*? Presumably after exhausting every other field—in my case the scientific modes: science, its tail comes off in your hand like a scared lizard. ("The response to shadow in the common flat-worm is still a puzzle to biologists. Then again, in the laboratory, inside a sealed test-tube the gravitational pull of the tides still obtains, together with the appropriate responses.")

Yes, he was right, I was going to try and free myself. "*Start*" Koepgen used to say wryly, sharply, lifting his glass, little drops of ouzo spilling on to the cheap exercise book which houses the loose nerve ends of poems which later, at dead of night, he would articulate. "Tap Tap, the chick raps on the outer shell in order to free itself—literature! Memory and identity. *Om.*"

* * * * *

But before leaving I did what I have so frequently done in the past—paid a visit to Victoria Station, to stand for a while under the clock. A sentimental indulgence this—for the only human fact that I know about my parents was that they met here for the first time. Each had been waiting for someone quite different. The clock decided my fate. It is the axis, so to speak, of my own beginning. (The first clocks and watches were made in the shape of an egg.) Seriously, I have often done this, to spend a moment or two of quiet reflection here: an attempt perhaps to reidentify them among the flux and reflux of pallid faces which seethes eternally about this mnemotopic spot. Here one can eat a dampish Wimpy and excogitate on the nature of birth. Well, nothing much comes of this thought, these moments of despairing enquiry. The crowd is still here, but I cannot identify their lugubrious Victorian faces. Yet they belonged I suppose to this amorphous pale collection, essence of the floating face and vote, epitome of the "90 per cent don't know" in every poll. I had the notion once of inventing something to catch them up, a machine which solidified echoes retrospectively. After all one can still see the light from technically dead stars. . . . But this was too ambitious.

Perhaps (here comes Nash) I might even trace my obsession with the construction of memory-tools to this incoherent desire to make contact? Of course now they are a commonplace; but when I began to make them the first recording-tools were as much a novelty, as the gramophone appears to have been for primitive African tribes in the 'eighties. So Hippolyta found them, my clumsy old black boxes with their primitive wires and magnets. The development of memory! It led me into strange domains like stenography, for example. It absorbed me utterly and led me to do weird things like learning the whole of *Paradise Lost* by heart. In the great summer sweats of this broken-down capital I used to sit at these tasks all night, only pausing to play my fiddle softly for a while, or make elaborate notes in those yellow exercise books. Memory in birds, in mammals, in violinists. Memory and the instincts, so-called. Well, but this leads nowhere I now think; I equipped myself somewhat before my time as a sound engineer. Savoy Hill and later the BBC paid me small sums to supply library stock—Balkan folk-songs for example; a Scots University collected Balkan accents in dialect in order to push forward studies in phonetics. Then while messing about with the structure of the human ear as a sound bank I collided with the firm. Bang. *Om.*

Victoria, yes: and thence to the bank to transfer funds to Tahiti. Then to my club to pick up mail and make sure that all the false trails were well and truly laid: paper trails followed by vapour trails traced upon the leafskin of the Italian sky. Then to drift softer than thistle-down through the violet-chalky night, skimming over the Saronic Gulf. Charlock on a planned leave-of-absence from the consumer's world. Second passport in the name of Smith.

"Hail, O Consumer's Age" the voices boomed,
But which consumer is, and which consumed?

As might have been expected I caught a glimpse of one of the firm's agents hanging about the airport, but he was not interested in the night-passengers, or was waiting for someone else, and I was able without difficulty to sneak into the badly lit apron where the creaking little bus waited to carry me north to the capital.

The taste of this qualified freedom is somewhat strange still; I feel vaguely at a loss, like a man must who hears the prison doors close on his release after serving a long sentence. (If time had a watermark like paper one could perhaps hold it up to the light?) I quote.

Yet the little hotel, it is still here. So is the room—but absolutely unchanged. Look, here are the ink stains I made on the soiled marble mantelpiece. The bed with its dusty covers is still hammock-shaped. The dents suggest that Iolanthe has risen to go to the bathroom. In the chipped coffin of the enamel bath she will sit soaping her bright breasts. I am delighted to find this point of vantage from which to conduct my survey of the past, plan the future, mark time.

Iolanthe, Hippolyta, Caradoc . . . the light of remote stars still giving off light without heat. How relative it seems from Number Seven, the little matter of the living and the dead. Death is a matter of complete irrelevance so long as the memory umbilicus holds. In the case of Iolanthe not even a characteristic nostalgia would be permissible; her face, blown to wide screen size, has crossed the continents; a symbol as potent as Helen of Troy. Why here on this bed, in the dark ages of youth. . . . Now she has become the 18-foot smile.

Junior victims of the Mediterranean *gri gri* were we; learning how to smelt down the crude slag of life. Yes, some memories of her come swaying in sideways as if searching deliberately for "the impacted line which will illumine the broad sway of statement".

The grooves of the backbone were drilled in a tender white skin which reminded one of the whiteness of Easter candles. On the back of the neck the hair came down to a point, a small tuft of curl. The colouring of Pontus and Thrace are often much lighter than those of metropolitan Greece—vide Hippolyta with her ravenswing darkness and olive eye. No, Io had the greyish green eye and the hair tending towards ash-blonde which were both gifts from Circassia. The sultans used to stock their harems with toys such as these; the choicest colourings were such, lime-green eyes and fine fair curls. Well, anyway, these tricklings through the great dam of the past cannot touch her now—the legendary Iolanthe; she may have forgotten them even, left them to litter the cutting rooms of gaunt studios in the new world. For example, I had trouble to get her to shave under the arms; in common with all girls of her class, the prostitutes of Athens, she believed that men were aroused by an ape-swatch under each arm. Perhaps they were. Now however when she raises her slender arms on the screen like some bewigged almond tree the pits beneath them are smooth as an auk's egg.

The young man that I was then cannot escape the charge of exercising a certain duplicity towards her; he condescended, letting his narcissism have full sway. Well, I don't know, many factors were involved. This little angel had dirty toes and was something of a thief I believe. I found some notes from this period whose irrelevance proves that even then Charlock had an obstinate vein of introspection running along parallel, so to speak, with his mundane life of action. The second, the yellow exercise book—the one with the drawings of the cochlea and the outline for my model deafness-aid—had other kinds of data thrown about in it.

Walking about Athens at night he might note: "The formication, the shuddering-sweet melting almost to faintness. . . . Why, the structure of the genitals is particularly adapted to such phenomena, Bolsover. (Bolsover was my tutor at Kings. I still converse with him mentally in prose and worse.) The slightest friction of a white hand will alert the dense nerve ganglia with their great vascularity. The affect disperses itself through the receiving centres of the autonomic nervous system, solar plexus, hypogastric plexus, and lumbosacral or pelvic. . . . Hum. The kiss breaks surface here. The autobiography of a single kiss from Iolanthe. Note also, Bolsover, that in embryology the final organ is progressively differentiated from an anlage—which may be defined as the first accumulation of cells recognisable as the commencement of the final organ. This is about as far as one can go; but even this is not far enough back for me. Surely once in the testes of my old man, in the ape-gland once, *I was*?"

These problems brought sadness and perplexity to my loving. I would light a candle and examine the sleeping figure with concern for its mysterious history; it seemed to me that it might be possible to trace back the undermeanings of pleasure and pain, an unreasonable wish I now recognise. Ass. Ape. Worm.

Her teeth were rather fine and small with just a trace of irregularity in their setting—enough to make her smile at once rueful and ravenous. She was too self-indulgent to husband her efforts in the professional sense—or perhaps too honest not to wish to give service? She could be blotted out sexually and retire into an exhaustion so extreme as to resemble death. Poor Iolanthe never got enough to eat so it was easy for a well-fed man to impose orgasm after orgasm on her until she reached the point of collapse. In our case the thing worked perfectly—indeed so perfectly that it puzzled her; we ignited each other like engines tuned to perfect pitch. Of course this is purely a technical question—one of perfect psychic and physical fit—queer there is not a science of it, nor a school in which one can try it out experimentally. If we could apply as much exactitude to sexual habits as, say, a machine turner to his toys, much unhappiness in love could be avoided. In an age of advanced technology it is surprising that no attention is given to such problems. Yes, even with her eyes closed, piously trying to think about something else in order to avoid exhaustion: even then, the surf carried her irresistibly to the other beach, rolled her up into the blessed anonymity of the fading second. Sometimes he shook her awake simply to stare into her eyes. But if at such moments she had asked him what he was thinking he would probably have replied: "The true cancer cell, in the final analysis, an oxygen-deficiency cell, a poorly breathing cell, according to Schmidt. When you coughed I suddenly saw in the field of my instrument a patch of tubercule bacilli stained with eosin to a pretty red—anemones in some Attic field." People deprived of a properly constituted childhood will always find something hollow in their responses to the world, something unfruitful. You could accuse both of us of that, in order to explain the central lack. The weakness of the marrow. A racing heart. Of course other factors help, like environment, language, age. But the central determinant of situations like this is that buried hunger which is only aggravated by the sense of emotional impotence. *Om.*

II

The Parthenon left stranded up there like the last serviceable molar in some poor widow's gum. Ancient Grief, my Greece! "Art is the real science." Well, well. Where they made honey cakes in the shape of female pudenda. Yes, but the Acropolis then was our back-garden —hardly a corner of it where we didn't make love. The smallness of its proportions gave it a monumental intimacy. In that clear hard enamel air the human voice carried so far that it was possible to call and wave to her from the top while she walked the Plaka streets below. "I-O-lanthe!" Note that the stress falls upon the second syllable not the third, and that its value is that of the *omega*. Now she is known to the world in a hideous Erasmic pronunciation with the stress on the third syllable. Actually I don't mind, as it makes her real name private property. She belongs, then, to Number Seven, and to the Nube, to the eternal Athens which miraculously still survives outside memory. In that mirror over there she wrestled with her eyebrows which had a tendency to grow too thickly. You should see them now—single soft lines of the purest jet. Though the room squints out on the marbles we dared not open a shutter until dusk; we lived all day in brown shadow like carp in a cool pool. Until sunset.

Sunset! Wake suddenly against the lighted wall and you have the momentary impression that the whole marble spook has taken fire and is curling up like burning cardboard. You put your hand to the hideous wallpaper and feel the actual heat of the mere reflection—or so you imagine. Up there outside the honey-coloured marbles, after a full day's exposure to the sun, echo on the heat long after nightfall, temperature of mammals' blood. Gradually the light sweats dried . . . stomachs gummed together like wet leaves. Yawning and smoking they lay about in whispers. She has a toy vocabulary and an island accent.

The marbles still reflect back, translated into the whiteness of flour, the dying day's burnish. Bit by bit she keels, veers, founders. The sun slithers down the nether side of Hymettus and into the sea with a huge inaudible hiss, leaving the islands to glow like embers which the young moon will soon reillumine. (They lie beside each other as quietly as legs; no kiss but would break the curvature of the unperfected thought.) Gradually leaks up from Salamis the smell of baked bread, melons, tar, borne on the breath of the evening freshets which will soothe wet armpits and breasts.

They had been refugees from Pontus, and had trekked down with a dancing bear to settle in Crete. When the bear died (their only means of livelihood) they had a last tearful meal of the paws in oil. A smallholding barely sustained her parents. To lighten the burden she had come to Athens in search of work—with the inevitable result, for work there was none. When she described these days she stood up and acted the bear, the padding and jingling of paw and bell, the harsh panting. The froth gathered at its snout where the iron ring ran through. It was half blind, the whip had struck out an eye.

The sheet had lipstick-marks on it, also the tooth-mug; our shoes lay side by side like fish. But she was gay, friendly, almost mannish in her directness and simplicity. A gaily coloured little parrot from an island. In those days for a whole summer black fingernails were *de rigueur* among her friends and workmates. This beastly shellac stuff used to peel off on to the sheet. Her one brother had "gone to the bad"; her lip shut on the phrase, framing it instantly in the harsh rectangle of peasant judgement. Had she, then, "gone to the good"? It was an attempt at a pleasantry which miscarried; her long underlip shot out, she was in tears. During the microfield tests on Abel I sifted a good deal of this stuff about her through the field, and the king of computers came back in oracular fashion with some chunks taken from another field—Koepgen I think. It was all about love, its scales. (After Io leaves I can watch her from the window. She takes the crooked path up the side of the Acropolis, swaying a little, as if she were a trifle tipsy, hand to heart.)

Thus Abel: "If we could only make all time proximate to reality we could see a little more deeply into the heart of our perplexities; the syzygy with its promise of a double silence is equally within the grasp of man or woman. If ever they combine forces in their field you might speak of loving as something more than a term for an unclassifiable animal. It is unmistakable when it does happen for it feels as if the earth had subtly shifted its epicentre. How sad it seems that we, images of insipid spoonmeat, spend our time in projecting such strange figures of ourselves—delegated images of a desire perfected. The mystical gryphus, the 'perfect body' of the Alexandrian psychology, is an attempt on a telenoetic field. (What space is to matter, soul is to mind.) Some saints were 'dry-visioned'. (Jerk, jerk, but nothing comes; taking the 'distressful path' towards after-images of desire.) They were hunting, poor buggers, for a renovated meaning or an infantile adoption by a God. Unhappily words won't carry the charge in these matters, hence the deficit of truth in all verbal fields. This is where your artist might help. "A craft is a tongue, a tongue is a key, a key is a lock." On the other hand a system is merely the shy embrace by which the poor mathematician hopes to persuade his bride to open up." Koepgen never met her, I think, yet at his best he seems to be talking about her.

* * * * *

My frail old black recorders with their clumsy equipment were a source of the greatest concern; jolting about as they did with me on country buses, on caiques, even on mules. My livelihood depended on their accurate functioning, and this is where Said came in. The little watchmaker was a friend of Io. One-eyed, mission school, Christian Arab, he had his little workshop in a rotting hut in the Plaka, more fitting for rabbits than for a workman capable of craftsmanship of such extraordinary delicacy. Mud floor, fleas jumping in the straw and nibbling our ankles; we spent hours together, sometimes half the night, at his little workbench. He copied from any drawing. One-eyed Said with his watery optic pressed to a butter-coloured barrel, among the litter of fusees and escapements and hairs. Eager and modest in discussion of trade topics such as the use of invar etc. He made my echo amplifiers in a couple of weeks. Small as a garden pea, and beautifully done in mother of pearl. Graphos now! But I will be coming to that.

It was the recorders that brought me to the notice of Hippolyta. Vivid in a baroque hat like a watering can she dispensed tea and éclairs in the best hotel, coiling and uncoiling her slender legs as she questioned me about the mysteries of the black box, wondering if I could record a speech which was to be made by some visiting dignitary. My impression squared with all I heard afterwards of her public reputation. It was typical of back-biting Athens that she sounded so unsavoury a figure; the truth was that she was a mixture of naivety and wrong-headedness punctuated with strange generosities. The hard voice with its deeper tones and the fashionable boldness of the dark eyes were overcompensating for qualities like shyness which even her social practice had not enabled her entirely to throw off. The green scarf and the blood-red fingernails gave her a pleasantly old-fashioned vampire's air. "O please could you do that for me?" She named a figure in drachmae so high that my heart leapt, it would keep me for a month; and held my hand a trifle longer than formality permits. She was a warm, pleasantly troubling personage. Despite the impressive jewellery and the orchids she seemed more like a youth than a girl. Of course I accepted, and taking an advance made my way back to the Plaka delighted by such good fortune. She promised to let me know when the person in question—the speech-maker—arrived. "I can't help liking slightly hysterical women" I confided to the Parthenon.

At Spiro's tavern, under the vine-trellis, I paused for a drink and caught sight of a familiar object at an empty table; the little yellow exercise book which Koepgen used for theology and musing alike. It lay there with his pen and a daily paper. He must have gone to the lavatory. At this time Koepgen was a theological student embarking on the grim path of monkhood. A typical product of white Russia, he spoke and wrote with equal ease in any of four languages. He taught me Greek, and was invaluable on out-of-the-way factors like the phonetics of this hirsute tongue; things like the Tsaconian dialect, still half anc. Doric. Well I sat and riffled while I waited.

"The *hubris*, the overweening, is always there; but it is a matter of scale. The Greeks traced its path with withering accuracy, watching it lead on to *ate*—the point at which evil is mistakenly believed to be good. Here we are then at the end of the long road—races dehumanised by the sorceries of false politics." Koepgen weeping for Russia again. I always want to shout "stop it!" At last he stood before me, full of a devout nonchalance. He was a small dapper man, contriving to look clean despite the threadbare soutane and grotesque smelly boots. His long hair, captured in a bun, was always clean. He seldom wore his stovepipe hat. He reproached me for my inquisitiveness and sat down smiling to hear my tale of good fortune. Of Hippolyta he said: "She is adorable, but she is connected with all sorts of other things. I came across her recently when I did some paid translation —O just business letters—for an organisation, a firm I suppose, in Salonika. She organised it. But something about it gave me an uncomfortable feeling. They offered me very large sums to keep on with the work, but I let it drop. I don't know quite why. I wanted to keep myself free in a way. I need less and less money, more and more time."

There are other data, floating about like motes in a sunbeam, waiting to find their place: the equipment in the abortioner's leather bag. The needle-necked appurtenances which mock the spunk-scattering troubadours of a courtly love. The foetus of a love-song. ("One way" wrote Koepgen "might be to take up Plutarch's idea of the Melisponda. This should be within the grasp of anyone.") Mara the hag with a pair of tongs worked off a car-battery. I am not so sure whether in the brothels of Piraeus he did not achieve the *mare pigrum* of the philosophers and alchemists. Here one bares one's sex to a whole landscape—internal landscapes of empty sea, nigger-head coral, bleached tree-trunks, olive-pits burnt by lye. Islands (each one a heart and mind) where the soft spirals of waves shoulder and sheathe floors awash with the disquiet of palaces submerged in folded ferns. Symbol of the search is the diver with the heavy stone tied to his belt. Sponges!

Then lying about among my own records I come upon some stone memoranda like altars and tombs; stuck in among them some moments of alarming happiness. If the portly Pausanias had seen the city's body through that of a young street-walker his catalogues would have had more life. Names and stones would have become the real fictions and we the realities. After dark we often sneak through the broken fence and climb to the cave below the Propylea. Her toes are fearfully dirty in her dusty sandals, as are mine, but her hair is freshly washed and scentless. We are never quite alone up here. A few scattered cigarette-points mark the places where other lovers wander, or lie star-gazing. Up on these ledges in winter you will find that the southern gales carry up the faint crying of sea-mews, sacred to Aphrodite; while in the spring the brown-taffeta nightingales send out their quiet call-sign in the very voice of Itys. "Itú, Itú, Itú" they cry in pretty iteration. Then by moonlight come the little owls. They are tame. (No more!) Turning their necks in strange rhythms—clearest origin for ancient Greek masked dancing.

Down below in the later sequences of the play the tombs face east with their pathetic promise of resurrection. The modern town rolls over it all like surf. Prismatic gleams of oil-patches on macadam; coffee-grounds and the glitter of refuse (fish-scales) outside the smelly taverns with their climbing trellises and shelves of brown barrels. Once a golden apple was a passport to the underworld, but today I am only able to buy her a toffee-apple on a stick which she dips in sherbet, licking it like a tame deer.

A true Athenian, free from all this antiquarian twaddle, she knows and cares nothing for her city; but yes, some of the stories alert a fugitive delight as she sits, sugaring her kisses with her apple. It is pleasant to babble thus, floundering among the telescopic verb-schemes of demotic; telling her how Styx water was so holy as to be poisonous, only to be safely drunk from a horse's hoof. They poisoned Alexander this way. Also how Antony once set up his boozing shop in the Parthenon, though his was a different sort of poisoning, a chronic narcissism. (She crosses herself superstitiously as a good Orthodox should, and snuggles superstitiously up to me.) Then . . . about embalming bodies in honey—human toffee-apples: or curing sick children by making them swallow mice coated in honey. Ugh! But excited by this she responds by telling me of witches and spells which cause nausea and impotence and can only be fought with talismans blessed by a priest. All this with such earnestness that out of polite belief I also make the sign of the Byzantine cross, back to front, to ward off the harms of public utterance from us both. ("There is no difference between truth and reality—ask any poet." Thus Koepgen sternly, eyes blazing, a little drunk on ouzo.) The quiet wind blew dustily uphill among the moon-keepers. To make love in this warm curdled air seemed an act of unpremeditated simplicity that placed them back once more in the picture-book world sacred to the animal kingdom where the biological curve of the affect is free from the buggerish itch of mentation. Warm torpid mouth, strong arms, keen body—this seems all the spiritual instruction the human creature needs. It is only afterwards that one will be thrown back sprawling among the introspections and doubts. How many people before Iolanthe? Throats parched in the dry air we drink thirstily from the sacred spring. She washes the sugar from her lips, washes her privates in the icy water, drying them on my old silk scarf. No, Athens was not like other places; and the complicated language, with its archaic thought-forms, shielded its strangeness from foreign eyes. Afterwards to sit at a tin table in a tavern, utterly replete and silent, staring at each other, fingers touching, before two glasses of colourless raki and a plate of olives. Everything should have ended there, among the tombs, by the light of a paraffin lamp. Perhaps it did?

* * * * *

The news of Caradoc's coming was conveyed to me by Hippolyta one fine Sunday afternoon; once more bidden to tea, I found her in a corner of the Bretagne where she kept a suite permanently available, playing patience among the palms. She looked a little less forbidding this time I thought, though she was fashionably turned out in the styles of the day. Bejewelled, yes, but this time without much warpaint. Moreover she was short-sighted I noticed; raising a lorgnon briefly towards me as I advanced, she smiled. The optic changed her clever aquiline face, giving it a juvenile and somewhat innocent expression. The eyes were noble, despite their arrogance of slant. She was immediately likeable, though less beautiful this time than last. I compared her mentally to her reputation for extravagant gesture and detected something which seemed at variance with the public portraits, so to speak. Somewhere inside she was a naif—always a bad sign in a woman connected with politics and public life.

"You remember we spoke? He is coming—you may have heard of Caradoc, the architect? No? Well. . . ." She suddenly burst out laughing, as if the very mention of his name had touched off an absurd memory. She laughed as far back as a tiny gold stopping on a molar and then became serious, conspiratorial. "The lecture will be on the Acropolis—will your machine be able . . .?" I was doubtful. "If there is wind it won't be very clear. But I can make some tests in the open air? Sometimes very small things like dentures clicking, for example, ruin the quality of the sound and make the text difficult to recover on playback. I'll do what I can, naturally."

"If you come to Naos, my country house, in the garden. . . . You could practise with your instrument. He will come there. I'll send you the car next Friday." I reached for a pencil to give her my address, but she laughed and waved away my intention. "I know where you live. You see, I have been making enquiries about you. I did not know what your work was or I would have offered my help. Folk-songs I can get you two a penny." She snapped white fingers as one does to summon a waiter in the Orient. "On my country properties I have singers and musicians among the villagers. . . . Perhaps this would interest you later?"

"Of course."

"Then first make this speech for us." She laughed once more. "I would ask you to stay and dine but I have to go to the palace this evening. So goodbye."

That evening the fleet came in and Iolanthe was summoned back to the naval brothel in Piraeus leaving me alone to pursue my studies with Said. Three of my little orient pearls had been manufactured now, and I was mad keen to find a deaf man to try them out on. Koepgen had said that he knew a deaf deacon who would be glad of a mechanical cure so that he would not flounder among the responses! But where was Koepgen? I left messages for him at the theological school and at the tavern he frequented.

* * * * *

Naos, the country house of Hippolyta in Attica, was large enough to suggest at first sight a small monastery skilfully sited within an oasis of green. By contrast, that is, to the razed and bony hills which frame the Attic plain. Here were luxuriant gardens rich with trees and shrubs within a quarter of a mile of the sea. Its secret was that it had been set down, woven round a double spring—a rarity in these parched plains: oleander, cypress and palm stood in picturesque contrast to the violet-grey stubbled hills, their fine soils long since eroded by weather and human negligence. The dangling rosegardens, the unplanned puffs of greenery made full amends for what was, at close sight, a series of architectural afterthoughts, the stutterings of several generations. Barns climbed into bed together, chapels had cemented themselves one to another in the manner of swallow-nests to unfinished features like half-built turrets. One huge unfinished flying buttress poked out nature's eye, hanging in mid air. One step through the door marked W.C. on the second floor and one could fall twenty feet into a fishpond below.

A series of gaunt and yet dignified rooms had been thrown down pell mell about a central cruciform shape, rambling up two floors and petering out in precarious balconies which looked out on the ravishing mauve slopes of the foothills. On reflection one established the origins of the whole place. Clearly Hesiod had started it as a grange for his cattle; Turks, Venetians, French, Greeks had carried on the work without once looking over their shoulders, enlarging the whole place and confusing its atmospheres. In the reign of Otho utterly nonsensical elaborations had tried to render it stylish. While one corner was being built up, another was crumbling to ruins. Finally those members of the family lucky enough to have been educated in France had added the ugly cast-iron features and awkward fenestration which would, one presumes, always make them nostalgic for St.

Remo in the 'twenties—Marseille tile, Second Empire furniture, plaster cherubim, mangy plump mouldings. Yet since every feature was the worst of its epoch and kind the whole barrack had a homogeneity, indeed a rustic dignity which endeared it to all who came, either to visit or inhabit it. It was here that Hippolyta held court, here that her old friend, sheepish Count Banubula, worked in his spare time cataloguing the huge library hurled together rather than collected by several generations of improvident noblemen more famous for their eccentricities than their learning. Woodrot, silverfish, death-watch beetles—all were active and industrious though nobody cared except the poor Count, tip-toeing along creaking balconies or shinning up precarious ladders to rescue a rotting Ariosto or Petrarch.

Here Hippolyta (the Countess Hippolyta, "Hippo" to us) lived when she came home—which was rarely; for the most part she preferred Paris or New York. Other members of the family (with whom she was not on speaking terms) also came from time to time, unheralded, to take up residence in various dusty wings. (There was one ancient and completely unexplained old lady, half blind, who might be seen crossing a corridor or scuttling off a balcony.) Two younger cousins were ladies-in-waiting at court, and also occasionally put in an appearance attended by beaky husbands or lovers. Hippo made a point of not letting her own visits coincide with theirs; it was we, the members of her little court, who usually ran into them—for there was always someone staying at Naos; permission was freely given for any of us to spend a summer or winter there.

Here then in Naos, of a spanking summer evening, I was carried to the lady with my devil machines. (Tapes A70 to 84 labelled G for Greece have been fed back into Abel.) Well, she was clad in Chinese trousers of fine Shantung, inlaid Byzantine belt, and an impossible Russian shirt with split sleeves; she lounged in a deck chair by the lily pond while a hirsute peasant clumsily assuaged our thirst with whisky and gin. She was smoking a slender cheroot, and was surrounded by a litter of fashion papers and memoranda gathered in coloured folders—esoteric Greek pothooks which I feared might be the beginnings of a book. Two huge pet tortoises clicked across the paths and came bumping into the legs of our chairs, asking to be fed;

and this Banubula undertook with an air of grave and scrupulous kindness shredding lettuce from a plate. My little toy was greeted with rapture and some amusement; Hippolyta clapped her hands and laughed aloud like a child when I reproduced a strip of conversation harshly but clearly for her consideration, while old Banubula cleared his throat in some surprise and asked whether it wasn't rather dangerous, such a machine? "I mean one could take copies of private conversations, could one not?" Indeed one could; Hippo's eye shone with a reflective gleam. The Count said in his slow bronze-gong voice: "Won't Caradoc mind?" She snorted. "He knows these machines; besides if he is too lazy to write it all out, if he prefers to extemporise . . . why, it's his affair."

There was silence. "I saw Graphos today" she said, a sudden expression of sadness clouding her face. Presumably she was referring to the politician? I said nothing, nor did they. In the moment of embarrassment that followed we heard the noise of the car drawing up, and the figure of Caradoc emerged among the oleanders—the stubby frame hunched up with a defiant and slightly tipsy-looking mien; he carried a much-darned Scotch plaid over his arm, and in his hand a leather-covered flask from which he drew encouragement as he advanced. No greetings followed, much to my surprise; Hippolyta just lay, the Count just stared. Staring keenly, menacingly under shaggy white eyebrows, the architectural mage advanced, his deep voice munching out segments of air with a kind of half-coherent zeal. At first blush he seemed far too sure of himself, and then as he came closer the impression changed to one of almost infantile shyness. He spread his arms and uttered a single phrase in the accents of a Welsh bard: "What it is to work for these beneficed Pharisees!" Giving a harsh bark of a laugh full of ruefulness he sat down by the pond, turning the bottle over thoughtfully in his fingers before pushing it into the pocket of his cape. A heavy air of constraint fell over the company and I realised that it was caused by my presence; they could not speak freely before me. I unshackled my machine and excused myself. But through the window of the ramshackle lavatory on the ground floor I heard, or seemed to hear, Hippolyta give a low cry and exclaim: "O Caradoc, the Parthenon! Only Graphos can fight it." Caradoc gave an incredulous roar in the accents of the Grand Cham. "They told me nothing, they never do. Simply to come at once and bring Pulley for costings. I was hoping to build Jocas a seraglio. But this.... No, I won't believe it."

"Yes. Yes." Like the cry of a sea-bird. That was all. By the time I returned the whole picture had changed; the constraint had vanished. They had exchanged whatever they had needed to, and though there were still tears in the eyes of Hippolyta she was laughing heartily at something the Cham had said. Moreover his assistant Pulley had now joined the company—a lank north-country youth of yellowish cast, with huge hands and teeth. He said little. But he yawned from time to time like an eclipse of the sun.

A dinner table had been set out among the oleanders on a nearby terrace; the still air hardly trembled the candles in their silver sockets. Wine soon oiled the hinges of the talk. The Cham, after a short period of reservation, frankly gave me his hand.

"Charlton, you said?"

"Charlock."

"Well, Charlton, here's my hand."

Then he turned in business-likefashion and began to mash up his food with vigour, talking in loud and confident tones as he did so. No reference was made to my function, and I made none, treading warily; but towards the middle of the meal Hippolyta made a gesture inviting me to record, and I obeyed unobtrusively, while Caradoc continued with a grumbling one-cylinder monologue. He was in a curious mood it seemed, uncertain whether to allow the wine to make him gay or whether to become testy and morose; presumably he was still troubled by whatever she had told him, for he suddenly said, in an aside: "Of course I shall never cease to be grateful to the firm—how could one not be? It has allowed me to build all its cathedrals, so to speak. But one can build cathedrals without being a religious man? Anyway I don't propose to be upset until I know for certain what is in Jocas' mind." Then, as if to pursue the metaphor he turned to me and said: "I'm talking about Merlins, my boy. Easy to join but hard to leave. Nevertheless there comes a day...." He sighed heavily and took Hippolyta's hand. "Now" he said "we must make a real effort to enjoy ourselves tonight. No good can come of worrying. I propose to lead an expedition to the Nube, and I invite the lot of you as my guests. By the navel-string of the Risen Lord we shall have a marvellous time. Eh? Do you know the Nube, Charlton?"

"The Blue Danube? By repute."

"It is a home from home for us, eh Pulley?"

He consulted the circle of candle-lit faces as he barked out the phrase. There seemed little enough response aroused by this proposition. He was pained. As for the Blue Danube, it enjoyed a mild repute among frequenters of houses of ill fame. Its name, in frosted bulbs, had been changed for it by wind and weather; the letters had either fallen out of their frames or gone dead. All that remained for the wayfarer to read against the night sky now was the legend The Nube, ancing, aberet. "I should like to come" said I, and received a friendly thump from the Cham. He was delighted to receive support from some quarter. His good humour returned. "It is run by an adorable personage, daughter of a Russian Grand Duke, and sometime wife to a British Vice-Consul, most aptly so entitled, and she calls herself Mrs. Henniker." Hippolyta smiled and said: "All Athens knows her." Caradoc nodded. "And with justice; she has the cleanest girls in Attica; moreover there is one Turk called Fatma." He embraced a large segment of air to suggest her dimensions. "A heroine is Fatma."

All this was becoming less and less esoteric. Caradoc dished us all a stoup of red Nemean and cajoled us with prophecy. "You will see," he said "Graphos will get in and save our bacon." She smiled, yes, but sadly; shaking her head doubtfully. "I'll give you the big car" she said. "But I won't come. In case he phones or comes to see me. But I expect you'll find all your friends at the Nube, including Sipple. He knows you are arriving today." Caradoc registered approval, commended the cheese he was cutting up ("This Camembert has lain a long time, not in Abraham's bosom but in the hairy armpit of the Grand Turk himself") and added, with his mouth full: "Give me Sipple the clown any day." Pulley explained that Sipple was an "undesirable".

"But irresistible, my favourite *numéro*" insisted the Cham. "A man of parts."

"Second-hand parts" said Pulley. He seemed from his facial expressions to live in a state of furious though repressed disapproval. Caradoc, by now distinctly mellow, turned aside in disgust and confided some thoughts of the first magnitude, so to speak, to the mild and tentative Count, who had registered an expression of pained alarm at the mention of a house of ill fame. It was clear that he would not be joining us in this bacchanal. Caradoc, feeling perhaps an unexpressed reservation, tried to cajole him with high thinking to concede some virtue to low living. This sort of stuff. "The Nube is the perfect place for self-examination, better than a church. Why not, after all? The nearest vicarious approach to death is by the orgasm which produces its temporary simulacrum." ("Ow!" exclaimed Hippolyta with superstitious disgust.) The Cham warmed to the pulpit, his tone now tinged distinctly with Welsh tabernacle. "That is why it has been surrounded with prayer, poetry, propitiation, tabu. The Greeks saw a clear relationship and in their wisdom compounded temple and brothel. We haven't the imagination. Fools! The priest has tried to harness its power, dynamo fashion, to make more braindust. A foul repression is written all over our mugs. Look at him, him, her. *Look at me!* In the East we are told he has managed to crack the mould and liberate the statue of the silver man. But in the West our methods have failed—the silly reticule of the human brain can only generate a sterile flight of symbols and concepts which have given us certain insecure powers over matter but none over ourselves."

Pulley began to express his disapproval of all this bardic verbosity by beating himself about the chest and biceps and making animal noises and monkey faces. This delighted the Cham, who now stood up and in the pleading accents of a Welsh preacher admonished and cajoled him. "Now which is wiser, Pulley my dear fellow: to wear all nature like a suit of clothes, or to rape and tame it?"

Pulley gave a thin yowl and said: "Pack it up Carry, like a good fellow. I've had nothing but this all day in the plane." He turned to us for support. "Can you bear it when the bloody Druid comes out in him?"

"Of course they can" said Caradoc majestically, still poised for flight. "Only just" said Hippolyta.

"It gives me the bloody shivers" said Pulley.

"Very well." Caradoc sat down unsteadily. "Very well you Philistine. Very well." He took my hand and began to recite.

If a monumental mason
Carved a monumental turd
As a symbol of humanity at prayer,
We could cast it as a bronze
And distribute it to dons
As an article of college table-ware

He was sufficiently pleased with the response to threaten us with a ballad beginning:

How nugatory and how glum
The endomorphs of scholarship
Like hippos on a sinking ship
Stay bum to silly bum.

But he could push the matter no further, and submitted to Hippolyta's amused disapproval with mock contrition. She had kicked off her sandals and was smoking a Turkish cigarette in a black bone holder. Caradoc helped himself to a rose from the bowl on the table. "The moon is late tonight" he observed with petulance. He had been watching the little dab of whiteness on the horizon which marked its point of emergence. He had been here before, then? Supposedly.

The night had been still down in this garden with its unhovering candles, its slow-moving warm currents of scent. Now came a small gust which blew out the light and left us in half-darkness.

"A fitting end to our dinner" said Caradoc. "And a sign that we should be about our business. How shall we arrange matters?"

Hippolyta was staying; Banubula elected to be dropped off in Athens, "if we could face the detour". That left the three of us. I left my sacred boxes in a safe place against a future return and joined them. Pulley had taken the wheel of the car, sitting beside the chauffeur whose air of misgiving showed that he knew he was in for a long night's work. "Drive carefully" cried our hostess from the gate.

Caradoc sang softly to himself, beating time with a finger.

Drinking, dicing and drabbing
Drabbing, drinking and dice,

You can say what you like they are nice
You can say what you like they are nice

Faces with nothing behind them
Or behinds with nothing before. . . .

Pulley nearly ran into an unlighted cart and threw us all about widdershins. Banubula made turkey-noises. He was obviously a timorous man and was relieved to be deposited on the outskirts of the capital, pausing only to retrieve a silver-knobbed walking stick and to bow a ceremonious good-night. Then down towards the sea we turned, and now the young tardy moon was rising; it rode with us along the whole circuit of the long walls, past the rabble of dingy villas nestling in sterile palms, the beer factory, the refuse-encumbered Ilyssos. Below the Acropolis the olive groves melted away downhill towards the little railway. No horizon was ruled as yet, only a point at which stars began to prickle up out of the darkness. The last curve of the coast road sprang out like a branch in full blossom and elated by the moonlight and the silver spangles of the mild sea Pulley increased speed until we were whirling down towards Sunion—stars cool now as cress and shining waternibbled rock. Caradoc's rose was black. The night was placid and reassuring. Caradoc had decided for the time being to stop acting the rhetorical mountebank; the lightly varnished night-sky was a narcotic. In an absent-minded fashion he tried to catch a moonbeam in his cupped hand.

Nor was it long before we swerved off the pitted macadam of the main road on to hard dune: thence on to flaky sand dunes, to bump and skitter and slide into the rotting garden of the Nube and come to rest hull down under a single balcony where the one and only Mrs. Henniker awaited us in the attitude of a gaunt Juliet in retirement. The electric sign throbbed weakly: though for reasons of economy or aesthetics the current had never been taken inside where the lighting was by paraffin lamp or candle. Caradoc announced our arrival and at once Mrs. Henniker bobbed out of sight, only to reappear a minute later at the front door, arms extended in welcome. The long horse face with its patchy pink skin inspired confidence. She exhaled rectitude and forthrightness like the best sort of seaside landlady. Her tones were tart and martial, her back as straight as a ramrod. She was at once fearful and endearing. Behind her one could sense the long and thankless lifetime spent in putting up with the lopped-off capacities of her typical clients. ("The Goddess of Sex, who, like the multiplication table, repeats her demands, always trying to raise herself to a higher power, perhaps in order to precipitate a true self?" Who the devil was that? Yes, Koepgen.)

At any rate it was to the Nube that humanity shuffled, lugging its heavy baggage—the interior pains and massive depressions. Among Mrs. Henniker's girls they were exorcised. Not us, mind you, for we were heartwhole and in sportive mood—to judge by the tone set by Caradoc. He introduced me as Mr. Chilton and added agreeably "He is a man of the world like us." Mrs. Henniker, who took everything with deadly seriousness, fluffed out her feathers like a bird and said, with intense feeling, "My poy. My poy"; taking as she did so, my right hand between scaly palms. It was all very formal, very graceful, very relaxed. Pulley gave a German professor's bow.

We entered the Nube with well-bred enthusiasm to go through the statutory ritual with the big wooden statue of the Curé d'Ars—a cordelier with an unhealthy leer. This came as rather a surprise to me. Caradoc embraced the statue warmly, addressing it as Saint Foutain. Then he indicated a slot in its shoulder large enough to admit a drachma. "Initiate yourself" he cried jovially, tendering me the coin. It tinkled into the body of the Curé and there was a whirr followed by a click. All at once a hatch in his robe flew open and he thrust out a beautifully hand-painted penis the length of a sermon. "Don't reel, don't recoil that way" said Caradoc reproachfully. "Put your hand on it and wish." I obeyed, offering up a shadowy half-formulated wish, fragile yet iridescent as a soap bubble, in the general direction of the absent Io. Pulley followed suit. "He's an infallible fellow. You only have to ask him and it comes true. He was bequeathed to the Nube by a commercial traveller in French wine, as mark of his esteem and entire satisfaction." So, feeling suitably shriven, we advanced upon the candle-lit interior through a succession of dusty curtains; here the girls waited, yawning—about half a dozen dressed in baggy Turkish trousers and no tops. They looked nice and tame, if rugged; and dying of boredom.

Time hung heavy, one gathered, when there were no clients in the Nube. A gramophone, yes, but the discs were few and scratched. Film magazines in plenty, but ancient. So it was that our majestic appearance on the scene evoked a burst of energy and merriment that was spontaneous and unfeigned.

But wait, we were not completely alone. In one corner of the room, on a table, lay a red-headed man apparently dead, and clad in nothing but his underpants. A large and heartless-looking fellow of Celtic cast, he was still sentient for he breathed stertorously through his nose. Not dead, then. The girls giggled as they examined him like some entomological specimen, lifting an arm to let it drop plump, peering into a glazed eyeball, up his nose. "I don't know who he is" said Mrs. Henniker in dismay. "We will have to wait until he comes round." One of the girls explained how the eyeballs of the corpse had suddenly rolled upwards into his skull like a doll; she mimed this horribly. Caradoc approached the figure with an air of medical knowledgeableness and said: "Aha! Cheyne-Stokes respiration. My diagnosis is Merchant Navy. Have you looked in his clothes?"

"He has none. He arrived on a bicycle with some money in his hand. Nothing but his underpants."

Caradoc tutted sympathetically. "You see" said Mrs. Henniker piteously "what we are up against all the time? How to run a respectable house what I mean? Tomorrow I will ring the Consul."

They submitted the corpse to a further series of tests, tickling its privates with a quill, smacking its cheeks, rubbing it with Cologne—but all to no purpose. Finally with a sigh they drew a bead curtain over the figure and Mrs. Henniker led us away among the further alcoves where, among the dusty divans, siphons and bottles awaited us together with plates of various comestibles. Here Caradoc was very much *en pacha*; Fatma had already discovered her lost love in him. I pitied and admired him, for she was a fearsome golliwog of negroid cast, though amiable in a pockmarked way. A shelf of gold and tin teeth adorned a cheerful and matronly grin.

The girls closed in now with chatter and laughter, piling themselves around us on the cushions like stray cats. It was all very domesticated and soothing. In the far corner Miki played a tune on a tinny piano which evoked dim and far-off things. There was no disposition to hurry, except in the case of the playful Fatma who made many a playful grab at the Cham's cods to see, as she said, "if there was any fruit on the branches as yet". Pulley said with an unmerited acerbity, "She's got a hope she has"; and in truth Caradoc seemed to derive more satisfaction from conversation than anything else. The sound of his own voice filled him with a vivid auto-intoxication. "They always ask me" he said somewhat sadly "if I am not married and why and how many children and so on. I try and explain that I was never convinced about the state. But at long last I got so fed up that I began to carry around a wallet-full of children just to humour them. Look." He tipped out of a wallet a series of grotesque pictures of nude children of various ages. "This is my youngest" he explained, holding up the most hideous. "He must be a man of forty by now; but this poor damsel won't know any better." Fatma crooned over the pictures. They were passed round the eager circle of baby fanciers. They had the effect of increasing enthusiasm. Eager to entertain, someone started to scratch a mandolin and croon. Others in a burst of baby-worship produced their knitting and fell to work in aid of an imaginary seventh-month foetus. Tina dabbed us all with scent from a bottle labelled *Phul* and exhorted us to have *kephi*—joy. Somewhat to my surprise Mrs. Henniker also relaxed and laid down with her head in Demetra's lap, allowing the girl to brush her harsh hair and massage her temples. She kicked off her shoes and extending thin arms in rapturous abandonment allowed two other girls to knead and palp them slowly. A fine fat peasant girl closed in on me, polite and nonchalant. Of course in those fine free pre-salvarsan days nobody could help being slightly nagged by syphilophobia. I thought of Schopenhauer's "*Obit anus Abit onus*" and sighed into my flowing bowl. As if she read my mind Mrs. Henniker opened one eye like a chameleon and said: "She is all right; we take no chances here; the safety of the client is our guarantee." I tried to look as if I needed no such reassurance, allowing myself to be fed like a pet bird with aromatic scraps of entrail on toothpicks. "I want to see Sipple," said Caradoc "that velvet prick in an iron mitt, that specialist in all the unwashed desires." "Later" said Mrs. Henniker, "he always comes later"; and then as if the word had reminded her of something she consulted her watch and rose to excuse herself. "I am hiring some new girls" she explained. "The doctor is coming to examine them." So saying she filtered through a wall of curtains and disappeared. Dispersing slowly upon our various trajectories I heard, as if in a dream, Caradoc admonishing me with: "I hope Charlton that you are not one of those Englishmen who forever dream of some sodomy-prone principality with a fringe of palms where the Arabs wear nothing under their nightgowns."

Silence, dispossession, plenitude. The little rooms on the first floor of the villa were spotlessly clean and bare of all ornament. Scoured wooden floors and enormous old-fashioned beds squatting like sumpter camels, with mattresses too tough to be dented by our bodies. Outside the sea sighed along the strand. "Some magi among the barbarians seeing Harpalus despondent persuaded him that he could lure the spirit of Pythonice back from the Underworld. In vain, despite the voice which issued from the bronze bay-tree." She came from no island but from the mulberry-starred plateaus where the Vardar flows, and where the women have voices of steel wire. The fish-markets of Salonika had been her only school. Pitiful black eyes of a mooncalf adorned this kindly personage. Her freshly washed hair, though coarse, was delicious as mint. But then ideas turn sideways in their sleep, seduced by the lush combing of waves upon sand, and one turns with them, sliding towards the self possession of sleep and dreaming. Once more I saw Harpalus among the tombs. "Harpalus the Macedonian, who plundered large sums from Alexander's funds, fled to Athens; there he fell madly in love with Pythonice the courtesan and squandered everything on her. Nothing like her funeral had ever been seen, choirs, artists, displays, massed instruments. And her tomb! As you approach Athens along the Sacred Way from Eleusis, at the point where the citadel is first seen, on the right you will see a monument which outdoes in size every other. You halt and ask yourself whose it is—Miltiades, Cimon, Pericles? No. It is Pythonice's, triple slave and triple harlot."

On my way downstairs—I took a wrong turning and lost myself, blundering down at last into a sort of cellar which must once have served as a kitchen when the villa had been a normal habitation. Here a strange scene was taking place, illustrated, so to speak by the shadows which whirled and loomed upon the dirty ceiling. A group of starkly silhouetted figures stood grouped about a deal table on which lay the figure of a girl. It was their shadows which lobbed about up above like daddy long-legs: fascinating cartoons, travesties of ordinary gestures magnified to enormous size. Mrs. Henniker occupied the foreground of the animated Goya. Her friend the doctor was bent intently over the girl on the table whose parted legs suggested a fruit tree in espalier. To one side, seated along a bench, fading yellowly away from the centre of lamp light sat half a dozen candidates with cheap handbags. They looked contrite and hopeful, like extras at an audition.

Abashed and curious I hestitated in the open door. Mrs. Henniker, who stood holding a bull's eye lamp, turned with nonchalance and beckoned me in with: "Come in my poy, we are just finishing." The doctor grunted as he inserted some kind of oldfashioned catheter with a bulb—or a swab. His bent head obscured for me the face of Iolanthe as she lay there like some taken sparrow-hawk. I was handed the torch while Mrs. Henniker busied herself with some documents, reciting the name and state of the subject. "Samiou Iolanthe, maid-servant in Megara." The doctor wound up his gear and threw a towel over the exposed parts. "This one is also clean" he said and sitting up abruptly the girl gazed into my startled face. Her features sketched a mute imploring expression—almost she put her fingers to her lips. The doctor seized her thumb and stuck a syringe into the ball. She gasped and bit her lips as she saw him draw off a teaspoonful of venous blood to fill a tiny phial. Mrs. Henniker explained her pre-occupations to me in a series of thorny asides. "I have to be careful they don't come from other places, dirty places, what I mean. Specially the sailor's brothel in Piraeus. So I take every precaution, what I mean." I did see what she meant—for that is precisely where Iolanthe came from; nor did she, nor had she ever hidden the fact from me, for there was no promise of exclusiveness between us. On the contrary it was thanks to her that I had visited the place when the Fleet was away.

We clattered down one summer dusk in the ill-lit and musty little metro; it was not a long run to Piraeus—a ragged and echoing town-ship aboom with sirens and factories and the whimpering of seagulls. The place lay some way outside in a crepuscular and unsavoury quarter picked out in old bluish street-lamps obviously left over from the Paris exhibitions of '88. It was traversed by a squeaky tram-line so sinuous that the occasional tram bucketed and swayed about as if stricken by palsy. The establishment had more than repaid my curiosity. It was built like a barrack around three sides of a wide flagged courtyard with a fountain in the centre, suggesting nothing so much as a khan at the desert's edge. The flamboyant fountain, choked and dribbling, trickled down into a basin full of green slime and moss. On all three sides of the long low blocks stood the cubicles of the girls, somewhat like a row of bathing cabins; now of course, the place was empty, all doors lying open. One or two of the cells had been left still lit by cotton wicks afloat in saucers of olive oil—as if their tenants had just slipped out on an errand and would soon be back. But the only inhabitant of the place seemed to be the janitor—an old half-crazy crone who talked cheerfully to herself. "Soft in the head" said a gesture of Io's.

Outside every door stood a pair of wooden clogs, or pattens. It was extraordinarily beautiful in a story-book way—the dense shadow, the elfish yellow light, the dark velvety sky above. All the doors had the traditional Judas cut in them, but this time heart-shaped, which enabled the clients to peer in on the lighted girl before making their choice. Moreover on each of the doors was painted, in crude lettering, the name of the girl—all the names of the Greek anthology, the very perfection of anonymity! The furniture of each cubicle was identical, consisting of a clumsy iron bed, small dressing-table and chair. The only decoration was personal—tortoise-shell mirror, tinsel strips from biscuit tins, postcards of far-away ports, an ikon with a bottle of fresh olive-oil beside it. The oil performed a double service both religious and laic—for the only instrument of contraception was a slip of Kalymnos sponge dipped in it. Thus the sacred juice celebrated its historic ancestry by a double burning, igniting up man and saint alike. On the back wall, innocent as a diploma on a seminary wall, was the medical certificate of health with the date of last inspection. On this figured the girl's real name.

Her cell now (Antigone) was occupied by someone called Euridice Bakos according to the chart. But she too was away on some mysterious errand, though the wick burned in the alcove before a misty

St. Barbara. This ikon was however Iolanthe's—for she blew out the wick and reclaimed it. In the drawer of the rotting dressing-table with its gaudy oilcloth cover she rummaged purposefully to disinter a comb and brush of doubtful cleanliness and a few shabby articles of wear. Lastly in a corner, under the bed with its tin chamber-pot, she picked over a bundle of cheap magazines—*Bouquetto, Romanzo*, and the like—to trace a serial she wanted to continue; also a French grammar and an English phrase-book.

The pattens she had not wanted to take, although they were hers; but I was loath to surrender the clumsy things and slipped one into each pocket. Later the ikon stood upon the mantelpiece in Number Seven. They lighted an expensive candle before it and turned off the harsh electric light. The clogs served later as book-ends. Then disappeared. Here they are again. The persistence of objects and the impermanence of people—he never ceased to reflect upon the matter, as he lay there listening to the distant music of the Plaka taverns and the nearer heartbeats of his watch. She slept so lightly, with such a shallow respiration, that at times she looked dead, as though her heart had stopped. Then to lie back under that shadowing ceiling and yonder into introspection once more, allowing his mind to fill up with all the detritus of thought—things far removed from fornication's rubber pedal; and yet with the idle side of his mind he could go over her points like a mare or a hare. Reflecting I should suppose upon the unconscious alchemist he might one day become, the lion-man. But no, this is a perverse attempt to read back from memories which have faded. About sex? No. About death? Never. This young man never thought of making a will. No he thought in fields, fields which he hoped that one day Abel would arrange in valencies. Some document! It would ideally record how one day he, like everyone else, began to face the disruption of the ordinary appetites, the changing electric fields of the impulses, so hard to place, to tame, to convert into practical usage like, say, the orgasm of electric light in a bulb, or a wheel moving under a lever.

Koepgen used to say that human life is an anthology of states; chronological progression is an illusion. And that to be punished for what one does not remember except in dreams is our version of the tragedy the Greeks invented. The poetry is in the putty, as Caradoc used to say!

Patterns of fading music from the south; early cocks compose their infernal paternoster. Clytemnestra lopped off the heavy limbs and carefully wiped her fingers in the thing's hair. Delicate white fingers with their enormous vocabulary of gestures. The shadows on the cave of Plato lobbed and bounced now upon the walls of Mrs. Henniker's dungeon. The performance was at an end. My smile of friendly complicity had reassured Iolanthe. But to my surprise I suddenly felt the pricking of a puzzling jealousy. The scientist does not like to see his algebra get up, shake itself, and walk away. I promised myself another banquet of Greek twilight soon, though it hardly allayed the absurd sensation. On the dirty wall I thought I descried moving ideograms of other love-objects living in their Platonic form—"man" "rose" "fire" "star". All the furniture of Koepgen's poems, which he claimed were really "acts, the outer skin of thought". All this had passed over the head of the recumbent Charlock; now he had come back to take up the dropped stitch, so to speak, to recapitulate it all for Abel. All this vulgar data when "screened out" by the sign-manuals of the computer, or "panned out" (as if for gold), would be sifted down through the spectrum of language itself, punctuated and valued, to yield at last the vatic tissue which owes little to ordinary looms. Now I know that everything is remediable, that finally somehow somewhere memory is fully recoverable. These thoughts then bursting on the surface of the mind in little bubbles of pure consciousness would provide red meat for the Lion—Abel's raw aliment.

Life is an image (Koepgen) of which everything is the reflection. All objects are slowly changing into each other—dead man to dead tree, to dead rock, to vine, to marl, to tan sand, to water, cloud, air, fire . . . a movement, not of dissolution but of fulfilment. (To fulfil is to fill full.)

Chemical reincarnations by the terms of which we all become spare parts of one another—excuse the biblical echo. Abel roars and roars. Our modern oracle like the ancient is this steel animal: bronze bull, steel lion. His diagnosis is as follows: "This young man should read Empedocles again. Complexity, which is sometimes necessary, is not always beautiful; simplicity is. Yes, but after the last question has been asked and answered there will always remain something enigmatic about a work of art or of nature. You cannot drain *la dive bouteille* however much you try."

The object of Abel's operation you see was never the manufacture of a factitious literature, no; but a way of remodelling sensation in order to place one in a position of "self-seizing". Such words then become merely a novel form of heartbeat as they do for the poet. In "real" life. Has not Koepgen always called his poems "my little prayer-siphons"? Gradually I find my blundering way back through the stale curtains....

Caradoc was there, musing over a drink, and looking somewhat gibbous after his exertions; Fatma had produced a manicure set and was touching up his square fingernails. He indicated a siphon and said: "Drink, boy, until you detonate the idea within you." He was I thought a trifle detonated himself already. Inconsequential ideas trailed through his mind. He stroked the golliwog and extolled her "great bubbles of plenty". Ugh! He enjoined her to give us a tune on her zither, and then without waiting for accompaniment sang softly, wearily:

Ah take me back once more to find
That pure oasis of neurosis called
The Common Mind
To foster and to further if I can
The universal udderhood of man.

Obscure associations led him to speak of Sipple. "Sipple was a clown once, a professional clown. Aye! I have seen him at Olympia come on with boots like soap-dishes and a nose like a lingam. His trousers furled like a sail and the whole man was held together by a celluloid dickey which rolled up like a blind and knocked him down. His greatest moment was when the second clown set fire to his privates with a torch. Talk about Latimer's ordeal: you should have heard the ladies screech. But his proclivities were not those of the refined. His habits were rebarbative. There was a scandal and he had to retire. Now he lives in honourable retirement in Athens—don't ask me on what. Even the firm can't tell me that."

He broke off and gave a surprised roar, for in the furthest alcove in the room a figure which had been lying completely buried in cushions suddenly sat up and gave a yellow yawn. It was a dramatic enough entry on cue to satisfy Sipple's sense of theatre—for it was he. His pale lugubrious face was creased with sleep; his small bloodshot eyes, full of a kind of street-arab meanness, travelled round the room in dazed fashion. Only when he saw Caradoc advance upon him with outstretched arms did a vague smile wander into his countenance. "So you got here" he piped, without much relish, hitching his tubular trousers on to sagging braces, and laughed *chick chick.* His face was alive with little twitches, tics and grimaces—as if it did not know into what expression to settle. No, it was as if he needed to stretch out the sleep-creased skin. He submitted to some massive thumps of welcome from his friend, and yawning hugely accepted to come and sit in our corner of the room. A tame sloth I would have said: with a queer pear-shaped furry head.

The Cham pushed and pulled him about as one might a pet. I was introduced and shook a damp octopoid hand; bizarre was Sipple, and rather disturbing. "I was telling the boy here" said Caradoc "about why you had to leave the motherland." Sipple shot me a doubtful and cunning look, unable to decide for a moment whether or not to pick up this gambit, an obvious comedian's "feed". His eyes were far too close together; "made to see through keyholes" a Greek would have said. Then he decided to comply. "It was all Mrs. Sipple's fault, sir" he whimpered with just the suspicion of a trembling underlip. "Yes" he went on slyly, moistening his lips and gazing sideways at me with a furtive and timorous air. "She didn't hold with my exhibitions. We had to part."

Caradoc, who appeared to hang on his lips, struck his knee with massive sympathy. "Wives never do. To the ducking stool with them all" he cried in jovian fashion. Sipple nodded and brooded further on his wrongs.

"It was the lodger" Sipple explained to me in a painstaking undertone. "I can only do it in exceptional circumstances, and then it all goes off in spray." He looked woebegone, his underlip swelled with self-commiseration. Yet his ferret's eye still watched me, trying to size me up. I could see it was a relief when I decided to find him funny, and laughed—more out of obedience to Caradoc than from my own personal inclination. However he took courage and launched himself into his act—a recital obviously much-rehearsed and canonised by repetition. Caradoc added rhetorical flourishes of his own, obviously keenly appreciative of his friend's gifts. "You were right" he cried. "Right to leave her, Sippy, with dignity intact. Everything you tell me about her fills me with dismay. God's ruins! Covered in clumps of toc. Ah God to see her haunches stir across the moon at Grantchester. No, you were right, dead right. A woman who refuses to tie up a Sipple and thrash him with leg-irons is not worth the name."

Sipple gave the stonehenge of a smile exposing huge discoloured teeth with some extensive gaps. "It wouldn't fadge, Carry" he admitted. "But here in Athens you can do as you would be done by, as the scripture has it." I suppose you could call it extra-suspensory perception.

"Tell me again" said the Cham eager for further felicities of this kind, and the little pear droned on. "It came over me very gradual" said Sipple, raising his arms to pat the air. "Very gradual indeed it did. At first I was normal as any curate, ask my mates. Give me an inch and I took a mile. And I was never one for the boys, Carry, not then I wasn't. But suddenly the theatrical side in me came to the fore. I was like a late-blooming flahr, Carry, a retarded flowering. Perhaps it was being a clown that did it, the magic of the footlights, I dunno."

It was funny all right, but also vaguely disquieting. He put his head on one side and winked with his right eye. He stood up and joined his fingers to say, with a seraphic sadness: "One day I had to face reality. It was quite unexpected. I pulled out me squiffer when all of a sudden it abrogated by a simple reticulation of the tickler. I was aghast! I went to see the doctor and he says to me: 'Look here Sipple, I must be frank with you. As man to man your sperm count is low and the motility of your product *nil.*' I reeled. There I had been, so young, so gay, so misinformed. 'Sipple' went on the doc 'it's all in your childhood. I bet you never noozled the nipple properly. You never had seconds I'll avow.' And he was right; but then what little nipper knows how to tease the tit properly and avoid abrogation in later life when he needs all the reticulation he can get, just tell me that?" He wiped away an invisible tear and stood all comico-pathetico before an invisible medico. "You have all my sympathy" said Caradoc, drunk and indeed a little moved. He swallowed heavily. Sipple went on, his voice rising to higher more plaintive register: "But that was not all, Carry. The doctor had drained away my self-confidence with his blasted medical diagmatic. Yet there was a crueller blow to come, 'Sipple' he said to me 'there is no way out of your dilemma. You are utterly lacking in PELVIC THRUST.' "

"How unfair" cried Caradoc with burning sympathy.

"And thank God untrue" squawked Sipple. "Under the proper stage management it is a wanton lie."

"Good."

"I have shown you haven't I?"

"Yes."

"And I'll show you again tonight. Where is Henniker?"

"I'll take your word for it, Sippy."

Sipple poured himself out a massive drink and warmed to his tale, secure now in his hold over his audience. He must have been a very great clown once, for he combined the farcical and the sinister within one range of expression. "Some day I shall write the story of my love-life from my own point of view. Starting with the dawn of realisation. One day the scales dropped from my eyes. I saw love as only a clown could: what struck me was this: the *position*, first of all, is *ridiculous*. No-one with a sense of the absurd could look at it frankly without wanting to laugh. Who invented it? If you had seen Mrs. Arthur Sipple lying there, all reliability, and fingering her ringlets impatiently, you'd have felt your risibility rise I bet. It was too much for me, I couldn't master myself, I laughed in her face. Well, not exactly her face. She was too heavy to turn over, you'd need a spade. It was only when her night-dress took fire that she realised that all was over. I couldn't help laughing, and that made her cry. 'Farewell forever Beatrice' I said turning on my heel. I sailed away and for many a month I wallowed in the dark night of the soul. I reflected. Gradually my ideas clarified, became more theatrical. I had found a way through.

"So I went back to the doctor, all fulfilment, to tell him about my new methods. He jumped and said I was a caution. A caution! 'It's very very unBritish, you know' he said. I hadn't thought of that. I thought he'd be so pleased with me. He said I was a traitor to the unborn race. He said he wanted to write a paper on me, me Sipple. I grew a trifle preremptory with him, I'll allow. But I hadn't come all the way back to Cockfosters to be insulted. He called me an anomaly and it was the last straw. I struck him and broke his spectacles." Sipple gave a brief sketch of this blow and sank back on to the sofa. "And so" he went on slowly "I came here to Athens to try and find peace of mind; and I won't say I didn't. I'm assuaged now, thanks to Mrs. Henniker's girls and their broomsticks. No more abrogation of the tickler."

Caradoc was having one of his brief attacks of buoyancy; drink seemed to have a curious intermittent effect upon him, making him tipsy in little patches. But these were passing clouds of fancy merely from which he appeared to be able to recover by an act of will. "Once," he was saying dreamily "once the firm sent me to build a king a palace in Burma and there I found the menfolk had little bells sewn into their season tickets—believe me bells. Every movement accompanied by a soft and silver tinkle. Suggestive, melodious and poetical it was to hear them chiming along the dark jungle roads. I almost went out and ordered a carillon for myself. . . .

Come join the wanton music where it swells,
Order yourself a whopping set of bells.

But nothing came of it. I was withdrawn too soon."

A large scale diversionary activity was now taking place somewhere among the curtains; Pulley appeared looking sheepish and incoherent, followed by Mrs. Henniker who was greeted with a cry from Sipple. "What about it, Mrs. H?" he cried. "I told you I wanted to be tortured tonight in front of my friends here." Mrs. Henniker clucked and responded imperturbably that there had been a little delay, but that the "torture-room" was being prepared and the girls dressed up. The clown then excused himself with aplomb, saying that he had to get ready for his act but that he would not be long.

"Don't let him fall asleep" he added pointing to the yawning Pulley. "I need an audience or it falls flat."

Nor did it take very long to set the theatrical scene. Mrs. Henniker reappeared with clasped hands and bade us follow her once more down into the same gaunt kitchen where the shadows still bobbed and slithered—but a different set of them; moreover the dungeon now was full of the melancholy clanking of chains. More lights had been introduced—and there in the middle of things was Sipple naked. They had just finished chaining him to a truckle bed of medieval ugliness. He paid no attention to anyone. He appeared deeply preoccupied. He was wearing the awkward oldfashioned leg-irons of the cripple. But most bizarre of all were the party whips, so to speak. The three girls who had been delegated to "torture" him wore mortar-boards and university gowns with dingy fur tippets. The contrast with their baggy Turkish trousers was delightful. They each held a long broom switch—the sort one could buy for a few drachmae and which tavern keepers use for sweeping out the mud-floored taverns. As we entered they all advanced purposefully upon Sipple with their weapons at the ready while he, appearing to catch sight of them for the first time, gave a start and sank kneeling to the floor.

He began to tremble and sweat, his eyeballs hung out as he gazed around him for some method of escape. He shrank back with dismal clankings. I had to remind myself that he was acting—but indeed *was* he acting? It was impossible to say how true or false this traumatic behaviour was. Mrs. Henniker folded her arms and looked on with a proud smile. The three doctors of divinity now proclaimed in very broken English, "Arthur, you have been naughty again. You must be punish!" Sipple cringed. "Nao!" he cried in anguish. "Don't 'urt me. I swear I never."

The girls, too, acted their parts very well, frowning, knitting black brows, gritting white teeth. Their English was full of charm—such broken crockery, and so various as to accent—craggy Cretan, singsong Ionian. "Confess" they cried, and Sipple began to sob. "Forward!" said Mrs. Henniker now, under her breath in Greek, adding the further adornment of a thick Russian intonation. "Forward my children, my partridges."

They bowed implacably over Sipple now and shouted in ragged unison, "You have again wetted your bed." And before he could protest any further they fell upon him roundly with their broom switches and began to fustigate the fool unmercifully crying "Dirty. Dirty."

"Ah" cried Sipple at the stinging pleasure of the first assault. "Ah." He writhed, twisted and pleaded to be sure; he even made a few desultory movements which suggested that he was going to fight back. But this was only to provoke a harsher attack. Anyway he would have stood little chance against this band of peasant Amazons. He clanked, scraped and squeaked. The noise grew somewhat loud, and Mrs. Henniker slipped into the corner to put on a disc of the Blue Danube in order to mitigate it. Bits of broom flew off in every direction. Caradoc watched this scene with the reflective gravity of one watching a bullfight. I felt astonishment mixed with misgiving. But meanwhile Sipple, oblivious to us all, was taking his medicine like a clown—nay, lapping it up.

He had sunk under the sharpened onslaught, begun to disintegrate, deliquesce. His pale arms and legs looked like those of a small octopus writhing in the throes of death. In between his cries and sobs for mercy his breath came faster and faster, he gasped and gulped with a perverted pleasure. At last he gave a final squeak and lay spread-eagled on the stone flags. They went on beating him until they saw no further sign of life and then, panting, desisted and burst into peals of hysterical laughter. The corpse of Sipple was unchained, disentangled and hoisted lovingly on to the truckle bed. "Well done" said Mrs. Henniker. "Now he will sleep." Indeed Sipple had already fallen into a deep infantile slumber. He had his thumb in his mouth and sucked softly and rhythmically on it.

They surrounded his bed filled with a kind of commiserating admiration and wonder. On slept Sipple, oblivious. I noticed the markings on his arms and legs—no larger than blackheads in a greasy skin: but unmistakably the punctures of a syringe. The shadows swayed about us. One of the lamps had begun to smoke. And now, in the middle of everything, there came a sharp hammering on a door somewhere and Mrs. Henniker jumped as if stung by a wasp and dashed away down the corridor. Everyone waited in tableau grouped about the truckle bed until she should reappear—which she did a moment later at full gallop crying: "Quick, the police."

An indescribable confusion now reigned. In pure panic the girls scattered like rabbits to a gunshot. Windows were thrown open, doors unbolted, sleepers were warned to hurry up. The house disgorged its inhabitants in ragged fashion. I found myself running along the dunes with Pulley and Caradoc in the frail starshine. Our car had disappeared, though there seemed to be another on the road with only its dim sidelights on. Having put a good distance between ourselves and the house we lay in a ditch panting to await developments. Later the whole thing turned out to have been a misunderstanding; it was simply two sailors who had come to claim their recumbent friend. But now we felt like frightened schoolboys. Concern for the sleeping clown played some part in Caradoc's meditations as we lay among the squills, listening to the sighing sea. Then the tension ebbed, and turning on his back the Cham's thoughts changed direction. Presumably Hippolyta's chauffeur had beaten a retreat in order not to compromise her reputation by any brush with the law. He would be back, of that my companions were sure. I chewed grass, yawning. Caradoc's meditations turned upon other subjects, though only he and Pulley were *au courant*. Out of this only vague sketches swam before me. Something about Hippolyta having ruined her life by a long-standing attachment, a lifelong infatuation with Graphos. "And what the devil can she think we will achieve by my giving a Sermon on the Mount on the blasted Acropolis?" Nobody cared what savants thought. Graphos might save the day, but his career was at its lowest ebb. He had had several nervous breakdowns and was virtually unable to lead his party even if the government fell, as they thought it would this winter. And all because he was going *deaf*.

I perked up. "Can you imagine a worse fate for a politician raised in a tradition of public rhetoric? No wonder he's finished."

"Did you say *deaf*?" I said.

"Deaf!" I had become very fond of the word and repeated it softly to myself. It had become a very beautiful word to me.

"And I have to sermonise on the Mount" repeated Caradoc with disgust. "Something to give ears to the deaf, something full of arse-felt greetings and blubberly love. I ask you. As if it could avert the worst."

"What worst?" I asked; it seemed to me that for days now I had done nothing but ask questions to which nobody could or would provide an answer. Caradoc shook himself and said: "How should I know? I am only an architect."

Lights were coming down the road. It was Hippolyta's car. We signalled and galloped towards it.

* * * * *

Somewhere here the continuity becomes impacted again, or dispersed. "I was the fruit of a mixed mirage" said Caradoc, dining Chez Vivi with a group of money-loving boors with polish. Laughing until his buttonhole tumbled into his wineglass. "We must work for the greatest happiness of the highest few." I had by then confided my orient pearls to the care of Hippolyta for Graphos. A queer sort of prosopography reigns over this section of time. Arriving too early, for example, I waited in the rosegarden while she saw Graphos to his car. I had only seen his picture in the paper, or seen him sitting in the back of a silver car, waving to crowds. I had missed the club foot; now as they came down the path arm in arm I heard the shuffling syncopated walk, and I realised that he had greater burdens to carry than merely his increasing deafness. His silver hair and narrow wood-beetle's head with those melancholy incurious eyes—they were set off by the silver ties he wore, imported from Germany. Somewhere in spite of the cunning he gave off all the lethargy of riches. I came upon exactly the quality of the infatuation he had engendered in an ancient Greek poem about a male lover.

He reeks with many charms,
His walk is a whole hip dance,

His excrement is sesame seed-cake
His very spittle is apples.

Insight is definitely a handicap when it comes to loving. (His rival shot him stone dead with a longbow.) On the lavatory wall someone had marked the three stages of man after the classical formula.

satiety
hubris
ate

"The danger for Graphos is that he has begun to think of himself in the third person singular" she said sadly, but much later. All this data vibrates on now across the screens of the ordering condensers in Abel, to emerge at the requisite angle of inclination.

Nor was my experiment with Caradoc's voice less successful; amongst the confusion and general blurr of conversation there was a brief passage extolling the charms of Fatma to which she listened with considerable amusement, and which I found centuries later among my baggage and fed to A. "She may not be a goddess to everyone" he begins a trifle defensively "though her lineaments reveal an ancient heritage. An early victim of ritual infibulation was she. Later Albanian doctors sewed up the hymen with number twelve pack thread so that she might contract an honourable union. No wonder her husband jumped off a cliff after so long and arduous a honeymoon. In their professional excitement the doctors had by mistake used the strings of a guitar. She gave out whole arpeggios like a musical box when she opened her legs. Her husband, once recovered, sent her back to her parents with a hole bored in her frock to show that she was no virgin. Litigation over the affair is doubtless still going on. But meanwhile what was Fatma to do? She took the priapic road like so many others. She walked in peace and brightness holding the leather phallus, the sacred *olisbos* in the processions of Mrs. Henniker. Nor must we forget that these parts were *aidoion* to the Greeks, 'inspiring holy awe'. There is no special word for chastity in ancient Greek. It was the Church Fathers who, being troubled and a trifle perverted, invented *agneia*. But bless you, Fatma does not know that, to this very day. When she dies her likeness will be in all the taverns, her tomb at the Nube covered with votive laurels; she will have earned the *noblissima meretrix* of future ages. Biology will have to be nudged to make room for Fatma."

But the rest scattered with the talk as gun-shy birds will at a clapping of hands. Something vague remains which might be guessed to concern the Piraeus brothel where many of the names live on from the catalogues of Athenaeus—like Damasandra which means, "the man-crusher": and the little thin ones, all skin and bone and saucer eyes, are still "anchovies". Superimposed somewhere in all this Iolanthe's just-as-ancient moral world out of Greek time. Skins plastered with white lead to hide the chancres, jowls stained with mulberry juice, blown hair powdering to grey, underside of olives in wind but not half as venerable. The Lydians spayed their women and did their flogging to the sound of a flute. Depilatories of pitch-plaster battling desperately against the approach of old age. . . . The appropriate sounds of the fountain whispering and of a leather-covered bottle being decanted. Then amidst yawns C's declamation of a poem called The Origen of Species

One god-distorted neophyte
Cut off his cods to see the light,
Now though the impulse does not die
He greets erections with a sigh.

Somewhere, too, room must be made for the scattered utterances of Koepgen—his notebooks were always to hand, not a drop was spilt. Records from some Plaka evening under a vine-tent, mewed at by mandolines. "First pick your wine: then bleed into it preciously, drop by drop, the living semen of the resin. Then pour out and drink to complete the ikonography of a mind at odds with itself here below the lid of sky. The differences can be reconciled for a while by these humble tin jars." Singing has blurred the rest of it, but here and there, like the glint of mica in stone, the ear catches a solidified echo. "Have you noticed that at the moment of death a man breathes in through both nostrils?"

These simple indices of acute anxiety, racing pulse, incontinence, motor incoordination (wine jar spilt, flowers scattered, vase broken) involve the loss of reflexes acquired within the first year of infant life.

Iolanthe cannot be to blame. She sleeps like a mouse-widow with her hair in her mouth, black fingernails extended on the pillow like grotesque fingerprints. Bodies smelling hot and rank.

Somewhere here also, among the shattered fragments recovered from old recordings, Abel has the germ plasm of Hippolyta's voice, vivacious and halting, running on like a brook in a dry river-bed. The black of that perfumed hair when set seems to be charcoal, carved and buffed—or a Chinese ink which holds its sheen even in darkness. She walks naked, unselfconscious, to the balcony to find the car keys, and when he has driven off without a backward glance she goes barefoot down the garden path to the small Byzantine chapel at the end to consult the hovering Draconian eyes of the ikons, the reproachful smile of St. Barbara. Here to light the lamps and mutter the traditional prayers.

It never ceases to amaze me that throughout all this period, unknown to me, Benedicta was approaching; she was sliding down the mighty Danube whose feeble headspring crawls out of a small opening in the courtyard of some German castle. Lulled by the voices of the Nibelungs she sees great castles in ruins brooding on their own reflections in the running water. Trees arch over Durnstein: then Vienna, Budapest, Belgrade and down through the Iron Gates to scout the Black Sea coast of Bulgaria in a Rumanian packet slim as a cigarette; and so down the Bosphorus to where the crooked calligraphy of mosques and spires waited for her in Polis. And for Charlock.

The journey had been arranged for her by the firm; young widows must do their forgetting somehow.

Little eddies of thyme and rosemary lay about in parcels among the columns; one walked into them. There was no breeze. The sun had completed its impressive weight-lifting act and plunged into the darkness. Violet the Saronic Gulf, topaz Hymettus, lilac bronze the marbles. The oncoming night was freshening towards the dews of midnight and after. Here we were assembled, some two hundred people, at the northern end of the Parthenon. *Tenue de ville,* dark suits, cocktail dresses. It seemed a fairly representative lecture audience—members of the Academy and the Temple of Science, professors and other riff-raff of this order. In this cool stable air everyone was relaxed and informal, indeed mildly gay. Except Hippolyta, who was in a high state of nerves, eating valerian cachets one after another to calm herself. On the top plinth, among the columns, stood a lectern with a lamp. It was from here that Caradoc was supposed to be lecturing. The general disposition of the chairs for the audience was pleasantly informal. They were dotted about in groups among the shattered rubble. Everything promised—or so I thought. Doubtless the site itself was responsible for these feelings for who can see the blasted Parthenon at dusk without wanting to put his arms round it? Moreover in this honeyed oncoming of night with its promise of a late moonrise, an occasional firefly triggering on the slopes below, the owls calling?

Below the battlements glowed the magic display of precious stones which is Athens at night: a spilled jewel-casket. The shaven hills like penitents bowed around us and domed the whole in watchful silence. Yes, but what of the lecturer?

"I haven't been able to reach him all day. He's been out with Sipple, drinking very heavily. They were seen on bicycles at Phaleron this afternoon, very unsteady. I've hunted everywhere. If he doesn't come in another five minutes I shall have to call the whole thing off. Imagine how delighted the women will be to see me humiliated like this." I took her arm and tried to calm her. But she was trembling with anxiety and fury combined. It was true that a slight restlessness had begun to make itself felt in the audience. Conversation had begun to dwindle, become more desultory. The women had taken stock of each other's clothes and were becoming bored. "Give him time" I said for the fourth time. People had started to cough and cross their legs.

At this moment a vague shape emerged from among the distant columns and began to move towards us with a slow, curmudgeonly tread. At first it was a mere shadowy sketch of a man but gradually it began to take on shape as it approached. It held what appeared to be a bottle in its left hand. Head bent, it appeared to be sunk in the deepest meditation as it advanced with this lagging unsteady gait. "It's Caradoc" she hissed with a mixture of elation, terror and doubt. The figure stopped short and gazed at us all with amazement, as if seeing us all for the first time, and quite unexpectedly. "He's drunk" she added with disgust gripping my arm. "O God! And he has forgotten all about the lecture."

Indeed it was easy to read all this into the expressions which played about those noble if somewhat dispersed features. It was the face of a man who asks himself desperately what the devil he is supposed to be doing in such a place, at such a time. He gazed at the lectern with a slowly maturing astonishment, and then at the assembly grouped before him. "Well I'm damned" he said audibly. At this moment the despairing Hippolyta saved the day by starting to applaud. Everyone took up and echoed the clapping and the ripple of sound seemed to stir some deep chord in the remoter recesses of the lecturer's memory. He frowned and sucked his teeth as he explored these fugitive memories, sorting them hazily into groups. The quixotic clapping swelled, and its implications began slowly to dawn on him. It was for him, all this! Yes, after all there was some little matter of a lecture. A broad smile illumined those heroic features. "The lecture, of course" he said, with evident relief, and set his bottle down on the plinth beside him—slowly, but without an over-elaborate display of unsteadiness. It was impossible to judge whether he looked as drunk to the rest of the audience as he did to us. They did not perhaps know him well enough to detect more than a desirable flamboyance of attitude—the nonchalance of a great foreign savant. Moreover his tangled mane of hair and his rumpled clothes seemed oddly in keeping with the place. He had appeared like some sage or prophet from among the columns—bearing perhaps an oracle? A ripple of interest went through us all. The Greeks, with their highly tuned sense of dramatic oratory, must have believed this to be a calculated entry suitable to a man about to discourse on this most enigmatic of ancient monuments. But it was all very well for him to remember the lecture at this late date—it must have been gnawing at the fringes of his subconscious all day: but if he had prepared nothing? Hippolyta trembled like a leaf. Our hands locked in sympathetic alarm we watched him take a few steps forward and grip the lectern forcibly, like a dentist about to pluck out a molar. He gazed around in leonine fashion under frowning eyebrows. Then he curtly raised his hand and the clapping ebbed away into silence.

"All day," he said on a hoarse and delphic note "I have been locked in meditation, wondering what I was going to tell you tonight about this." He waved an arm towards the columns behind. Hippo sighed with growing relief. "At least he is not completely out." Quite the contrary. His speech was thick but audible and unslurred. He was making a rapid recovery, hand over fist. "Wondering" he went on in the same rasping tone "how much I would *dare* to reveal of what I know."

He had unwittingly fallen upon a splendid opening gambit. The hint of mysteries, of the occult, was most appropriate to the place as well as to the gathering. There was a stir of interest. Caradoc shook his head and sank his chin upon his breast for a long moment of meditation. We, his friends, were afraid that he might indeed doze off in this attitude—but we did him an injustice. In due course he raised his leonine head once more, and with the faintest trace of a hiccough, went on in oracular fashion. "Time must inspirit us with all the magniloquence of the memories which hover here. Who were they, first of all, these ancestors of ours? Who? And how did they manage to actualise the potential in man's notions of beauty, side-step history, abbreviate eternity? Perhaps by prayer—but if so to whom, to what?" He licked his lips with relish and raked his audience with flashing eye. Hippolyta nudged me. "This is good stuff" she whispered. "But most of them don't know English and they won't realise that it means nothing. But the tone is perfect, isn't it?" It was; he was clearly beginning to surmount his infirmity rather successfully. If only he could keep up the oracular note it wouldn't matter much what he actually said. Hope dawned in our hearts.

"Anyone can build, place one stone on another, but who can achieve the gigantic impersonality of such art? The cool thrift of that classical indifference which only comes when one has stopped caring? In our age the problem has not changed, only our responses are different. We have tried to purify insight with the aid of reason and its fruit in technics: and failed—our buildings show it. Yet we are still here, still full of sap, still trying, grafted on to these ancient marble roots. They have not disowned us yet. They are still lying in wait for us, the selfish and indifferent nurselings of matter, yes; and their architecture is the fruit by which ye shall know them. It is the hero of every epoch. Into it can be read the destiny, doctrines and predispositions of a time, a being, a place, a material. But in an age of fragments, an age without a true cosmological notion of affect and its powers, what can we do but flounder, improvise, hesitate? A building is a language which tells us all. It cannot cheat."

"The only trouble" whispered Hippolyta again "is that all this is useless for my purposes. It's all gibberish, damn him."

"Never mind. At least he's here."

Caradoc's self-possession was gaining ground. He had retrieved his bottle by a stealthy sideways movement, and placed it on the lectern before him. He seemed to draw courage from an occasional affectionate glance at it. He pursued his way, adding judicious and expressive gestures.

"What can I tell you about him, this man, these men, who realised and built this trophy? Everything, in fact. Moreover everything which you also know full well, though perhaps without actually realising it. For we have all done our spell in the womb, have we not? We were all inhabitants of prehistory once, we all squirmed out into the so-called world. If I can give you the autobiography of this monument it is only because it starts with my own birth; I will give you its pedigree in giving you my own.

"In the first twenty-four hours after birth we must recognise a total reorganisation of the creature in question from a water to a land animal. No transformation from chrysalis to butterfly could be more radical, more complete, more drastic. The skin, for example, changes from an internal organ, encapsulated, to an external one, exposed to the free and abrasive airs. This little martyr's body must cope with a terrific drop in external temperature. Light and sound pierce eye and ear like gimlets. No wonder I screeched." (At this point Caradoc gave a brief but blood-curdling screech.)

"Then, to pursue the matter further, the infant like an explorer must supply his own oxygen requirements. Is *this* freedom? Nor could the stimulants of his puny machine be less irksome to come to terms with—small whiffs of deadly carbon monoxide, with its inevitable slight hypoxia. *Aiee!* Can you wonder that my only wish was to retreat, not only into the sheltering maternal pouch, but right back into the testes of the primeval ape for whom my father merely acted as agent, as representative? I can tell you that Caradoc found this no fun at all. My respiratory centre was labouring heavily. I lay on the slab, the mortuary slab of my immortal life—twitching like a skate in a frying-pan. But even this would have been too much if it had not been enough. Within a few hours an even more drastic reorganisation was to be forced upon me. My whole cardio-vascular system, so cosily established and equilibrated in the socialist state of the womb, had to change from the dull but munificent throbbing of the placental intake to a new order of things—a whole new system. From now on my own lungs were to be the primary, indeed the only source of my oxygen supply. Think of it, and pity the shuddering child." Here the lecturer provided a few illustrative shudders and took a brief pull at the bottle, as if to seek warmth and consolation against these memories.

"At birth the heat-regulating centres are sadly immature. It takes weeks of running-in for the motors to improve. At birth, as I said, there is the calamitous temperature-fall, but as yet no teeth to chatter with. It takes overcoming, and somehow I did it. I achieved the state known as poikilothermic—a shifting of temperatures to respond to the degree outside. The doctor was in raptures at the very word. Poikilothermic! He pushed a dynamometer up my behind and began to read off the impulses, beating time with his finger. But already I was dying to retire from this unequal struggle, to draw my pension and relinquish the good fight. But I must not deny that I had already had a little practice in swallowing during my period *in utero*. There had also been a few languid movements of the gastro-intestinal tract —a mere dummy practice. But I knew no more about its meaning than a conscript knows about the intentions behind intensive arms-drill; less, even, I should say, much less. He may guess—but how should I guess my own future?

"Of course some sucking motions had been present before there was anything to suck on, so to speak. Ah the teat, when it came—what an inexpressible relief! What a consolation prize for the surrender I had made!

"All this is essential to realise if we are to think seriously about the Parthenon, my friends. The inside of a baby is sterile at birth; but a few hours afterwards . . . why, it has apparently taken in all the germs that make human life so well worth unliving among our mortal contemporaries. As you can imagine I found all this most distasteful, and made it plain with whatever vocal chords I possessed. In the meantime however the skin had started to influence fluid balance by evaporation. But the whole thing felt so damn precarious—the capillary system is so liable to dilatation and contraction. Yet I went on—not consciously, by my own volition—but propelled by my biological shadow. Slowly the respiration began to stabilise. But how slowly the systolic blood-pressure comes up during childhood. The pulse-rate, so high at birth, slowly comes down to the average adult beat of 72 to the minute. But meanwhile I was also developing an enzyme system for digesting the various chemical entities I should be required to ingest in order to keep body and snail together. How slow! I mean the evolution of the body membrane in order to filter proteins adequately. At birth the lining of the intestinal tract is a hopelessly inadequate barrier which allows the more complex of the proteins to be absorbed in the blood-stream undigested. The key to later allergies may well be here; to this day I cannot face crab unless it is marinated in whisky. Then, too, the filtering and concentrating powers of the kidney are woefully immature at birth.

"Up to twenty-six weeks after the fatal event I was struggling with the shift-over to an entirely different chemical type of haemoglobin. You see, my respiration was far more diaphragmatic than intercostal. I had to be patient, to let it settle into intercostal. I did. I have never had any thanks for this. Of course *some* muscle-tone had been present *in utero*. I am not boasting. This is normal. At birth the infant presents itself with a hypertonicity of muscle which gradually levels off. Mine did. I will not dilate on all the other skills which had to be mastered if I was ever to hope to live on to build cities or temples: bowel-control, feeding, self-feeding. I passed through all these phases until by the end of late infancy the homeostasis of my physiology had become more or less established. Biting and chewing had replaced sucking—but with great reluctance. Teeth, which begin to appear after six months, gradually reach the normal size of the first deciduous set at about two years. By then, of course, I had already marked my mother with my personality by biting her breasts to cause more than one attack of nipple inflammation.

"I should add here that by the time I could utter one word I had passed through the university of a human mother's care and absorbed from her—from her voice, taste, smell, silences—a complete, overwhelmingly complete, cultural attitude which has cost me half a century or more to modify, to objectify. A cultural stance derived from every scintilla of her own anxieties, disgusts, predilections, moral and mental prejudices. All this was conveyed to me as if by massage, by radio-wave—in a fashion quite independent of the reasoning forebrain. Mould-made, then, and with the classical penis in a state of erection I capered upon the scene to play my part—a remarkable and distinguished one—in the charade of people who believe themselves to be free. 'Woman,' I cried in parody 'what have I to do with thee?' She did not need to answer. In the confessional intimacy of these first few months of absolute dependence I had received an impress, a mould-mark, a sigil which will perhaps never be effaced. My very body-image I owe to her—my slovenliness, lubberliness, my awkward gait, propensity for strong drink—responses she bred in me by leaving me alone too long to cry: by going out of the house and leaving me alone. . . . How can I thank her? For all my cities have been built in her image. They have no more than the four gates necessary to symbolise integration. The quaternary of resolved conflicts—even though it is harder to construct creatively upon a rectangle than upon the free flow of a curve or ellipse.

"And yet, even here, after so much struggle, can I say that I have succeeded? What is the education of the adolescent, the adult even, compared in power to this primary school of the affect which leaves its pug-marks alike in human minds and the marble they quarry? The notion of education, used in its ordinary sense, is surely nonsense. O perhaps it once might have connoted some sort of psychic training towards freedom from this chain, this biological prison within which all mothers want their sons to be sexual bayonets and encourage them to be such, while all fathers want their daughters to be merely fruitful extensions of their wives. Yet bayonets end in battles and deep graves—look about you: and women in order to mask their satisfactions end up in lustful widows' weeds, tailored for beauty.

"How soaring an act of insolence, then, was a construct of this order, and my god, how fragile an act of affirmation! with all the dice loaded against him this man one day stood upright in his mother's shadow and evolved this terrifying stone dream. He dared not yet conceive of the existence of another shadow, an unfettered one, the soul. A meaningless but fruitful placebo. Aye! For this early conception of a soul of the dead presupposed at first a subterranean continuation of life on earth, and led inevitably to tomb-building . . . the stone-age binding up of corpses symbolising their tethering to one dwelling place. The first house, the tomb, became the outer casing for the dead soul, just as the first house proper (its windows breathing like lungs) was a case for man—as indeed his mother's body had been a case to house the water-rocked embryo. But from all this to the temple—what an imaginative jump! It takes him soaring beyond the chthonian tie; for here at last is a bus-shelter, and an ark for the immortal and the divine.

"Somehow he managed, for one brief flash, to get a glimpse of the genetics of the idea and to break the incestuous tie. Hurrah, you might well say; well, but to escape chthonos is one thing and to face your own disappearance (without mummy there to help) is quite another. His tomb becomes a boat to sail him over the dark waters of the underworld. Poor little embryo, poor mock-giant. This recurring flash of vision is eternally lost and found, lost and found. His cenotaphs are battered into ruins as this has been.

"But if you can't take it with you, you can't entirely leave it behind either—the inheritance. Now comes the big historic dilemma. His sense of plastic had to cling to the morphology of what he now, tactually as well as factually, knew. The scale of his vision, however much it might include past, present and future, had to remain human. The fruit of this struggle, and this dilemma, you can see partly resolved here in this stone cartoon. Vitruvius has told us the story—how when Ion started to found the 13 colonies in Icaria he found that the memories of the immigrants had begun to fail them, to turn hazy. The workmen entrusted with the task of setting up the new temples found that they had forgotten the measurements of the old ones they wished to imitate. While they were debating how to make columns at once graceful and trustworthy it occurred to them to measure a human foot and compare it to a man's height. Finding that an average foot measured one sixth part of a man's height they applied this to their column by laying off its lowest diameter six times along the overall length, the capital included. Thus did the Doric column begin to mimic and represent the proportions and compressed beauty of the male body in temple-building. And the female? You cannot have one without the other. Our author tells us that when they came to the problems raised by Diana's temple they thought of something which might symbolise the greater slenderness of the female form. The diameter would be one-eighth of the length in this case. At the bottom, then, a foot representing the slender sole. Into the capital they introduced snails which hung down to right and left like artificially curled locks; on the forehead they graved rolls and bunches of fruit for hair, and then down the shaft they made slim grooves to resemble the folds in female attire. Thus in the two styles of column one symbolised the naked male figure, the other the fully dressed female. Of course this measure did not remain, for those who came later, with finer critical taste, preferred less massiveness (or taller women?) and so fixed the height of the Doric column at seven, and the Ionian at nine, times the mean diameter.

"How to forbid oneself to elucidate reality—that is the problem, the difficulty. How to restore the wonder to human geometry—that is the crux of the matter. I do not feel that this marble reproaches us for a finer science, a truer engineering, but for a poorer spirit. That is the rub. It is not our instruments which fault us, but the flaccid vision. And yet . . . to what degree were they conscious of what they were doing? Perhaps like us they felt the fatal flaw, saw ruin seeping into the foundations as they built? We shall never know the answer to this—it is too late. But we, like them, were presumably sent here to try and enlarge infinity. Otherwise why should we read all this into this bundle of battered marble? Our science is the barren midwife of matter—can we make her fruitful?

"But what, you will ask, of the diurnal man? What of his housing? We can of course see that the individual house bears the shadowy narcissistic image of himself embedded even in its most utilitarian forms. The head, the stomach, the breast. The drawing room, bedroom, the kitchen. I will not enlarge on this. All the vents are there. I would rather consider the town, the small town, whose shape can embody both trade and worship. Now Vitruvius, in common with the whole of classical opinion, describes the navel as the central point of the human body. For my part the argument that the genital organ forms the *real* centre has more appeal to one who has always kept a stiff prick in an east wind. But I have only once met with it, and then in a somewhat corrupt text—Varro! But perhaps this was mere Roman politics, an attempt to oust the Delphic omphalos as the true centre of the world? That would be very Roman, very subtle, to try and oust the deep-rooted matriarchal principle and set up father-rule in order to promote the power of the state. This is as may be. Let us deliberate for a moment on the little town itself.

"Do you remember the rite practised specially by the Mediterranean nations in town-building? It was established around a previously marked-out centre, the so-called *mundus*. This centre was a circular pit into which they poured the first fruits and the gifts of consecration. After this the limits of the town were set by a circular boundary line drawn round the *mundus* as a centre of ritual ploughing. The simple pit or *fossa*, the lower part of which was sacred *dis manibus* to the spirits of the dead and the underworld Gods—was filled up and closed in with a round stone, the *lapis manalis*. Do you see the connection establishing itself between the two ideas—*urbs* and *mundus*?

"Then came other factors, deriving perhaps from old half-forgotten complexes—like the propitiatory building sacrifice, for example, which has hung on until today. On your way home look at the skeleton of the new gymnasium in Pancrati. Today the workmen killed a cock and smeared its blood over the pillars. But even closer at hand—do not the caryatids over there speak clearly of such a sacrifice? If ever they should be opened or fall down will we not find the traces of a woman's body in one of them? A common and deeply rooted practice. In your great narrative poem on the bridge of Arta the same ceremony is mentioned—the girl bricked into the piers. It has hung on and on in the most obstinate fashion. Stupidity is infectious and society always tries to maintain the illness in its endemic state.

"Now comes the important question of orientation to be considered so that the inhabitants or worshippers might find themselves within the magnetic field (as we should say today) of the cosmic influences pouring down on them from the stars. Astrology also had a say in the founding of temples and towns. Spika was the marking star for the ancients—people far earlier than the sophisticates who built this sanctuary. In those times it was accurately done by the responsible agent, the king, with the aid of two pegs joined by a cord, and a golden mallet. The priestess having driven one peg into the ground at a previously consecrated spot, the king then directed his gaze to the constellation of the Bull's Foreleg. Having aligned the cord to the hoof thereof and to Spika, as seen through the visor of the strange head-dress of the priestess, he drove home the second peg to mark the axis of the temple to be. Boom!

"Mobego, the god of today, does not require any such efforts on our part. Yet perhaps defeat and decline are also part of an unconscious intention? After all, we form our heroes in our own likeness. A Caligula or a Napoleon leaves a great raw birth-mark on the fatty degenerate tissue of our history. Are we not satisfied? Have we not earned them? As for the scientific view—it is one which drags up provisional validities and pretends they are universal truths. But ideas, like women's clothes and rich men's illnesses, change according to *fashion*. Man, like the chimpanzee, cannot concentrate for very long; he yawns, he needs a sea-change. Well then, a Descartes or a Leibniz is born to divert him. A film starlet might have been enough, but no, poor nature is forced to over-compensate. We are all supposed to be pilgrims, all supposed to be in search; but in fact very few among us are. The majority are mere vegetables, malingerers, fallers by the wayside. All the great cosmologies have been stripped of their validity by human sloth. They have become hospitals for the maimed, casualty clearing stations."

Hippolyta, understanding little of all this, was in a state of deep depression though tinged with relief. But Caradoc swept on, hair flying, voice booming. My only concern was for my devil box. I was anxious lest the faint wind in the mike should give me boom as well as rasp.

"There is no doubt in my mind that the geometries we use in our buildings are biological projections, and we can see the same sort of patterning in the work of other animals or insects, birds, spiders, snails and so on. Matter does not dictate the form but only modifies it in order to make sure that a spider's web really holds the fly, the bird's nest really cherishes the egg. And how much the whole matter is dependent on sexual factors is really a dark question. Among squids and octopods, for example, the males have a special arm with which to transfer the semen to the female, inserting the spermatophore into the cloak or mantle of the lady. In the chambered nautilus the female clutches and retains the arm which breaks off. Spiders are differently catered for; the end of the pedipalp is used as a syringe to suck up and transfer the sperm; but before this can be done the male must discharge this into a special web which he weaves for the purpose. In fact the female does not have to be present. In the axolotl however the female picks up the sperm case with her hind feet and inserts it—a labour-saving device which Mrs. Henniker's young ladies would be prepared to perform for elderly clients. In birds sometimes, by fault an egg can produce weird gynandromorph forms, half male and half female. Aye! In the smallest thing we build is buried the lore of centuries.

"All this and much more occurred to me in my youth as a prentice architect playing about among the foundations of Canberra with Griffin, one of Sullivan's lads. It has occurred to me all over again here in Athens among the girdling shanty towns like New Ionia which your refugees from Turkey have run up, almost overnight. In these provisional and sometimes haphazard constructs you will find many a trace left of the basic predispositions we have been discussing. They have woven them up spider-wise out of old kerosene tins, driftwood, scraps of bamboo and fern, rush matting, cloth and clay. The variety and inventiveness of their constructions are beyond praise. Though they are unplanned in our sense of the word these settlements are completely homogeneous and appropriate to their sites and I shall be sorry to see them vanish. They have the perfection of organism, not of system. The streets grow up naturally like vines to meet the needs of the inhabitants, their water-points and sanitation groupings intersecting economically and without fuss. All the essential distances have been preserved, needs sorted and linked, yet everything done unprofessionally, by the eye. A micro-climate had been established where a city could take root. Streets of soft baked earth into which has soaked urine and wine and the blood of the Easter lambs—every casual libation. Flowers bloom everywhere from old petrol cans coaxed into loops and trellises, bringing shade to the hot gleaming walls of shanties. On a balcony of reed mats a cage of singing birds whistling the tunes of Pontus. A goat. A man in a red nightcap. There is even a little tavern where the blue cans go back and forth to the butts. There is shade where bargainers can fall asleep over their arguments and card players chaffer. You must compare this heroic effort with the other one we are contemplating tonight. They have much in common. A city, you see, is an animal, and always on the move. We forget this. Any and every human settlement for example spreads to West and North in the absence of natural obstacles. Is there an obscure gravitational law responsible for this? We do not know. Some law of the ant-heap? I cannot answer this question. Then reflect how quarters tend to flock together—birds of a feather. Buildings are like the people who wear them. One brothel, two, three, and soon you have a quarter. Banks, museums, income groups, tend to cling together for protection. Any new intrusion modifies the whole. A new industry displaces function, can poison a whole quarter. Or the disappearance of a tannery, say, can leave a whole suburb to decay like a tooth. Think of all this when you read of the shrine of Idean Zeus, floored with bull's blood red and polished—as in South Africa today.

"And now that we have spoken at length about womb-building and tomb-building it is time to consider tool-building and perhaps even fool-building."

Here the transcript became blurred and faulty for as he spoke an extraordinary interruption had begun to take place, a completely unexpected diversion.

A large white hand, with grotesquely painted fingernails, appeared around the column directly behind Caradoc's back. It advanced in hesitant snail-like fashion, feeling the grooves in the stone. The speaker, noticing the thrill which had rippled through his audience at this sight, and following the direction of everyone's gaze, turned his own upon this strange object. "So there you are, Mobego" he muttered under his breath. "Good."

We all watched with intense concentration as the hand became an arm clothed in a sleeve of baggy black with a preposterous celluloid cuff attached to the wrist. Hippolyta drew several sharp breaths of horror. "It's Sipple" she whispered with dismay; and indeed it was, but a Sipple that none of us had ever seen, for the creature was wearing the long since discarded equipment of his first profession. Slowly the apparition dawned among the columns of the temple, and the singularity of his appearance was dumbfounding in its wild appropriateness to the place—like some painted wooden grotesque from an ancient Greek bacchanalia which had suddenly stirred into life at the rumble of Caradoc's words. First the face, with its rhinoceroid proboscis of putty, the flaring nostrils painted on to it as if on to a child's rocking-horse: the bashed-in gibus with the coarse tufts of hair sprouting from it: a tie like a cricket-bat; huge penguin-feet in bursting shoes: ginger hair pouring out of rent armpits. . . .

A shiver of apprehension ran through us all as this semi-comatose little figure stepped shyly blinking into the soft lamplight. Hippolyta's shiver was naturally one of social apprehension; but the audience stayed mumchance, unable to decide whether to laugh or cry out. Here and there one heard a few giggles, quickly repressed, but these were purely hysterical reactions. We were riveted to our seats.

Still blinking, this grotesque advanced slyly on Caradoc, who for his part seemed also to be immobilised by surprise and indecision. Then, while we were all in this state of suspended animation, hardly daring to breathe, Sipple made a sudden rush in the direction of the bottle. Caradoc, awakened from his trance, tried to counter this somewhat ineffectually by grabbing at the clown's wrists. But with a dexterity one would hardly have expected from this strange batrachian, Sipple secured the heavy bottle, and with a single wild leap jumped into the audience and began to run like a hare towards the north battlements, scattering deck-chairs and the ladies in them on either side of his passage.

The spell was broken. There were some shrieks now from the tumbled womenfolk. Everyone else was on his feet gaping. Some began to laugh, but not many. Caradoc had lost his balance and fallen forwards off the plinth, still holding on to his lectern. Knocked almost insensible he lay motionless among the historic stones. His oil-lamp exploded and set fire to a chair; fortunately this was rapidly extinguished. But while a few concerned professors moved forward, impelled by compassion, to pick up the body of the lecturer, the greater part of the audience, still screaming, watching the dramatic trajectory of the figure with the bottle held high above his head as if it were an umbrella. The speed of his flight was astonishing; one wondered how he would manage to brake it by the time he reached the outer wall.

But Sipple had other ideas. With one wild cry, like a demented sea-bird, he gave a leap clear into the sky and . . . crashed down into the lighted city far below him. It was a tremendous acrobatic leap, his knees drawn up almost to his chin, his coat-tails spread upon the night sky like bats' wings. He seemed to hang up there for one long moment, outlined upon the shimmering opalescence of the capital below: and then plummeted down and vanished, his terrible yell fading behind him. More ragged screams went up and half the audience rushed to this high corner of the battlements to look down in the expectation of seeing the crumpled body lying far below. But just under the crowning wall there was a decent-sized ledge; relief and doubt began to mix, for surely this is where he would have fallen, out of sight of his audience? Or had he overshot it and actually fallen into Athens? They hung here pondering, hearing the deep burr of the traffic below and the soft honking of klaxons. From the ledge itself, too, there seemed to be no way down the cliff. Where the devil was he, then? The watchers craned, and turned perplexed faces to each other. The whole episode had been so strange and so sudden that some must have wondered if the whole thing was not an illusion. Had we dreamed up Sipple? His disappearance was so sudden and so complete. One could see nothing very clearly.

But by now the keepers had been summoned, and a number of chauffeurs as well, to examine the slopes of the Acropolis for the supposed body of the clown. Torches were pressed into service. A line of glow worms appeared along the fringes of the cliff. It was all to be in vain, however, for the clown had clambered down a steep goat-track and made good his escape.

Attention turned to Caradoc who had cut his forehead slightly and had the wind banged out of him. He was too incoherent still to answer questions about the episode and showed signs of being still a trifle drunk as well. Hippolyta herself was almost weeping with vexation. But with great presence of mind she delegated some of the local savants to conduct him lovingly down the staircases and ramps to her car. He went out like a hero, to ragged applause. Meanwhile Hippolyta bade her guests goodnight, fighting back her tears. But in fact, she found to her surprise, the whole evening had been—for all its strangeness: or perhaps because of it—a great success. People still stood about in excited thunderstruck groups, discussing what they had seen and trying to evaluate it. Accounts differed also, and arguments followed. I collected my boxes which had unaccountably escaped damage and followed her down the long staircases. She walked at a furious pace and I feared she would sprain an ankle.

In the bushes below the wingless victory a figure approached her and muttered something in an undertone. I took it, from its ragged clothing to be a beggar soliciting alms. But no, it handed her a letter. She seemed filled now with a sudden new concern. She tore open the envelope and read the message in the light of the car, and it seemed to me that she turned pale, though this may have been an illusion caused by the beam of light. I loaded my gear into the boot. Caradoc was asleep in the front seat now. We climbed in and she laid trembling fingers upon my arm. "Will you do something for me tonight, please? It is very urgent. I will explain later."

The car swirled us away towards the country house. I smoked and dozed, listening to the rumble of Caradoc's voice; he was apparently continuing the lecture in his sleep. Hippolyta sat stiff and upright in her corner, lost in thought.

At Naos all the lights were on, and she stalked rapidly through the rosegardens into the house where we found the sleepy-looking figure of the Count half dozing by the telephone. She handed him the slip of paper, but it seemed that he was already *au courant*. "Yes, they phoned here" he said, and added "What is to be done?"

"Is your passport visa'd for Turkey?"

"Yes."

"Then take the car to the Salonika border; it will be easy to get him over if we lose no time."

The Count yawned heavily and pressed his ringed hands together. "Very well" he said mildly. "Very well."

Hippolyta turned to me and said: "Will you find Sipple for him? You know where he lives."

"Sipple?"

"We must get him out of Athens as swiftly as possible. The Count will drive him to Salonika if you can find him and persuade him to pack in a hurry."

"What has Sipple been doing?"

"I'll explain everything later." But she never did.

Banubula took the wheel of the big car after having stowed away a small dressing case, containing I presumed a change of clothing; he would be away a night at least. Somewhat to my surprise he proved a powerful and fastish driver, and it was not very long before we were back in the streets of the capital. We proposed to divide the labour; he would go to Kandili and draw oil and petrol, while I crossed the Plaka and alerted Sipple. We should meet at the Tower of the Winds as soon as may be. It could not be too soon for me, I reflected, for I was very tired and the hour was late. A faint grey pallor on the sea-horizons of the east suggested that the dawn—which breaks very early in summer—was not far off. In the meantime . . . Sipple. I crossed the Plaka rapidly, using my pocket torch whenever necessary in the unlighted corners.

I had never been inside Sipple's quarters; but I had had them pointed out to me during one of my walks about Athens at night. He occupied the whole of the first floor of a pretty ramshackle building of a faintly Byzantine provenance. Long narrow wooden balconies looked out towards the Observatory and the Theseum—a pleasant orientation. Two long wooden staircases mounted to the first floor from the street level—and these were a mass of flowers and ferns sprouting from petrol tins. There was hardly a passage to be pressed between them. As I made my way up, however, I noticed that the glass door at the end of the balcony was ajar, and that a faint light shone from somewhere inside the cluster of gaunt rooms. This would offer some encouragement—I should not have to knock and wake up all his neighbours.

The first room was dark and empty of everything except some rickety bamboo furniture. The walls were decorated with esoteric objects like pennons, flags of many nations, and photographs of

Sipple in various poses. Two large bird cages, muffled against the light by a green shawl, hung in the window. All this my pocket torch picked up with its vivid white beam. I half whispered and half called his name, but no answer came out of the inner room, and I made my way towards it after a decent interval, pushing open the door with my hand.

The light—dimmer than I had supposed—came from a fanlight which marked, no doubt, a lavatory. In the far corner of the room stood a rumpled and disordered bed. I did not at first look at it carefully, deeming that Sipple himself was to be found beyond the lighted door attending to the calls of nature. Indeed I could hear him breathing. More to mark time than anything I swept the cheap deal table with my lamp. On it stood a half-packed suitcase and a British passport made out in the name of Alfred Mosby Sipple. So he was already packing! I advanced to look at a framed photograph on the chest of drawers, and then something impelled me to take a closer look at the bed. I was not prepared for the shock that followed. I suddenly became aware that there was a figure in the bed lying with its face turned away towards the wall and the bedclothes drawn up to its chin. It was Iolanthe! Or at first sight it seemed to be her—so remarkable was the facial resemblance between her and the sleeping figure. One would have said her twin brother—for it was a youth, his style of haircut showed it. Intrigued, I advanced closer, feeling my curiosity turning to a vague alarm at the silence and pallor of the face—this face of Iolanthe. A glimpse of white teeth showed between bloodless lips. Then, as I touched the sheet, drawing it back, my blood began to curdle for the youth had had his throat cut like a calf. The pallor and the silence had been those of death, not sleep. There was no immediate trace of blood for it had all drained downwards into the bed. The deed then had been carried out in this same position while the youth lay sleeping. I recoiled in horror and as I did so I heard the clumsy bang of the home-made watercloset. A bar of sallow light entered the room through the open door frame in which stood Sipple, doing up his trousers. We stared at one another for a long moment, and I suppose he must have seen from my expression that I knew what had taken place in that soiled and rumpled bed. His face seemed to float in the yellow light like a great yolk. Traces of greasepaint still clung to it, grotesquely outlining one eye and his chin. His fingers depended from his wrists like cubist bananas. He gave something between a sob and a giggle; then taking a step towards me he held out a pleading hand and whispered: "I swear I didn't do it. He's mine, but I swear I didn't do it." We stayed fixed in this tableau for what seemed an age. Somewhere a clock ticked. The dawn was advancing. Then I heard the first sleepy chirping of Sipple's birds under their covers. My throat was parched and aching. Moreover something else had begun to play about the corners of my mind in disquieting fashion. In lifting the sheet I had noticed traces of something, just a few grains here and there, scattered on the sheet and pillow; I thought at first of powdered graphite which can give off a sheen. And then I was reminded of the black nail varnish of Iolanthe, the dark shellac mixture which set hard and glossy, but also chipped easily. It was not a thought or observation I pushed very far—my mind was like that of a startled rabbit. But it stayed, it nagged. Meanwhile here before my eyes was Sipple, apologetically shortening his braces and pouting at me, like a man who has been wronged and feels upon the point of tears. Behind him the sky was whitening over the sleeping city. Far off came the buzzing tang of a semantron from the Theological Seminary, calling the students to early prayers. The birds stirred, half asleep. Sipple said brokenly, but under his breath, talking purely to himself, "It's leaving the birds that really hurts." Now I heard the whimper of the big car climbing the steep slope by the temple, and reversing into position.

The tiredness which had been overwhelming me had been banished at a stroke. I walked about the city for more than an hour, drinking a raki or an ouzo in the few taverns which opened at dawn in preparation for the market carts rolling into the city with their produce. I could not get the picture of Sipple's empty bedroom with its silent recumbent figure in the corner, out of my mind. I even returned and circled the quarter like a criminal returning to the scene of his crime, gazing up at the silent windows, wondering what I should do, if anything. Finally I fell asleep on a park bench and woke when the sun was up, stiff with rheumatism from the heavy dew which had soaked my clothes.

I limped back to the hotel, relieved to find the clumsy front door already open; the porter Nik, still in his underclothes, was brewing coffee in a little Turkish coffee spoon. He jerked his head sleepily—a gesture which had become formalised both as a greeting and as an indication that Iolanthe was at present upstairs in Number Seven. Yawning with fatigue I shuffled my way up. The door of the room was ajar, and so was the door of the bathroom. Her handbag and clothes were on the bed, but I could hear her stirring next door. She had not heard me come in. I walked to the half-open door and once more my heart turned a complete somersault. She was lying in the dry tin bath covered from head to foot in fresh blood—for all the world as if she had been brutally murdered and cut to ribbons. I almost cried out but abruptly caught sight of her rapt and happy face. She was crooning to herself in a soft nasal tone, and I could just catch the words of an island song which was very much in vogue at that time: "My father is among his olive-trees." As she sang she was dabbing the vivid menstrual blood on her cheeks, her forehead, her breasts—literally painting herself in it. I recoiled before she caught a glimpse of me, and retreated on tiptoe into the corridor whence I re-entered Number Seven, this time making a characteristic noisy entrance. I heard her call my name. The bathroom door was abruptly closed, and with a swish the bath-taps went on.

I took off my shoes and lay half drowsing on the bed until she had finished. She emerged wearing my old green dressing-gown, her face radiant with a kind of defiant elation. "I have news" she said breathlessly. "Look!" She took up a key from the mantelshelf and held it up, tapping the air with it. "The key of a villa!" She sat down by my feet, bubbling over with joy. In the absurd phrasing of newspaper demotic she added: "At last! I have been solicited by a great personality! Think, Charlock! A salary, clothes, a little villa in the Plaka." For the girls of her persuasion this was the ultimate dream realised—to find oneself the mistress of a rich man. My congratulations seemed to her somewhat tepid—though in truth they were heartfelt enough; it was simply that I was dazed, half asleep, and with my mind swimming with the events of that evening. She put a sympathetic paw on my thigh, misinterpreting my lukewarmness, and went on: "Mind you, I would have stayed with you if you had really wanted. If you had spat in my mouth and said you owned me. . . . But it is better that we should be good friends like we are, is it not?"

Her sincerity was so disarming that I almost began actively to regret the intrusion of this "great personality" upon the blameless youthful life we had enjoyed in Number Seven. I saw, so to speak, rapidly thrown down upon one another—or fanned out like a pack of gaily coloured cards—the thousand and one glimpses I had obtained of Athens entirely through her kind offices. I saw her buying fish, or Easter ribbons, or coloured chapbooks containing the shadowplay texts, or swimming in a cove with towed hair fanned out behind. "It's really excellent news." She crinkled her laughing eyes up, relieved. "And it may lead to other things. This man has great influence." I could not then imagine what other things such an assignment might lead to.

"Who is he? Do you know?"

"Not yet." This was a lie, of course.

The trouble with memory, and its prolix self-seeding process, is that it can always by-pass the points of intersection at which we recognise, or seem to recognise, the action of a temporal casuality. Is it a self-indulgence to want to comb it out like a head of hair? Reminded of the severed heads of Turkish traitors prepared so scrupulously for exhibition—the hair washed and curled, the beard pomaded, the eyesockets massaged with cream by terrified Greek barbers. Or the shrunken heads in bottles of spirit which still fetch great sums as talismans in the High Taurus. Well, and among these fugitive snapshots I found a faded one of Io on her island, helping her old father with his small crop of maize. At one blow she could shed the city with all its spurious sophistications and revert to the healthy peasant. Once on holiday I had seen her barefoot walking the deep dust of the road, bronze-powdered from head to foot, with a poppy between her teeth. Given the means this would have been her idea of advancement—to help the little man with his walnut-wrinkled face on some burning hillside, among the banded vipers. The key to the stuffy villa in Pancrati was the sesame which might lead her homewards, though not before she had endured all the vicissitudes and privations which come from exclusive ownership. Months later appearing, dressed like a typical adulteress in a voluminous scarf and dark glasses, to announce that she was going away—traded presumably to some wealthy client on the Nile. But no, something better, far better. Then in a tone appropriate to the comic side of Athenian life—its Aristophanic simplicities. "Ouf, I can hardly sit down; he has a taste for the whip, this one."

I did not go back to Naos until I was summoned, a week or two later; nor, by some curious chemistry of the unconscious, did I mention anything at all about Sipple, or about my visit to his rooms. Neither did Hippolyta. Nor, most perplexing of all, could I find any reference to the matter in the newspapers which I so diligently perused in the Reading Rooms of the local library. Not a word, not a breath. It was to be presumed then that the whole thing had been a bad dream? Hippolyta was alone in the rambling house, lying almost waist-deep in newsprint, her cheeks pink, her voice crackling at the edges with triumph. She embraced me with a curious reverential, a devotional tenderness—the precise way that the Orthodox peasants salute an ikon. "Graphos" she cried, the tears rose to her blackbird's eye. "O do look. Have you read it?" I had not. The press was plastered with it. "It is the greatest speech he has ever made—all Athens is thrilled. He has found himself again."

These esoteric matters concerning the vicissitudes of Athenian political life were of no concern to me; or so it then seemed. "But you don't understand. His party is reformed at a single blow. He is certain now to carry the autumn election and that will save the day."

"For whom? For what?"

"For us all, silly."

She poured me a drink with shaking hand, wading through the bundles of newsprint with their vivid many-coloured letterpress, all bannering the name of Graphos, all carrying cartoons of him, photographs of him. "He wants to see you, to thank you. He will receive you whenever you wish."

And receive me he did, in one of those high-ceilinged rooms in the Ministry with polished parquet floors and beautiful Baluchistan carpets—receive me moreover at a magnificent rosewood desk containing nothing but an empty blotter and his own silver cigarette lighter. It was the sort of desk which is only used to initial an occasional treaty. He was paler, thinner and a good deal sadder at close quarters than I had imagined him to be—but the thin man gave off a sort of excited candence. It was gratitude partly, but also mixed with curiosity. Touching his ear with a tapering finger he asked if anyone knew of my inventions, and whether I had taken any steps to profit by them. I had only thought vaguely of the matter—the first thing was to perfect the idea. . . . "No. No" he said emphatically, standing up in his excitement. "My dear friend, do not lose your chance. There may be a great fortune in this for you; you must protect yourself somehow." His rapid and fluent French conveyed better than English could have done the temper of his excitement; I suppose I must have presented myself badly, vaguely, for my apparent indifference piqued him. "Please," he said "I implore you to let me express my gratitude by putting you in touch with my associates who would be glad to help you put the whole thing on a proper basis. I am determined that you must not lose by this thing. Or must I plead with Hippolyta to convince you? Reflect." I confess I thought he exaggerated somewhat, but what was there to lose? "You could at least examine their proposals; if you agreed with them you would find yourself well protected. There could be a great fortune in this device."

I thanked him and agreed. "Let me take it upon myself to send you to Polis for a few days to meet them and discuss with them. No harm can come of it; but at least my conscience will be at rest. I owe you a debt, sir."

I was indeed a little puzzled by my own hesitation in the matter. Certes, I had vaguely thought of patenting the device one day and licensing it perhaps; but several reasons came into play here. First, it seemed to spoil all the fun, second I could not be sure that other devices of the same order had not been thought of—the principle was spade-simple. But these considerations seemed to carry little weight with Graphos who brushed them aside with the remark that within a week he could find out and have the matter put upon a professional basis. Well, I let it go at that, but before leaving congratulated him somewhat sychophantically upon the speech which I had not read. He winced and became shy, and I suddenly saw what an effort it must have cost this shy, reticent and orderly mind to launch itself into public affairs. He had the soul of a grammarian, not a demagogue. When I spoke, for example, of the poetry I pretended to discover in it he held up thin hands to his ears and protested. "Rhetoric, not poetry. You could not convince with mere poetry. Indeed there has always been something a little suspect about the latter for me since I read that Rimbaud insisted on wearing a top-hat in London. No, our objectives are limited ones. If we get in again it will be to try and prove only that the key to the political animal is magnanimity. A frail hope I agree." And he smiled his pale sad smile, moistening his lips with his snaky tongue. His fine small teeth were turned inwards, like the spokes of a lobster-pot. "So you will agree to let me send you?" I nodded and he sighed with unfeigned relief and rose to shake my hands with a surprising gratitude. "You don't know how much pleasure it will give me to send you to see my associates; even if nothing should come of it I shall feel I have discharged my obligation to you. Certainly you will have nothing to complain of from the firm."

The blue sunlight of Athens seemed so firm and stable a backcloth to my restless ideas that I was not conscious of having made any kind of decision, far less a momentous one. Hippolyta slept in her cane chair under a fallen triumphant newspaper, showing a tip of tongue, smiling like a javelin-thrower who has scored a hit. Caradoc, beside her, put a finger to his lips and smiled. It was still early, the bees dew-capped from the flowers they visited. "An olive-branch nailed to the inn-door of the world." Far away in the harbour the sirens went bim and their echoes bim bim to slap the buttocky waters of the sound, scattering from one steel surface to the next. "I am going to Turkey." Caradoc gestured. "Shh!"

So we sat, hushed in sunlight, until I felt a drowsiness creeping over me—compact with fragments seeded from recent memories of conversations jumbled and jostled—switching points like express trains as they roared through deserted junctions. Hippo, for example, in a reported speech: "I cannot sleep alone, yet no-one pleases me. It is a real dilemma." The turntable spinning away into sleep, lips parted. Then with equal suddenness some articles from Sipple's rooms which I was not conscious of having noticed at the time: cold prunes and custard in a chipped soup-plate, a blue enamel teapot, and a large pair of dressmaker's scissors. Then some unidentified naked woman from the Anthology, "of delicate address and lovely insinuation". Dead notes on a classical keyboard—or might it have been already Benedicta? Here is a love-letter. "Benedicta, I love you. The collection of delta spacings for several radiations permits the identification of spurious peaks resulting either from target contamination or incomplete filtration of K alpha radiation. Your Felix". Yes, on some mutinous machine like Abel, will dawn one day the cabyric smile. Idly drifting, thistledownwise came Koepgen with his "promissory notes drawn upon reality". Monks with impetigo, their heads shaved, arousing his pithy sarcasm with their great leather-bound octavo farts. "Must one, then, negotiate with God?" he exclaims oddly; hunting as if for a thorn one can't quite locate—this is not in my line. Some tiny tufts of north wind rise now and shuffle the roses. Caradoc is trying to keep awake by writing a Mnemon, as he calls it. We have promised to collaborate on a macabre pantomime to be called "The Babes in the Food". As sudden but less distinct comes the scorching rain of white roses in *Faust*—whole epochs of redemption or desire. Caradoc saying with much severity about K: "He has been slumming among the Gnostics, selling his birthright for a pot of message. He will end by becoming an Orthodox Proust or a monarcho-trappist. All monks are grotesque lay figures—figures of funk."

Then away beyond Cape Sunion towards those distant lighthouses of sorrow across the waters, memories of Leander, where the Moslem dead await us with an elaborate indifference. Sweet, aquiline and crucial rise the stalks of the women's tombs, the soulless women of the Islamic canon. In marble one can see the pointed conciseness of a death which promises no afterlife—without the placebo of soul or resurrection. My own faint snoring matches that of C's and the soft even breathing of Hippolyta in that Athenian sunlight.

III

Well, and so it was that the little Polybus alternately leeched and strode across the mountainous yet sunny Aegean, buffeted by a fresh north wind—a sea rolled into episodes, into long spitcurls of sea-sodium. The dirty little steamer was used to this and worse—the shrapnel bursts of spray along her grimy spars. On we went bounding like a celluloid duck. Mountains of excrement and vomit accompanied the dazed passengers, and the sea held until the straits were reached and we turned down the long brown sinus with its darned shrub—its hint of an alimentary canal leading to the inland sea. Here we gathered a hard-earned knot or two of speed. So upwards at last into a misty gulf and thence, wheeling now in a long arc to the left, to paddle into Kebir Kavak for *pratique*. Here, while they were hauling the yellow flag up and down and exchanging the windy garble of mariners' talk, I first set eyes on Mr. Sacrapant who had been detailed to meet me. He sat in the stern sheets of the quarantine cutter gazing with a kind of sweet holiness up into my face, watching my expression as I fingered the engraved visiting card. It had been sent aboard by a sailor and it read

Elias Sacrapant
B.Sc. Economics London (*external*)

I ducked and he ducked back; a faint smile illumined that pale clerkish countenance. The infernal noise of engines precluded more intimate exchanges. But presently he was allowed aboard. He negotiated the gangway with an erratic and somewhat elderly spriteliness. His hands were warm and tender, his eyes moist with emotion. "We have been waiting for you" he said almost reproachfully "with such impatience. And now Mr. Pehlevi is in the islands for the week-end. He asked me to look after you until he comes. I cannot express my pleasure, Mr. Charlock." It seemed a bit overdone but he was charming in his white drill suit, elastic-sided boots, and white straw hat. A very large tie-pin gathered the wings of his collar over his scraggy neck. His eyes were very pale blue. Once they may have been very beautiful, almost plumbago. He spoke English as it is learned in the commercial schools of the Levant, a sort of anglo-tradesman; but very accurately and with a pretty accent. "You may relax, Mr. Charlock, for you are in my hands. I will answer any questions you put. I am the firm's senior adviser."

And so it was with Sacrapant as a companion that I came upwater at last to dangle in view of the Golden Horn where the immense inertia—the marasmus of Turkey—drifted out with sea-damps to finger my soul. Cryptogram, yes, these huge walls of liquid dung baked by the sun into tumefied shapes. It all had a fine deliquescent charm—the coaxing palms, the penis-turreted domes, the lax and faded colouring of a dream turning to nightmare. Mr. Sacrapant pointed out all the sights and explained them carefully, with the exactitude of a book-keeper, but in kindly fashion, chuckling from time to time as he did so. Moreover he was splendidly efficient, darting here and there with tickets and passports, buttonholing officials, exhorting sailors and porters. "For tonight the Pera hotel" he explained "will enable you to rest. There is every luxe. Tomorrow I will come and take you to the Pehlevi *danglion*—a water pavilion. It is prepared for you. It will be very comfortable. You will be just fine, fine." He repeated the word with his characteristic pious effervescence, joining his hands together and squeezing them. Very well.

It was the least I could do to offer him dinner when at last we arrived, and he accepted the invitation with alacrity. I confess that with the sinking sun on that gaunt but beautiful terrace I was glad of company for I felt the death-grip of the Turkish night settling upon me—a sort of nameless panic wafted up with the smell of jasmine from the gardens below, from the chain-mail ramparts of forts and ravelins which enclose Polis like the scar tissue of old wounds upon which the blood has dried black. Sacrapant was someone to talk to—but not until our meal was well on its way. He addressed himself to the menu with the same fervour—indeed he removed his wrist-watch and placed it in a safe corner before picking up his knife and fork. Also he put upon his nose a pair of pince-nez the better to instruct me in the intricacies of the local cuisine. A small vermouth had brought a flush to his cheek. But at last, somewhat assuaged by the fare, he leaned back and undid his coat buttons. "I cannot tell you what pleasure it gives me" he said "to think of you joining the firm—O I know that you have only come to discuss with Mr. Pehlevi." Here he pointed his long forefinger at his own earhole to show that he knew the subject of our discussion. "But if you agree with him, you will never never repent, Mr. Charlock. Merlin's is a marvellous firm to work for—or to let it work for you." He chuckled and rolled his eye. "Marvellous" he said. "Whether one is its slave or its master." I stared at him, eager to know more.

Mr. Sacrapant continued: "Excuse me if you think my feelings are excessive, but when I look at you I can't help the thought that if I had a son he would be about your age. With what joy I would have seen him enter Merlin's." He spoke about the organisation as if it were a religious order. "That is why." And he gave my hand a shy pat, adding ruefully "But Mrs. Sacrapant can only make girls with me, five girls. And here in Stamboul for girls . . ." He rubbed finger and thumb together expressively and hissed on a lower note the word "Dowries". Then he once more lay back in a sort of infantile rapture and went on. "But there again, the firm, thank God for the jolly old firm. They will look after all. No detail is too small, and no organisation offers comparable status and benefits in the Levant. We are a hundred years ahead of our time." He poured himself a thimbleful of wine and drank it off like a hero.

It was puzzling, this string of homilies—as if he had been sent to soften me up before my negotiations with Pehlevi began. And yet . . . Sacrapant was so guileless and so likeable. He dropped his napkin, and in retrieving it inadvertently revealed a strip of sock and calf. I was intrigued to see, strapped to his thin ankle, a small scout-knife such as a girl-cub might use to pierce the tinfoil on a jampot. He followed the direction of my glance. "Shh" said Mr. Sacrapant. "Say nothing. In Stamboul, Mr. Charlock, one never knows. But if attacked by a Moslem I would give a good account of myself—you may be sure." He blushed and tittered and then all at once became grave, plunged in reverie. "Tell me more about the firm" I said, since it seemed his only topic. He sighed. "Ah the firm!" he said. "When will I ever cease to be grateful to it? But I will do better, I will show it to you. I have instructions to do so. At least as much of it as we manage from here—for we are only the Levant end. The firm is world-wide, you know, in London Berlin New York. Mr. Pehlevi's brother Julian runs the London end. Yes, you shall see it for yourself. It will take up the time until Mr. Jocas comes back from the islands on Monday." It sounded an interesting way of passing the time and seeing something of the city. As I walked him through the damp garden with its throbbing crickets he went on sincerely, rather touchingly. "You know—perhaps you don't—how hard it is in the Levant to have any sort of security, Mr. Charlock. It is hard to earn good money if you have children. That is why I am so happy. The firm has meant to me serenity for wife and loved ones. Yes, and insurance too, we are all covered. Believe me, outside the firm it can be . . . very hard cheese I think you say in English? Very hard cheese."

Before taking the one dilapidated taxi he lingered for some further chatter, unwilling to end the evening; and I was glad, thinking of the ghastly bedroom that awaited me. I had forgotten to bring something to read. For his part Sacrapant behaved like a man who had been deprived of any social life, who was hungry for company. Yet he had only this one topic, the firm. "You see it is very wide. Old Mr. Merlin the founder did not believe in building up and cornering one market; he preferred to build horizontally." He drew his hand along his body with a stroking gesture. "We are very wide rather than very tall. There is great variety of holdings, but few are exclusive to ourselves. That is why the firm is so wide, why there is room for everyone in it—well, almost everyone." Here he stopped and frowned. "There are some exceptions. I forgot to tell you that Count Banubula is staying in your hotel. Now he is one. He has tried for years to join the firm but with no hope. It is nothing to do with his behaviour, though when he is in Stamboul he behaves . . . well, very strangely. You know him I think."

"Yes, of course. But what has he done?"

"I don't know" said Mr. Sacrapant compressing his lips and shooting me a furtive glance. "But I expect the firm does. Anyway, they will not let him in; he has exhausted his nerves in pleading but Mr. Jocas is adamant. There are one or two like him. The firm makes an example of them, and they are blocked. It is a huge pity for him for he is a gentleman, though his behaviour in Stamboul would not let you think so."

"But he is a very mild and quiet man."

"Ah" said Mr. Sacrapant on a reproving note.

"And is Merlin still alive?"

"No" said Mr. Sacrapant, but he spoke in a whisper this time, and in a fashion that somehow carried little conviction. I had the impression that he was not at all certain. "Of course not" he added, trying to bolster the simple affirmative; but all of a sudden he looked startled and somewhat discountenanced, like a frightened rabbit. He took my hand and squeezed it saying: "I will come tomorrow and take you down to the offices for a look. Now I must go." On this somewhat ambiguous note we parted. I turned back into the hotel relieved to see that there were still a few lights on—notably in the bar. And here I was overjoyed to come upon Count Banubula, the only occupant of the place, gloomily consulting his own reflections in the tarnished mirrors.

His appearance had undergone a subtle change which had not been apparent when I entered the room. How to say it? He looked flushed, snouty, and somehow concupiscent. He swayed ever so slightly, almost imperceptibly, as very tall buildings do. "Ah" he said as he caught sight of me, in a new and rather insolent fashion. "Ah Charlock!" I echoed his "Ah" on the same note, my curiosity aroused, for this was certainly not the Count Banubula I knew. "What about a little drink?" he went on sternly. It was virtually an order and I obeyed gladly. His waistcoat was undone and his monocle tinkled loosely against the buttons. The light was too bad to enable me to be sure, but it seemed to me that his lips and eyebrows had been discreetly touched up. This is, of course, a service which any barber will perform in the Orient on request. Banubula raised the sad plumes of his heavy eyebrows and closed his eyes, breathing slowly through his nose. Yes, he was drunk.

The barman produced two whiskies and disappeared through a hatch. Still with eyes shut the Count said: "I knew you were coming. I have been here some time. Ah, my goodness, if you only knew. I can't leave till Thursday now." He started an involuntary spin like a top, and just managed to find his way to a chair. "Sit" he said, in the same authoritative way. "It is better so." I obeyed, and sat opposite him, staring at him. There was a very long silence, so long indeed that I thought he would drop off to sleep but no, he had been setting his mind to the problem of conversation. "Do you know what Caradoc said about me?" asked the Count with slow sad tones. "He said I looked like a globe artichoke, and that I would die, a whisky-stiffened mummy in some Turkish bagnio." He gave a sudden squawk of laughter and then sank back into this oozing gloom, eyeing me narrowly. "Cruel man" he said. "They are all cruel men. For years I have done their dirty work. There have never been the small rewards I asked for. Nothing. No hope. I go on and on. But I have reached the end of my tether. I am in despair, Charlock. At my age one can't go on and on and on and on. . . ." his voice sank into a mumble. "But who are these people?" I said.

"It isn't anybody special, it's just the firm."

"Merlin's?"

He nodded sadly. "O Lord" I said "does no one talk about anything else in this city?"

The Count had taken a leap into autobiography and did not heed my remark. "I love my dear wife" he said "and I esteem her. But now she sits all day with her hair done up in a scarf and curl papers writing long letters about God to Theosophists. And I have become abnormal, you see Charlock? Without wishing it. In these hot climates one cannot be deprived of one's rights without something happening. Since she became religious all is ended; yet I could never divorce her because of the scandal. My name is an ancient one." He blew his nose violently in a silk handkerchief and dibbled a finger in his right ear to clear it. Then he shook his head with equal violence, as if to clear his brain. "And then all these negotiations, all this pleading. It has made me a very superstitious man, Charlock. I feel I must try and avert a horrible fate—unless they relent. Look!" He threw open his waistcoat to reveal a plump white chest to which was attached an iodine locket. He waited for my comment, but it was somewhat difficult to find words; the iodine locket was the talisman of the day, much advertised in the vulgar press. It promised health to the wearer for a very small outlay. "But health is no good" said Banubula sadly "if one's fate is wrong. I have been a student of Abraxas for several years now, and I know my fate is wrong. Do you know how I defend myself?" I shook my head. He detached from his key ring a small Chaldean bronze leaf inscribed after the fashion of amulets thus:

S A T O R
A R E P O
T E N E T
O P E R A
R O T A S

Banubula nodded like a mandarin. "It is only to prove to you that I have tried everything. I even tried love potions on my spouse, but they made her violently ill. I meant well. That much you will grant me." I nodded, granting him that much.

"O God" said Banubula, drinking deeply, thirstily. "My sorrow seems bottomless, bottomless." The choice of phrase seemed to me bizarre, but I did not comment. "Just how would things change if... if all these negotiations were successful?" I asked. At once his large hairless face changed its expression, became animated with a fiery enthusiasm. "Ah then everything would be different, don't you see? I should be *in*!"

The officious barman started to bang shutter and door and indicate brusquely that the bar was closing; he refused us another drink. "You see?" said the Count. "My whole life is like that—one refusal follows another, everywhere, in everything." His lower lip dipped steeply towards a self-commiserating burst of tears, but he restrained them manfully. "To bed I think" I said, with as much cheerfulness as I could muster. And I did what I could to steer the yawing bulk of the Count upstairs to bed. "I won't bother to undress" he said cheerfully, falling upon his bed. "Goodnight."

I turned at the door to find that he was regarding me with one eye open with the air of a highly speculative jackdaw. "I know" he said "you are dying to question me about him. But I know so little."

"Could Sipple be working for Merlin's?"

"Certainly. At any rate it was they who cabled and telephoned to Hippolyta asking her, us, to get him over to Polis as swiftly as was humanly possible."

"What on earth could Sipple do? Spy?"

Banubula yawned and stretched. "As for the boy you said you . . . found; that has nothing to do with the case. I mean it's a quite independent fact which has nothing to do with the firm. It's Sipple's own business."

"But how do you know about it?"

"Sipple told me. He denied having anything to do with it."

"There was no mention in the newspapers; somebody *must* have found the body. Who hushed the whole matter up?"

"In the Middle East" said Banubula sighing "a London detective would go out of business; there are so many people with such unusual motives. . . . I mean, look, suppose Sipple's landlord thought that the discovery of a corpse would prejudice him letting the room to someone else. What would he do? He would put it in a sack and slip it into one of the sewers, or take it to the top of Hymettus and fling it into a crevasse—there are some hundreds of feet deep, sheer falls, never been explored." Banubula cleared his throat and went on in a shyer tone of voice. "Once I was forced to get rid of a rival for my wife's hand in somewhat the same fashion; though in my case it was complicated by blackmail and menaces."

"You killed a man?" I said admiringly.

"Yes . . . well . . . rather" said the Count with modesty.

He lay back, closing his eyes and breathing coolly through his nose. Then he said in somewhat oracular fashion: "Haven't you noticed Charlock that most things in life happen just outside one's range of vision? One has to see them out of the corner of one's eye. And any one thing could be the effect of any number of others? I mean there seem to be always a dozen perfectly appropriate explanations to every phenomenon. That is what makes our reasoning minds so unsatisfactory; and yet, they are all we've got, this shabby piece of equipment." He would doubtless have had more to say, but sleep gained on him steadily and in a while his mouth fell open and he began to snore. I slipped off the light and closed the door softly.

* * * * *

Sacrapant was as good as his word and appeared next morning on the dot—but this time with a big American car driven by a Turk dressed in a sort of bloodstained butcher's smock. He was all frail animation and charm as we bumped and careered down towards the waterside sectors of the town, through souks rendered colourless now by the dreadful European reach-me-downs worn by the inhabitants of this artificially modernised land. At the best the Turks of the capital looked opium-ridden, or as if clubbed half insensible; the clothes set off their mental disarray to perfection. Of course I did not voice my sentiments as strongly as this, but my hints were enough to convey the general drift of my thoughts to Mr. Sacrapant. To my surprise he expressed stern disapproval. "They may be ugly" he said. "But thanks to them we brought off one of our biggest *coups*. The firm was in touch with Mustafa's party when it was still a secret society. It knew his plans, and that when it came to power it would abolish the fez and the Arabic script. It waited. By skilful bribing we made an agreement, and the very day the *firman* was launched, we had six ships full of cloth caps standing by in the roads! We swamped the market. We had also collared the contracts for printing of stamps and the national stationery—we had been importing presses for months. You see what I mean? Doing business in the Levant is rather a special thing." He bridled, flushed with pride. I could see that all right, O yes.

The oldfashioned counting-house, down among the stinking tanneries of the yards, was rather impressive; the interior walls of three large factories had been taken out and replaced by a huge acreage of tile floor. Here, cheek by jowl, worked the Merlin employees, their desks brow to brow, practically touching one another. A deep susurrous of noise rose as if from a wasp's nest, deepened by the throaty echo of electric fans. Here there seemed to be no sleep—I could hardly see one face that did not signal itself as belonging to a Greek, Jew, Armenian, Copt, Italian. A sort of dramatic electrical current seemed to have generated itself. Sacrapant walked between the desks, bursting with a kind of hallowed civic pride, nodding to right and left. I could see from the way he was greeted that he was much beloved. He walked as a man might show off a garden, stopping here and there to pluck a flower. I was introduced to a few people, a swift sample, so to speak; they all spoke good English and we exchanged pleasantries. Also, in one corner—the only screened section—I was presented to three elderly men of Swiss accent and mien: they looked both authoritative and determined. They were dressed in formal oldfashioned tail-coats which must have been stifling to wear in summer. "They speak all our languages" said Mr. Sacrapant, adding: "You see here each man is very much head of his own section. We have decentralised as much as humanely possible. The great variety of our work permits it." He picked a bundle of ladings and C.I.F. telegrams off a desk and rapidly clipped out the words "Beirut, Mozambique, Aleppo, Cairo, Antananarivo, Lagos."

I accepted a traditional black coffee of the oriental variety and expressed my approval of all this creditable activity; afterwards we stepped out blinking into the sunlight. Sacrapant had taken the day off in order to show me something of the town and together we walked laterally across it, making clever detours to visit the choicer monuments. In the honeyed gloom of the covered bazaars I bought a few coins and some beaten silver wire of Yemeni origin, with the vague intention of presenting them to Hippolyta on my return. We sauntered through the courtyards of sunbaked mosques, pausing to feed the pigeons from a paper bag full of Indian *gram*. Thence to Al Quat for a really excellent lunch of pigeon and rice. It was late afternoon by the time we started to saunter back to the hotel, and by now I had come to see what an immense graveyard Stamboul is, or seems to be. The tombs are sown broadcast, not gathered together in formalised squares and rectangles. Graveyards were spread wherever humanity had scratched up a tombstone behind it, as in a cat-box; here death seemed to be broadcast wholesale in quite arbitrary fashion. A heavy melancholy, a heavy depression seemed to hang over these beautiful empty monuments. Turkey takes time to know.

Truth to tell, I was rather anxious to leave it and get back to the noisy but freer air of Athens. "You have brought your box, of course?" said Mr. Sacrapant. "I know that Mr. Pehlevi is most anxious to see it." But of course he would not be available for another twenty-four hours; yes, I had brought my box. Mr. Sacrapant accepted tea and toast and reminisced awhile about the business community of Smyrna where he had learned his English. In parenthesis he added: "By the way, Mr. Pehlevi told me to tell you that there is a commercial counsellor here and he will insist that any contracts we offer you should be seen by him. Just in case you have no business head. He wants everything to be above board and clear. It is part of our policy. I have told Mr. Vibart and he agrees to advise you. So all is in order." I have no idea why this remark should have seemed slightly ominous to me but it did. He sighed, and with great reluctance excused himself, saying that he had a dinner engagement. For my part, after so long and exhausting a walk, I was glad to go to my room and siesta—which I did to such good effect that it was after dark when I awoke and groped my way distractedly down to dinner. There was no sign of Banubula in the dining room, and there were few other guests whose appearance offered hope of time-killing conversation. But later I ran him down in the sunken billiard room playing mournful Persian airs on a very tinny cottage piano. Several large whiskies stood before him—a precaution against the barman with his capricious habits of shutting up the bar when drinks were most needed. He was, I should say, a little less drunk than he had been the evening before, though the number of the whiskies boded little good; he allowed me to take one and sit beside him. He was in a morose, cantakerous mood, and was hitting a lot of false notes. At last he desisted, banged the piano shut. "Well," he said, sucking his teeth "tonight I will be handing over Sipple, and then byebye to Polis."

"Handing over? Is he in irons?"

"He should be" said Banubula savagely. "They all should be."

He growled awhile into his waistcoat and then went on. "I suppose you have seen Pehlevi, eh? That swine!" Such an outburst from this mild, courteous and bookish man was astonishing.

"Tomorrow." Banubula sighed and shook his head with a gloomy star-crossed expression.

"Tomorrow you will be *in*, over my head."

It was my turn to get annoyed by this repetitive and meaningless reiteration—this eternal *mélopée.* "Listen to me" I said poking his waistcoat. "I am not in, not out, and will not be. This might be a commercial agreement over a small toy which may make me some money, that is all. Do you hear?"

"You will see" he grunted.

"Moreover any contracts will be vetted by the commercial consul" I added primly.

"Ha ha."

"Why ha ha?"

"Over whose dead body?" said Banubula inconsequentially. "Over mine, my boy. In you go and out I shall stay." He drained a tumbler and set it down with exaggerated care. Then all of a sudden the cloud seemed to lift a little. He smiled complacently and stroked his chin for awhile, looking at me sideways. "Caradoc does not spare our infirmities" he said.

"Is *he* in?"

Banubula looked at me incredulously. "Of course" he said with disgust. "Has always *been* in; but he wants to get *out*!"

"It's like a bloody girls' school" said I.

"Yes" he said with resignation. "You are right. But let us talk about something pleasanter. If I had not been on duty here I might have shown you some of the sights of the capital. Things that most people don't see. In one of the kiosks of the Seraglio, for example, is Abdul Hamid's collection of dildoes, brought together from all over the world; all carefully labelled and dusted. He was impotent, they say, and this was one of his few pleasures."

"Is old Merlin still alive?" I asked suddenly. Banubula shot me a glance and sat up straight for a moment. Ignoring my remark he went on: "They were kept in a long row of pipe-racks presented by the British Government in a vain attempt to curry favour with him. The names were so beautiful—*passiatempo* in Italian, *godemiche* or *bientateur* in French. No? They illustrate national attitudes better than anything else, the names. The German one was called the *phallus phantom*—a ghostly metaphysical machine covered with death-dew. Alas, my boy, I have not the time to show you this and other treasures."

"It's a great pity."

Banubula consulted his watch with pursed lips. "In another half hour they will take over and I shall be free. But I think I should just make sure that Sipple is all right. Do you want to come with me?"

"No."

"It won't involve us in anything, you know."

I looked and felt somewhat doubtful; depressed as I was at the thought of spending another evening here alone I did not want to become involved in any of the Count's escapades. On the other hand I was a bit anxious for his own safety. It seemed unwise to leave him alone. I must have looked as confused as I felt for he said, cajolingly, "Come on. It will take me a quarter of an hour. I will just peep through the curtain at the Seamen's Relief Club, and then we can return happy in the thought of duty well and faithfully done."

"Very well" I said. "First let me see that you can walk straight." Banubula looked wounded in his self-esteem. He rose heavily to his feet and took a very creditable turn or two up and down the room. His own steadiness rather surprised him. He looked somewhat incredulous to find himself navigating with such ease. "You see?" he said. "I'm perfectly all right. Anyway we will take a cab. I'll send these remaining whiskies up to my room for safety and we can go. Eh?"

He pressed the bell for the waiter, and gave his instructions in faultless Turkish which I envied him.

Once more we slanted down the ill-lit streets where the occasional tram squealed like a stuck pig. Banubula consulted a pocket notebook which appeared to have a rough plan pencilled into it. Why not a compass? I wondered. So like an explorer did he behave. We left the taxi on a street corner and set off in an easterly direction, skirting the bazaars. The Count walked in what I can only describe as a precautionary way, stopping from time to time, and looking behind, as if to see whether we were being trailed or not. Perhaps he was showing off? The town smelt heavily of tannin and garbage. We crossed a series of small squares and skirted the walled exterior of mosques. The city seemed to become more and more deserted and somewhat sinister. Finally however we reached a corner where light and noise abounded, where spits hissed and bagpipes skirled. A section of the sky had been cut out by the flares. There can be no mistake about the

Greek quarter of any town. An infernal industry and gaiety reigns. Here we entered a large café the interior of which was full of mirrors and birdcages, and domino players, and crossing it reached a courtyard where, in the dimness, a notice could just be discerned which read "Seamen's Relief Club". Banubula grunted as he addressed himself to a flight of creaky stairs. "How does one relieve a seaman?" I asked, but the Count did not reply.

On the first floor there was a sort of large drill hall full of smoke and the noise of feet and chairs scraping; there was also a good deal of laughter and clapping, as if at some performance or other. Banubula stopped outside a dirty door sealed by a bead curtain. "I'm not going in," he hissed "but we'll just see. I think he's acting the fool for them now." And with sinking feelings I heard the flat nasal whine of Sipple, punctuated by the roars of laughter of the merry tars. "Yes, you may laugh, my sirs, you may laugh—but you are laughing at tragedy. Once I was like you all, I wore me busby at an angle. Then came that fatal day when I found myself abrogated. I found myself all slantingdicular to the world. Up till then my timbrel was normal, my pressure quite serene. I lived with Mrs. Sipple in a bijou suburban house with bakelite elves on the front lawn. Not far from Cockfosters it was. (Cheers!) Every day I rose, purified by sleep, to bathe and curl my hair, and put on a clean artichoke. I travelled to Olympia in a Green Line bus like the public hangman with my clothes in a bag. It wasn't exacting, to act the clown—a pore fart-buffeted blorque. But when me whiffler abrogated I lost all my confidence. (Clapping.) Ah you may laugh, but when your whiffler becomes a soft lampoon what's to be done? I found my reason foundering, gentlemen. I started drinking tiger-drench. I had become alembicated. I had begun to exflunctify. Then when I went to see the doctor all he said was: 'Sipple you are weak in Marmite.' "

All this must have been accompanied by some fitting stage business of an obscene kind for it was greeted with roars of laughter. From where we stood we could not see Sipple; the balcony overhung him. He was immediately beneath us; all we could see was, so to speak, his reflection in the semicircle of barbarous faces, expressing a huge coarse gratification. Banubula consulted his watch. "Four more minutes" he said. "And then he's off. Phew, what a relief!" He stretched in the gloom and yawned. "Now let's go and have a drink, what?" We went downstairs again and crossed the courtyard; as we reached the lighted café a large black car drew up in the street outside and two men climbed out, yawning, and made their way directly past us, looking neither to right nor left. Banubula watched them pass with a smile. "That's the committee" he whispered. "Now we are free." And in a heavy jolting way he started to hurry along the street towards the corner of the square where the taxis were, coiling and uncoiling long legs.

"I can't tell you the relief" he said sinking back at last on the back seat cushions and mopping his brow. Indeed his face had become almost juvenile and unlined. "Now you can come and watch me pack, and I will share my whisky with you." I was puzzled by my own equanimity, by the ease with which I seemed to be accepting this succession of puzzling (even a little disquieting) events. "I've stopped asking questions" I said aloud to myself. Banubula overheard me and gave a soft chuckle. "Just as well to save your breath" he said.

I sat on the bed and watched this infernally clumsy bear-like man trying to fold a pair of trousers and squeeze them into his suitcase. He was a trifle tipsy again, and his little performance would have almost done credit to the clown Sipple. "Here," I said "let me help you." And gratefully Banubula slumped into a chair and mopped his white brow. "I don't know what it is about clothes" he said. "They have always eluded me. They seem to have a life of their own, and it doesn't touch my life at any point. Nevertheless I wear them very gracefully, and pride myself on being quite smartly turned out. These shoes come from Firpo in Bond Street." He stared at them complacently.

I had shaken a batch of notepaper out of his coat pocket; it fell on the floor. "O dear O dear," said the Count "how forgetful I am." He took the papers, set them alight in the ashtray and sat watching the flame like a child, poking at it with a matchstick until the paper was consumed and the ash broken up. Then he sighed and said: "To-morrow I shall return to Athens and my dear. To resume my old life again."

"And Sipple?" I asked, curiosity getting the better of me. "What will become of him?" Banubula played with his lucky charm and reflected. "Nothing very special" he said. "No need for dramatic imaginings. Hippolyta says she was told that he was an expert on precious stones; that would give him a connection with Merlin all right. Then someone else said he was retained by the Government to supply political intelligence. There again . . . much can be learned in the brothels of Athens. Politicians build up dossiers about each other's weaknesses and there is hardly one who hasn't some pretty little perversion up his sleeve which could lay him open to political pressure, or even blackmail. Graphos makes them dress up and whips them mildly, so they say; others have more elaborate needs. Pangarides insists on the 'chariot'. . . ."

"What is the chariot?"

"It's really a Turkish invention I suppose. A sort of *en brochette* effect. I've never tried. It's having a small boy while the small boy himself is having a girl. With clever timing it is supposed to. . . . But heavens, why am I telling you all this? I am usually so discreet."

He sighed heavily. I could see that he was possessed by a heavy sense of regret that he should soon be called upon to resume the trappings of respectability in Athens. "Why don't you stay here, and live in a bagnio?" I asked and he sighed. Then his expression changed: "And the Countess, my wife? How could I?" Affection for her flooded into him; tears came to his eyes. "She is devoted to me" he said under his breath. "And I have nobody else in the world." His tone touched me.

"Well. Goodnight, then" I said, and he shook my hand warmly.

Next morning I slept late, and when at last I came downstairs I found that the Count had left for Galata; he had favoured me with a last communication in the form of a visiting card with a crown below the name Count Horatio Banubula and a few words pencilled on it. "Above all be discreet" he had written. But what the devil had I to reveal—and to whom?

Sacrapant was not due to appear before dusk so I lazed away the heat of the day in the garden under the shining limes watching the shifting hazes of the skyline condense and recondense as the sun reached its meridian. As it overpassed and began to decline the army of domes and steeples began to clarify once more, to set like jelly.

Light sea airs from the Bosphorus were invading the Horn now, driving the damp atmosphere upwards into the town. It must have been some sort of festival day, too, for the sky was alive with long-tailed kaleidoscopic box-kites—and by the time we reached the water under the Galata Bridge to pick up the steam pinnace which had been sent for me, I could look back and upwards at a skyline prepared as if for some mad children's carnival. In such light, and at such a time of day, the darkness hides the squalor and ugliness of the capital, leaving exposed only the pencilled shapes of its domes and walls against the approaching night; and moreover if one embarks on water at such an hour one instantly experiences a lift of the senses. The sea-damp vanishes. God, how beautiful it is. Light winds pucker the gold-green waters of Bosphorus; the gorgeous melancholy of the Seraglio glows like a rotting fish among its arbours and severe groves. Edging away from the land and turning in a slow half-arc towards Bosphorus I allowed Mr. Sacrapant to point out for me features like the seamark known as Leander's tower, and a skilfully sited belvedere in a palace wall whence one of the late Sultans enjoyed picking off his subjects with a crossbow as they entered his field of vision. Such were the amenities of palace life in far-off times. But now our wake had thickened and spread like butter under a knife, and Sacrapant had to hold on to his panama hat as we sped along, curving under the great placid foreheads and wide eyes of two American liners which were idling up the sound. It grew mildly choppy too as we rounded the cliffheads and turned into the Bosphorus. The light was fading, and one of the typical sunsets of Stamboul was in full conflagration; the city looked as if it were burning up the night, using the approaching darkness as fuel. Sacrapant waved his arm at it and gave a small incoherent cry of pleasure—as if he had momentarily forgotten the text of the caption which should go with such a picture. But we were near in to the nether shore now and travelling fast; stone quays and villages of painted wooden houses rolled up in scroll-fashion and slipped away behind us. Here, rising out of a dense greenery, one caught glimpses of walled gardens, profiles of kiosks smothered in amazed passion flowers, marble balconies, gardens starred with white lilies. Then higher up again small meadows shaded by giant plane-trees, leading to softly contoured hilltops marked with umbrella pine or the slim pin of a cypress, eye-alerting as a cedilla in some forgotten tongue. Thickets of small shipping passed us, plodding industriously into the eye of the sunset, heading for Galata. Somewhere hereabouts, in one of the small sandy coves with high cliffs, would be the wooden landing stage which marked the entry to that kingdom Merlin had called "Avalon". Sacrapant explained that it was a ruin when Merlin bought it—part Byzantine fortress and part ruined Seraglio which had belonged to a rich Ottoman family that had fallen into disgrace. "The sultan expunged them all" said Sacrapant with a kind of sad relish. "It was named thus by Mr. Merlin himself." He made a motion with his slender hand.

It was still light when we came into the landing stage where the small group of servants awaited us, two of them with lanterns already lighted against the approaching night. They were supervised by a fat bald-headed capon of a man whom I had no hesitation in identifying as a eunuch. It was partly because of the unhealthy lard-coloured pallor of his skin: partly because of the querulous spinster's voice which inhabited the fat body. He bowed in deeply submissive manner. Mr. Sacrapant waved him away with my suitcase as together we walked up a steep path into the garden of a small villa, with charming vine-trellises on three sides, and a fine balcony overlooking the sound. This was apparently where I was to stay, and here I found my case already lying on the bed open; two servants under the supervision of the bald majordomo were hanging up my clothes. Sacrapant had a good look round and satisfied himself that all was well with me before taking his leave. "I am going back with the boat" he said. "Now in half an hour a man with a lantern will come to lead you to the villa where Mr. Jocas will be waiting for you—both of them in fact."

"Both brothers?"

"No. Miss Benedicta arrived last night. She is staying for a few days here in the other villa. You will meet her also."

"I see. How long do I stay?"

Mr. Sacrapant looked startled. "As long as . . . I don't know sir . . . as is necessary to conclude your business with Mr. Jocas. As soon as you see him all will become clear."

"Have you ever heard the name Sipple?" I asked.

Sacrapant thought gravely and then shook his head. "Never to my knowledge" he said at last.

"I thought perhaps as you knew Count Banubula you might also know Sipple, an aquaintance of his."

Sacrapant looked desolated, and then his face cleared. "Unless you mean Archdeacon Sipple. Of course! The Anglican clergyman."

It did not seem a fruitful line of enquiry to pursue, and I let it slide out of the picture. I strolled back with him towards the landing stage, along the winding paths which smelt of some powerful scent—was it verbena? "One more thing" I said, in spite of myself. "Who was the young woman watching us as the launch pulled in? Up there among the trees. She turned back and slipped into that little copse there."

"I saw no one" said Sacrapant. "But that is where Miss Benedicta's villa is; but you know, Mr. Charlock, it might have been anyone from the harem. There are still quite a lot of old aunts and governesses living there. Mr. Merlin was very generous to both relations and servants. Why, it could have been her English or French teacher—both live there still."

"She was youngish, handsome, dark."

"Well it was not Miss Benedicta, then."

He said goodbye with a shade of effusive reluctance; I felt that he would very much have liked to accept an invitation himself to the Pehlevi table. But it was not to be; he sighed twice, heavily, and once more took his place in the pinnace. The crew was Turkish, but the captain was Greek, for he spoke to Sacrapant in his mother tongue, saying something about the wind freshening. My friend answered impatiently, placing his hat safely beside him. He gave me a small genteel wave as the distance lengthened between us.

I stood for a moment or two watching the light dying out along the mauve hills and combs of the Asiatic shore. Then I walked back to the little villa. Someone had already lighted the petrol lamps and their white fizzing flame carved black shadows out of the rooms around them. I shaved my jumping reflection in the bathroom mirror and put on the only summer suit I had brought with me. I was sitting, at peace with the world, on the side terrace when I saw a lantern coming slowly down through the trees towards me. It was held by the fat majordomo who had been present at the landing stage. He bowed, and without further words spoken I followed him slowly upwards through the gardens and copses towards where in some room (which I could not readily imagine) my host Jocas Pehlevi awaited to offer me dinner.

(If it gives me vague pleasure to recount all this, dactyl dear, it's because it seems about 100 years ago.)

It was eerie as well as rather beautiful to pass in this fashion up the hill, guided only by the single cone of light which threw up silhouettes of buildings without substance or detail. Owls cried among the bushes, and in the heavy night air, the perfumes hung on, insisted. We crossed a ruined quadrangle of some sort, followed by a series of warrens which suggested kennels; ducked through an arch and walked along the side of a ruined turret on a broad flagged staircase. Now lights began and the bulk of the main house came into view. It suggested to me a huge Turkish khan built as such caravanserais were, around a central courtyard with a central fountain; I heard, or seemed to hear, the champing of mules or camels and the whine of mastiffs. Up through a central massive door and along a corridor lighted with rather splendid frail gas-mantles. Jocas was sitting at a long oak table, half turned sideways towards the door which admitted me, staring into my eyes.

In those disproportionately huge hands he held a piece of string with which he had constructed a cat's cradle. As we looked seriously at each other I received a sudden flock of different impressions—almost like a shower of arrows. I felt at once a feeling of being in the presence of someone of great virtue, of psychic goodness, if you like; simultaneously, like an electric current passing in me, I felt as if the contents of my mind had been examined and sifted, and as if all my pockets had been turned out. It is a disquieting effect that one sometimes runs into with a medium. Side by side with this however I had an impression of a naive and almost foolish man, half crippled by nervousness. He was wearing, goodness only knows why, the traditional three-quarter frock coat and the Angora bonnet of wool—articles of attire which, on such a night, must have been a torture to support. Perhaps it was his desire to show some little formality towards a stranger? I don't know. I stared at that strange face with its swirling peruke of hair, and the tiny piratical rings in the ear lobes, and felt unaccountably reassured. When he stood up one saw that, though thick set, he was on the short side; but he had extremely long arms and huge hands. The hand that grasped mine was moist with anxiety—or perhaps just heat generated by the absurd clothes? He wore a couple of ribbons—a Légion d'Honneur and something else I could not identify. He said nothing; we just shook hands. He motioned me to an empty chair. Then he threw back his head and gave a laugh which might have seemed sinister had I not already taken such a liking to him. His canines were tipped with gold points which gave his smile a somewhat bloodthirsty effect. But his teeth were beautiful and regular and his lips were red. He was of a swarthy cast of countenance—a "smoked" complexion: and while he seemed a hale middle-aged man there was quite a touch of grey in his hair. "Well" he said. "So at last you have come to us." I excused myself for my dilatory habits and the delay I had caused. "I know, but you have other things to do, and are not interested in making money." I assured him that he was in error. "So Graphos says" he said, dropping the string into the wastepaper basket and moodily cracking a knuckle. He seemed plunged in thought for a moment; then his face changed expression. He became benign. "You see he was right, Charlock; there was no time to be lost, there never is in matters of this kind. You were distributing these things free, were you not? Well, I had one copied, and took our drawings and articles on it for a patent. In your name, of course. That means that whatever happens —you may not want to let us handle it—the invention is yours and can't be stolen." He waited a long time, staring sorrowfully at me. "My brother Chewlian did it for you. He runs the European side of the firm in London. He is an Oxford man, Chewlian." A haunted, wistful look came into his eye. "I have never been further than Smyrna, you see. Though one day. . . ." I thanked him most warmly for this kindly intervention on my behalf; he knew full well that I would not know how to go about patenting such an object. He got up to adjust a wavering gas-jet, saying as he did so: "I am very glad you are pleased. Now at the same time Chewlian drew up a contract offer for you to study. Benedicta brought it with her, you will have it tonight. Myself I think it errs on the side of over-generosity, but that is Chewlian all over!" He sighed in admiration at his brother. An expression almost maudlin in its affection crossed his face. "He behaves like a Prince not a businessman." Then all at once he grew tense and serious and said: "That remark has made you suspicious. Why?" It was perfectly true; and he had read my mind most accurately. I said lamely: "I was thinking how incompetent I am to understand business documents, and hoping you would give me time to think them out." He laughed again and slapped his knee as if at an excellent joke. "But of course you shall. Anyway you have already taken your precautions haven't you?" I saw from this that he knew I had decided to take Vibart's advice before signing anything.

I nodded. "Come, we will have a drink on it" he said cheerfully, going to the corner of the room where decanters and plates glimmered. He poured me a glass of fiery mastika and placed a cheese pie beside me on the arm of the chair. "But there is something much bigger than this one small thing. Chewlian says we should try and enter into association with you to handle all your inventions. You have others in mind, have you not?" He got up impatiently and strode up and down the room again, this time in a fit of vexation, saying: "There! once again I have made you suspicious. I am going too fast as always." He spoke a curious English with a strong Smyrna intonation, slurring the words as if he had picked them up by ear and had never seen them written. "No" I said. "It is just that the idea is completely novel to me."

He snorted and said, "My brother would have put it to you much more . . . gentlemanly I suppose. He says I am always like a carpet seller." He looked rueful and absurd in his black curate's tail coat. "Anyway he has sent us a draft paper—articles of association—for you to look at." He fingered the dimple in his chin for a moment and stared at me narrowly. "No" he said at last. "It is not suspicion so much. You are slow. To understand."

"I admit it."

"Never mind. When you understand you can see if you want to join us or not. The terms are generous, and nobody yet has been dissatisfied with the firm."

I tried my hardest not to think of Caradoc and his strictures lest my thoughts be read by this disarming yet determined little man. I nodded, attempting an air of sageness. He crossed to the door and called "Benedicta" once, on a sharp hawk-like note which was at once humble and imperious. Then he came back and stood in the centre of the room staring down at his own shoes. I looked about me studying the jumble of furniture and decoration which gave it the air of a store-room. An expensive chronometer on one wall. A case of chased silver duelling pistols. Then I identified the slightly sickly smell of rotting meat. In one corner on a tall perch slept a falcon in its soft velvet snood. From time to time it stirred and very faintly tinkled the small bells it wore. While we were waiting thus the door opened and a dark girl appeared, holding a briefcase which she placed in an armchair. I thought she bore a resemblance to the girl who had watched the launch come in to shore from the grove of trees up the hill. She stopped just outside the radius of the lamplight and said, in somewhat insolent fashion: "Why are you dressed up like that?" The note of icy contempt withered Jocas Pehlevi; he shrivelled to almost half his size, ducking and joining his hands almost in a gesture of supplication. "For him" he said. "For Mr. Charlock." She turned a glance of indifferent appraisal upon me, echoing my bow with a curt nod. It was a cold, handsome face, framed in a sheeny mass of dark hair twisted up loosely into a chignon. A high white forehead conferred a sort of serenity upon it; but when she closed her eyes, which she did in turning her head from one person to another, one could see at once how her death-mask would look. The lips were full and fine, but most of their expressions hovered between disdain and contempt. She was, then, as imperious as only a rich man's daughter dares to be: and noting this I conceived a sort of instant dislike for her which rendered her interesting.

Her entry had reduced Jocas to the dimensions of a small medieval playing-card figure; he scratched his head through the woollen bonnet. "Go and change at once" she said sternly reducing his self-esteem still further; he slipped away with an ingratiating bow in my direction, leaving us face to face. If she had moved forward a pace I would have been able to identify the peculiar blue of her eyes. But half in shadow like this they glowed with a sullen blue magnetism. She looked at me as if she had the greatest difficulty in mustering any interest in me or my doings. Then in a low voice she excused herself and turned aside to the dark corner of the room where the great falcon sat in the manner of a lectern-eagle. She was wearing a long, stained garment of some sort of leather or velveteen. Now she pulled on an extra sleeve and worked her hand into a gauntlet. Somewhere in the shadows there came the dying fluttering of some small bird, a quail perhaps, and I saw with disgust that she was busy breaking up the body with her fingers into small tid-bits. She suddenly began uttering a curious bubbling, crooning sound, uttering it over and over again as she drew a long plume softly over the legs of the peregrine; then the gloved hand teased the great scissor beak with the bleeding meat and the bird snapped and gorged. As it ate she reiterated the single word in the same crooning bubbling fashion. Slowly, with the greatest circumspection, she coaxed the falcon on to her wrist and turned to face me, smiling now. "He is the latest to be taken" she said. "I don't know as yet whether I shall succeed in bringing him to the lure. We shall see. Do you hunt? My father was a great falconer. But it takes an age to break them in."

At this moment the tall doors at the end of the room openedand I saw a long dinner table laid upon a wide balcony. Jocas had already arrived upon the scene after a change of clothes. He wore now a comfortable Russian shirt of some soft silky material. His mane of hair was brushed back above his ears. "Lights" called Benedicta sharply, and at once the servants diminished the amount of light by blowing out half the candles. This left a small lighted area at one end, with two places set. "Don't move please." Still softly crooning the girl advanced to the balcony and crossed it towards the shadowy end of the table where she was to sit throughout the meal, eating nothing herself, but from time to time feeding the falcon. Jocas and I sat at the other end of the table, served by the expressionless eunuch. Out of the corner of his eye the little man kept glancing at the girl with a professional curiosity. For her part she now removed the easy fitting rufter-hood for brief intervals, and then slipped it back into place. "It needs the patience of the devil" said Jocas. "But Benedicta is good. If you like we can take you for a day's sport—francolin and woodcock. Eh Benedicta?" But the girl sat absorbed before her plateful of bleeding odds and ends and did not deign to look up or answer. Presently she rose—it was part of the routine it seemed—and announced that she must "walk" the falcon; bidding us good-night she walked softly down the marble staircase into the garden and disappeared. It seemed to me that Jocas addressed himself to his dinner with a sort of relief after this—and he also became more voluble.

"Merlin was a great one for peregrines" he said. "And we have all taken after him—even down to small things. By the way, have you got the papers? In that briefcase Benedicta brought." He jumped up and fetched the article. "Here they are, you see, the two schemes set out separately. One is for the hearing device only; the other is a more detailed scheme—to manage all your work. You would become part of the firm, on a fixed retainer, with royalties etc." He replaced the documents carefully in the briefcase and patted it. "At your leisure: the patent is safe—only your signature is needed. But first you must see your advisers. Tomorrow I will send you back to Polis for the day, yes?"

"Tell me about the firm" I said, and Jocas twinkled with pride and pleasure, in a manner which reminded me a little of Sacrapant. "Well," he said "where to begin? Let me see."

"Begin with Merlin."

"Very well. Merlin was what you would call a merchant prince, a self-made prince. He arrived in Stamboul perhaps in the eighties of the last century on board a British yacht. He was a cabin boy. He deserted his ship, settled in the capital and began business. Much later when it had grown almost too big to handle he found myself and my brother and offered to let us become associates. How I bless the day." He joined his huge hands together and, laughing out loud, squeezed them until the knuckle joints cracked. "He was really a genius—you know all through the period of Abdul Hamid he never failed in his negotiations, he always got his firmans through. You know of course that Abdul Hamid was mad—mad with a fear of assassination. He lived up in the Yildiz palace in absolute terror. Loaded pistols lay in every corner, on every table. If startled by a sudden move he would open fire. Once his little niece ran into the room while he was dozing and he shot her. Merlin used to take special precautions when he went to see this madman—to walk slowly, talk slowly, sit quietly. He also worked out elaborate flatteries. Sent him a life-size sculpture of himself in butter, in ice-cream. Sent him clocks of extraordinary workmanship specially designed in Zürich. It was he too who achieved other objectives for the firm by skilfully planted rumours. Abdul Hamid was very superstitious and had his horoscope made afresh each day. The firm suborned the court astrologer. In this way Merlin became in a sense the most important man in Turkey. But he was as wise as he was foreseeing. All the time he was giving money to the revolutionaries, to the Young Turks. And then the fleet—it was allowed to lie there and rot in harbour because Merlin told Hamid a pack of rumours about the use the allies would make of it—playing on his fear and credulity. Why, I have seen those battleships rusting there all my life. They grow flowers on the decks. So gradually, even during the bad period, the firm grew and grew. Now of course times have changed, it is easier for us. Then when Merlin . . . left us, we two brothers took over the responsibility for Benedicta. We became her uncles." He laughed very heartily, wiping his eye in his sleeve. "And his wife?" I asked. All of a sudden Jocas looked nonplussed. His face grew serious. He thrust out his bearded chin and spread his hands in a gesture of inadequacy—as if he were powerless to answer the question satisfactorily. "There were many compromises made" he said, a trifle defensively. "There had to be. Merlin, for example, adopted the Muslim faith when he was in his fifties. Inevitably there were rumours of his wives and . . . ladies; but there was nothing very concise, very clear. This place was like a little walled city, and when you live *à la turque* the secrets of the harem are guarded from strangers. Benedicta was brought up in the harem, with foreign governesses first: then Switzerland for some years, that is why all her languages are so perfect." "But she is English?" Jocas nodded his head rapidly. "Yes. Yes. But I have never discussed with her, nor has Chewlian. Merlin never spoke with us about his private things. He was a very secretive man. I know that Chewlian also knows nothing because once he asked me."

Coffee, cigars and brandy found us removed to the further end of the terrace where a sort of belvedere had been improvised out of carpets and cushions, and here the conversation turned to the recording machine which I had put at the service of Hippolyta in Athens. "I heard about it from Graphos," admitted Jocas "and I could easily ask Chewlian to get me one and send it; but I understand that they are very hard to *drive*, no? And very delicate. So I waited to speak to you, to ask you about the matter."

"What would you use it for?" I asked, thinking of board-room meetings and the like. Jocas plucked his lips and looked sideways at me, with an air of exaggerated cunning. He considered. "I will tell you. We do not meddle in politics, as you know, but so often politics meddles with us that we really have to be up to date, to know what is afoot. At the moment there is a secret branch of the Young Turk officers having secret meetings. I do not want to spy on what they actually have to say; but I am on the look-out for one voice I know very well. If he has joined them, then I know all the rest. I would like a box to make a short talking of such a meeting. Would you do that for me? This has no connection with any of the other matters?" I agreed, but with every professional reservation. My little mikes were not powerful enough to record through thick walls or at a hundred metres. He shook his head. "There is a fireplace in their room; beneath one of the big cisterns. I will have a brick removed for you to put your instrument."

"In that case very well."

"I will tell Sacrapant to take you, then" he said, with considerable unfeigned relief, touching my hand. "So very good."

He rose now and gazed out across the dark garden. A heavy sea fog had been rolling up as we talked and settling over the waters of the sound below; we could hear the muffled horns and bells of the sea traffic as it moved cautiously down towards the city. It had turned a trifle cold and damp. I thought it time to take my leave of my host, but he would not let me go without a visit to the old dark barn which had been turned into a "mews" for his hunting birds. I fell in with the suggestion out of politeness: indeed there was nothing to see for the place was kept in almost total darkness. Vaguely I saw the shapes of the birds stirring on their wooden cross-bars. Jocas went among them with the assurance of long familiarity. He made a low hissing noise with tongue and teeth as he went from one to the next, checking the jesses which bound them to their perches. The smell of rotting meat was almost unbearable; and I could feel the fleas jumping from the dirty flagstones on to my ankles. "This week end we shall have some sport with them" he cried cheerfully. "If you are interested."

I agreed, for despite my personal indifference to the sport I found myself recalling to mind the image of the dark girl with the falcon on her wrist. It stirred me in some way—perhaps it was only curiosity taking fire. Nevertheless it would be interesting to go out with them, if only for the ride, and I said so. "Fine" he cried. "Fine."

We had a last whisky on the terrace, and then the majordomo appeared with the light to conduct me back to the guest house. I found that I was quite unsteady on my legs, though my head was clear enough. We had agreed that I should spend next day in Polis consulting my advisers and return once more at nightfall by launch. The old eunuch led me slowly and steadily downhill, suiting his pace to mine, until at last I stood once more upon the little terrace. He entered the house to light the lamps. I stood, breathing the damp fog-bound night air. There was no sky, no water, no stars. I floated in the swirling mist on my little balcony as if on a raft. His task completed the servant bowed and made his way up the hill. He was swallowed with the suddenness of a shutter falling. Then it was I heard the voice of the girl in the copse above the house. I could not see her in the darkness; but I could hear the low crooning of her voice as she addressed the bird on her wrist "Geldik gel ulalum", over and over again, varying the monotony of the phrase by small changes of intonation. The disembodied voice moved across the hill and faded on the ear. I was tempted to call her name once—and the thought surprised me very much indeed. Instead I went to bed and lay in a tangle of damp sheets dreaming fitful and discontinuous dreams in which the voice came from a great bird not a woman. A strange bubbling croon, like rose water agitated in its bowl by the drawing narghile; a sound at once tender and obscene. On the one hand as sweet as the calling of turtledoves, on the other as incisive as the hiss of a snake. Great wings hovered over me in a dark sky; huge talons of iron entered my shoulders and I cried out. Then the long staggering fall earthward. But I fell into one of the kiosks of the Seraglio and was chased down dark corridors and into deserted ballrooms by three blind men. They operated by sound; when I made no move they halted, nonplussed, scimitars in hand. Then my breathing would alert them and they would rush towards me once more. I woke in a fever of perspiration and anxiety. The fog had lifted somewhat and there was a frail horned moon afloat in the water. Once more to bed where I wrestled awhile with insomnia before sinking once more into the grim quagmire of the dream.

I was awoken by the sun in my eyes. It was pouring across the terrace and into the windows of the little room. Moreover, to my surprise and confusion, Benedicta Merlin was there, sitting on the stone balustrade of the verandah, staring in at me as I slept. Beside her stood the briefcase which I had forgotten the evening before. Her face was serious, almost intense, almost as if she had been deeply concentrating as she watched me asleep. I uttered an incoherent good-morning as I ran my hands through my hair, and she nodded. Her expression was still serious, almost a little puzzled. "You've been watching me asleep" said I with some vexation. "Why didn't you wake me?" She sighed and said: "I was counting up to a hundred. Then I was going to." She stood up and brushed some pollen or leaf mould from her hands. "I brought you this" she said, pointing to the briefcase. "The boat has arrived already and is waiting."

"Are you coming to Polis with us?"

She shook her head. "No. Not today. Why?"

"I don't know: we could talk."

"Talk?" she said in a higher register, and with a look of genuine suprise—as though the idea of someone wishing to talk to her was a novelty of the first magnitude.

"Why not?"

She turned on her heel almost shyly now and whispered "I must go." She crossed the path and went slowly up the hill. I stood in my pyjamas and watched her. At the edge of the copse she turned and looked back at me. I raised my hand in a greeting and she responded, but in a curious way—abbreviating the gesture, breaking it in half. Then she turned and vanished out of sight among the trees.

I retrieved the briefcase, and dressed in a hurry, knowing that the patient Sacrapant would be waiting for me in the stern-sheets of the *Imogen*, elegant yet stiff like some praying mantis or a tall crane in the docks.

I was suitably apologetic for having kept them all waiting and was heartily forgiven on all hands; soon we were skirling along the Bosphorus coast, scoring deeply into a marble sea and throwing out a wake of white chips as we went. Everything—the great drop curtain of the city coming up before us—was hesitant, milky, tentative, mirage-edged. It was beautiful to sit within inches of the water, intently passive, so to speak: watching the glossy surface slide by under us. At such moments idle thoughts drift in star clusters, in cloud formations, across the nodding mind. I thought of Jocas' capacity for mind-reading and compared it to my own: neither was very esoteric. If one concentrates on a human being, really concentrates, one can see his astral shape, so to speak, unfolding and progressing forward into his future: can divine the shape of what he might become. Well, I thought to myself wryly: aren't we being the little Faustus, now? And tell me cher maître, what would you divine in the smooth pious visage of Mr. Sacrapant who sits beside you holding the sacred briefcase which is to have such a strange effect on my life? "Sacrapant?" I replied to myself. "Hum. Let me see." All this was long before he fell out of the sky. The phrases came unbidden. "Case 225 Elias Sacrapant. He has listened all his life to Turkish music—music of a transcendental monotony. His wife loves with such piety that she has driven him steadily towards a nervous breakdown." But Mr. Sacrapant was talking, pointing out places of tourist interest. (How travel narrows the mind!) I nodded and took refuge in the steady hum of the engines. Then, still engaged with my Faustian self, I presented another figure for analysis for an X-ray, so to speak: Benedicta! Here my self-possession quite deserted me. I saw a succession of snapshots of that cold face—the unselfconsciousness of beauty of its lines and planes and expressions. Case 226, so to speak. "She is living in absolute terror—and there is no reason for it. She has not realised that just as art is not for everyone so other subjects like lovemaking or mathematics can only come to fruition in the hands of their adepts. Her case is so hopeless that one must, absolutely must, love her." These ideas frightened me so much that my hair almost stood on end.

Vibart occupied a modest but comfortable little villa in a palm-filled garden beyond Pera whence he conducted a good deal of his business which concerned business men for the most part. The front room had been converted into an office with a few files and a hospitable sideboard full of bottles. He scanned through the documents from the briefcase with care but at speed, his mouth open with astonishment. Then he pushed his horn-rimmed glasses up on to the top of his head and said: "Jesus Christ, man—have you read them?" I nodded, adding: "But I'm no lawyer and wouldn't spot any catches."

"Catches!" he laughed in exasperated amazement, and took an agitated turn up and down the room. "My dear sir! Have you seen the sliding royalty scale, the size of the retainer? You should have signed the articles of association *at once*, do you hear? They not only offer to pay you royally for what you do, but to market it; and as if that weren't enough to provide ways and means for you to experiment to your heart's content." He sat down and held his ears briefly. "I don't know what to say. I'll look at them in more detail if you like but really, on the face of it. . . ."

"I felt it was almost too good to be true: as if there were something fishy behind it all."

"Merlin? Fishy? You must be mad, Charlock. The firm is as sound as a rock and highly respectable. You are damned lucky to have got into it at your age and in your line of business. I wouldn't hesitate if I were in your shoes. As a matter of fact I know quite a lot about Merlin because I was once asked to do an article for *The Times* on our Levant merchants, and I started to research on him. But somehow or other I got sidetracked, couldn't get enough material; Pehlevi raised some trivial objections—not this one, Julian, who runs the London end. I was sorry because the story was a most romantic rags-to-riches one. It started very modestly with this naval cadet deserting his battleship, and going to ground in Polis. Then, bit by bit, with his headquarters in a wine-shop he started dealing with true Scots judgement: hides, coal, corn, poppy from Lebanon, qat from the Yemen, tobacco, perhaps a touch of slaving on the Red Sea. . . . It grew up slowly but steadily into a giant he couldn't handle alone. Hence the two Pehlevi brothers, God knows where Merlin found them; they couldn't be more unlike each other in temperament and background. Jocas . . . well you've seen him. Julian I have never seen but only heard about. A tremendous career at Oxford, a spell in the Bank of England, and then he took over London for Merlin. With the disappearance of Merlin from the scene the firm divided by a sort of binary fission—rather like the division of the Eastern and Western churches: only of course they work hand in glove the two brothers. Julian is all banking, investment schemes, manufacturing, stocks and shares and so on: while this end you have chiefly trade based on marketable raw materials. Istanbul is still a conventionally strategic entrepôt for whatever comes down the Black Sea into the Med. Don't look so gloomy Charlock. With one scratch of a pen you can secure more than financial independence, man, but *riches* as well as the security to go on doing your work in peace. It makes me feel hysterical to think of your luck."

"What of Benedicta Merlin, the brunette daughter?"

"Brunette? She's blonde—or one of us is colour blind. No, I remember now that she is given to wearing wigs of various colours. But she is blonde I swear, and very handsome. There, my boy, is another prize worth carrying off. I should say she's one of the richest women in the world."

"But she's a widow. Yet they never use her married name."

"Yes, so it seems. I never saw her husband."

I stood up and finished my sherry thoughtfully. "Well," I said "I'll leave the papers with you for the time being, for a closer look into them. Then, if you still think . . . I don't know." I had an obscure but obstinate feeling against tying myself down with such finality—though I could bring no reasoning to bear on it. I could not elucidate it.

"Righto" said Vibart, disappointed. "Only in a world where almost everyone has compromised and is doing a job he doesn't like or want in order to eat—one can't help envying a chap an offer like this."

"What would you do if you could?"

"Get out of diplomacy, where everything is so much smaller than life and . . . no, I won't say the word, Charlock, I won't say it."

I sighed for him, having heard all this bleat before. "I know" I said. "You want to write." Vibart groaned and ran his hand through his blond hair; he smiled that attractive smile of his and agreed shyly. "My dear Charlock," he said "I have always been big with book, but it will never get written unless I WAKE UP." He shouted the last three words and banged on his desk so loudly that I was startled. "Sorry" he said. His wife called from the other room to ask if he was all right. "Of course I'm all right" he cried indignantly. "That is the whole trouble." Under the foolery I could sense a very real anger and frustration. Vibart was a charming and highly articulate victim of his education. "I must escape before I contract the diplomatic pruritus" he went on. "Better anything than to live forever in terror of committing a mere imprudence." I laughed and invited him to walk off his ill humour and he readily agreed to accompany me back to my point of rendezvous with Sacrapant. In the course of his long rambling self-decortication he threw in small scraps of hearsay, tid-bits of information which sometimes struck me as false—or if not false, then on the face of it at variance with what I would have myself surmised as true. For instance, that Sacrapant was a crack pistol-shot and had won a number of cups thereby; that Julian had ordered some Corinthian columns for the Merlin estate and had them broken up and scattered about in order to imitate a Greek temple. "But let me talk about myself" said Vibart, still seething with the desire of self-castigation. "It is my only real subject. I come, Charlock, from an interesting family with a record for profligacy, degeneracy, philistinism and selfishness which stretches back to Tudor times. But where are all these qualities? The strain has gone thin and sour, for I am wise and good. I can show you nothing worse than sloth, shoddiness, self-delusion and sanctimoniousness. Bad enough, you may say: but all negative things. What, shall I stay on forever, and lobby myself a dwarfdom by dancing the Boaconstrictor with a Councillor's wife?"

"Well why not begin?" I asked.

"That's the whole point" he said sadly. "I would not be content with anything less than perfect. And you cannot, it seems to me, do it simply by being nice and well conducted and full of notions—though why the hell not? It's as if my parents had bought me an expensive wheelbarrow when they sent me to Winchester—and here I am too lazy to garden. It's despicable." He struck his calf with his cane and uttered an oath. "On the other hand how can one believe in literature? Nor is the contemporary scene very reassuring for the newcomer. Crowns of rhubarb 1st Class, parsley, sage, rue. Tinsel for the new boys. Then the allocation of honorary titles like 'The Thrush of Finchingfield'. This is more than a little dispiriting."

"Well I don't know what to suggest."

"Of course you don't: nor do I. And here is time flying by and I'm putting on weight. Soon I shall be only fit to write the history of Adipose Rex—sorry!"

We arrived at last at the intersection of streets where Sacrapant had promised to meet me; Vibart hung on, talking, unwilling to relinquish a listener.

"I have mislaid myself" he announced with a grandiose gesture of his stick in the direction of the Grand Bazaar. "E quindi uscimmo a riverder le stelle—but where do I fit in, please tell me? Shall I carve myself a niche among the waterbabies of socialism—the songsters of the back passage? Or contract criticism, that superior form of blood poisoning? Shall I present as a Protestant Radical—one who will not take yes for an answer? Or is reticence the better part of valour? Shall I focus my 200 rabbit power eyes on the future and stay mum?"

I persuaded him to allay his vexation somewhat by entering a café with me to have a mastika; here he continued with this unwearying self-examination for my benefit. "I have mapped out my whole career more than once. I have even written my own press book. 'Full of characteristic felicities and written at gale force. Who is this Vibart? We must know.' (*Sheffield Clarion*): or 'Subtle, thought-provoking and full of lovely mince' (*The Times*): or 'Ecstasy to riffle and give away' (*Vogue*). I am already at the height of my career. How did I achieve this transcendent position? I became so thin they gave me the Nobelly Prize and a whole page in the Literary Sacrament. . . ."

"It won't do, Vibart."

"I know it won't. Comely of form was he, but with the temperament of a field-mouse. Damn. Damn."

All this of course masked a very real dilemma; I saw that to accuse himself of vainglory, narcissism, selfishness and so on was something more than just a defence; on the one hand it earned him kudos for honesty and insight—on the other it absolved him from *doing* anything about it. But then, on the other hand, why should he? I liked him the way he was. Besides one day he might shake the drops off and address himself honestly to life. "Well keep trying" I said. "And I'll get in touch with you in a day or two about the contracts." He took his leave with many a sad cautionary head-shaking, and I watched the tall athletic figure slipping away through the warrens of the souk. And here, as if by magic, Mr. Sacrapant appeared at my elbow with his characteristic air of piety. He gazed moistly at me and clasped his hands together. "Have you joined us, Mr. Charlock? Have you signed?" For some reason this incessant harping had begun to get on my nerves. "No I have not" said stoutly with a mulish expression. "I have left them to be carefully examined. It will take a day or two."

He gave a disappointed sigh, and then shrugged his shoulders. He looked inexpressibly saddened and pained—I suppose by my suspicious hesitations over joining the firm. I saw him suddenly—a grey-haired, winged and ithyphallic little man off some shattered Phrygian marbles, standing there eternally with that look of sadness, but silent now, silent as rain on fleece. Elias Sacrapant Esq. He stood upon the axis drawn by intersecting arcades, silent and friendly. "Let us talk of other things" I said. "What about this political meeting you want monitored?"

Sacrapant came down to earth at once and took on the aspect of a conspirator; he leaned forward, after a glance around him, and said: "I was going to bring that up today. I knew you had been approached. It would be just a minute or two. They meet every evening, about six, all this week. So you could choose your time." I reflected. "You know," I said "I have left one of my boxes in my room at the Pera. If you like we could get it and do the job this very evening. What do you say?"

Sacrapant's eyes kindled. "Good. Excellent. The sooner Mr. Pehlevi knows the truth the better for the firm. I will go down and tell the launch to wait for us, and then taxi up to join you at the hotel. You will walk I presume? Well, we have time, we have time."

I fell in with his wishes, and woolgathered my way back to the hotel where I tested my machine and the spare microphone. Then I lay on my bed and dozed off incontinently—to dream a confused dream of childless blue-stockings lecturing to Vibart on the novel.

Little bas bleu
Come blow up my horn
And sanction a tumble
Amid the green corn,
My pretty blue stocking
My supercherie
With prune and with prism
Fandangle with me.

I awoke with a start to find myself looking down the barrel of a pistol. I cried out incoherently and Mr. Sacrapant burst into a thin peal of delighted laughter. "It isn't loaded of course" he said. "But how was I to know that?" He became all contrition. "I am sorry. But I have been told to take some weapon with me. In case."

"In case what?"

"You never know."

I began to feel indignant. "Look here, I wasn't told that there was any danger about this performance."

"There isn't theoretically. None at all."

He slipped the weapon shyly into an inner breast pocket and pulled his coat down. "In a while we can start" he said.

It was my first introduction to the fantastic honeycomb of ancient cisterns upon which the city appears to have been built. Afterwards I returned to explore them in some detail, but on this occasion we found our way to the Yeri Batan Serai—the Underground Palace built by Justinian under the portico of the Basilica itself. Its entry was an obscure hole—like a shaft dug into a tumulus. A leather and wooden door, fastened with wire, marked the entry to the long flight of steps which led downwards at a steep angle to the water's edge. Here Mr. Sacrapant, true to form, produced a couple of pocket torches. It was awe-inspiring to plunge down all of a sudden into this watery cathedral. The symmetrical rows of columns stretched away on all sides in extraordinary perspectives, picking up the light and shadow simultaneously. The depth, the gloom, the reverberation of our footsteps on the staircase swelled the sense of mystery; moreover from one of the darker corners—across the long lanes of dark water which threw wobbling shadows into the heavy vaulting overhead—I saw a light. Mr. Sacrapant whistled, but very softly; and he was answered after a pause by a replica of the sound, soft and mellifluous. The light approached us now, and I saw that it was on the prow of a small skiff, being rowed by a single old Turk who wore a fez. "Come" breathed Mr. Sacrapant, and held the nose of the boat steady for me to climb in with my gear. Then lithe as a lizard he leaped in after me, and we set off down these long dark galleries of water. The rower propelled his boat noiselessly with a simple twisting motion of the oars, standing upright and never letting the blades rise to the water-surface. It was fearfully damp; the least sound—crepitation of water in the caverns, peppering of sand falling from the roof—became blown up, magnified, hazy. None of us spoke. The rower seemed to know his destination. Mr. Sacrapant sat forward flashing his torch upon the darkness ahead. His lips moved. He was it seemed counting the columns, for presently he muttered a figure under his breath and tapped a signal on the back of the Turk, who turned the boat at a sharp angle, and set off down a side-gallery. We came at last to a shallow flight of stairs—a sort of water-gate—which led upwards into the throat of the cistern, so to speak; it pierced the ceiling with a rotten trap of wood. This was our objective, or so it seemed. Here Sacrapant began to behave with a good deal of muffled circumspection, using gestures and mime wherever they might replace spoken words. The staircase was solid enough, but the heavy recorder was a clumsy thing to man haul, particularly in the dancing uncertain light of the little torches. However we managed the operation without mishap; and now I followed the lanyard-like figure upwards into the gloom, along a cob-webbed corridor, and then upwards again. He was hunting along the wall of a particular place. The white light jumped and flicked along the gloomy stone facings—the ground floor of a deserted subterranean Venice I thought to myself as I followed him, by this time feeling more than a touch of apprehension. Blind man's fingers. I had not visualised this sort of exploit when Pehlevi spoke to me about my recorders. But it was now too late to withdraw and show a white flag. Sacrapant skidded along the corridors in lizard fashion until at last he came to a marked stone in the wall. He produced a pocket knife and, beckoning me to preserve an absolute silence, inserted it in the interstices of the stone to exercise leverage on it. It came away with relative ease and on his invitation I took a look into a sort of flue which I was soon to realise was that of a vast fireplace. The hole, admirably camouflaged, stood about six feet above ground level.

As far as the room was concerned there seemed to be a meeting already going on; chairs scraped, the hum of voices swelled and subsided. It was all barks and glottal stops to me. For my part all I had to do was to let a microphone dangle as low as possible above the hearth and start printing this medley of sound. Pertinacious Mr. Sacrapant seemed now to be in an agony of apprehension; he stood on one leg and then on the other. Why? The operation was a simple one and it was not very long before I saw my blue pilot nodding away at me in the gloom, and heard the soft whirr of the machine "taking". Down below in the board room or officers' mess or whatever the place might be, new voices came up. Some sort of speech of welcome was made; measured and sententious sentences without subsidiary clauses, following one another in dactylic progression. I had copied for about ten minutes when Sacrapant signalled me to cut out. It was quite enough, he contorted; and so I began to pull in my line like some benighted fisherman and swash up my equipment. And here all at once there was a hitch. My line must somehow have dislodged a small stone or pebble from the interior of the flue—for something fell into the fireplace with a clatter, bouncing on the iron firedogs. At once I was aware that the inhabitants of the room below had been alerted by this sound. Voices came up the flue now—they were trying to look up the chimney. I hauled in like mad; it was not a moment to hang about. Sacrapant hopped and cajoled me to hurry up. For my part I did not even wait to replace the stone, so infectious was the little man's anxiety. I hulked the stuff down and jumped into the boat; Sacrapant followed, but as he did so his little pistol slid out of his pocket and into the dark water with a splash. The Charon-like Turk was now urged to carry us away from the place at all speed; but he was typical of his leaden unhurried race, and so we set off at the same funeral pace, moving at right angles to one set of pillars. We had extinguished the light of the boat, and depended for direction on an occasional torch-blink from Sacrapant. So we scored our slow way across the inky water of the cavern. Suddenly, far away to the right, there came a gleam of yellow light—as if from a door which had been thrown open—and one heard the nibble of voices. After a moment's delay—perhaps for deliberation—we heard the snickering of pistol-shots ricocheting from the vaults and falling in the water. It was not clear whether they were aiming at us or not but the sound was ominous. Mr. Sacrapant with great prudence lay down in the bottom of the boat and complained about feeling sea-sick. The Turk was completely unmoved and plodded on towards our own landing-stage. I tried as far as possible to sit in a position which would have shielded me from our aggressors, though their exact whereabouts as well as the direction of their fire was somewhat in doubt. It seemed to take an age before we grazed the landing-stage and bumped to a halt. By now we were far away from the scene of our imprudence and it seemed possible to use the torches again; we paid off the old man and clambered out into a surprise—for darkness had already fallen upon the city. Nor did it seem possible even at this early hour to find a taxi so we were forced to content ourselves with a horse-drawn cab which jogged us, juddering and swaying, down to the Galata bridge where the launch waited, its captain smoking patiently on the bridge.

We dined late that night, but on the same balcony overlooking the darkened garden, and this time my host was in high spirits at the success of our operation of the evening; Sacrapant was invited to dinner throughout which he sat in a daze of self-congratulation. "We were shot at" he repeated wonderingly more than once. "Mr. Charlock and I were shot at." I said nothing about him lying in the sheets, or about my heroic attempt to shield myself behind the rower. We were heroes. Bravo, Felix! I was only sorry that the mysterious Benedicta was not there to share in all this grandeur; but she had crossed over to the Asiatic side, and was to meet us next morning for a day's falconry. "You know, don't you, that she has been very ill?" said Jocas Pehlevi in what seemed on the face of it an inconsequential aside. It had nothing to do with the preceding conversation. I could not quite decide whether his tone implied a warning or the registration of a simple piece of information. But the phrase cracked open a new area of comprehension. Pausing for thought, I understood now the secret source of that striking and distracted gaze—the source of what I called her beauty. It was not simply the happy disposition of features, it was the sadness and withdrawnness of her illness—the fragmentation of neurasthenia—which gave her the air of someone distractedly listening to an interior monologue, a private musical score. The total solipsism of . . . but I won't say it: why offend the doctors? But if she had not had this she might have seemed as commonplace as half a hundred good-looking blonde girls; with it she achieved a kind of legendary quality—a sick muse embedded in a statue of flesh and bone. This realisation so kindled my sympathy that I hardly heard Jocas saying: "Now can we hear your records please?" I came to myself with a start. "Yes, of course."

I had been somewhat doubtful about the quality of my recording, but here again luck held. It was pronounced clear. Jocas listened with intense concentration, smoking a cigar, head down; but after the fourth repetition he said with a sigh of relief: "It was not Mahmud was it?" Sacrapant shook his head joyfully. "Then we will not have to act for the time being" said Jocas. "Good. Good."

The conversation shifted crabwise to other and more impersonal matters which did not concern me, and I turned my attention adrift, not surprised that it wandered off in the direction of Benedicta, recalling all the minutae of her behaviour and appearance as if to find in each fragment a specimen of the sick beauty which had once become her master. I excused myself early that night, as we were due to set off before dawn, and made my way back to my waterside bungalow. I took off all my clothes and went over my body point by point, holding up the light in the mirror the better to study it. I did not know why I was doing this—nor did I ask myself any questions. But afterwards I sat down in despair on the bed and said aloud: "Is this what it is like?" What was I talking about? I don't know. I found my beauty unconvincing I suppose! Moreover to add to this feeling of horrible dispersion and inadequacy there came its twin—the conviction that I had made a choice that was as bad as it was irrevocable! But, O dear, how clearly I saw that face! Nevertheless the realisation must have cleared the air, so to speak, for that night I slept the dreamless sleep of early childhood. Iolanthe must have been dreaming about me.

As for Benedicta herself I must confess that I had seen her before, in a manner of speaking. The gesture with which Iolanthe sank down upon the carpet and drew forth the greasy little pack of playing-cards always heralded a prolonged scrutiny of the auspices, an evaluation of her future and mine; she kept them separate even then, out of who knows what sad tact? And, youthful and self-sufficient boor that I was, I hardly noticed the crestfallen tones in which she might say: "Our story is coming to an end for many years. Soon I shall go from you, and the other will come, the widow. She will be sadder than I, much sadder. I see many doors around her, and all of them closed." I yawn, of course, in the manner of one who has known (as Caradoc would say) "*des femmes de toutes les catégorilles*". We scientific chaps cannot countenance divination by aces and spades. "My story is one of riches, riches, but much dissatisfaction, much unhappiness. Then look, we meet again in another country—but it will be too late to start again. Meanwhile the widow will hold you. She is fair. You will recognise her by her right foot—something is wrong with it."

"A cripple? Does she limp?"

"No. I see her dancing with you, beautifully."

Regarding with distaste the hot and crumpled sheets upon which Iolanthe gazed with such tenderness. Now when I think of it I go all-overish. All this for me was mere pleasure which never exploded into insight, couldn't disturb the egocentric flow of my hugged imaginings. The arts of introspection nourished on a junior loneliness and too much bloody education. Sentient beings for me were still almost convincing dummies, that was all. Am I typical then? A thousand little acts of attachment passed over me unnoticed. Well, later memory takes them and turns them into spears. One cries out in one's sleep, one curses. Like, I mean, taking the spectacles off my sunburnt nose as one lifts the lid from a jar of olives—to kiss me. Made foolish by too much knowledge I did not see her then as she was, namely in her natural state; I only began to "see" her when she had created her artificial self, the actress. Then she hit me between the eyes. But then one can't start loving retroactively—or can one? Too little, Felix, and then too late. Matter of fact or fact of matter? With Benedicta I chewed off my own tail in a cloud of unknowing. For better or for hearse. But wait. It was not all so vague, for she had deep and pitiful experiences to chew upon, and was gifted with a strange aberrant insight, as when she was describing early sexual experiences once and came out with: "If you push passion to extremes you are bound to tumble into mere mysticism." What a strange use of the word "mere"! But wait a minute.

It was well before dawn when I woke with a jolt to find Jocas standing over me, jack-booted and spurred, holding a lighted candle and grinning like a dog. "Sea fog" he said oracularly, and I heard the engines of the pinnace warming up, ticking over, in the obscurity below. Over his arm he carried a miscellaneous collection of clothes and boots—gear more suitable for a day of riding than the suit I had brought with me. I foraged about amongst it all and equipped myself with a good pair of boots, ill-fitting riding-breeches, an empty bandolier and such other sundries as seemed to me to be to the purpose. Then before climbing down the hill to the boat he poured us each a small cup of scalding sage-tea backed by a sip of gasping mastika. So we careened out of harbour into an olive drab mist which coiled around us, condensing upon hair and eyebrows. The dispirited dogs drowsed and yawned among the tarpaulins. "She went over early with the old falconers," said Jocas "and we'll meet later today. Hullo! What's that?"

The channel even at this early hour was full of ships labouring cautiously down towards the Horn, their bells clanging out warnings, soft wet lips of fog-horns, etc. In smaller craft the lookout banged upon a saucepan and shouted from time to time to mark position. As we had to cut directly through the middle of this traffic to reach the Asiatic side the operations of the pinnace were delicate in the extreme, although we were equipped with engines of great power and a fog-horn whose melancholy resonance was enough to set the dogs ululating. Jocas smoked a short pipe and waited patiently as his pilot trod cautiously among the indistinct shapes and sounds on this dark waterway. This funeral pace was imposed on us for nearly an hour and then, in the most dramatic fashion, the fog was peeled aside by a scurry of wind and we were in the full light of an early sunrise riding down along the low purple headlands of the nether shore where our drumming wake rippled down upon sleeping villages to set the coloured boats bobbing at deserted landing-stages. Everything was still sticky with fogdamp and Jocas would not let the guns out of their cases until the sun was fully up. The dogs were rubbed down with straw. We drank black coffee in tin mugs and watched the chromatic scale of yellow Byzantine light loop up the eastern end of the sky—until it ran over and raced everywhere, spilling among the shady blue valleys, and touching in the vague outlines of the foothills. Sunrise. Carob, sweet chestnut, oak—and plaintive small owls calling.

We were running along the low toothy headlands of the coast now, in view of the country which we were to hunt. Clumps of swaying bamboos marked the points where shallow streams had nosed their way down into the bight. The land soothed itself away to the girdle of foothills, the shallow intervening valleys wearing their scrub and green screes bravely, pin-pointing here and there a cypress plume or a regiment of olives; but for the most part dwarf oak, juniper, myrtle and arbutus—the classical combination so easily negotiable (so it seems) until one tries to follow a gun-dog into the impenetrable jungle of interlocking roots and thorns. Jocas swept the land with a powerful glass, grunting with satisfaction; then he handed it to me, pointing out here and there a shattered fragment of an abandoned temple, or a cluster of pruned stone where a seamark had been allowed to dribble into a heap of rubble under the rubbing water. But away to the north his blunt finger directed me to a small landing-stage, a tiny harbour carved in shale, where the horses awaited us. Then, moving away to the right over the green land he indicated a tall hillock, with a fine tall stand of oak-trees where, in the shadow, one saw the movement and glitter of what seemed to be an encampment. "Benedicta is up there" he said. "She will have the birds. We won't use the guns today unless . . . I suppose a boar might be tempting. But they are not very numerous now."

We were met by a little group of horsemen whose repellent ugliness and strange attire suggested to the mind the inhabitants of remotest Tartary. They were clad in greasy duffle, with jackboots of soft leather crudely sewn. Their rifles were antiques, muzzle-loaders. Their little round hats with the shallow brim emphasised the almond-shaped eyes. They greeted Jocas with an awkward curtness which suggested not so much discourtesy as the shy manners of remote mountaineers. There wasn't a smile between the lot of them.

We mounted and set off across the fields feeling the sun hot upon our backs. I had not ridden for a long time—not indeed since a bit of mild hacking at university—and felt very much of a novice. Jocas rode sturdily but without elegance: indeed he sat like a sack of meal. But his huge hands and his grip on the reins suggested that a troublesome horse would receive no quarter from him.

We crossed a half-dry marsh and began to climb the hill. Here the sun had started to make the wet land steam, and the rising mist swept upwards into the trees. It was through this abrupt dimming of our vision that Benedicta appeared, mounted dramatically on a bronze stallion, her yellow hair flying loose. She was a different woman from the dark girl with the heart-shaped face; this was someone imperative, assured, even perhaps cruel when one thought of the dense blue eyes under frowning brows: periwinkle-blue, large, fierce, finely formed. "You're damned late" she said to Jocas, reining in and turning into a slow-plunging, arse-banging reorientation in order to come alongside us. Then still unsmiling she reached out and pressed my wrist in a gesture of greeting which was, to say the very least of it, puzzling: I could not decide if it were descended from some oriental form of greeting—or was an expression of personal intimacy. I was tempted to raise my wrist to my lips but refrained. The gesture itself may also have meant nothing; but it illuminated something for me in a flash. I understood what the meaning of my strange behaviour on the night before could be: I mean examining myself so carefully in the mirror, measuring so to speak the degree of my own narcissism in the face of this reflected man, I had been thinking of something like this: "Yes, but then we are modified affectively by the contents of our skulls, by what we think. This science nonsense has reduced your ability to affirm yourself. You would, faced by a challenge like this—I mean a girl who sets herself down in front of the target—turn the whole thing into hollow propositions which you would lodge in the conscious mind. You couldn't just bite into her like a fresh apple. Yum, Yum. And if you did try to warm up your feelings in a more generous direction why you'd go soft, you'd go sentimental. Too much scientific thinking has poisoned feeling, has reduced your pulse-rate so to speak. What will you do if she embraces you?" Fall off my horse I suppose.

This is where the extraordinary melancholy came over me. (At this moment my heart was simmering, my blood had turned to quicksilver. I saw her then in some almost legendary form—this slender woman riding down upon us like some drunken queen of the Iceni.) It was the melancholy subject of the night before which reflected and told himself that perhaps we are forced to choose as lovemates, shipmates, playmates those that best match our inward ugliness—the sum of our own shortcomings. No, I did not know that as yet. Not then.

There was sweat upon her upper lips and temples; her cheek was red, little blonde hairs twinkled. The eyes didn't have any particular expression—perhaps a touch of disdain. But when they turned upon mine a whole new world of feeling darkened them. Incredibly enough, I could have sworn she was in love with me. Riding like that through the mist I had a sudden feeling that I was about to faint, to fall out of my saddle into a bush. It did not last long, this vertiginous feeling, but it altered the whole scale of my sentiment. All of a sudden I was sure of something, I knew where I was; I longed to escape as a fish longs to escape from the hook. If one could apply some rational system to subjects like these how nice it would be: instead one must always talk as provisionally as possible and in terms of poetry. But damn it Charlock is a scientist—and scientists, moved by pure reason, never let themselves get into such awkward positions. Was it Koepgen who said that science was built upon defensive measurement and art upon propitiation?

"I knew you would have to come to me" she said in a low voice. A minatory note, a little too intense: I did not like it one little bit. This again did not need saying now: at the touch of her fingers on my wrist I had realised that she had been willing me to return once more in a slow curve to that point of reference in time at which our natures had ignited each other. Heavens, what a way to express it! But we *are* modified affectively by what we think. (Charlock, cool your mind with the calculus.) Benedicta waited for me to answer her—but what was I to tell her about the whole deathscapade of lovemaking? The soul of modern man is made of galvanised iron. She turned away, biting her lips. I felt sad to have to wound her by a silence and an awkwardness at a time when our feelings had defined themselves, grouped themselves, were waiting only to be honourably avowed and recognised. Thoughts incoherent and dispersed floated through my skull as the horses undulated up the slope. I heard for example (why?) the disembodied voice of Sipple say: "Blowed if I see any culture in the Parthenon. To me it's just a marble birdcage. They say it's old but how is one to tell? There are no maggots in marble." But if I could see her so clearly as she was that day I could also see, by simple extension of her look, her manner, the Benedicta who could sit for hours before a mirror with a finger to her lips, her eyes wide with fright; I could see those cupboards full of fancy-dress costumes, the masks. Puppetry! Among the cartoons of monks and demons there hung whips with knotted thongs. Yes, I saw Benedicta always elaborately gowned and cloaked, always wearing some fabulously expensive bracelet over a left-hand glove: Benedicta dressed like an Infanta to welcome me to the white walls and glassy balconies of the Sanatorium in Zürich which her father had once endowed. If I had dared then to say simply: "Benedicta I love you" it would have been like the report of a gun, the discharge of a firearm that blows the top of your skull off. The hero of the New Comedy will be the scientist in love, grappling with the androgynous shapes of his own desire. Wouldn't you say?

But we had come now to a shady clearing among the trees on the nether side of the hill which dipped down towards flat green country of simple brush, iodine coloured. Here the old falconers were gathered about the awkward wooden cages which held their choicest birds. They looked like all specialists look—all members of bowling clubs, artisans, artists, tend to look. Old wrinkled specialists who spent their whole time hanging about the falcon market in Istanbul waiting to pick up a bargain—an eyas tiercel or a peregrine or a jack Merlin (strange that should have been the name of Benedicta's father). Did he look rather like the bird? The little group talked in low moping tones, they had all of them grave bedside manners, walking among the unfidgeting birds. A single cigarette passed from hand to hand. The gunbearers stood about in dispirited fashion, but with our arrival all was animation; the horses were trimmed, girths checked. Jocas elected to fly the largest of the falcons, his favourite, while the girl chose a smaller short-winged bird—one that could be discharged from the wrist at the first sight of prey almost in the manner of a shotgun. We wound down the hill in single file before fanning out the beaters and the dogs, trained skilfully not to overrun. Once down the hill Jocas looked over our dispositions and released his hawk with a shrill musical cry, slipping the hood from its eyes. After a swift look about the great bird rose magnetically, its wings crushing down the air as it rustled upwards in a slow arc, to take up its position in the sky. This one would "wait on" in the higher air to have the advantage over far-flying quarry. But as yet we had hardly begun the beat, moving with the sun at our backs; a couple of woodcock rose with a rattle and began their crashing trajectory across the lower sky. At once the shrill ululations of the falconers broke out, encouraging the great falcon: sometimes these sounds reminded one of the muezzin's call to prayer from a minaret in the old city. So the battle began. One of the woodcocks went to earth in the bracken and refused to be flushed, but the second put up a struggle characterised by tremendous speed and finish. It seemed to be able to judge the moment when the falcon had positioned itself for the stoop; instantly it would dive for cover, only to be flushed once more by the ever advancing line of beaters. After the third or fourth repetition of this tactic it began to tire; its flights became shorter and more erratic, its plunges for cover more desperate. The hunt had now broken into several parties, interest being divided by other quarry, by new birds taking the air. I saw Benedicta discharge the short-winged hawk from her wrist at the sight of something rising among the holm-oaks. It flew at incredible speed—fired like sling-shot.

But the battle between Jocas' falcon and the woodcock had drawn us on ahead of the rest. It was exciting, the gallop across the flat plain after the failing woodcock. It was after about a mile and a half that one saw the falcon shortening its gyres, closing the space between it and its quarry. It was winding it in almost, as a fisherman winds in a fish. The woodcock despite its fatigue was game and rose again and yet again, but falteringly now. It was becoming clear that the end was not far off. The falcon once more positioned itself, helped now by a slight change of the wind's direction. It took careful aim and suddenly came plummeting down at incredible speed, adding impetus to its own great weight. Too late the woodcock tried to evade it by a feint, sliding sideways as it fell. The falcon struck it a devastating blow with its hind talons—must have struck it stone dead in fact. Down they both went now in a tangle of wings, leaving a trail of slow feathers in the amazed sky. At once the horsemen shrilled and ululating broke into a ragged gallop to retrieve. Jocas, red faced and sweating, was radiant now. "It was that shift of wind" he said. "Game won't fly upwind under a hawk. What elegance eh?"

So the day wore on; the quarry was rich and various, and the incidents of the kill quite absorbing. I quite forgot my saddle-soreness. The longest and dourest battle Jocas fought was, strangely enough, with one of the slowest birds of all, a marsh-heron. One would not have believed that this slowcoach of a bird could outwit a trained hunting falcon, but this was very nearly the case. Indeed the heron proved so cunning that it had Jocas swearing with admiration. Though in lateral flight it is slow, the big concave wings give it the power of rising rapidly in the perpendicular, almost in balloon-fashion: meanwhile the falcon has the task of trying to gain sufficient height for her swoop by circling. The old heron used this advantage so skilfully that the battle ranged over several miles. Twice the hunter misjudged its distance, or the heron sidestepped it in the sky: for the falcon, missing it, lost the superiority of altitude and was forced laboriously to circle once again until it could take up the required position. But at last—and both birds were tiring—it found its site and with a swoop "bound to" the heron and both came tumbling out of the sky together with a crash and scream.

The sun was well past meridian when we broke off the sport, all parties converging once more on the hillside where, on the eastern side, there was an old abandoned marble fountain in the denser part of the wood. Here a spring boomed and swished among the rocks and the air was sweet and dense with moisture. Here we lounged and ate the food which had been sent up from the boat in a wicker hamper. The cool shade was luxurious and sleep-inducing—and indeed Jocas had dozed off for a few moments when a messenger rode into the camp from the boat and summoned him back on urgent business to the town. He left at once, with a resigned good humour, promising to send the pinnace back to collect us that night. I was left alone with

Benedicta. Watching her move among the falconers, smoking a cigarette, I felt the same tightening of the heart-strings as I had when she rode out of the mist towards me. That, and also an awkward sense of premonition: the sense of having embarked upon a course of action which would reward me perhaps by the very damage it might do to my self-reliance, or my self-esteem. Rubbish. And yet at the heart of it all there was a magical content—for there seemed to me to be absolutely no alternative to make me hesitate. Apart from the greed of the eyes and the mind which contemplated her bright abstract beauty there was a kind of inner imperative about the matter —as if this was what I had been foreordained to execute. Yes, I had been born to get myself into this extraordinary, this bewitching mess. So that it was with a complete calm assurance of happiness that I merely nodded and agreed when she said: "I am sending them all down to the boat this evening, but I shall stay here tonight with you. Yes?" The "yes" was quite unnecessarily wistful, and now I repaid the debt of my earlier negligence by taking up the slender fingers and pressing them back to life. So we sat side by side on the grass eating a pomegranate, surrounded by all the bustle of the encampment breaking up. They were to leave us sleeping bags, wine and food; torches, cigarettes, and horses. It took them hours to pack up. We stood side by side in the green evening light to watch the cavalcade straggle down the valley towards the sea. Then, thoughtfully stripping off her clothes, she turned slowly towards the broken marble cistern where the water drummed, she walked into it, seizing the foaming jets with her hands, crying out with joy at its intense cold. So we lay rolled about and were massaged by the icy spring, to climb out cold and panting at last, and lie down as wet as fish in each other's arms. But before making love or attempting any kind of intimacy, lying mesmerised like this, still trembling from the cold water, she uttered a cautionary phrase which to my bemused mind sounded as normal, as natural, as the bustle and boom of the water in the marble dish below us. "Never ask me anything about myself, will you? You must ask Jocas, if you want to know anything. There's a great deal I do not know. I mustn't be frightened, you see."

It seemed to me perfectly logical and I accepted the proposition, sealing the pact there and then with kisses that grew ever more breathless, refining themselves, exploding like oxygen bubbles in the blood. It was like that, the sun shone, the water drummed: everything had become explicit. We sank, deeper than pain, into this profound nescience. And here again (as always when we made physical love) her teeth were drawn back in a kind of agony under her lips, and she said: "O help me, please help me, you must help me." An awkward Galahad was born. I vowed to help her—how I did not know. And mentally I replied—as I have continued to reply ever since—"Of course, my darling, of course: but against what, against whom?" There was never any answer to my question, only the pain swelling up between us; she pressed ever harder upon me as if to blot it out, as if to still the ache of some great bruise. Thus our sensuality was touched by a kind of unconscious cruelty—kisses inflicting pain, I mean, rather than pleasure. It was all very well the "Help me": but afterwards she lay like the ghost of rigor mortis itself, her lips blue, her heart beating so that she could hardly breathe. But at last her eyes unclouded by the invading terror. Sex cleared the brain, if only for an instant. She ached in my mind like a choice abstraction.

A flock of ignorant chattering birds, perhaps starlings, crossed our middle vision and settled in a cloud in a nearby tree. Benedicta foraged for the little carbine which they had left behind with the horses and began shooting at them. She shot in a brilliant unpremeditated way, like a woman making up her face, and with an unerring exactitude. The birds began to fall on the ground like overripe fruit. She emptied the magazine before throwing the hot gun down on the sleeping bag. How easily she could fill me with disgust. It was beautiful, the polarity. Then she went and lay face down by the spring, almost touching the foaming tumbling cataract with her lips. It seemed to me then, smoking and watching her, that she was something the heart must desire and I grew afraid of the depth of my feelings. I had never before actually feared to be parted from a woman; the novelty was overwhelming. Tomorrow I must leave for Pera, I decided; if only to get away from this suffocating network of ambiguities. After all, with her wealth etc. etc. I could hardly keep her as a mistress. . . . The ideas rose in clouds like sparrows to a gunshot. But even before they had fallen back into place she was saying:

"I feel this is decisive—that you'll never leave me. I have never felt that before." She always said this: she felt men expected it. All introspection now seemed little more than a fruitless mental debauchery. I closed up my mind and searched ever more frantically for that tame and now touchingly tremulous mouth. We fitted into each other like Japanese razors.

I had collected a couple of huge leeches which had settled on the back of my thigh; by the time I felt the slight discomfort their bites caused, they were already gorged with my blood and fit to burst. Benedicta found a salt cellar in the basket and dosed them until they spewed out the blood they had sucked and fell writhing into the dust. She seemed to like this. I went to wash in the spring. It was her turn now to sit and watch me which she did with a discomforting intentness.

Then she nodded to herself and came to sit beside me to dangle her long legs over the marble parapet. With a long stealthy look about her—as if to make sure that there were no interlopers about in the wood to oversee her—she bent down towards her right foot. I had already noticed that the small toe was bound up with a piece of surgical tape, perhaps to protect a scratch. It was this tape that she now stripped with a small slick gesture, holding out the foot for my inspection. The last toe was double! They were both perfectly formed in their twinship, but joined together. She watched me watching her with her head on one side. "Does it disgust you?" she said. It did, but I said that it did not; I bent to kiss it. Moreover I understood why she kept it bound away, out of sight of the superstitious inhabitants of the place—for it was a clear mark of witchcraft in popular oriental belief. The vestigial toe, known to the medievals as "the devil's teat". She flexed her feet, stretched, and then wandered away to sit under a tree with an air of morose intentness. "What are you thinking, Benedicta?" Her grave, unwavering abstraction melted; she put a stalk of grass between her teeth and said: "I was wondering what they will think when they know. But what can they do, after all?"

"Who?"

"Julian, Jocas, the firm; when they know what I have decided. About you, I mean."

"Has this anything to do with them?" She looked surprised at the question and turned her head away to frown at the darkening sealine. "Besides," I went on "just what have you decided?"

But to this her only answer was to beckon me down among the blankets where we lay luxuriously cradled between snore and wake. For much of the night we talked quietly between snatches of sleep. She spoke about a youth spent in Polis—but haphazardly, at a venture. And from these imprecise snatches of dialogue a sort of picture emerged of a childhood full of loneliness like my own, but spent in the sunken gardens of the Seraglio, in the glittering emptiness of the harem with its shallow female sensualities. In the summer heats of the old capital she had learned everything there was to be known about the sexual appetites before she reached puberty. Learned and forgotten. Perhaps this was why for her there clung about the act of lovemaking a hollow, disabused quality? I don't know. She behaved as if her feelings, her private mind, were enclosed in the frailest of eggshells easily smashed by an indiscreet question. I asked her, for example, if her father was still alive; the idle question made her stiff with anxiety. She sat upright like a frightened hare and admonished me savagely for breaking the rule she had made. I must ask Jocas, she said. I had quite a task in calming her.

At dawn, or just after, we heard the purring of the ship and saw the long white furrow lengthening towards the harbour. She bound up her toe in haste. It was time to gather up our gear and leave. Benedicta was sunk in deep thought as the horses negotiated the shallow slopes of the hill. At last she said: "When are you going to sign those contracts?" I had completely forgotten their existence, and the question startled me. "I hadn't really decided to in my own mind. Why, do you want me to?" She considered me gravely from under frowning brows. "It is strange that you should doubt us" she said. "But I don't," I protested "my hesitation hasn't been due to doubts about the validity of the contracts, no. They are overgenerous if it comes to that. No, it was something else. You see, it isn't easy because I am in love with you." She raised her quirt and struck me across the wrist. "Reflect," she said "reflect."

"I'll see" I said. She looked at me curiously but said no more. The ride back was smooth and uneventful. Jocas was waiting for me with a hospitably decorated table; but Benedicta disappeared, after saying that she would lunch in the harem. I tried to visualise it—a sort of glass and pink satin *bonbonnière* looking out over the calm straits, the light filtered by the intricately carved wooden screens; to this I added some cage birds singing away in melancholy fashion and a few old deaf women, all clad in black, and a few wearing clumsy and ill-chosen frocks from Paris and London. Lots of gold-leaf and mirrors. There would be a horn gramophone with a pile of outdated waltzes and other jazz, and bundles of old picture papers. . . . I wondered how near the mark this was. There did not, for example, appear to be a book anywhere. "You are wrong" said Jocas sharply. "She has a very smartly decorated suite of rooms, satin and gold mouldings; brilliant chandeliers, and electric pianola, two black cats, and a bookcase full of beautifully bound books by Loti and company."

"Thank you" I said ironically, and he made a mock bow.

"At your service" he said. "We are not all equally gifted alas. I should have been a fortune teller in the bazaars I suppose. That's what my brother Chewlian says. I was very backward as a boy; even now, do you know, I read and write with difficulty. I have to pretend that I have mislaid my glasses. It has hampered me very much. It kept me a trader whereas Chewlian is truly a merchant prince. I stayed here, but he went on to brilliant studies. He found a patron, one of the monks who ran the orphanage found him a rich man to stake his education. But I was always ill, always wet my bed until my twentieth year. Had no head and no taste for paper. Only in middle age did I calm down, when Merlin found us."

"But you were orphans?"

"Yes."

"And *brothers*—how would you know?"

"It's only presumption, partly a joke; we shared the same door-step on the same evening. What more is a brother? I love Chewlian and he loves me."

"I think I shall go back to Pera this evening."

"Yes, why not?" he said equably, pressing my arm. He was a most lovable man. "You will see nothing of Benedicta for at least two days now. She has a treatment. But she will get in touch with you if she wants. I think she has to go back to Zürich this coming week."

I found the idea curiously chilling. "She didn't say anything?" I asked, in spite of myself.

"I am not Benedicta's keeper" he said frowning, in a chewing way.

This line of conversation seemed to come up against a brick wall; I felt that perhaps I had unwittingly offended him and strove to be a trifle more conciliatory as I went on. "Tomorrow I'll have a last session with Vibart and decide about the contracts. I will certainly sign for the little ear device—which I call a 'dolly'. About the more general terms of association I'll have to see."

"I know the cause of your hesitation" he said, and burst suddenly into a peal of clear laughter. "It is perfectly justified. Once when I mentioned something I saw from your expression that you were surprised: because it meant that someone had been through the papers you had left behind in Athens. The new device for electric Braille remember?"

He was dead right. I looked at his jutting nose and laughing eyes. "You thought it was us, didn't you? Well, it wasn't. It was Graphos, one of his hirelings who went through your stuff; what they expected to find I don't know. But they photographed everything—all the parts in shorthand and the mathematical materials. Now, when I asked Graphos for details about you after this first idea came along, he was able to supply quite a number of them—things you are working on. I saw at once that we needed you as much as you need us. We can shorten your labours by years if we give you the right equipment, by years. How, for example, can you work on the firefly and the glow-worm without a chemist, indeed a big laboratory to help? We have such a place—Lunn Pharmaceuticals belongs to us. Do you see?"

"The firefly produces light without heat" I had written once, unwisely. "Note. If we could find just *how* chemically we would be on to a new light source perhaps." But of course he was right, one could hardly conduct this kind of experiment from Number Seven. Jocas was watching me intently, still smiling. He said "The trembler fuse, the iodine and sodium bath experiment—how will you ever do it?" All of a sudden the lust for this vocation—of tampering with the universe and trying to short-circuit its behaviour—grew up in me and seized me by the throat. I drank my wine off at a thrust and sat bemused, staring through him. O God! There was also the danger that they might sow these idle speculations broadcast behind my back, that other talents with bigger means might scoop me. I was ashamed of the idea, but there it was! Pure science! Where does the animal come in? "Also a passage where you ask why bats can navigate in the dark and not blind men in the light, eh?"

"Hush," I said "I'm thinking." I was, I was furiously thinking of Benedicta, sitting here trapped between conflicting hesitations.

Jocas said softly: "I do not see that the matter of Benedicta alters anything." He was doing his mental lip-reading act again. Here he was wrong; she hung above all these abstractions and ambiguities, like a wraith, an *ignis fatuus*. That long cobra face seemed to symbolise everything that this vast organisation of talents stood for. I was looking fame and fortune in the eyes, and the eyes were adding the promise of love to these other riches. "Yes" I said at last, surprised to find how very hoarse my voice sounded. "Yes, I am a fool. I *must* sign on."

In retrospect this epoch, these scenes, astonished me very much when I recalled them; I mean after everything went to wrack, the period of illnesses and confusion, the period of intemperate recriminations, quarrels, fugues. Once, when she was hovering on the outside edges of logic I even heard her say: "I only really loved you when I thought you were determined to be free from the firm. It seemed to promise me my own freedom. But afterwards I saw that you were just like everyone else." Then in my fury I shouted back. "But you made me sign on, Benedicta. It was you who insisted, remember?" She nodded her furious head and answered: "Yes. I had to. But you could have stuck to your guns and that would have altered everything. For us both."

"Then why, knowing this, did you insist on having the child? There was no need, was there?"

"There were several reasons. Partly because Julian said so, Nash said so, it was a question of cure as well. Then also the question of succession, inheritance. Then me. All those miscarriages were a challenge I had to face. Above all I wanted a Merlin of my own, of my very own." She paused and gazed about her as if to identify a small sound, audible only to her inner ear. "You see," she added tonelessly "hardly anyone saw my father in the flesh—though everyone saw Julian at some time or another. Then the firm—O Felix, Benedicta is only a woman, she has always tried to be just." Nearly sobbing.

"You talk about yourself as if you were a *product*."

"I am. I am." That was the *tu quoque*!

Then later when I was speaking to her about love she could say with burning indignation: "But love is a reality not a recipe." As if in offering her mine under any other guise I had tricked her. Woman!

But all this lay far in the future on that day when Jocas walked down to the landing stage beside me with his choppy deliberate tread. "You will go back to Athens and wait" he said and his tone was one of delighted relief. He embraced me warmly and added "Benedicta will come to you very soon. You may find her the key to everything. Sacrapant will deal with all the contractual details. I myself am going to the islands for a week. Felix!"

"Yes, Jocas?"

"You are going to be very happy."

But I felt bemused still and shaken by my own decision. Sacrapant gazed at me with lachrymose tenderness; it seemed that he too knew, without being told, that I had agreed to sign, but tact held him silent. We roared away across the opalescent water towards the dim horizon where the city lay half asleep, embedded in time as in a quagmire—the Orient Venice snoring its life away.

Vibart was at his habitual desk, only today he was blowing an egg to add to his collection. He had pierced the blue crown with a needle and was blowing with soft absorption into the tiny hole; from the opposite hole the yolk was being gradually expelled to fall with a plop into his waste-paper basket. "There" he said with relief, placing the tiny object in a velvet hollow among others like it. He closed the casket reverently and joined his fingers together as he gazed at me. The contracts lay on the corner of the desk among his papers. Without saying anything I picked up the pen from its slab of marble and signed in all the required places. "Well" he said in great good humour "I should bloody well think so. Fame and fortune, my boy, and all for the price of a signature. The luck some people have." I sat, staring into the middle distance, still confused and somehow fearfully sad. Somehow he must have felt it (he was a discerning young man under his flippant exterior) for his tone changed to one of quickening sympathy; the drink he poured out with which to celebrate the event was a stiff one, and I needed it, or felt I did. Though why?

I seemed to hear the voice of Sacrapant saying: "The firm is wonderful, Mr. Charlock, sir. When I could not find anyone for my wife's womb the firm found me someone."

The telephone rang squeakily. "It's for you" said Vibart. I recognised the voice of Jocas, distant and crackly. "Felix I forgot. I have a message for you to give your friend Koepgen in Athens. He is your friend, isn't he?"

"Yes. I didn't know you knew him."

"I don't personally. But when you see him will you tell him that we have located the ikon he has been hunting for?"

"The ikon?"

"Yes. We know the monastery now."

"I'll make a note of it."

"Thank you very much Felix."

I drew a deep breath and said: "Jocas, I have just signed the articles of association."

"I knew it" he said. "I felt it. I was sure."

Vibart sat sipping his drink and staring at me. "I think" he said "you need cheering up. I shall invite you to dine with me and hear all the details of my literary career. It's really moving forward. And by the way, I have found a good *French* tavern. You know the French will eat anything and everything? If the sky rained corpses' legs they would become cannibals without a second thought. Moreover it would be doubly enjoyable because it was all free. Will you?"

"Very well. But I must first take these down to the firm and draw some money."

This I duly did, walking through the crowded and insanitary streets among the snarling bands of dogs. Mr. Sacrapant was waiting for me: but oh, he looked so grave and tender, like an undertaker's mute on his best behaviour. He took the documents and cashed me a voucher for what seemed to me an immense sum of money which I stuffed into my slender wallet with cold fingers.

"You'll be going back to Athens I have no doubt" he said. "I shall treasure the memory of our association. Mr. Charlock."

"Thank you. In a day or two I expect." The truth of the matter was that I was reluctant to leave the city before I had seen Benedicta once more—and yet, there seemed to be no chance of that. Should I perhaps send her a message? Perhaps the mere information that I was still in Polis might.... "I think I shall be here another full week if you should need me" I told him. "At the Pera as usual."

The malignant tumour of a passive love! All of a sudden the gloomy steamy city seemed peopled with ghosts. I was still numb from the astonishment of finding myself freed at a stroke from all the smaller preoccupations that beset ordinary men—financial dependence, occupation, etc. It was puzzling too because anyone in my place would have felt exultant, bouyant. I felt absolutely nothing. I took a cab back to the detestable hotel, confirmed my reservation, and ordered lunch in the garden. There were no familiar faces there, much to my regret. I would be grateful for Vibart's company while I was waiting. Waiting! But suppose Benedicta did not come? There was Zürich of course.

At dusk Vibart called for me and together we wandered through the city towards his newly discovered eating-house. His wife would join us there later. As usual he was preoccupied with the building of this imaginary career upon which he was too hesitant to embark; the self-rebukes multiplied in all directions. He had decided to reverse the usual order of things and start by writing his own reviews. "Why not the obits?" I suggested. "They are always the warmest reviews. The one consolation about death is that everyone will be forced to be nice to you behind your back."

"I never thought of that" said Vibart settling his napkin round his neck with the air of a man putting on a cummerbund. "And I think it's too late. My novel *The Asparagus Tree* comes out this week. ('A novel of surpassing tameness'.) The press will be very mixed. I console myself by saying that the jealousy of opinionated dunces is the finest of literary compliments. I have arranged a good sales picture however. What do you think of thirty thousand in the first week? On a sliding scale that should be a clear thousand, no?"

"Too good by half" said his wife with the resignation of one who has been forced to live with an obsession. She was a handsome brunette with shy green eyes. Her name was Pia.

The food was excellent. "I should give it up" I said "and go for criticism. Grudge yourself off in the weeklies. Loll your way to fame. Tell yourself that you are not really a bad man, just unprincipled."

"Can I" said Vibart in envious tones "tell my wife about your terrific coup—the new job?"

"Of course." He did so at once and at some length. She watched me curiously, surprised by my lack of animation. I suppose I looked guilty. I tried to explain. "You see, Vibart, in a sort of way I am in the same boat as you. I didn't want to be just an artificer, I wanted to go for abstractions: use the calculus as a springboard. Like you, I have not got the talent. I shall be forced to confine myself to tinkering with nuts and bolts instead of dealing with poetic abstractions, new universes. And I did *so* want to be the age's little Copernicus. Hence the apathy you criticise. I am the wrong kind of scientist. I shall have to be content to try and do something about the faulty five senses in this smaller way."

He reeled off, in quotation: "An eagle for sight, a hart for hearing, a spider for touch, an ape for taste, and a dog for smell."

"I would have liked to achieve in my line whatever would correspond to a work of art—which my friend Koepgen has defined as an act of disciplined insubordination. But if one isn't up to it?" My God, we were getting drunk.

"Oh dear," said his wife "here I am surrounded by failures." But she was grateful for this self-identification with her husband's private myth.

Vibart was put into a very good humour now, and decided that all further self-recrimination should cease until he had reached the coffee. The food, he said, was too good to poison, and besides the only metaphysical problem for the gourmet was: is there a life beyond the gravy?

A freak thunderstorm had sprung up and rain was needling the tragic arcades; we sat long over our brandies, waiting for it to stop, and once more the consuming restlessness beset me. My wristwatch purred on in tireless itching iteration and I found myself wondering about Benedicta and the new equivocal pattern of relationships which she alone could disentangle and sort out. Time is the only thing that doesn't wear out. "I think I shall probably leave for

Athens tomorrow" I said, since Vibart was planning a picnic for the week-end and I had suddenly tired of him. The rain was thinning off now, and a fresh wind was flapping at the awnings of the cafés. By luck we found a cab to take us back to Pera, where I dropped off at my hotel. Here all my doubts were resolved for on the mantelpiece of my room I found a single joss stick burning in a vase and a visiting card of Jocas' with a few words written on it in that curiously shapeless and hesitant hand which I was to come to know so well—Benedicta's. She was coming to visit me on the morrow at noon. All at once—like the wind dispersing storm cloud at a single puff—I felt the whole weight of my preoccupations lift and disperse. I fell asleep almost at once, but it was to dream elaborate and intricate dreams, worthy of Vibart, about the long life-lines of the firm which channelled all the riches of the Orient into the huge granaries over which Jocas presided—furs and skins and poppy, caviar and salt and wax, amber, precious stones, porcelain and glass: dreams of such fervent inaccuracy that even while I dreamed them I was forced to correct the picture, to bring it up to date with less romantic commodities like pit-props from Slovenia, oil and wheat from Russia, bauxite and tin and coal. And somewhere in the middle of this meretricious romancing I saw the pale face of Benedicta staring down at me as if from a lofty window: and I woke with a start with a question on my lips, namely, "You must be sure that her riches play no part in any decision you make." But riches cannot be side-stepped; they mark one like a hare-lip. I studied her handwriting with misgiving. A graphologist would have hinted at glandular imbalances. But I loved her, I loved her, I loved her.

Then in the morning, following out in some obscure fashion the train of thought which had dribbled through my sleep, I went out to the fashionable Pera shopping area with the scientific intention of spending a very large sum of money: in order to see exactly how it felt. I thought I might buy a sporting gun or a wrist-watch or a fountain pen of abhorrent splendour. Accustomed to live meagrely if decently, to find myself frequently short, not of necessities, but of luxuries, I wanted to taste the sensation of pouring out some of my own fairly earned gold over some merchant's counter. But my desire for these unnecessary objects ebbed away as soon as I sighted them. What the devil would I do with a gun? Hippolyta would always lend me one. A wrist-watch? I should forget to take it off when I swam. A pen? No sooner bought than lost. In desultory fashion I mooned about the souk, allowing myself to be plucked and cajoled and lectured by the swarthies. I did not know enough then about precious stones. (Now of course my artificial diamonds flourish all over the globe.) Nor perfumes. But finally, with Benedicta in mind I allowed myself to be tempted by a small and lovely carpet—an authentic Shiraz according to the label. With this rolled up under my arm I walked back to the hotel in time to see a flock of hamalis—the grotesque cow-like public porters of the capital—carrying a string of black suitcases and hat-boxes all marked with the gold monogram I was to come to know so well. But she was already there, dressed like a fashion-plate, sitting upon the terrace with her gloved hands in her lap. Gloves! Her large fine straw hat cast dancing freckles of amber light over her features.

She was staring at her gloves and her lips were moving as if in prayer or in a secret conversation with her own mind. Everything seemed to warn me, but I walked up to take her hands—remove them from her field of vision, claim them and with them her attention. She responded, when I uttered her name with a glance full of abstraction—as if she were seeing me for the first time. "Everyone is agreed" she said softly—the most desolating words that a man in love can hear. "But everyone, without exception, even Julian. They are all on our side." She trembled a little when we embraced; slender and pliant, and fragrant with a scent I could not identify. "I want you to say my name; to hear how it sounds: I haven't paid attention before." I repeated her name twice. She sighed and said "Yes, it is just as I thought." It was as if something had been put to the proof. I sat beside her and unrolled my gift. "I brought you a small Shiraz" I said proud of my acquisition, only to be dashed by her smile as she said: "It's Afghan. You've been cheated." She laughed and clapped her hands as if at an excellent jest.

All my gear had been moved from my room into a very large suite on the second floor; it mingled oddly with her collection of shining suitcases. A Turkish maid was busy hanging up her dresses. A lunch table had been laid upon the balcony. She stood with her probationary eyes narrowed critically as she surveyed the room with its huge four-poster and velvet baldaquin. Then she turned suddenly to me and said: "I can only stay three days this time. Then I must go north. But I will come to you in Athens or in London later. Yes?"

"Very well."

Three nights, three days of calendar time; to the bemused (and it *was* reciprocal) it could have been three centuries, so marvellously did the spilled seconds transform my view both of her and her melancholy city of historic afterthoughts: it had become a sort of extension of her childhood and its memories, a coherent demesne. All the stagnant beauties, its repellent corners of dirt and disease, the marsh gas thrown off by the rotting corpse of Byzantium—they all coalesced into a significant shape. She walked about it with the unconscious assurance of long familiarity. It was a wicked place to fall in love with a woman, an unmanning place: or was this simply Benedicta, and the obstinate alarm bell sounding in the back of my mind, muffled by the sweet minaret-calls, the sage boom of sirens from the Horn? Let us say that I saw her reflections in it—imprint of the imago which underlay the kisses which were not blithe and free, as they should have been, but concentrated, perverse, bewitching. The central enigma hasn't changed from that day to this; I could have seen her even then, if I had tried, as someone born to be loved yet doomed to die, in solitude like a masterless animal. Yet how lucky I was myself—for I was able to surrender—and this gave me the illusion that I could however briefly cross the distance that she put between us. The victories of applied science! I gave her everything that I had learned from Iolanthe! For one moment had the conviction that I had stopped the great moving staircase of the heart! I stubbornly averted my face from the notion that in all this first encounter what I really saw was the first sketch, so to speak, of a more massive alienation. Did I? I don't know. Anyway, making love with a sort of breathless resignation—or else desperately, like someone trying to pull an arrow from the flesh before the poison has time to spread. And she knew ways to excite, the praying mantis, like "tie up my wrists" or less judiciously "O it is too big, I shall split." Incitements to the furies let loose in men when they love an aggressive woman. To couple so perfectly and yet be denied any sort of initiation! Kisses were warnings I did not recognise; but the feeling of finality was delicious, vertiginous—things could not have fallen out otherwise could they? Gentlemen of the jury, we should tackle reality in a slightly joky way, otherwise we miss its point. It isn't solemn at all, it's *playing*! It's all very well telling poor Felix that now; he too is wise after the event. Suppose we could make the electric chair into a romantic symbol? If you section the olfactory gland of the rabbit you condemn it to impotence; snick off the salamander's head while it is coupling, and it feels nothing; caught in the divine rhythm it continues as if nothing had happened. Perhaps nothing has? Benedicta! Rapidly cooling worlds, we lie asleep in each other's arms. The mysteries do not matter. I come upon her sitting on the balcony in a flood of tears. "Why, Benedicta?" She doesn't know, staring up at me with tear-laden lashes, tears running down her long subtle nose. "I don't know." Yet ten minutes later laughing heartily at the antics of a monkey on a barrel-organ.

Well then, as I say, her city began to borrow some of her colours; our excursions and promenades became the unfamiliar delight, and she knew corners and nooks which escaped the industry or perhaps taste of other guides like Sacrapant or Vibart. It is not possible for me now to think of Polis again without seeing Benedicta's face superposed upon whatever it is—mosque, graveyard, tilting forest of shipping in the Golden Horn. She owns it as Io owns Athens. There were puzzles, of course, and singularities: I remember that wherever we went we found someone to receive us—someone waiting outside a mosque with the keys for example. The difficulty of gaining entry to the smaller mosques, the difficulty of tracing the guardian with the keys, is too famous an aspect of Polis to need elaboration; every visitor has complained of it. Yet wherever this fateful couple went—and so often on foot—the guardian was there waiting. Had she warned him, or caused him to be warned, I asked? "No, it is just that we are lucky, simply that."

Then again, with the same equivocal air—an expression of pride and sorrow almost—she led me through the beautiful cemetery at Eyub, among the marble incantations with their tell-tale-turbans and flower-knots. We came to one grave set in a small grilled enclosure of its own. I could not read the flowing Arabic inscription, of course; but below it, in small Roman letters, I saw the name Benedicta Merlin. There was no date. "Who is it—your mother?" I asked; but she only turned away abruptly, picking a stalk of green with which to tease her lips as she walked down the hill. "Benedicta, please tell me." She stared at me intently, and then once more turned away and resumed her slow progress among the graves. It was useless to press her. At the edge of the cemetery she turned and embraced me, pressing me to her with a strange sort of fury, as if to extirpate some unhallowed memory of the past. But no words, do you see? And then with a soft kind intensity she took out her handkerchief to rub the lipstick marks from my mouth. Never, it seemed, had anyone looked at me with so much overflowing love, vulnerable tenderness; what did it matter that she should have her secrets? The stern mask of the priestess had slipped. Briefly I saw a woman.

So the time passed, dense with the special fulfilments of physical possession; I averted my mind from the prospect of her vanishing back into Europe—dragged by the slow Orient Express through the great walls of the city towards Zürich. Then in the middle of everything—or rather at the end, for it was the last evening—came the most singular event of all: the death of Sacrapant. It was so sudden and so unexpected that it deafened the mind—though afterwards of course it was explained satisfactorily. Events of this kind are always clothed in a factitious causality when we see them in retrospect. Was it, though?

Sunset is the finest hour; with the city nimbling softly away towards darkness while the sun fights its lion-battle against the skyline driving the dense mists higher and higher into brief priceless colours and shapes. To sit in the darkening garden of the hotel quietly drinking an aperitif and waiting for the blind muezzin to climb into his perch among the buildings and send out his owl-cry to the faithful—this was the best way to spend this hour, watching the lights beginning to twinkle over by Taxim, and the shipping rustle and moo on the darkening water.

This particular eloquent evening we were very silent; the express left just before midnight, her packing was done. We sat there between two worlds, neither cast down nor elated: existing in a curious abstraction of certainty about the future. One side of the mind turned towards that quiet call which must soon come from the mosque—the old blind face of a bird uttering the quiet nasal cawing of the Ebed. And I saw in the gathering dusk a slim figure in white limping among the distant trees; it walked with just a trace of unsteadiness but with resolution as if towards a predetermined destination. I recognised my friend, though I did not comment on the fact; so, I think, did she, following the direction of my gaze. There would have been nothing unusual about that; but then to my surprise I saw him pause, squint upwards into the sky, and enter the circular staircase of the mosque. But now his pace had changed; he walked slowly, wearily, as if bowed under a great weight. I saw him appear at the little window-slit half way up and could not resist a puzzled gasp. "What the devil, it's old Sacrapant. . . ." She looked at her watch and at the sky.

It was still early for the muezzin. The frail figure appeared at last at the balustrade, raising small fern-like hands as in an invocation to the darkening world about the tower. It was indeed an invocation, but a frail and incoherent one; the sense of the words hardly penetrated the heavy layers of the damp night air. I thought I heard something like "will find fulfilment in the firm. Give it your best and it will be returned an hundredfold." One could not be absolutely sure, of course, but among the wavering incantations I thought I heard so much. Then I jumped to my feet for the frail figure had started to lean forward and topple. Mr. Sacrapant started to fall out of the night sky in a slow swoop towards the dark ground. A crash of a palm tree, and then a thud of unmistakable finality, followed by the splintering jingle of broken glass and small change. I was transfixed by the suddenness of it all. I stood there speechless. But already there were running feet everywhere and voices; a crowd gathered in no time, as flies will do about an open artery. "My God" I said. Benedicta sat quite still with bowed head. I turned to her and whispered her name; but she did not move.

I shook her gently by the shoulders as one might shake a clock that had stopped and she looked up at me with an intense unwavering sadness. "Come away quick" she said, and grabbed my hand. Away among the trees the sounds had become more purposeful—they were gathering up the loaves and fishes. Blood on marble. I shuddered. Crossing the dark garden hand in hand we moved towards the lighted terraces and public rooms of the hotel. Benedicta said: "Jocas must have given him the sack. O why must people go to extremes?" Why, indeed! I thought of the pale humble face of Sacrapant shining up there in the evening sky. Of course such an explanation would meet the case, yet. . . . The evening lay in ruins about us. The silent dinner, the packing away of the luggage into the office car which had appeared—these operations we performed automatically, numbed by the sadness of this sudden death. My mind reverted continually to the memory of that pale face leaning down from the tower; Sacrapant had looked like someone who had been carefully deprived of an individual psychology by some experiment with knife or drug. For one brief moment his coat tails had flattened out with the wind of his fall giving him the shape of a dart—like a falling mallard. But he had fallen, so to speak, slap into the middle of our emotions; the widening rings of his death spread through our minds now, alienating us from each other.

We embraced, we parted, almost with disgust. The hideous station with its milling tortoise-faced mob of Turks mercifully precluded speeches of farewell. I stood holding her hands while the carriage was found and the luggage stored in it by the chauffeur. "Or else" she said gravely, in the tones of one continuing an inner monologue "he suddenly learned that he had cancer, or that his wife had a lover, or that his favourite child. . . ." I realised that any explanation would do, and that all would forever remain merely provisional. Was this perhaps true for all of us, for all our actions? Yes, yes. I studied her face again with care, with an almost panic-stricken intentness, realising at last how useless it was to be loving her; she had climbed into the carriage and stood looking down at me from the open window with a hesitant sorrowfulness. We could not have been further apart at this instant; a cloud of anxiety had overshadowed all emotion. I felt my heavy despairs dragging at their moorings. Tomorrow I should return to Athens—I should be free from everyone, free even from Benedicta. My God, the only four letter word that matters! The train had begun to move. I walked beside it for a few paces. She too was looking almost relieved, elated. Or so it seemed to me. Perhaps because she felt sure of me—of her hold over me? She wound up the glass window and then, with a sudden impulse, breathed upon it in order to write the word "Soon" on the little patch of condensation. At once the pain of separation came back.

I turned away to let my thoughts disperse among those sullen crowds of featureless faces. The car waited to take me back to the hotel. That night I slept alone and for the first time experienced the suffocating sense of loneliness which came over me with the conviction that I should never see Benedicta again. This whole episode would remain in my memory, carefully framed and hung, quite self-subsisting: and quite without relevance or continuity to anything else I had ever done or experienced. An anecdote of Istanbul!

Nor did this feeling completely leave me even when, from the windy deck-head, I saw the white spars of Sunion come up over the waters. The season had turned, autumn was here, the marbles looked blue with cold: and I had turned a corner in my supposed life. It was baffling, the sense of indecision which beset me; I supposed that the novelty of this new life was what had numbed me—simply that. Simply that.

Hippolyta met me at the dock with her car, bursting with excitement and jubilation. "We're saved" she cried as I clambered down the gangway with my suitcase. "O come along do, Charlock; we must celebrate, and it's all due to you. Graphos! He has swept all the provinces. My darling, he's changed completely. He is certain to get back into power." Apparently something had been averted by the resuscitation of the great man's party and its electoral successes. Well, I sat by her side, letting her babble on to her heart's content. We headed for the country directly because they were all "waiting to congratulate" me. I was returning like a conquering hero to the hospitable country house. "Moreover" she said, taking my hand and pressing it to her cheek "you have joined the firm. You are one of us now." In the back of my mind I had a sudden snapshot of Benedicta walking alone in some remote corner of an untended garden, among rare shrubs and flowers which discharged their pollen on her clothes at every step, like silent pistol-shots. In the house great fires blazed and champagne-glasses winked. Caradoc was there and Pulley; and the immaculate spatted form of Banubula. Everyone burst into a torrent of congratulatory rhetoric. I drank away the feelings of the past weeks, lapped around by all this human glow. It was only when, as an afterthought, I said: "By the way, I am going to marry Benedicta Merlin" that the great silence fell. It was the half second of silence at the end of some marvellously executed symphony, the mesmerised rapture which precedes the thunder of applause. Yes. That sort of silence, and lasting only half a second; then the applause, or rather the storm of congratulation in which, to my surprise, I strove suspiciously to detect a false note. But no. It rang out in the most genuine manner; Caradoc indeed seemed rather moved by the news, his bear-hugs hurt. I surrendered myself to my self-congratulation invaded by a new sense of confidence. It was late when at last I gathered my kit and borrowed the car to return to Athens; I was curious to see Number Seven again, to riffle my notebooks. Yet I noted with some curiosity that all of a sudden the absence, not of Benedicta but of Iolanthe, weighed. Some obscure law of association must be at work; I had not give her a thought in Istanbul, she was not appropriate to the place. Nor would Benedicta ever be to Athens. I looked up from under the shaded light and imagined her entering the room as she always did, punctual as a heartbeat. These sentimental polarities of feeling were new to me; I disapproved of them thoroughly. Frowning I returned to my scribbles. I roughed out a schema as a basis for my work for the firm when at last I should be summoned. Then I noticed a letter on the mantelpiece, a letter addressed to me. It was from Julian, written in an exquisite italic hand; it congratulated me most gracefully on the excellent news and told me that I need not move from Athens for the time being; but I should map out a work-scheme and submit it. Did I wish to start with the mechanical end of my research? A limited company called Merlin Devices would be set up as part of a light-engineering subsidiary of the firm. I would find the technicians and the tools ready to hand for whatever I dreamed up. It was a marvellous prospect, and I fell asleep happily that night in the stuffy little room, with my counterpane littered with notes and formulae and diagrams.

At seven, when the porter brought me my coffee I found that dapper Koepgen had followed hard on his heels and had taken up his usual watchful position in the armchair. Koepgen of the elf-lock and the lustrous eye. For the time of day he looked unnaturally spruce and self-possessed. "Go on" he said with ill-concealed excitement. "Tell me what it is." For a moment I had forgotten. "Jocas cabled me that he would give you a message for me." Then I remembered. Sleepily I repeated the message to him. He drew a long hissing breath, his face at once rueful and amused. "What a cunning old dog, what a swine" he said admiringly, and struck his knee. "I only worked a few weeks for them but it was enough for the firm to find my weak point. They are incredible." He chirped his loudest laugh.

"What's it all about?" I asked; there was a small bottle of ouzo on the mantelpiece; Koepgen made a by-your-leave, drew the cork and tilted a dose into a toothmug. He drank it off quite slim and said: "He's holding me to ransom, the old devil. He wants me to go back to Moscow and deal with some contracts for the firm; I refused, it doesn't interest me. Now I see I will have to go if I'm ever to get my hands on the bloody thing."

"What bloody thing?"

"The ikon."

"What next?" It sounded to me as if the firm were busy doing some elaborate trade in antiques; but no, said Koepgen, no such thing. What they were after were some contracts from the Communist Government for wheat and oil in exchange for machinery. Nothing could be more prosaic. And the ikon—where did that come in? Ah. He burst out laughing again and said with exasperation, "My dear Charlock, that is a piece of Russian folklore which will sound to you quite silly; but nevertheless it has cost me several years and hundreds of miles on foot." He sat down suddenly with a bump in the chair.

"But wouldn't it be dangerous, I mean Communists and all that?"

"No. One of my uncles is Minister of Trade. No, it isn't that. I just didn't want to work for the firm; but I made the mistake of telling them my fairy tale, and of course this is the result. You see, when I started this theological jag I chose one of the great mystics, a big bonze of Russia as a guide. As you know, absolute obedience is required, even if one is set a task that seems an idiocy. I was set a task which turned unwittingly into a pilgrimage on my poor flat feet. There was an ikon once in the private chapel of my mother; when the estate was confiscated it had vanished. I was told to find it or else."

"Or else what?"

Koepgen grinned. "Or else no progress, see? I should be stuck in the lower ranks. Never get my stripes. Don't laugh."

"What fantasy."

"Of course you'd think that; but there is more than one kind of truth, Charlock."

"O crikey," I said "don't do the theological on me."

"Well, anyway, hence this bloody long walk across Russia into Athos. I traced it there. After that I drew a blank for a while. It was a Saint Catherine of a rather special kind. And of course the woods are full of them—Saint Catherines. It might be somewhere in a way-side shrine on Olympus or stuck in some great monastery in Meteora. In spite of all the help I got I drew blank after blank. The Orthodox Church is an odd organisation or perhaps I should say disorganisation; what is the good for example of an encyclical when half the minor clergy are illiterates?"

"Offer a reward."

"We did all that. I sorted through hundreds of them big and small; but I couldn't get the one belonging to my mother. You see? Now the firm has stepped in found it and will tell me where it is on condition. . . ."

"I have never heard such rubbish in my life" I said. Koepgen nearly burst into tears. "Nor have I," he said "nor have I."

"I should damn well refuse to go."

"Perhaps I shall. I must see. On the other hand I suppose it isn't such an arduous undertaking; it might cost me a month or two in Moscow, and then at least I would have found it and satisfied my *staretz* old Demetrius. O dear." He took another swig from the bottle and fell into a heavy melancholy silence, turning over these weird contingencies in his mind. I drew a bath and lay in it awhile, leaving him to brood in the armchair. I had decided, on the strength of my new-found fortune, to move all my belongings today to the best hotel in the town—to take a comfortable suite. I did not need more space but I was most anxious to experiment with the notion of spending a lot of money. Yes, of course the grub would be much better. I was drying myself slowly when Koepgen appeared in the doorway. He was still sunk in a kind of abstraction, and gazed at me with unfocused eye. "You know" he said slowly at last "I have a feeling that I shall have to obey Julian. After all sacrifices have to be made if one's going to get anywhere in life, eh?"

"Hum" I said, feeling very sage and judicial, yet indifferent.

"You will see," he said "you will see, my boy. Your turn will come. Have you ever met Julian?"

"No." I dressed slowly; it was a lovely sunny day, and we walked across Athens on foot, stopping here and there in the shadow of a vine arbour to have a drink and a mézé. Koepgen made no further reference to his ikon and I was glad; the whole thing seemed to me to be a burdensome fairy tale. After all if a man of such sharp intelligence in his forties allowed the firm to play upon these infantile superstitions, well good luck to it. But such reflections filled me with shame when I glanced at his sorrowful and now rather haggard features. I had come to like him very much. As we parted, I to reserve my new quarters and organise the move, he to return to his seminary, he said under his breath: "I fear there is no help for it. I shall have to go. I'll cable Jocas today."

He started to walk down the winding street and then, on a sudden impulse, ran after me and caught my sleeve. He said in a humble, beseeching tone "Charlock, can I leave my notebooks with you if I decide to go?" His manner touched me. "Of course." And that evening when I got back to my new hotel, rather aware that my shabby wardrobe would have to be replaced if I were ever to match the splendour of such surroundings, I saw the familiar pile of school exercise books on the mantelpiece. A rubber band held them together. But there was no word with them; I must presume that Koepgen had fallen in with the wishes of the firm, perhaps he was already on his way north. I rather envied him the journey in a queer sort of way. My dinner had been left in the alcove to await me. I could not help touching the smooth expensive napery which enveloped it. In Athens such costly and beautiful ironed covers and napkins were quite a rarity. I had decided to work that evening on my crystals, and had set out my white china trays in the bathroom. But the telephone rang and when I picked it up Benedicta stood before me, so to speak; her voice was so clear that I thought she must be calling me from the floor below. But no, she was in Switzerland.

"Darling", the endearment made my heart suddenly turn over in its grave. Every doubt, every hesitation, was puffed away on the instant and I realised with a reviving pang how much I wanted her here, right here. The enormous inadequacy of words belaboured me. "Never have I missed anyone so much. It confirms everything." So it seemed to me also as I sat, gripping the black telephone, grimacing into it. "We will be married in April. Julian has arranged everything. In London. Do you agree?"

"Why wait so long, Benedicta?"

"I have to. I am under orders. I won't be free to move until then. O how much I miss you, miss you." The clear magnetic voice took on a note of familiar despair. "Julian is arranging the terms of the settlement, the marriage contract."

"What settlement?" I said in perplexity.

"Well, about my share in the firm. We must have perfect equality in love, my darling." All of a sudden the line went dead and a thousand other voices came up, trying to restore the broken communication. "Benedicta" I cried, and I could still hear her voice, though what she was saying was indistinct. An operator squashed her out and promised to call me back. I went and lay on my bed in a confused frame of mind—a mixture of rage and euphoria.

Gentlemen of the jury, now I can tell you that I have loved a woman who sat on numberless committees for the emancipation of other women, never speaking, and with the bitten nails of her left hand sheathed in a glove. Actually what women need is to be beaten almost to death, enslaved, raped, and forced to cook meals when they are heavy with child. Bite through the nape of the neck, Wilkinson, stick her with a bayonet, and she's yours forever. A bottomless masochism is all they seek to indulge; the penis is too kind a weapon by far. No, the emancipation of this creature is a joke. (Benedicta, look into my eyes.) They are waveborn, slaveborn; and yet somewhere among them may be one, just *one*, who is different, who fills the bill. But what bill, Felix? Love! We never had before nor never since, seen it, I mean. Burp! Pardon my parahelion.

Perfect equality in love, I thought. God! Tomorrow I would go out and buy the most expensive microscope in the world and a Stradivarius and some strawberries and a car.... But in love there is never enough equality to go round. We will have to settle for equity among men and women—a humbler target. Benedicta ached on. After half an hour of futile suspense I tried to restore the broken communication from my own end, but this proved impossible. They could not trace the number from which she had called me. The hall porter brought me a bottle of whisky and a siphon. I tried to resume the precious train of thought about crystals—the fragile line of reasoning which, after so many years, has given Merlin's a near monopoly in the field of lasers. Benedicta kept intruding among my scribbles. ("The ordering of their atoms is never quite perfect or they would not be able to form, to grow.")

Then the phone did ring again and I leaped at it. But it was only Caradoc, rather drunk and indistinct, calling me from the Nube, his gruff voice framed in a background of mandolin music. "Charlock," he said in his usual growling vein "we are waiting for you down here. Why don't you come?" But Benedicta had covered me in a sheath, a caul of discontent. I could not think of the sweaty Nube, the dust-filled curtains, without distaste. "I am waiting for a phone-call, and doing some work" I said, fearful lest our own conversation might be holding up a long-distance contact. Caradoc growled on reproachfully. "Ah you scientists in love! Soon you will be accusing nature of a moral order. Push!"

"Push to you" I said. "Now for godsake hang up and leave me alone will you?"

He did so, but with evident reluctance. "Well, hard cheese" he said as a parting shot, and I had the sudden vivid image of Mr. Sacrapant leaning over a desk looking gravely at me and saying "You are right to be precautionate, Mr. Charlock." And what was the other expression? Yes, "I have inaccurised the document, sir." Presumably he meant that he had been through it for inaccuracies. Ah, pale Sacrapant, falling out of the air like these autumn leaves tumbling into the parks. Again the phone rang and this time Hippolyta's clear youthful voice sprang from the mouthpiece as if from the ear of a goddess. "Charlock, I heard you'd moved. How does it feel to be really loved?"

"O leave me alone" I cried in anguish, much to her surprise. "Hang up. I'm waiting for a call."

But Benedicta did not ring again.

Indeed I had no word from her throughout the months which lay ahead. However, filled with the *gai savoir* I buckled down to my plans for the little Merlin subsidiary which I should virtually run single handed from London. Or so I thought. Two members of its hypothetical board flew out to meet me, Denison and Broad, and I was glad to find them both accomplished and experienced men. Needless to say I knew nothing about company law, patent claims, and similar esoteric subjects, and was glad to delegate this side of things to them; when everything was ready I should transfer myself to London with a basketful of preliminary ideas. This little respite was useful; it enabled me to map out my own objectives more clearly and to get them down on paper. Moreover I had nothing to fear from the Athens winter while I was lodged in such warm and comfortable quarters.

I sorted not only my papers but also the vast collection of tapes, fragments, dialects, etc. and transcribed them on to matrices; many were the felicities I had culled from the conversations of my friends. (The voice of Sipple saying, gravely: "You might say that I belong to the Purple People. In the case of Mrs. Sipple now—although I didn't know this till later—she used to come up every Wednesday from Broadstairs where she had been playing with the mighty organ of a DSO with Bar.")

I saw a good deal of Caradoc who was marking time before being sent off on a new assignment. As I've said, he had invented what he called the mnemon which he insisted was a literary form—"an art-form in which free Freud and solipsism marry and make merry. You might say it was a soft cotton pun dressed up in the form of a *Times* personal." They were indeed *Times* Personals of a slightly surrealist tinge, and I had the pleasure of helping him father a few. To my surprise he actually had them printed in the newspaper where they doubtless passed completely unnoticed or were supposed to be an obscure code, a love-call for some religious sect.

> Jewish gentleman in Romford, expert on
> vibraphone, urgently seeks father figure.
>
> Small pegamoid man, fond of soft clinics,
> seeks tangible rubber acme. Own plug.

No poet ever derived greater pleasure from seeing his work printed, and Caradoc spent a good deal of money on these confections. Then came his sixtieth birthday and he woke up to find himself knee deep in telegrams of congratulations and press cuttings. There were long articles on his work everywhere, photographs of the Hoarah Bridge, the University of Tobago, and other masterpieces of his implausible genius. To my surprise all this backslapping made him sad and plaintive, and once more he began to talk about leaving the firm. "About twice in your life you get a chance to change everything, to jump over the side; but a moment's hesitation and the chance slips away. It's late in the day for me but who knows? I might get another yet. I'm keeping my eyes skinned." Meanwhile the firm had found him a new assignment with which he could hardly quarrel: a new university and senate in the Cook Islands. He would be entirely his own master. Already his fingers itched when they were near a pencil and he spent much of his time, absorbed as any child, modelling in plasticine. "The game of volumes, my boy, the most intoxicating of them all. They've promised me aerial pictures of the site, I can't wait to get my hands on them. And think of new settings, palms, volcanoes, surf."

"When will you leave?"

"As soon as I can. There's nothing more to be done here."

The season was shifting, our little group was dispersing slowly; Hippo moved back into Paris with her sails spread and only occasionally sent us a postcard. Banubula went to the New Year's Eve ball dressed up in a quaint oldfashioned stock of Edwardian provenance with a twinkling pin, looking very much like a vampire on his evening off. "He is dark umber, the bloody Count" said Caradoc who enjoyed parodying his friend's exquisite and lapidary English. "I'm sure he would subscribe himself as 'Your Umber Servant'." The poor Count made no allusion to his Turkish excesses, and nor did I. He had resumed his Athenian persona. The Countess still sat alone for the greater part of the day in a dressing-gown and slippers, her hair caught up in a purple scarf: playing patience, and writing letters to Gurdjieff. "Horatio has been so strange this winter" she might say stretching out long phthisical fingers towards her coffee cup. "So strange." Did she see him as we did who were not privy to his innermost secrets? I mean dark brown voice, cotton gloves, silver-capped stick with heavy rubber ferrule, one ring-seal, iodine-locket, rebus. . . . It was hard to say. Benedicta wrote disturbingly "I have been ill, I have had a small absence": in French this time.

Then Caradoc was summoned to London to establish his team of draughtsmen for the new project, and I realised that I was going to be very lonely without him. Worse, I did not realise that we should never meet again—though in retrospect I cannot see the logic of such a sentiment. We had a farewell party in the Nube where I successfully masqueraded as sufficiently unwell to spare myself the culminating pleasures of the bed. An idiocy, I suppose—but what is one among so many? Here Sipple intervened, or rather the memory of him for Caradoc entertained a fantastically high opinion of his friend's gifts and much regretted not to see him before he left. I questioned him about the incident of the dead boy, but found that he knew little more than I did. It may have been something to do with blackmail. "I think Sipple must have been working for someone, perhaps Graphos, who knows?" "The Purple People no doubt" I said.

"On the other hand Banubula thinks it was purely and simply a family affair—an affair of honour. The boy's father had said he would punish him for soiling the family honour. This *is* the Balkans after all."

"What does Hippo think?"

Caradoc drained his glass and said oracularly "It's like everything else in life—those who know can't tell."

And at this moment Mrs. Henniker came into the room whinnying like a polo pony and waving a tattered magazine which the girls had been reading; it was a magazine devoted to film. "Look" cried Mrs. Henniker with a triumphant flourish, waving it under my nose. "One of my girls." To my surprise there she was, Iolanthe, all sepia and deckle edged, staring out at the world with a kind of forlorn lascivious grin. She was tricked out as some sort of Eastern houri and appeared to be bearing the head of the Baptist upon a trencher. The letterpress concerned a new film made by a Frenchman in Egypt. Apparently she had lobbied herself a small part in it. I was delighted and amused, unaware that we were witnessing the beginnings of so formidable a career. Mrs. Henniker was beside herself with pleasure. "One of my girls" she kept repeating in a dazed sort of way. I was obscurely touched as I looked at the gruesome inexperienced face of young Samiou. Why "inexperienced" though? Caradoc set the paper aside with a grunt of surprise. "Well, may they all prosper" he said at last. "The little dumplings."

Pulley came in with a huge watch dangling. It was time to be going home. It was freezing in the car, the Attic plain was all glittering under hoarfrost; the sewers steamed up through the manholes all the way along Stadium Street like so many geysers. Caradoc pressed my hand and declined a parting drink, showing unwonted resolution "Just time to pack my traps" he said "and then hey for the Virgin Isles. Think of me basking out there, eh? And remember that all perfected cultures have depended upon a high infant mortality." No, he wasn't drunk: he was full of the sadness of farewell. "As for you, Charlock, everything is moving in your direction now. You have only to spread your sails a bit. You are going to be very happy. O yes. Very happy indeed. A future full of sperm my boy."

I could see nothing illogical in the proposition, and yet I was filled with a sudden nagging nostalgia for the days of solitary poverty, the days before the firm took me up. But then the memory of Benedicta swept over me like a landslide; she was worth everything. I did not feel as if I had a separate existence any more.

"Caradoc bless you."

"Goodbye."

Om

IV

Konx. Ah! the brave new chrysadiamantine world of Charlock's nuptial London! O world of delegated sympathies, of mysteries, of great achievements. The expensive cars that soothed away the roads moving like ointments; the clothes that fitted like second skins. And in the midst of it all the white wand, the blind man's dowsing-rod, Benedicta. It is not I who speak, Lord: it is my culture speaking through me. It is hard to disentangle this first time from the others—for she was always going away, always coming back. In the Paulhaus everything has been catered for—chapels for six denominations. People are never too ill to pray. Either she appeared at airports clad in mourning; or else delivered in a white ambulance, laughing, cured, joking with the driver: to run up the steep steps into my arms. Try as you will, there is no explanation for madness, happiness or death. At first it would have been silly to speak of souls darkened by troubling presentiments, of dialogues bathed in strange lights. Later of course, one has all the time in the world to study the fatal metastases of the idea of love.

I counted upon her for very much, I discovered, sorting through my emotions with a new, a rather disgusting humility bordering on self-abasement. She would develop me like some backyard province perhaps, promulgate a charter. I did not even know her husband's name: whom could I ask? And then, where should we meet at last but under the backward clock at Victoria. Yet at once the Turkish image, brilliant as a postage stamp, gave place to another; she had become very thin now, very tense. She vibrated in my arms like a high-tension wire; her eyes were over made-up which increased her pallor, deeped the dimple in her cheek. But with such relief, such passion, after so long an absence. "And all this time you never wrote, Benedicta." "I know." (But afterwards she would write every day for weeks on end in her mirror hand: things like "It is snowing again. They have tied me to the same chair.") But here she only gave a small sweet groan as we broke apart to plunge our eyes into one another. "Felix!" She had managed to capture my very name and make it her own; it emerged newly printed. I had never liked it very much: now I hoped she might go on repeating it. "At last it is over." At last it had begun.

I had already been here alone for nearly a month, living at the beautiful house in Mount Street among the sumptuous impersonal furniture. There had been no signal of her arrival. I contemplated with superstitious awe the huge wardrobe which filled the glass cupboards in our room—my own new wardrobe. The devil! I recalled that one day long ago Jocas had asked me, as a personal favour, to allow his tailor to take my measurements: and though puzzled, I had complied. As one among so many ambiguous happenings this small trifle had hardly seemed worth troubling about. Now I understood. I stood, biting my lip, and contemplating myself in the mirror both ashamed and delighted at my own splendour. The silver-backed brushes were good to the scalp; the bathroom was crowded with expensive toilet waters and monumental soaps. It was perfectly understandable, I told myself, that I should dress appropriately, to match my new, my enormous new salary, and in general my new role in affairs. For Benedicta's sake, as well as the firm's... nevertheless. Nor was it too soon, for I had already taken possession of my new suite of offices at Merlin House in the City; I had already met everyone—except of course Julian who was away. Things had begun to move forward with irresistible momentum. Yes, I had even seen the fangled Shadbolt and initialled the preposterous marriage settlement. And now all these scattered elements were knitted together and resolved by her phone-call from Victoria. "I'm here at last. Please come to me at once." It was a familiar creature of course, her perfume was the same. All the signals of recognition the same. Yet a difference lay perhaps in the fact that so much time had passed and circumstances had subtly altered—this foggy soot-bellowing grime-tank of a station. And then her tremendous assortment of luggage which followed in a second taxi with her maids and manservant. Some lines of Koepgen drifted idly across the back of my mind like these mushrooming winter clouds. Something like "the human face upon its stalk perpetuates only the type of a determined response; there are so few elations and so few dismays to wrinkle between a laughing or a crying death, between a truthful or a lying breath." Benedicta sat gripping my manicured hand and staring unseeingly out of the window watching London lumber by, keeping its viscous slow coil. "You have seen Shadbolt, haven't you?"

"Yes."

"He explained and you agreed. Now we are really one." It was only the context that made the phrase sound extraordinary.

"I signed the document, though really I remained unconvinced inside. It's too generous, my dear. Why should I share everything so completely?"

"O God" she cried vehemently "I was afraid you wouldn't see."

"It was too generous; after all I'm earning my own way now. Why shouldn't you keep your fortune? We could have had a *separation des biens* arrangement."

"No. Never. Besides didn't he tell you that I have no personal fortune outside the firm? It's all I have, the firm. Darling, I want to possess you utterly, without reserves of any kind. I can't believe in myself in any other way." Well, so did I, so did I. "But I also wanted you to feel a little independent. Room to breathe."

She began to mutter under her breath, as if she were swearing *sotto voce*. Her knuckles grew white as she gripped my hand. A strange, rather ominous sense of impending misunderstanding cast its shadow over us. It might be possible to embrace it away, to exorcise it. As I kissed her I thought of Shadbolt. He was one of the five solicitors who dealt with the firm's affairs; he had presented for my perusal a thick handbook listing all the firm's holdings and all its subsidiaries. A heavy-breathing slothful little man with plum-coloured countenance, whose spectacles were attached to his lapel by a heavy black ribbon. When he put them on he did so reverently, as if he were in mourning. Voice of an old bugle full of spit. The marriage contract was an elaborate document couched in the sort of phraseology which made the trained mind swim. I was too intimidated by his air of being a papal emissary to prevail upon him to explain in too great detail. His grinding humourless voice grated upon me. "Everyone in

Merlin's seems to be obsessed by contractual obligations" I said somewhat peevishly. Shadbolt removed his spectacles and stared at me reproachfully. "How else shall one do business?" he asked with surprise, almost tenderly.

"But this isn't business" I said.

"Frankly," said the little man rising with infinite slowness to gaze out of the window "I would have hesitated had I been in Miss Benedicta's place. You will allow me to be frank? But she insisted. From your point of view Mr. Charlock, you have everything to gain and nothing to lose by it. It's a most generous gesture, a gesture of faith and trust and if I may use the word without immodesty, love. It fully incorporates you in all her fortunes. But if you wish we can tear the document up."

He crossed the room cumbrously with his penguin-like gait. I hesitated for a long moment, feeling very much out of my depth. "I somehow don't like to think about relationships, our marriage, in these terms." Yes, that was really the full extent of my reservations. The lawyer gave a bleak smile. "The sentiment does you much credit. I understand your feeling as you do. On the other hand there is nothing so very strange about making a marriage contract. Many people do. I was rather more concerned about her position than yours. All this" he tapped the white papers against his knee "would not be easily revoked if ever there were need. She is, in a sense, putting herself entirely at your mercy and the firm as well."

"That is what worries me; there isn't any need."

But, after all, since the whole thing was merely a whim on her part . . . I took up my new gold fountain pen and signed the document. Shadbolt sighed slowly as he pressed the blotter down upon the wet ink. "You are a lucky man," he said "a very lucky young man."

Now it seemed to me, as I sat beside her with her slender arm through mine, that the phrase might qualify as the nadir of understatement. Those nervous, tender blue eyes turning to grey in this pallid cloudlight met mine with such burning candour that I felt ashamed ever to have felt doubts or reservations about these paper conventions.

"What is it, Benedicta?" But still staring at me she only shook her head as she continued to explore her own inmost feelings—preoccupied, like someone trying to locate a hollow in a tooth. It was in this euphoric trance that we drew up at last in Mount Street. Baynes opened for us and ran down the steps to greet her; but she hardly acknowledged his presence, stalking past him into the hall with what might have seemed an insolent air, had her preoccupation not been so evident.

She threw her gloves on to the table and consulted her appearance in the tall mirror with a careful disdainful air. There was a big bowl of flowers on the side table by the wall, near the silver salver which held some engraved visiting cards and tradesmen's bills. "I told you I did not like the smell of flowers in the house" she said icily to the butler. "Take them out at once." As a matter of fact it was I who had ordered the flowers; but the kindly Baynes, after a glance at me, simply swallowed and decided to take the blame. "Yes, Madam."

Benedicta turned with a dazzling smile and said: "Now let's go through the house shall we? I love coming back here." And so we went from room to room in order to greet the more choice of her possessions—the little statue of Niobe, for example, and the wonderful gallery of golden heads of Greek gods and Roman, modern work by *cire perdue*. It was only when we were climbing the staircase that she said: "There's no one else here is there?"

"Of course not. I'm quite alone."

But now she walked with an air of quaint precaution, letting me enter each room ahead of her to draw the curtains. Nodded smiling, as if satisfied; so we perambulated the densely carpeted floors to come at last to the fine bedrooms where I had been sleeping. Here, at last, she experienced a sort of relief, clapped hands softly before my face and laughed as I trapped them. Well, then, whatever it was we had outwitted it. She walked about, opening cupboards, bed-bouncing, opening cupboards full of my gloatworthy clothing. Then abruptly she paused and said: "My God, I'm tired and dirty. I must have a bath."

I locked the door and drew her one in my scarlet bathroom, tossing in bunches of salts; simple and swift she undressed and stepped into it and all of a sudden I was carried back in a flash to the Benedicta who had once walked into the foaming cistern of "The Copious Waters" in distant Turkey; her preoccupations were gone. I sat beside her, touching the pale shoulders with my fingers. Afterwards she rolled herself in the great towelling kaftan and lay on the bed, flushed rosy from the heat. "Tell me now." And so I told her all about the thrilling activities of Charlock in London, unable to disguise the triumph and excitement in my voice. She listened nodding from time to time, but the nods were only part approval—she was like to doze off at any moment. Well, about the two small factories which had been set up near Slough to start production on two of my "devices"; about a study group which had been convened to test the more nebulous experimental stuff. Intoxicating stuff. I really could not blame her if her eyelids fluttered and drooped. "And as soon as Julian gets back I shall make contact and. . . ." But she was suddenly snapped sharp awake. She looked at me curiously for a moment and then, yawning, ran her fingers through my hair with a queer little gesture—that of a mother, ever so faintly commiserating, who hears her small son boasting about matters he could not as yet understand. "Ah Julian" she said, and I thought of the empty chair in the board room faced by the little marble plaque and the virgin blotter. "He's amazing really," I said, "despite his absence in New York; you know, he gets the minutes of all our meetings, annotates them and bangs them back within twenty-four hours sometimes. He must be a glutton for work. One feels his presence very strongly despite the empty chair."

Yawning, she went to the telephone, unlocking the door en route; Baynes answered hoarsely from the kitchen. She ordered him to bring some champagne in a bucket and to tell the office that she would use her box at the opera. "Do you agree?" over her shoulder. "It's my first night in London for so long? And Baynes bring us *The Times*. We must see what's on; and a car, please." A patrician simplicity, both authoritative and endearing. I consulted my watch. There was lots of time. She began her lingering toilet, slipping through the secret panel into her own mirrored rooms. Soon Baynes came, bringing all these trophies of a fashionable life, and I scanned the paper absently. "Ah!" I said. "An obvious mnemon by Caradoc! I wonder where he is now." And I read out: "Continental type orgy sought by plain living British family, Hornchurch area. No agents."

"Ask the office; they'll tell you" she said, and then in the same breath "You know they want to send us round the world for our honeymoon? Think, round the world."

"Who do?"

"The firm. Julian. Everyone." I reflected on this a moment. "Isn't it a marvellous idea?" She eyed me.

"Yes" I said, but rather doubtfully, and my tone seemed to puzzle her, for she stopped in front of me as she combed out her hair. "Well, isn't it?" she insisted. I lit a cigarette and said: "Yes, enormously kind of them. But, you know, I was rather hoping we'd sneak off all alone, by ourselves, like a couple of students. I know a dozen little places in Italy and Greece where we could be quite alone, quite out of touch—even with the firm. Besides, why put them to the expense? Think of the cost!"

"Cost?" she said on a chilling note of interrogation, and with a singular expression on her face. "How do you mean—'cost'?" I would perhaps have laughed had her strange expression not struck me so forcibly. All this became clearer later on when, after the marriage, I made the intoxicating discovery that we had no real income whatsoever against which to calculate our costs. I mean that there was no ceiling, no budget, no margin. She simply drew money as one draws breath. Any one of the four banks owned by the firm honoured her cheques; notes of hand—the merest scribbles on the back of a postcard or on a page torn from an address book—were honoured by Nathan, the administrative secretary. She never saw a bill in connection with any of the houses she owned. This contributed a vertiginous singularity to her dealings with money. And now that our fortunes were merged by the Shadbolt document I woke up to find that I too was in the same situation. I had no money of "my own"—yet what the devil does the phrase mean? At first it was intoxicating, yes, of course, not to have to reflect on costs; but later (I am talking of the period of the crack-up) I began to feel this as a major factor which contributed to her general confusion of mind. She was capable of buying a bracelet for ten thousand pounds and of leaving it in a taxi. When I grew alarmed about her general state of health, and found myself unable to see the elusive Julian face to face,

I remember writing a long eloquent memorandum to him which finally wound up on Nash's desk. I emphasised that even the Queen had a budgetry ceiling voted by Parliament, yet Benedicta had none. The confusion and waste were simply due to her total lack of knowledge as to what money might conceivably mean. Julian merely replied to my memo with another, neatly typed and signed in that inimitable hand: "Her doctors have been consulted, and also the principals of the firm. No change need be contemplated for the present." But at this moment I only saw the childish, endearing expression of puzzlement on her face and longed to kiss her. What is more endearing than the capriciousness of a rich woman? O, it is lovely. I might answer the rhetorical question very differently today I suppose. And heavens, I have had eight years or more in which to ponder the matter, along with more recondite subjects—Charlock sitting at his massive desk in Merlin House, drawing on his blotter with the golden pen which lived in a fat agate slab. Scribbling on a blackboard in coloured chalks.

She turned her white shoulders to me with a sigh. "Do me up at the back, would you please?" And for better or for worse, in sickness and in health, I did, stooping to touch the white skin with my lips. So hand in hand we sauntered downstairs casting admiring glances at ourselves on every landing. Baynes had made up a brown paper parcel of my prehistoric clothes, baggy grey trousers and tweed coats with leather elbow-patches and so on: the uniform of the poor sage! He asked me reverently what he should do with them. I was about to tell him to offer them to the nearest jumble sale when Benedicta intervened with an air of crisp decision and said: "Burn them in the furnace, Baynes." Baynes bowed to the heavenly will, and so did I, though I opened my mouth as if to speak. What did it matter? He had found an old French briar in one of my pockets, and this he had set aside. I was glad to see it again, though it was pretty much burned out; yet under the cool glance of Benedicta I found myself strangely incapable of reclaiming possession of it. I thought of the sweet-smelling box of cigars in the drawing room. From now on nothing but the choicest Juliets would touch the lips of Charlock. There was a conveniently placed leather case, already filled, upon the mantelpiece. "I think it had better go—it's pretty used up" I said treacherously to Baynes. He bowed again. "The boots and shoes I have given to the gardener" he said. "They fit him."

So we equipped ourselves with coats and wraps and floated through the front door to find the office Rolls—flatus symbol of the new Charlock—lying at anchor, waiting for us.

Memory refuses to recover the rest of that evening in any detail—behind the stripes and bars of Busoni's music; only towards dawn, lying exhausted beside each other, I awoke with a jerk to find her talking Turkish in her sleep—the strange crooning bubbling tongue which I had once heard her use to her hawk. She was feverish, tossing and turning in bed like someone trying to throw off, in her sleep, the imaginary bonds of some painful dream. But by morning the shadow had fled with the fever, and she was in sparkling spirits again. I walked half the way to the office across the spring-fermenting city with its frail sunlight, revelling in the green of the parks, the light rime of hoarfrost on the grass. Well, I was dense with happiness—the poor scientist could have trumpeted his joy like an elephant. Jevons the commissionaire was on duty as usual, stamping and chomping with the fresh cold, clad in his green coat with polished brass buttons, his billycock hat; his huge umbrella lay beside the directors' lift. He lavished his customary hearty pleasantries upon me, and even went so far as to tip me a conspiratorial wink as I passed him with my own black umbrella. It is amazing how quickly one can develop the condescending wave of an umbrella which somehow goes with city clothes. And a bowler! In stately fashion the lift bore me up to the third floor, to the silent and comfortable office from which one could glimpse a corner of St. Paul's far away to the left of the invisible river line. My despatch-box had already been brought up by Miss Tee, its contents neatly arranged in the metal tray for my perusal. The memorandum of the latest meeting upon the subject of the new light bulb project was already here, duly annotated by the absent Julian and signed by his secretary in his absence. How did he do it, I wondered? I supposed that the minutes were sent to him by Telex. "I am extremely eager to see this project realised," he wrote heart-warmingly "as it seems one of the most imaginative we have ever undertaken. Please keep it upon the secret list until production department is ready to market. Only one consideration comes to mind. We must remember the prohibitive price of mercury at £150 per 75 lb flask when costing. In this context however I hope shortly to have good news of negotiations going forward in Moscow for supplies of mercury. If we can capture this new market and thus sidetrack the chlorine plants which are responsible for the shortage and high price of this element we should be well on our way towards a signal success. Please press ahead with the first five hundred prototype bulbs."

I rang the manservant in the buttery and told him that for the eleven o'clock break I would very much like a bowl of strawberries and cream with a glass of the finest sherry. Corbin was perfectly used to requests of this kind; he would despatch an office boy at once in search of the strawberries. I put in a call to Slough to find out how the engineering department was dealing with the new filament and what the first tests had demonstrated. All was well; there was no deterioration in spite of the tremendous load. It was almost too good to be true, things were moving with such speed and smoothness. There was no meeting today and hardly any paperwork, so I opened the newspaper and sank into a pleasant daydream about Benedicta and the future—a daydream compounded of such various elements that it would not have been possible to sort them all out into a coherent pattern. At any rate not then.

Later she rang up and said she missed me. *She missed me!* I was overcome. And as far as Benedicta was concerned I found that I liked her all the better for knowing so little about her; this factor contributed something enigmatic to her—to her strangely withdrawn personality which flourished in privacy like some heavy-perfumed magnolia. Everything therefore was a surprise. Had I felt that she was deliberately keeping secret things she might have shared it would doubtless have been different; but her prohibitions and retreats into panic did not suggest this at all. She had thrown up simply the defences which over-sensitive, perhaps even rather neurotic, people throw up consciously against experiences too deeply felt to be the subject of open discussion. Of course at first the tabus were a little bewildering—but then why should someone not wish not to discuss their fathers or past husbands and so on? It was perfectly defensible; doubtless as we got to know each other better these defences would melt and give way to new understandings. (The strawberries were watery, the sherry indifferent, but I did not care. I was tied to a comet's tail.) And when I arrived back at Mount Street in the evenings there was no shadow of doubt about the warmth and eagerness with which she threw open the door, forestalling Baynes, to run down the steps and embrace me, almost ravenous for my embrace. Thus arm in arm to the warm fire crackling on the hearth, the winking bottles and decanters, and the prospect of a whole evening spent alone together. "Julian telephoned today and told me to send you his warmest greetings." Everybody loved me.

I had noticed that even in the first few days a flock of white envelopes addressed to her had landed like doves upon the hall table. In the morning the office sent her a social secretary to deal with such correspondence, so that when I arrived back I found an equally massive bunch of envelopes stamped and addressed for despatch. I sifted somewhat ruefully through them. "Heavens, you seem to know everybody worthwhile in London."

"Those are all refusals" she said. "Besides, I don't see people any more. I want you to myself. I haven't for ages. Besides you don't want to go out and about do you?"

"Good Lord no."

"And then after April I shall be in the country where nobody ever comes. Do you see? And you will drive down for week ends or whenever you get a chance. We'll be married there, too, if you agree. Julian has arranged it. Just the two of us I mean, with nobody."

"So you didn't want to escape with me?"

"It wasn't that, Felix. It's just that I can't just disappear like that. I have to stay in touch, you know."

"With whom, with what?"

She looked at me curiously, as though the question were an unexpectedly foolish one: as if she had not expected it from me. "I mean" I went on "you are not working for anyone; you don't have any real obligations, have you?"

"None at all." She gave a small sharp laugh, a sad laugh as she sat down on the hearthrug before the fire to rest her chin upon her drawn up knees and stare into the burning coals. Then it occurred to me that it might be something to do with her doctors, and I kicked myself for a prying fool, kneeling down beside her to put my arms about her shoulders. "I'm sorry Benedicta" I said. She had a trace of a tear in the corner of her eye, but she was still smiling. "It's of no importance. Come, sit beside me and tell me what you have been doing for the firm. Will you? I want to share everything."

This was more easy to do, and most congenial to my mood; and yet, as I started talking about the three first devices which Merlin was to put into immediate production, I could not but feel a sort of helpless despair that they were not more interesting and revolutionary than they were. They were only mechanical contrivances which, however useful, provided crutches for people in need. In the back of my mind I was thinking along more abstract vectors, groping towards something of which Abel is still only a shallow prototype. A behaviouristic abacus of patterned responses which might respond to the very oscillations of the nervous system—something which might both prophesy and retroprophesy. . . . Nothing was clear as yet; there was so much as yet to be done on the theory of mathematical probability. It made me dizzy thinking about it. But meanwhile my *alter felix* continued his lucid exposition of the toys for which the firm were to be responsible, and all the time Benedicta listened avidly, as if to music, her head thrown slightly back, eyes closed. And when I had finished—when I had even shown her one of the tiny filaments as some people will show the relics of an operation, a calculus in a bottle—she sighed deeply and put her arms round me, pressing herself to me as if all this prosaic recital had been almost sexually rousing.

"It's going to be marvellous" she said. "You will see."

There was no doubt of it in my mind; nor anything but overwhelming gratitude to this extraordinary golden creature whose head had sunk now to my knees, half fire-tranced. "I'm determined you are going to be happy" I said. "Happy and not scared." Put down that goblet, Felix!

She jumped up at once, startled, and said: "Who said I was scared?" She made as if to walk towards the door but I captured her hands and drew her gently back to the fireplace. "Did Julian say anything?" she said sharply and I answered in the same tone: "Nobody said it; besides I have never met Julian. I thought sometimes you seemed worried, that was all. But it's over now for good. You have got me to rely on." I caught sight of my face in the mirror and suddenly felt foolish.

For good! My clumsy advocacy worked at last; she seated herself beside me once more, relaxed and calm again. Beside the bed that evening I found a couple of books of essays, beautifully bound in green morocco. "I borrowed them from Julian's flat" she explained. She didn't say when. Each bore a pretty bookplate with the owner's initials entwined and a rebus—an ape climbing a pomegranate tree. Here and there passages of the books had been underscored, presumably by the owner. "Out of the present we manufacture the future; what we dream today becomes tomorrow's reality. All our ills come from incautious dreaming. Trivial or impure dreaming literally rots the fabric of the future. But the dreams of a rarefied psyche help to resolve tensions and build up good sources." I yawned, she was already asleep, curled up beside me with her head under her wing. Drifting now in her direction with half-shut eyes I dreamed I was addressing the politely subservient members of my board on topics of the greatest moment. "The sails of fancy, gentlemen, swell with the following wind of good fortune." I was learning how to raise my voice, to suit gestures to the words, to perorate....

So the brightly etched days rolled by. Julian had apparently returned from his trip abroad, but still put in no appearance at the boards, though his comments upon our lucubrations were as prompt and cogent as ever. I gathered that he did much of his work at home and was hardly ever in his office. It seemed to me strange that he did not make personal contact, if only to shake my hand. In fact I rather looked forward to meeting him. I even suggested to Benedicta that she might ask him to dine with us, but she shook her head doubtfully and said: "You don't know Julian. He is tremendously shy. He hides himself away. I'm sure he wouldn't come. He'd just send a huge shelf of flowers with a last minute excuse. You know, Felix, hardly anyone in the office has so much as seen him. He prefers to speak to them on the phone." It was intriguing to say the least, and at first I was inclined to think that she was exaggerating; but not so. Then one day he phoned me to discuss some point or other—but from the country. His voice had a thrilling icy sauvity. He spoke slowly, gently, in a dreamy way which suggested more than a hint of world weariness—one imagined Disraeli dictating a state paper in just such a disenchanted tone. I expressed my eagerness to meet him and he thanked me, but added: "Yes, all in good time, Charlock. We certainly must meet, but at the moment I am simply worked off my feet; and you have so much other fish to fry—I refer to your marriage to Benedicta. I can't tell you how happy that makes us all."

There seemed nothing for it but to bow to his whim for the time being. But one morning my own phone rang at the office and I could tell from the timbre of his voice that the call was coming from somewhere inside the building. It was Julian all right—by now I was quite familiar with his voice, we had already spoken to each other frequently; moreover I knew that he had an office at the end of the corridor where Nathan, the general admin. sec. presided over his papers. Why, I had even recorded him once or twice for my collection. I thought in playful fashion that I might surprise him, meet him in the flesh. So while he still spoke I put down the receiver on my blotter and stalked down the long corridor to throw open the door of the office in question. But there at his desk sat Nathan only; a small dictaphone, attached to the telephone, was still playing. "Ah you've hung up, Mr. Charlock" said Nathan with mild reproach, cutting off. I felt something of a fool. Nathan switched over and said. "He was in very early this morning and recorded half a dozen conversations. He often does so."

I recounted this incident somewhat ruefully to Benedicta; but she only smiled and shook her head. "You'll never catch Julian on the hop" she said. "Until he decides."

"What does he look like, Benedicta?" I asked. She gazed at me thoughtfully for a moment and then said, "There isn't anything special about him. He's just like anyone else I think."

On a sudden impulse I asked: "Have you ever seen him?" The question was quite involuntary, and the moment it was out I knew it to be absurd. But Benedicta swallowed and answered: "Of course, quite definitely." But the tone in which she said it struck me as curious. If I had had to "interpret" it in the manner of the inimitable Nash I should have taken it to mean: "I think that the person I have seen is Julian, but I am not absolutely sure." The thought as it crossed my mind however seemed to be ever so slightly disloyal, so I stifled it and changed the subject. "Ah well" I said "I expect we shall see him for the wedding at any rate." But once again I was to find myself in error, for neither Julian nor anyone else came to the wedding though the house was bursting with presents and telegrams of congratulations.

The wedding! What could have been more singular? I had asked no questions, of course; but then on the other hand I had been asked none. The arrangements were not of my making, but it was to be presumed that Benedicta (if she were not herself responsible for them) had at least been consulted. I supposed that she had decided to get married in the strictest privacy, that was all. Only that and nothing more. Nor had I anyone that I wished to invite. No family. An uncle in America, some cousins in India, that was all.

But it was my first visit to "Cathay", that preposterous, gloomy country house which was to be our home; moreover by night, for the marriage was arranged for midnight. "Cathay" forsooth! With its turrets and fishponds, great park, cloth-of-gold chamber, huge organ by Basset. At the end of a normal office day my fellow directors came in one by one to wish me luck and a happy honeymoon—cracking the usual awkward jokes about visiting the condemned man in his cell etc. After these so amiable pleasantries I took a taxi home to an early dinner, to find the hall full of luggage and the office car already outside the door. It was piquant, mysterious, rather exciting to be motored down into the depths of the country like this. It smelt of orange-blossom and elopements in the dark of the year. I visualised some great house-party with Julian and some of his collaborators, perhaps with a wife or two present to balance the forces of good and evil. Indeed I thought that Julian could hardly do less than witness for us. We did not speak much as the car nosed its way slowly through the slippery gromboolian suburbs towards Hampshire. Benedicta sat close beside me with her gloved hand in mine, looking pale and somewhat contrite. After the ceremony we were to drive on directly to Southampton to board the *Polaris*—a Merlin Line cruiser. But the wedding itself was of course to be a civil one. No church-bells for Charlock.

It was a long coldish drive with fine rain glittering in the white beam of the headlights, prickling through the greenery of forest land and heath. My initial elation had given way to a certain tender solemnity. "Benedicta" I whispered, but she only pressed my hand tightly and said: "Sh! I'm thinking." I wondered what her thoughts might be as she stared out across the darkling light. Of a past she had confided to nobody?

At last we crackled down the long avenues towards the bowl of golden light which gleamed at the end of the long green tunnels. The house was ablaze with light, and crammed with people all right. A telephone was insisting somewhere. But to my surprise "the people" were all servants. In the rococo musicians' gallery with its mouldy Burne-Jones flavour a quintet played ghastly subdued music as if afraid to overhear itself. Butlers and maids moved everywhere with a kind of clinical deliberation—yet for all the world as if they were making preparations for a great ball. A staff like this could have mounted a wedding reception for four hundred people. But I could see no trace of any guests. But a mountain of telegrams lay unopened on the marble tables in the hall, and the preposterous Edwardian rooms leading with an air of ever greater futility into each other were bursting with presents—everything from a concert grand to silver crocks and gew-gaws of all sorts and sizes. The mixture of portentous emptiness and reckless prodigality staggered me.

But Benedicta moved about it all with a kind of fiery elation, moth-light of step, her face glowing with pleasure and pride. She held her head high against the forest of candle-branches and spectral Venetian lustres. It struck me then how foreign she was. I divined that this old house with its musty gawkish features offered a sort of mental association with Stamboul—those rotting palaces in *style pompier* copied and recopied, criss-crossed with mirrors set in tarnished mouldings. Shades of Baden and Pau—yes, that is what made her feel so at home, so at one with it all. "But is there nobody except the servants?" I asked, and she turned her dancing eyes upon me for a second before shaking her blonde head. "I told you, silly. Only us." Only us! But we had just passed an enormously long buffet prepared for a midnight supper: apparently the baked meats (I thought in muddled quotation) were destined to grace the servants' hall. It was marvellous, it was macabre. I felt quite a wave of affection for poor Baynes who now advanced towards us with a sheaf of telegrams—congratulations from Jocas, Julian, Caradoc, Hippolyta: his was a familiar face. These brief messages from the lost world of Athens and Stamboul gave me a little pang—they seemed almost brutally gay. Baynes said: "They are waiting for you in the library, madam." Benedicta nodded regally and led the way. The noise of the quintet followed us apologetically. Everywhere there were flowers—but big banks of flowers professionally arranged: their heavy scent swung about in pools among the candle-shining shadows. And yet . . . it was all somehow like a cinema, I found myself thinking. Baynes marched before us and opened yet another door.

The library! Of course I did not discover the fact until later, but this huge and beautifully arranged room with its galleries and moulded squinches, its sea-green dome, its furnishings of globes, atlases, astrolabes, gazetteers, was a fake: all the books in it were empty dummies! Yet to browse among the titles one would have imagined the room to contain virtually the sum total of European culture. But the books were all playful make-believe, empty buckram and gilt. Descartes, Nietzsche, Leibniz. . . . Here, however, all was candlelight and firelight, discreet and perhaps a trifle funereal? No, not really. A large desk, covered with a green baize cloth, conveyed the mute suggestion of an altar, with its flowers, candles and open registers. Here sunning his shovel-shaped backside stood the Shadbolt, beside the registrar for the district; their clerks stood by to act as witnesses if need be—mouldy and dispossessed-looking figures. We greeted each other formally and with much false cordiality. Benedicta gave the signal while I groped in my pockets for the ring.

To my surprise she seemed quite moved by the grim routine of the civil ceremony. It did not last long. At a signal the tremulous Baynes appeared with champagne on a tray and we relaxed into a more comprehensive mood of relief. Shadbolt toasted us heartily; and Benedicta made her slow way through the house to touch glasses with the servants who had also been provided with a little spray with which to respond. It all seemed to happen in a flash. Within an hour we were on our way again, down the long roads to Southampton. It was raining. It was raining. I thought of the blue gourd of the Mediterranean sky with longing. Benedicta had fallen asleep, her long aquiline nose pointing downwards along my sleeve. I cradled her preciously. She looked so sly. From time to time a tiny snore escaped her lips.

Dawn's left hand was in the sky by the time we negotiated the sticky dockland with its palpitating yellow lights and climbed the long gangplank of the sleeping ship to seek out the bridal suite on A deck. Benedicta was speechless with fatigue and so was I; too tired to supervise the stacking of the luggage, too tired to think. We fell into our bunks and slept; and by the time I woke I felt the heart-lifting sensation of a ship sliding smoothly through water—the soft clear drub of powerful engines driving us steadily seaward. There was too the occasional lift, and hiss of spray on the deck around us. I had a bath and went on deck—a wind-snatched deck with a light grizzle of rain falling upon it. The land lay far behind now in the mists of morning, a grey smudge of cloud-capped nothingness. We were on our way round the world. England hull down in the sea-mist of dawn. It was so good to be alive.

Just time to return to my cabin and finish the study of the mantis which Marchant had lent me. "Another theory was constructed on the physiological experiments of Rabaud and others; in these it was found that the superior nerve-centres restrain or inhibit the reflexive system. The control is weakened by decapitation. The visible result is that the reflexive-genital activity of the headless male is made more vigorous and therefore biologically more effective." Benedicta sighed in her sleep and turned to snuggle deeper into the soft pillows. The same goes for decapitated frogs, while any hangman will tell you that a broken spinal cord will produce an instant ejaculation. I put my book aside and smoked, lulled by the lilt of the ship as she manned the green sea. Then slept again to awake and find my breakfast beside me and Benedicta sitting opposite in a chair, naked and smiling. We were sliding back towards Polis, that was why perhaps—towards those first intimacies which seemed now to lie far back in the past. Did she suit her lovemaking to the country she found herself in? Now as she came to sit cross-legged on the end of my bed I thought back to those ancient kisses and little punishments—the water torture, the wax torture, the frenetic zealous kisses with their wordless pieties—all of them making a part of the bright fabric of the past which must be carried forward into a future bright with promise. And here I was with the creature within arm's reach. Moreover what could well be more delightful than the life of shipboard with its defined routines, its lack of demands upon one's personal initiative? And with it isolation, being surrounded by water on every side. It seemed so soon when we found ourselves sliding past Gibraltar into calmer seas, cradled by light racing cloud and water far bluer than we deserved. She had flowered into a kinetic laziness which suited itself marvellously to the holiday mood. The only interruption was an occasional long cable from Julian about the minor details of some industrial operation; but even these dwindled away into silence.

Three months! But they passed in a slow-motion dream; already the lazy life of the ship had bemused us, sunk us into a tranced nescience. Talk of Calypso's island—I forgot even to make notes, forgot to figure. I read like a convalescent. I was even able to find relief from those half-unconscious trains of reasoning which had always formed a sort of *leitmotiv* to my quotidian life—so much so that I could honestly say that there had not been a single moment until now when I was not fully occupied with my private thoughts. An invisible censor clad in gumboots strode up and down before Charlock's subliminal threshold—O a far more competent fellow than the greybearded Freudian one. A primordial biological censor this, rather like a beefeater in the Tower of London.

Of course there were interludes in all this uxorious sloth when my alter Charlock reproached me bitterly and pushed me into involuntary attempts to show a leg. At Monte, for example, I rallied sufficiently to consider playing the tables. I collected a mass of those long printed sheaves of paper which record the numbers thrown out by the wheels. They are of great interest to those unwary souls who wish to study form with a view to establishing a system and so breaking the bank. I was hardly less unwary and thought that a brief analysis might—I had been playing about with mathematical probability—ah wretched artificer! But when I suggested this Benedicta came back with a very decisive "Ah dear no. Have you forgotten that the firm owns nearly all the shares in the Casino? Do you think they would let me lose on my honeymoon? We'd win a fortune Felix—

what would be the point of it?" Indeed! I let the long sheaves float away in the wind and settle in the pale waters.

The firm was omnipresent, though in a queer tactful sort of way; nor do I mean simply that the captain and crew of the vessel knew who we were, and had received instructions to take specially good care of us. It went a bit deeper than that. At every point of disembarkation we were discreetly met by the resident agent and taken on a conducted tour of the place, much in the manner of visiting minor royalty. This was most welcome in countries where we did not know the language and habits of the natives—Cambodia, India for example. Nevertheless I could well understand this unobtrusive tutelage becoming oppressive in the long run. There were a number of state occasions to be observed as well which made me sigh for the anonymity of a hotel-room in Florence; a Governor here and there bade us to his table: those huge mournful Government houses full of sighing chintz and mammoth billiard tables, full of bad pictures and unpalatable cooking. Well, I sighed—we both sighed—but there was nothing to be done but accept and attend. This of course was more marked east of Suez: we were familiars of the Mediterranean, needing no help in Athens or in Jocasland of the tumbled minarets. But Athens was strangely hushed—everyone was away it seemed, either abroad or in the islands. Nor could I get any news of Banubula or Koepgen, try as I would. I had a small fugitive inclination to visit the Plaka and perhaps Number Seven as well, but I dismissed it, telling myself that time was short. But at Stamboul it was no surprise to see a little white pinnace scuttling across the sea to meet us with Jocas steering her—this long before the mists divided to reveal the ancient city trembling among the tulip-topped bastions. I saw the great confiding hand of Jocas come sliding up the gangplank rope like a deepsea squid; then he was before us, with his shy dancing eye. There was nothing equivocal in the tenderness with which he greeted us, pressed us to his heart. He had brought some small presents like newspapers, Black Sea caviar, Turkish cigarettes and some rare pieces of jewellery for B. So we spent the day a-gossip under a white awning, watching the city swim up from the deeps. Our lunch was served on deck and Jocas drank his champagne to us, uttering the familiar druidic toasts to bless our union. Benedicta looked ravishing in her new brown skin; the fine hairs shading from temple to cheek had already turned silkworm golden. "I have never seen her look so calm, so well" said Jocas softly in an aside, and indeed it seemed to me to be so. He was full of news of the property and of course the birds and their form. Benedicta questioned him eagerly. Indeed at one point she wanted to stay a week, but the itinerary was already so charged. . . . Omar the master falconer was dead, but Said had taken over and was doing very well. He had invented a new kind of lure. And so on. But mixed also in this animated exchange of fact were scraps of news about other friends and acquaintances—Caradoc in New York, for example, preparing to fly out to his new venture. Graphos was going from strength to strength, after having nearly ruined his career because of an infatuation with a streetwalker. And Koepgen? "He is doing well in Moscow; he will have a year or two yet. I know you have his notebooks." As a matter of fact I had one with me on the voyage. "And then what?" Jocas twinkled the gold smile and rubbed his hands. "He will get a large bonus and be free to pursue his studies."

"And that ikon?"

"Yes, we have found the one he wants; it is quite safe, waiting for him. But the firm comes first." Jocas giggled. "It's a lure, eh?"

The liner was scheduled to stay only a few hours; it was hardly worth going ashore for such a brief period; a gaggle of sightseers were rushed ashore, crammed into buses and given a swift glimpse of the great walls of smoking dung. But we sat on deck, talking drowsily, until they returned and the warning siren sent its herds of echoes thundering across the sky. Benedicta was leaning at the rail now, staring down into the water. "In the old days" Jocas was saying dreamily "they had bird-fairs all over Central Europe—singing birds I mean. Her father was a renowned breeder of songbirds, and won prizes everywhere with his exhibits. They say he was the first to think of blinding birds in order to improve their singing—you know, red-hot copper wire. It's easily and painlessly done they say. He built up quite a trade in cage-birds at one time, but the business outgrew it. Now only a few specialists are interested; the fairs have all lapsed. There is no room for them in the modern world, I suppose."

"Did it improve their singing?"

"It would improve anyone's singing; one sense develops to compensate for the loss of another—you know that. Why do they try to find a blind man always for muezzin? It needn't be eyes necessarily. The voice of the castrato, for example." He yawned heartily, by now half asleep. "Benedicta," he called "I must leave you, my dear. I wish I could come too but I can't."

The sightseeing passengers were panting aboard again led by two steatopygous priests—soutanes stuffed with blood-sausage. Benedicta came thoughtfully back to us and said, without any preliminary gambit: "Jocas, did you give Mr. Sacrapant the sack?" Jocas was surprised into a smile as he answered. "Of course not."

"Then why?" she said with a puzzled frown.

"His suicide? But he left a letter listing a number of reasons—mostly trivial ones you would say, even insignificant reasons. Yet taken all together I suppose they weighed something. Good Lord, the firm had no part in the matter." He looked shocked. She drew a sigh of relief and sat down. "Then?" Jocas went on, frowning, as if trying to puzzle out the matter for himself. "We look at things from the wrong point of view. I mean, how many reasons could you give for wanting to go on living? The list would be endless. So there is never one reason, but scores. You know in a funny sort of way he could never get used to the idea of security—it was almost as if he couldn't wait for his wife to get her pension." He burst out laughing in a strange half-rueful way and struck his thigh. "Ah! old Sacrapant!" he said and shook his head. "He will be impossible to replace." I saw the little figure falling.

A bell rang urgently and someone signalled from the deck house by the bridge. Reluctantly Jocas took himself off, to stand in the sheets of the little pinnace looking up at us with a curious expression on his face—a mixture of affection and sadness. "Be happy" he called across the separating water, as if perhaps he had scented some fugitive disharmony in us after all: and the little craft suddenly reared up and began its glib motion as it raced away towards the land.

"Come," said Benedicta, taking my arm "let's go down for a spell." She wanted to go down to the cabin, to lie about and talk or read—most probably to make love: until the first bell went for dinner. Well, but by dark we were crawling through the Straits again bound for the furthest corners of the world. Columbus Charlock! I do not believe that one can love without analysing—though I know that too much analysis can spoil loving: but here at least nothing but contentment found a place, a luxurious self-surrender which made death seem very far away. That was it, death!

Somewhere there is an album full of photographs of this royal progress—photographs taken, not by us, but by the captain and crew who shepherded us through all the adventures of travel with such docile assiduity. Later a handsome bound volume, with the record duly mounted and in the right order, arrived on the hall table with the compliments of the shipping line. Well then, on the back of bloody elephants bucketing up the holy mountain in Ceylon, wearing weird pith helmets against the sun. Then some tiger shoots in India—Benedicta lavender-pale and slender, with her triumphant little boot upon the head of the beast: the rigor had stiffened its snarl into a silent travesty of the last defensive gesture. Smack! Hong Kong, Sydney, Tahiti—the long ritual led us on, offering no demands upon us.

But these superficial records could not deal with everything, take account of everything. For example, unknown to either of us, Iolanthe was also aboard—or rather her image was, the public one, printed on celluloid. Among the films we were shown as we crossed the Indian Ocean was one made in Egypt, trivial and melodramatic, in which to my surprise Iolanthe had a small part. She swam up out of the screen without warning, moving into close-up which projected her enlarged face with its heavily doctored eyeshapes almost into my lap. My surprise made me sit up with an exclamation and grip Benedicta's hand.

"Good Lord."

"You know her?"

"It's Iolanthe of all people."

It was not much of a part, it lasted barely half a minute. But it was enough to glimpse an entirely new person grafted upon the one I had known. After all, the smallest gesture gives a clue to the inner disposition—a way of walking, position of hands, cant of the head. All right. Here she had to cut up food and put it on a plate; then to walk with the plate across a strip of sand, to bow, to serve. In this very brief repertoire of acts and gestures—some so familiar from which I recalled the old being—I saw a new one. "It's a common little face" said Benedicta with distaste and a contempt that extended itself with justice to the whole ridiculous film, with its sheiks and dancing girls. "Yes. Yes." Of course she was right; but how much less coarse, less common, than the original Iolanthe I had known. On the contrary these photographs suggested a new kind of maturity; her gestures had become studied, graceful, no longer impulsive and uncoordinated, fluent. Some of this I tried to express to Benedicta but she did not follow; she turned her cryptic smile upon me and pressed my hand confidingly. "But she is being directed and rehearsed by the *metteur-en-scène*, my dear: and he probably sleeps with her as well to get her to do things his way." Of course this was true and yet . . . entirely factitious? The change seemed to hold a whole range of significance for me. I was puzzled; more mysterious still, I felt wounded in an obscure sort of way—almost as if I had been tricked. Could I perhaps have missed the most interesting part of my little mistress by the merest inattention? I was nudged into surprise by that short insignificant scene. Moreover, in order the better to analyse my own response to it, I asked for it to be played over again the following afternoon while Benedicta was taking her siesta. No, the astonishment remained. The coarseness, the street-arab knowingness, had found a point of repose where it could manifest itself calmly as naked human experience. This gave point to a new angle of the head, to the resurrection of a smile which I knew on lips which I knew—but which I had never noticed. Or had they not then been there? Iolanthe! Heavens! I saw the rust-stained marbles rising against the keen skies of Attica. I rummaged, so to speak, among my stock of memories, to find correspondences to match this new personage—in vain. The screen-figure corresponded so little to the original that I felt as if she had somehow hoaxed me. My mood of puzzled abstraction lasted until dinner time, when Benedicta noticed it—for she missed nothing. "I hear you have been visiting your girl friend while I was asleep" she said with a rather cruel smile, her lips curving mischievously up at the corners. "Isn't it rather early in the day to start being unfaithful to me?" It was a joke, and should have been taken as such.

But I wanted to be serious, to explain how confused and puzzled I had been by this parody of nature. O yes I did. Benedicta would have none of it. "You can have all the women you want provided you tell me about it in detail" she said, and a sudden new light, a little grim this time, came into her eye. It was rather annoying for this was hardly the point. Besides nothing could be more distasteful than to provoke the sort of middle-class tiff common to middle-class couples in the suburbs of loathsome capitals. I was outraged by her vulgarity. "It was only a joke" she said.

"How idiotic to quarrel over a strip of film."

"I am not quarrelling. Felix, look at me."

"Nor am I." I obeyed. We kissed but with constraint. What the devil was wrong? But we finished the meal in silence and after it stalked up on deck to sit side by side in deck-chairs, smoking and musing. "How much do you know about this girl?" she asked at last; somewhat peevishly I replied. "Certainly more than I know about you, even after all this time." Benedicta's eye narrowed with anger, and when she was in this mood she set her ears back like a scared cat.

"I will answer any question you put to me."

"I have never insisted on you answering questions."

"How could you *insist*?"

"Or even ask. I want you as you are, exactly as you are at this moment; I don't care if you are still a bit of an enigma."

She turned her hard blue eye upon me with a new expression which I had not seen before and which I might describe as an amused contempt, and yawned behind her brown fingers. "My poor Felix" she said in a tone which made me long to strike her.

I took myself off to bed with an improving book, but when the clock struck midnight and she had not put in an appearance I dressed again and went on deck to find her. She was sitting alone in the deserted bar, leaning heavily upon it, dozing. "Thank God you've come," she said incoherently "I can't stand up." She was in fact dead drunk. It was all the more surprising because she was ordinarily a very modest drinker. I helped her laboriously along the deck to the cabin where she sat on her bunk, swaying slightly, holding her head in her hands. "On Thursday we touch at Macao" she said. "That is where Max died of typhoid fever. I do not want to go ashore." I said nothing. She went on: "He was a musician, but not a good one. But he had invented something which didn't exist until then—a copying machine for scores, for parts. It wasn't complete, and it took some of the best brains in the firm to develop and market it. Anything else you want to know?"

"Did you have a marriage settlement with him?"

Her eye lit with a sulphurous gleam, the embers of a queer triumph shining through the whisky daze.

"No" she said; but the tone in which she said it permitted me to construe the words "There was no need." (I jumped with guilt at so treacherous a thought.)

Then she held up her cupped hands pleadingly and said: "But even if he had been alive I'd have left him for you."

It was not possible to resist her when she was in this mood—sitting like some forlorn collapsing edifice, foundering among its own distresses. I felt crushed under the weight of my self-reproaches. I soaked her patiently in hot water, helped her to be sick, and towelled her back to some semblance of sobriety; afterwards she lay, pallid and exhausted, in my arms until daybreak when she was able once more to whisper the little phrase which had become almost a slogan for us. Always after making love she would say: "Let's always, Felix."

So Macao passed, and with it some of the weight of her private preoccupations; her mood lightened and made room for a new gaiety, a new responsiveness. We had become used to the ship by now and familiar with the habit of life. It was almost as if we had never lived land-life. And as we neared our final port of disembarkation we even started to take part in the absurd dinners and fancy-dress dances which we had found so distasteful during the first weeks of the voyage. In fact the night before we reached Southampton we went the whole hog and borrowed fancy dresses and masks from the extensive wardrobe of the vessel. I was Mephisto I think, with eyebrows of jet; she was a nun in a great white coif of starched linen. It was while she was making up her face in the mirror that she said, in an almost terror-stricken tone: "You know Felix I may be pregnant—have you thought about it? What shall I do?"

"How do you mean?"

About the blood and all that. It was not very consistent.

She was sitting there in front of the mirror staring into her own wide eyes with an expression of silent panic. Then she gave a long trembling sigh and shook herself awake from the momentary trance, turning away towards the door of the cabin with the air of someone leaving the condemned cell. And all that evening she hardly spoke; from time to time I caught her looking at me with an expression of inexpressible sadness. "What is it, Benedicta?" But she only shook her head and gave me a tremulous smile; and after the dance, when we reached the cabin, she tore off her coif and shook out her golden hair, turning upon me with a sudden air of agonised reproach, to cry: "O can't you see? It will change everything, everything."

That last night we lay side by side unsleeping, staring up into the darkness, our strange voyage almost over.

We stepped ashore in a mist of grey watered silk, to find the car waiting on the dockside. Someone had already been aboard to take charge of the luggage; we had nothing to do except to negotiate the gangplank and take refuge under the black umbrella the chauffeur held for us. "Welcome back!" We sat in the back of the car, hand in sympathetic hand, but quite silent, watching the ghostly countryside whirl away around us. Gusts of wind stirred the tall trees; heath moulded itself away into heath, dotted here and there by statuary of soaked forest ponies. At last we came to the big house, which seemed no longer full of people; but there were fires going everywhere, and the muzzy smell of oldfashioned central heating filled the air. A lunch table had been laid for us. It was a queer sensation to be on land again; I still felt the sea rocking in my semicircular canals. Baynes was there to greet us with his air of lugubrious kindness; he had mixed one of his excellent cocktails, Benedicta took hers upstairs for a while. I heard the telephone ring, and saw Baynes switch the extension lever sideways so that it would sound on the first-floor landing. I heard Benedicta speaking, her voice sharp and animated. When she came down she was all smiles. "It was Julian. He sends his love to us. He says that you'll have a pleasant surprise when you next visit the office. We've had a big success with your first two devices."

That afternoon I motored up to London to my by now unfamiliar desk, to be greeted with good news that Julian had promised me. Congreve and Nathan brought me the whole dossier, including all the advertising and promotion. "It's a landslide, Charlock" said Congreve happily, washing his hands with invisible soap. "You sit tight and watch your royalty scale; there seems to be no ceiling—the German and American figures aren't even complete and look at sales."

All this was extremely gratifying. But at the back of the dossier was another folder somewhat cryptically labelled "Dr. Marchant's adaptation of the filament to gunsighting". Neither Congreve nor Nathan could enlighten me as the meaning of it. When they left me I picked up the phone and asked the switchboard to try and unearth Julian for me; this took some time, and when at last I did locate him his voice sounded a good way off, as if he were speaking from the depths of the country. I cut short his conventional greetings and congratulations and at once broached the subject of the dossier. Julian said: "Yes, I was meaning to talk to you about it. Marchant runs our electrical side down at Slough. You may have met him, I don't know. But when we were going into production he at once seized upon your device and applied it to something he himself was working on—a vastly improved gunsighting system. It looks very promising indeed; the Services are most excited by it. We have not moved properly into prototype as yet, but in a month or two we'll have a trial shoot with the Army and see what we've got. I don't need to emphasise the importance of the contracts we might get; and of course your patent is fully protected. It would mean a terrific jump in your royalties. I hope you are pleased."

My silence must have disabused him of the idea, because he repeated the last phrase somewhat more anxiously and went on: "Of course I should perhaps have consulted you—but then you were somewhere on the high seas and Marchant was eager to get going with this infra-red electrical device...." His voice tailed lethargically away. "I feel" I said "as though my invention has been wrenched out of my hands." It was marvellous the way he managed to convey the notion of a sympathetic smile over the phone, the kindly touch upon the elbow. "O don't take it like that, Charlock. It isn't the case. It's your device differently applied, that is all."

"Nevertheless" I said stubbornly, spectacles on nose. "Nevertheless, Julian." He clicked his tongue sympathetically and went on with redoubled suavity. "Please accept my humblest apologies; I should have asked. But now the damage is done, so please forgive me won't you?"

There was in fact nothing to be done but bow to it. "Where is Marchant?" I said. "He is on his way up to you now" said Julian, his voice suddenly fading into a thicket of scratchy interruptions. There was a click and we were cut off. I looked up to find Marchant standing before my desk with the air of an aggrieved collie, tousle-haired and shortsighted behind steel-rimmed spectacles of a powerful magnification, basted with insulation tape. He held out a long limp hand with fingers heavily stained by nicotine and acid. "It's me" he said in his whining disagreeable voice, without removing the wet fag end from his lower lip. "Of course we've met." "Sit down" I said with as much cordiality as I could muster. His whole appearance spoke of the stinks labs of some provincial university—much-patched tweed coat and grey bags: extremely dirty and crumpled shirt with missing stud. He threw a bundle of drawings on to the desk and drew up a chair in order to explain them, pointing cautiously with a silver-hilted pencil. His tweed smelt of wet. I was disposed to adopt an attitude of somewhat boorish resentment towards him, but one glance at his papers showed me the marvellous elegance of his application; he had made full use of the new sodium-tipped contrivance and applied it, with slightly modified mountings, to the conventional sighting screen of a weapon. I listened to his lucid explanation with unwilling admiration. "But then weapons!" I could not help saying at last. "How disappointing. I was hoping my toys would help the human race, not . . . well, contribute to its quarrels." He looked me over, coolly, critically, and with some contempt. Then he lit a cigarette and said: "It's quite the opposite with me. I hate it. Anything I can do to make things harder for it I will, so help me." He exposed a row of uneven yellowish teeth in a ferine grin.

"Anyway" I said with unconcealed distaste "I must congratulate you I suppose."

"It's too early" he said. "Wait till we have our first shoot and see if this blindsighting device works out. Nor need you repine too much, Charlock; compared to some of the things the firm is working on, this is . . . why, virtually harmless." The little intercom panel below my desk lit up and buzzed. Nathan's quiet voice said: "Mr. Charlock, more good news. Mr. Pehlevi says to tell you that the mercury contract is secure; we can substantially reduce our price on the new costings."

Marchant was quietly wrapping up his plans and preparing to slide them back into the cardboard tube. His cigarette dangled from his lip. "Marchant have you ever seen Julian Pehlevi?" I asked curiously; I found I was addressing this question to more and more people these days. Very few could say yes—Nathan was one of the rare ones to have had the privilege. Marchant depressed his cheek in a grin and shook his head. "Can't say I have" he said. "He keeps in touch by phone."

He hovered for a moment, standing on one leg, as if everything had not been said on this particular topic. "I must say," I said with a laugh "his damned elusiveness is getting me down—he's like some blasted ghost." Marchant scratched his nose. "Yet" he said, surprisingly "he must exist somewhere—look at your paper today." There was a daily paper lying unopened in my in-tray. Marchant took it up and hunted for a moment before doubling it back at the financial page and handing it to me to read. Julian had made a speech to the Institute of Directors which was reported in full. "You see?" said Marchant. "Several hundred of those bloody directors must have listened to him for an hour yesterday."

Despite the long tally of successes on every front it was with a kind of subdued melancholy that I drove down to the country that evening. Benedicta had already gone to bed when I arrived. I went up and watched her sleeping by the rosy glow of the night-light, her breast rising and falling, her features relaxed by sleep into an expression of forlorn simplicity. It seemed to me that there were several thousand things I had to tell her, to ask her: yet they were locked up somewhere below the threshold of consciousness. I could not bring them out, rationalise them. What were they? I did not really know—but they swarmed and pullulated inside me like bees from some overturned hive. I watched her thus for a long moment, before turning away and moving silently towards the door. I had my hand upon the panel when I heard her voice say: "Felix." I turned, but she was still lying with her eyes shut fast. "You were watching me" she said.

"Yes."

"I have seen Nash and Wild. They think it is true, I am."

"Open your eyes."

"No."

Two tears welled slowly out from under the closed lids and ran down her aquiline nose. "Benedicta!" I said sharply. She sighed deeply. "But *you* said you wanted a child."

"I do. But I did not know it would be like this."

I dabbed her nose with my handkerchief and stopped to kiss her lips, but she writhed away on the pillow. "I can't bear to be touched, don't you see? Please don't touch me."

I realised in a confused sort of way that a whole new pattern of our relationship had come into being, ushered in by these words. "Go away. I must sleep now." Her tone might well have signified "I find everything about you repellent, disgusting." Her eyes were open now, and they said much that lips could not. In the hall I sat down in a chair and stared hard at the opposite wall, completely bemused and discountenaced. "It will pass I suppose."

I had just finished dining that evening when I heard the sound of a car upon the gravel drive outside the house. It was Nash, whom I had seen only once or twice before—small, pursy and pink: he stood before the fire somewhat self-importantly, rocking slightly on his heels, and drank a whisky. We spoke about Benedicta. "She often gets into states of mild confusion or hysteria—but this you probably know. There is nothing to be done, and as yet nothing to get unduly alarmed about. I've brought her a sleeping tablet or two; if you don't mind I'll go up and have a word with her in a minute. By the way, terrible thing about Caradoc."

"What about Caradoc?"

"Haven't you seen the *Evening Standard*? Killed in an air crash. I couldn't believe my eyes." Caradoc killed! It was like a hammer-blow in the centre of the mind. Nash extracted a paper from his briefcase and made his way up the long staircase, shaking his head and muttering to himself.

CLOSE MISS AS AIRLINER CRASHES

Sydney

An Australian airliner reported a very close miss with an Eastern Overways DC 7 which crashed into the sea off Sydney yesterday afternoon. The Federal Aviation Press has issued the transcript of an exchange between the plane and the control tower. The DC 7 was at 3,700 feet soon after take-off while the airliner was coming in at 3,500 feet, although not quite at the same time. The transcript reading was as follows: "We had a close miss here. We are turning now to three six zero. Did you have another target in this same spot? About the time you turned over?"

"That's right, Southbound, affirmative. However not on my scope at the present time."

"Is he still on scope?" "No, sir."

"It looked like he's in the bay, then, because we saw him. He looked like he winged over to miss us and we tried to avoid him and we saw a bright flash about a minute later. He was well over the top of us, and it looked like he went into an absolute vertical turn and kept on rolling."

"Air Japan reports a big fire going out on the water. Route traffic control keeps asking where is Eastern six thirty-three. I don't scan him any more."

There were 40 passengers in the crashed aircraft but only four survivors, one seriously injured. So far twelve bodies have been recovered. Units of the Australian Navy are on the scene to lend aid. Among those listed as missing . . . *Professor Noel Caradoc*"

The name swam out of the text with paralysing force, holding me to my chair with my untouched drink beside me.

Nash came downstairs once more to reclaim his drink and to stand beside me in sympathetic silence for a long moment. "Wretched bad luck for us all" he said at last. "I shall miss the old bastard." Then he replenished his glass and turned back to the topic of the moment. "You know, Charlock, on reflection I think I did right; I told her as long as she felt like this she should go away quietly for a while; recover her good spirits in Zürich, say. Get away from you—what do you say? I'm not unduly alarmed, but she has after all a bit of a medical history—and as you know women often get strange and hysterical when they are going to have a child."

"But it isn't even absolutely certain is it?"

"No."

"And besides she doesn't need to keep the damned child if it's going to unbalance her, need she? I don't want to be responsible for her cracking up."

"She wouldn't dream of losing it."

"Are you sure?"

Nash sat down and smiled his sad and wrinkled little smile which was always so unexpected, and gave him a sudden simian expression.

"Yes."

"I am not so sure."

"Anyway, humour her for a while."

"Of course."

No alternative line of action seemed to commend itself; listless and apathetic I walked the little man to his car and watched the headlights wander away down the long leaf tunnel. I walked back slowly into the house, still preoccupied by the image of Caradoc's sudden disappearance from the land of the living. Suddenly the huge house seemed stuffy, confining. I took the paper and started upstairs to bed. On the turn of the second landing a sudden impulse made me look up. Benedicta was standing staring down at me with a queer feverish expression which made her pointed features look almost wolfish. She moistened her lips and said: "Has Nash gone?" I nodded. "And you don't mind if I go away for a bit?" I shook my head. "Thank God" she said with relief. She turned away and disappeared on the instant and I heard the rattle of the key turning in the lock of her door.

By the time I returned the next evening she was already gone, though she had left me a few tender words on a postcard, ending with the phrase: "Believe me, it won't be for long. And then happiness again."

* * * * *

V

The new life, which displaced the old with such abruptness, had a somewhat hollow flavour coloured as it was by apprehension about Benedicta's fate with its sudden reversal of values. But Nash was kind and kept me in touch; she was well, it seemed, and living in a small chalet in the grounds of the Paulhaus near Zürich. She was always most composed when she inhabited a snowscape—clouds, pines, snow—and by now she had made up her mind about having the child, indeed seemed to welcome the idea. I wrote to her every week, giving her an account of our doings, but the letters sounded ominously hollow to my ear; the old scaffolding of such common intimacies and confidences as we had been able to build was summarily removed. Subconsciously too I suppose I must have felt that the raw new building exposed, like an aborted piece of architecture, the slack and insubstantial nature of my loving. Yes, something of that order. Also it was somehow humiliating to feel myself replaced by a series of couriers who brought me news of her without ever having a direct message to retail. Julian too was kindness itself and phoned me regularly to demonstrate how close he was keeping in touch with events. The weeks deepened into months, and yet time appeared to have slowed up, to be almost standing still. I had left the country and moved back to the town house in order to be nearer to my work, but I went out very little. I knew hardly anyone in London; and during this period I saw most of Pulley, perhaps, for whom I had developed a great friendship—due in a queer sort of way to our joint misfortune in the loss of Caradoc. The Cham, far from being absent, seemed to go on growing as we sorted out his effects and grouped his papers into some sort of order against the forthcoming publication of whatever might be publishable in all this diverse mass. A great deal of scabrous verse, limericks and the like, were scattered about in his notebooks, and these we supposed would hardly be found suitable—though they afforded us great amusement and pleasure: almost as if he himself were present. Strangely enough, too, the putative publisher of the essays on the history of architecture turned out to be—I would never have guessed it—Vibart of all people. One day he strolled into my office, fit and brown and smiling, to grip my hand and, sinking into an armchair, announced that he was "saved". "Saved?" I echoed; the word had all the flavour of religious conversion. "And all due to you, Charlock Holmes" he said, waving his hat and lighting himself, sumptuously, a cigar. This was surprising indeed. "As they say in stories written for housemaids, I have *found* myself; I have left the F.O. thus avoiding a posting to Sofia and I am now—why here, let me give you my card."

"A publisher!" I said, peering at it. "How is this?"

"Jocas Pehlevi" he said with his shy grin-frown. "Some while after you left he came to see me and said he knew all about my ambitions from you."

"But I never mentioned you to him."

"My dear chap, he could quote some of my conversations verbatim." Perhaps, then, I had recorded Vibart at some stage? My memory held no record of the event, but it is true that I usually made samples of everyone for my voice library—the five vowels etc. (More of that anon.) Perhaps Jocas had helped himself? "Well I'll be damned."

"But he went further; he said that in his view I was no writer but that I would probably make a good publisher. Now as the firm owned half the Norwegian paper stock. . . "

"Does it? I didn't know, but nothing surprises me nowadays."

"It does. It does. He offered to set me up in business with a young Frenchman here in London. Presto! The first fifteen titles are on the stocks already—among them the stuff you are digging out by your friend whatsisname, Caradoc. Do you see?"

"With no strings attached?"

"The firm never attaches strings" said Vibart in a vibrant histrionic register. "Why should it?"

"You really surprise me. But I am glad."

He became very serious now, putting on his most humble and endearing expression as he puffed his cigar. "So am I. Glad? O Lord, it goes deeper than that. I really feel I am going to fulfil myself. It's really saved everything—you know my marriage was going steadily on the rocks because of my incessant whining? And I was getting more and more costive instead of less. My life was terribly abortive; and now look at me! Aren't I a wonderful figure of a man, a publisher? Large cigar, slight *embonpoint*?" He rose and spread the wings of his coat, rotating slowly before me like a mannequin showing off a dress. We both laughed, and I ordered up some sherry to celebrate this surprising resurrection from the dead. "So you see" he said "I only dropped in to thank you, and to ask you in my official capacity when the manuscript will be ready for us."

"But I have all the material at home and we are still working on it; listen, you must dine with Pulley and myself and help us sort it—after all, it's your responsibility really, and there are decisions to be taken. Some of the stuff is characteristically comic, too."

A change. This meeting led to at least one or two delightfully congenial evenings in the Mount Street house, reading, sorting and reminiscing over this huge bundle of papers and notebooks. Moreover I was able to supplement much of this material by a series of recordings made at different times—yes, many of indifferent quality, but sufficiently clear for transcript. It was Caradoc alive who lumbered into the circle of firelight before our very eyes, growling and grumbling and perorating. Pulley at times had tears in his eyes, as much from laughter as from tears. "Pulley standing there like a cow, with his udders swollen out, needing to be milked of this abstract transcendental love of humanity—his religion of service. Eh Pulley, damn you? Ethics not based on metaphysics—that's what it is." "Whee" answered the static.

Deaf as a piecrust
Smooth as a sage
This old man is anyone's age.
Younger than a schoolchild
Older than a Norn
This old man was to the manna born.

This must have been the Nube at some point; criss-crossed with mandolin whirrs and tonic sol-fa and snicking of St. Foutain's painted penis. Then a sudden shift of venue, the noise of a tavern with its clanging cans against butts and the whistle of wind in the trees. Here, rather surprisingly, Koepgen's voice raised angrily—one can well guess against whom. "But you become what you hate too much, you attract what you fear too much." A series of piercing whistles drowned an altercation.

So we listened while the Cham roared on, and Vibart made notes on a pad; we would obviously need to have most of this set down on paper, but the only problem was to find a blushproof secretary capable of undertaking the task.

It was getting on for eleven when the doorbell rang; Baynes had gone to bed. On the doorstep stood the junior office messenger with a letter. It had come in that evening. I could recognise at once the handwriting of Benedicta—but it was mirror-writing; another hand had drawn a line through it and readdressed the envelope to me at the office. I tipped the boy, and excusing myself went upstairs to the bathroom where I opened the letter and unearthed a shaving mirror in which to decipher it. "My son" it opened shakily, with the words thrice repeated. "It is so dark here, down here. The darkest of the three nights and the train has not come in. It goes very slowly when you are waiting but the eyes will always be the same, watching. We will compare notes later, unless I am too bored to exist. In that case goodbye. Julian knows how I feel."

I returned to the firelight, to the room from which all the gaiety seemed to have disappeared. "What is it?" said Pulley. "You look pale." "Bad omens" I said. "Let's have a drink."

It was late when we parted—but for me all the pleasure had gone out of the evening; a massive anxiety had replaced it, anchored in frustration—for there was clearly nothing to be done, to be said, to be acted upon. I grabbed at the chance to walk Vibart across London to his new flat in Red Lion Square for the sake of his company; and when finally we parted I pursued my own walk, erratic and unstudied and frequently turning back upon itself. Vague notions of finding somewhere open which might provide a coffee to drink; but it was either too late, or not early enough. On a hoarding in Oxford Street the post-stickers had already begun to glue up the announcements of next week's film. On one hoarding there was half a poster already up, waiting for its twin to complete it, like the missing piece of a jigsaw puzzle; on it there was a girl dressed in black, but split neatly down the middle—half a face, one breast, one leg. It was Iolanthe—or rather so it seemed to me. I peered among the titles to see if her name was there among the credit lines. Yes, there it was, though it too was split in half; but its size indicated that she was a star of some consequence already. The dawn was swarming up now; wind-triggered, opalescent. A few people were out, walking with ghostly step and wearing cadaverous early-morning faces. A policeman eyed me speculatively as I stood, gaping at the poster; he was almost minded to move me on, but I saved him the trouble. I woke a sleeping taxi at the corner of Bond Street and made my torpid way home. The morning papers would bring the world the knowledge of her runaway marriage to the greatest box-office star in Hollywood. Reno. There was no such thing as a private life for her any more. In *The Times* she looked radiant. but in the evening paper she was more suitably crying with emotion.

* * * * *

Somedays later I received a phone-call from Marchant to tell me that his new gunsight was ready to be proven. "All things being equal day after tomorrow, early, Salisbury Plain. Can I ride down with you? We'd better take a thermos and something to chew. Oh, and you know what? Julian says he is coming, so at last you'll see him in the flesh." In the flesh! At last the promise of something to relieve the monotony of the passing days, something to pique my curiosity.

We set off together accordingly in the middle of the night—we were supposed to reach the proving grounds at seven. But as we neared our destination a thick fog began to settle over the world, and soon we were travelling at a snail's pace inside a frosty bowl of yellow light from the dashboard panel. Here and there a corner would lift and the chauffeur broke away and made a dash along the highway to gain ground before the thick white curtain closed again, submerging our powerful headlights in pools of whirling snowflakes. It was lucky there was no traffic at all to intensify our difficulty. Nevertheless we nearly ran into the little cluster of jeeps and staff cars which were waiting at the point of rendezvous. It was eerie to see the bustle of shapes and figures moving about upon this damp screen; the headlights yawned in the obscurity. The chauffeur was anxious about the plain, fearing he would get stuck in the mud; but Marchant was delighted. "What could be blinder than this?" he repeated. "The conditions are perfect." A tall figure emerged with startling suddenness from the veil around us; it was like a swimmer surfacing. "Brigadier Tanner?" called Marchant, and was relieved when the tall personage answered to the name. "I'm glad you've got here" he said. "I've detailed a staff car to guide. We're all set up on the side of that hill. . . ." He laughed in an exasperated way to find himself pointing into blankness. "The Minister is coming down I believe; God knows if he'll ever get here with this muck. How far along did you hit it?" We exchanged fog-information in a listless way. It had turned quite cold of a sudden. Marchant had unearthed an old sheepskin coat which gave him more than ever the air of an unbrushed collie dog. We did not dare to wander too far from our car in case we lost it altogether. "Julian is with the Minister" said Marchant. "But I don't propose to hang about; we'll get our shooting over and bugger off back to town after we've eaten, what do you say? They can come along any time and talk to the Army."

At first the Brigadier seemed rather reluctant to comply with this view but, when Marchant pointed out that the fog might hold them a prisoner indefinitely and that they might never arrive, he took the point; he would leave a picket on the main road to guide them if they turned up. We were to follow his string of glow-worms across the plain; there was no danger of mud, it was perfectly dry and safe.

We moved off in formation, our engines whimpering in bottom gear; the journey seemed endless at this pace. The scout-cars had to stop frequently to reassure themselves that they were on the right path; the light carrier behind us was working on a compass bearing which did not square with that of the leading picket car. A conclave of shrouded figures exchanged grim pleasantries and grimmer oaths. "The bloody thing's demagnetised" suggested a cockney voice. Shrouded up like this against the dawn-airs they looked like a group of Stone Age figures moving about in the whiteness, engaged on obscure tasks. Now and then a patch of curtain would lift, and the whole convoy would break into a canter, so to speak, for a hundred yards or so. It was getting lighter though; a kind of salmony tinge was beginning to run along the higher reaches of the whiteness—as if something were slowly bleeding to death in the upper sky. The variations in visibility gave human movements some of the quality to be seen in underwater swimming, or else in slow-motion film; the shifting depth of focus teased the eye and dazzled the mind. People seemed far away at one moment; the next they swam up in front of the car as if they had been fired by a cannon. The gradient had sharpened now and we were moving through patches of scrub; earth had changed to gravel on which our tyres sizzled agreeably. The chauffeur grunted with relief. He did not believe the Brigadier's tales about there being no mud. "You can never trust the Army, sir" he said to Marchant. "I was in it. I know." Marchant giggled and stumped out his nauseating cigarette, filling the car with acrid smoke. "So was I" he said.

At last they were there; suddenly and quite mysteriously materialised upon a lightly sloping hillock—the three tall weapons looking more like combine-harvesters with snouts cocked at the sky. The gnomes that tended them appeared first in a sort of tableau, leaning forward to identify us—in fear, I suppose, of being run down. Hoarse voices barked orders, answered one another; the Brigadier re-emerged from the nothingness and opened the door of the car. We followed him across the field to where soldiers in blankets now moved—but with the immortal listlessness of a typical apathy. The ground-glass tones of a sergeant major tried to stir them up with quaint oaths and elephantine jokes. But they moved like somnambulists. Marchant's toy was a clumsy great barrel-organ of an instrument whose panels glowed with a whole spectrum of coloured switches.

He lurched across to it with a welcoming gesture, arms open, almost as if it had been a girl; then he crouched over it with an over-elaborated delicacy, touching now this part now that, manipulating switches, patting it and peering about him shortsightedly as if seeking some sort of reassurance from the sky. Watching him thus so vulnerably exposing the whole range of his naive gestures, his anxiety, his frail hopes, I had a sudden pang of sympathy for him; and at the very same moment I was swept by a conviction that here was not simply a scientist, but a sort of genius. His whole waking mind moved among abstractions now, like a fish in its element. And I made an involuntary comparison with my own gifts—the mere tinkering with string and wire, the superficial meddlesomeness of the second-rate gift: and I realised that I would have given anything to be Marchant, to belong to his tribe. How trivial my string of elementary devices seemed to me as I took in the feverish engrossed state of my fellow inventor; the very skeletal posture seemed to have the pulse of a different sort of fever running through it—an electrical charge. "We'll have to modify the whole armature, of course" he said. "She's far too heavy. But first let's see if she works eh?"

We were surrounded by more figures leaning down to tend these metal engines with the air of men carefully watering plants in a high window-box. These were the flint arrowheads of our wretched culture!

I could watch all this activity with a certain bemused detachment, since I could not interpret all these diverse movements; I was like an amateur at a ballet or a bullfight. All I knew was that these stubby snouts raised in sinister elevation against the lightening sky would spit out a momentary stab of flame. The Brigadier was counting; he held something in his right hand attached to a long landline. His air was that of a doctor taking the pulse-beat of a patient. A plane drowsed languidly overhead, established radio contact, and moved off. More orders came harshly out of the mist and a thick snicking of oiled steel. Marchant produced a little box, such as air-lines issue to their passengers, containing ear-plugs, and urged a couple on me. Then came another interminable wait before the shoot began.

When it came I was quite unprepared for it; a tremendous pulse-beat ran through the ground under our feet and ran swiftly away to the horizon in an accumulating wave. The snouts recoiled slowly, with great elegance, hissing; only to return and flame again briefly. Fire and recoil, fire and recoil. The nearest part of the mist had been blown to bleeding patches; there were tears everywhere in the fabric now, it hung down and swirled slowly about. Marchant knelt down staring at his barrel-organ, hands over his ears, chattering to himself. A smear of sharp light illuminated a large-scale map over which hovered some disembodied moustaches. Then followed a silence during which a devout signaller communicated with the unseen through earphones, his box of tricks spluttering and crackling. I divested myself of my plugs and turned up my coat collar. Marchant was in a state of high elation. "It's going to be all right; the modifications are nothing" he repeated; he had grabbed the sleeve of the soldier who disengaged himself politely, his attention turned on his signallers. Again. There seemed to be a long moment of suspense now followed by a lot of jabbering in military argot. The Brigadier shook hands with Marchant, and as he did so an equestrian figure emerged slowly out of the mist on our left with a high degree of improbability and walked his tall horse over to the battery. "It's the General" said Tanner, and went over to give an account of his stewardship. "Well done" said the mounted figure in sepulchral tones. "You can wind it all up now. The Minister has got stuck somewhere along the road, waiting for this fog to lift. We'll have to wait and see what he says. I expect he'll put it off until next week."

"Well, that's the lot" said Marchant. We climbed back into the car; he sat beside the chauffeur to take advantage of the light from the dashboard, for he had already resumed notebook and pencil in order to cover the pages with hieroglyphics and drawings. "Sorry" he said apologetically over his shoulder. "But unless I get things down they have a habit of disappearing."

The fog was thinning out quite perceptibly and once upon the gravel road the chauffeur professed to know his way; we were able to dismiss the single jeep which had been delegated to shepherd us back to the main road. It turned aside with a roar and bounced back into the obscurity, leaving us to our own devices. We pressed on slowly with the headlights ablaze; from time to time the chauffeur sounded his melancholy horn—a desolating croak like that of some solitary marsh-bird. And then we found ourselves lost again; the gravel gave out and we were rolling softly along grass inclines. Marchant used a great deal of bad language, but added: "Thank God we brought some grub. This can't last for ever. Let's press on a bit eh? After all what is the worst that can happen? We might end up in Cornwall that's all."

"There's no mud yet, sir."

"Well, it's your fault for sending the Army back."

"I'm sorry, sir."

But even as we spoke a miracle started to take place; a wind started to flap from nowhere, lifting huge panels of fog almost bodily, rolling them back upon one another like so many strips of sodden newspaper. Huge rents and whorls and eddies began to appear all round us. In corners the white screen had begun to pour away like suds down a sink, to shiver and swirl like the dust devils of the desert. Huge slices of visibility were thrust upon us, and the sun started to shimmer through the opaqueness. It was like watching the scrambling retreat of an army. Even the terrain looked firm and promising; elated we moved into second gear and gave chase, squeezing down the soft inclines, further and further. "A compass damn it; we should have borrowed one" said Marchant, but I was breathlessly watching the bewitching phosphorescence of the mist retreating from us. Larger and larger grew the spaces, until with a last sudden flick of the wrist a whole valley burst open to the view, radiant with sun and green grass on which glittered a million diamonds of condensing fog. The theatrical effect was vastly heightened by the fact that there, right before us, glowed the melancholy and enigmatic pillars of Stonehenge. Involuntarily we all three exclaimed. We were alone, surrounded by a good square mile of radiant sunlight. "Marvellous" shouted Marchant. "We'll eat our grub here. Abandon ship, my lads." It was doubly lucky as the chauffeur could now reorient himself in relationship to the stone monuments—we had been travelling at right angles to the correct bearing. The fog was now vanishing with greater speed, restoring the whole landscape to us, stretch by stretch. So it was that in a state of high elation we took our provisions and devoured them among these mysterious blocks.

It was not unduly cold in this frail sunlight. Marchant fell upon the chicken and ham with ardour, speaking volubly as he chewed. "Well, it went off all right, Charlock, didn't it? The only fly in the ointment is that we didn't see Julian." He chuckled mischievously. "But I didn't expect to. I don't. I say, you are not much of a chemist are you? I'm not being rude, I'm asking." I shook my head ruefully. Alas. "All the better stroke of genius that guess of yours—but I'm not sure that sodium is your answer; I'll see what I can do to improve on it. It's marvellous that you are not a jealous person."

"Alas, I am."

He gazed at me wide-eyed, his mouth full of cress.

"O Lord" he said in dismay. "I did hope not."

We sparred good-humouredly for a while as we ate and gulped the scalding coffee; the chauffeur maundered off among the ruins, still wounded in his *amour propre* by having mistaken his road. "As for Julian . . . well damn him. I don't *want* to meet him any more." He chuckled. "As a matter of fact I once had the impression that I *had* met him—and I'm not given to fond fancies. But once he asked me to take some drawings up to his flat and leave them. When I arrived there was a singular-looking bird in the lift, very striking in a queer way. Deeply lined face, eyes like dead snails, medium to tall, dressed rather well in a stockbrokerish way, with a spotted bow tie. A brown signet ring. He was waiting for me in the lift. I tried to get him to speak, because then I would have recognised the voice, but he wouldn't. So I simply said: 'Second floor' and let him press the button. I addressed a question to him but he shook his head without speaking and gave me a sort of sad smile—a lost world of a smile. On the second I stepped out and up he went to the top floor. Well, I rang the bell, but the manservant was a hell of a while coming to open the door to me. All this time I could hear this chap just above me in the liftshaft—hear his breathing I mean and smell his cigar. He hadn't got out of the lift, he was just standing there waiting. Well, when my door opened and I was let in—while I was still standing in the hall having the front door closed behind me—I heard the lift coming down again. The servant said: 'You've missed Mr. Pehlevi by a few moments, sir. He's just gone out.' Well now, had I missed him? I wondered."

He laughed again with schoolboyish elation. "I say, you aren't depressed are you?"

"No." But really I was, depressed and confused. "As for Julian," he went on "I've given him up, as I say. But it's curious how a little thing like his obstinate Trappist-like refusal to manifest himself gives rise to rumours. You can never trace the source, of course, it's always at second hand. But someone had heard that he was disfigured by lupus and was too ashamed to show up; another chap in the office had heard that Julian was going through a long and complicated piece of facial surgery. There may be something in that one. The Institute of Directors were addressed by a man who had a huge dressing across his forehead, and wore dark glasses. It's rum, I suppose, but I've got used to it. Strangest of all was Bolivar, a weird painter fellow; Julian bought some of his things for the firm. You may have seen them. Well, he claimed to have done a sort of composite portrait of him based on the evidence of those who said they had seen him—what they call an Identikit nowadays I suppose. On the sly, of course. Bolivar was an awful drunk and lived on some repulsive cat-food in a basement room in Campden Hill. He's dead now, poor chap; but during his last illness he rang me up and said that he was going to leave this portrait to me, and that I should find it in the drawer of the bureau in his room. I went round, but he was already delirious and the drawer was empty. I say Charlock, cheer up. When a civilisation has decided to bury its head in the sand what can we do but tickle its arse with a feather?" Marchant raised his pale and grubby finger and apostrophised the sages of antiquity. "O Aristotle, your civilisation too was based on slavery and the debauching of minors."

It was almost noon before we piled back into the car to start the homeward journey, and by now almost the whole landscape had come back into sheer focus. The fog had banked up to the north and west but in our immediate vicinity visibility was virtually total. It was pleasant to feel the car at last able to slide up the scale into top gear, and to see the hedgerows sliding by. In the remote distance among the dangling coils of remaining mist moved an ant-line chain of Army cars crooning across the plains; but we had gathered momentum now, and our tyres whirred upon the fine macadam. I settled myself in the back, wrapped my coat collar around my ears and fell into a doze. I do not know how long I was asleep, but when at last I woke it was with a start of surprise. We were in the middle of a forest moving in almost total darkness through a fog much heavier than the one we had experienced; moving, moreover, in a long slow string of main-road traffic, tail-light after tail-light, in a slow forlorn processional. "It's come back" said Marchant angrily. "It'll take us weeks to get back to London at this pace." So it would seem.

We were advancing slowly and circumspectly in measured distances; at some of the cross-roads ghostly policemen walked up and down the lines with torches keeping the files as free for movement as possible. There were long inexplicable halts, followed by short advances, and then new halts. It was on one of these halts that I suddenly saw, in the whiteness of our headlights, the number of the car in front of us; it was Julian's Rolls! We had drawn up almost touching his rear number-plate. "My God it's Julian" I cried to Marchant. "He must have turned back." And before the matter could be discussed—indeed in quite spontaneous fashion—I opened our car-door and lurched into the road. I ran up alongside the Rolls, calling out "Julian" and rapping with my knuckles on the glass of the side windows. But the whole car, like our own, was virtually misted up. Only the windscreen wipers kept a triangle of visibility open in front of the chauffeur. I tried to draw his attention, but he was watching the road ahead and did not appear to see me. I tried the rear glass again, shouting once more, and from inside a hand lowered it about an inch. A voice, not Julian's, said: "Who is it?" I wiped a circle of mist from the outside and said: "Is Mr. Pehlevi in there?"; and from the misty interior the voice—probably that of the Minister—answered testily. "Yes, who wants him?" The glass was lowered slowly and I said, somewhat foolishly: "Julian, it's Charlock." There were two figures sunk in the dark depths of the limousine, and I could see the face of neither clearly. Just an etching of two black Homburg hats. "I was looking forward to meeting you at last" I went on naively. One hat turned to the other, as if waiting for it to take the cue and answer me; but Julian did not speak. I was still hanging there anxiously when there came a hooting of horns and the confused sound of traffic police shouting: "Move along there smartly please." A torch flashed moth-like from somewhere near. "Julian" I cried, I wailed. But the Rolls was moving forward now—the whole line sagged forward and peeled itself off softly into the obscurity. The window went up with a slap; I was forced to rejoin Marchant in our car, furious and disappointed. "It's his car all right" I said. "And he's in it. Next time we stop. . . ." But we had reached a double cross-roads with an island now, with slightly better visibility; the cars ahead were moving to left and right now, the file had thickened and started to disperse down the various lanes. By the time we came up to the faintly glowing beacons Julian's car had disappeared, and we were hard behind a charter bus, hemmed in on either side by small cars. A mournful hooting filled the air. Marchant laughed and slapped his knee. "I suppose you can't catch them" he said to the chauffeur; but the rejoinder was an obvious one. They could have slid away down any of four roads. Once again he had given us the slip.

Characteristically enough within the space of an hour the fog had dispersed again and we were racing away towards London in a fine clear rain. The chauffeur put on a turn of high speed in order to try and catch the Rolls if indeed it were travelling along the same road—

the main London road. But strive as we might we overtook nothing that looked like it. Marchant found my disappointment rather comical, and once or twice I found him glancing at me with his cruel sidelong smile. When we arrived back at Mount Street he invited himself in for a bath and a drink; a flock of messages waited for us. Congratulations from the office, presumably on the strength of Marchant's success with the Army; a note from Pulley to say he would come in after dinner—some of Caradoc's drawings had been washed ashore. But most surprising and heartening, there was a short note from Benedicta which was both coherent and very tender, promising that everything would soon be over and that she would rejoin me. I rang up to tell Nash the news, only to find that he was very much *au courant*. "Yes, she's had a splendid period now, a complete change, and the outlook is excellent. By the way, she is convinced it will be a boy. Women usually get what they want, have you noticed?"

Marchant had his bath, though except for damp hair awkwardly combed back towards his ears one would hardly have guessed it. We joined each other for a drink by the fire; and he asked if he might play the piano for a moment before taking himself off. He attacked several of the more complicated preludes and fugues of "the 48" with great assurance, but with a total lack of sensibility, working at them like a woodpecker or a cobbler at his last. "Poor Bach!" I said. "I know," he said cheerfully "I know." But he seemed to derive great enjoyment from this somewhat awkward operation; he wagged his head about as he played. When he stopped to light a cigarette I said: "You have never been married, have you, Marchant?" He looked at me slyly, his hands poised to resume playing. "Good Lord, what a question. No. Why?" I refilled his glass. "An idle question" I said. "I was wondering why not." "Why not?" he repeated, as if trying the question, so full of novelty, upon himself for the first time. "I've never felt the need. I doubt if real scientists ever do—the need for these charming articulated mummies. At least, I think we belong to a dispossessed tribe, all our affective life is passed in the head; and then, again, after forty you begin to feel out of date and out of sympathy. Do you care for this age particularly? I mean, once our hero was a St. George doing in a Dragon to free a damsel; but now our hero seems to be a spy doing in a damsel in order to escape the dragon. The genius of suspicion has entered the world, my boy. And then, what do you make of the faces of the young? As if they had smashed the lock on the great tuck-box of sex only to find the contents had gone mouldy. Sex should be like King's drinking, not piglets at teat."

"My goodness" I said, delighted. "You are an oldfashioned romantic, Marchant. I would never have guessed."

"I was once in love with a little female butcher, a pretty widow. But you know with all the handling of the meat her little paws had got the fat worked into them. White little plump mortuary fingers. When she touched me I could feel her handling those swinging carcasses. I was cured, but not before I had made some very valuable scientific observations on her. You know the pharmaceutical boys down at Lund's working on the firm's perfumes. I was able to turn out a cream for old Robinson which is second to none for rough or chapped skin. But I had to leave her all the same, the girl in question."

"A sad story."

"Perhaps; but it illustrates another extraordinary fact about this game. Your best discoveries are always accidental by-products of a search for something you never find; you set out to hunt something and presto, along comes something else, something quite unexpected. Did I tell you about our bottled sweat project—we call it that for a joke? It's still experimental which means non-existent. It's interesting in a farcical sort of way. Toller works on perfumes, as you know; well, Nash came up with some Czech psychiatrist's notion that all perfumes contained a kind of built-in echo of human sweat, and that some types of sweat, male sweat, contained a sort of paralyser which women could not resist—like cats with valerian. It was a complicated and wordy essay this, but it advanced the idea that the irresistibility of Don Juan was not due to looks or charm, but due to his smell. All Don Juan types are ugly and stunted, says this chap, who had run over a few psychoanalytically. But they all had a smell which spelt out danger. It sounded silly of course, and the team busy making things for women's armpits got a hell of a laugh out of it. But Toller and I ruminated a bit; we started to do a leisurely survey of sweats, every kind of sweat: a woman with her period, an athlete after a race, sun sweat, fear sweat. You will hardly believe how much smell changes according to circumstance, temperature and so on. For years we played about this notion; I can't say we were entirely serious. It was a by-product of the scent-business. It was a rest and a change from worrying about what smell makes women irresistible; what, we asked ourselves, makes a man irresistible?

"The actual chemistry, the analysis, was fearfully complicated, a real challenge; we had to devise a sort of scent-log. And for a long time we were at sea. We used what we knew of the rest of the scent range—from garlic to magnolia blossom. Then one day I had a glimmer; fundamentally women want to be raped I think, taken by force; things haven't changed much since the Stone Age. On the other hand, as the biological left hand of the partnership responsible to the tribe for childbearing, they had developed a heavy load of conscience about it. In order to really give in it had to be in a fashion which unequivocably excused the lapse. In other words they had to be *frightened* almost to the point of insensibility before they could clear themselves with their own consciences. Our hypothetical Don Juan, then, had this paralysing gift. He could scare them into surrender by his scent. All right, laugh; but sometimes these crazy ideas have a point. It was a sort of rape-mixture we were after. Where to find a laboratory of smell? It suddenly occurred to me (do you know the smell of schizophrenes, of epileptics?) that all of the kingdom's top rapists are locked up in Broadmoor! Nash arranged for us to send in a small team to hunt around among them, and see what we could find. Well, after four years' work we have, very tentatively, isolated something which might break down into this vital secretion. Women beware! From the sweats of paranoiacs we have husbanded something which will permit your lasciviousness full play and your consciences rest! It has no name at the moment and the quantity is small; but we have put it out on test for a try-out."

"Do you mean you have a lot of London bobbies walking around smelling like goats and making women drivers turn dizzy at the wheel?" Marchant gave his characteristic giggle. "Of course not. They would never get near enough to do the damage; what I *have* got is a willing experimental team of fifteen provincial hairdressers, women, who have agreed to wear nothing but this stuff for six months. Now they are always bending over their clients. Moreover there is always fug to help things along. We shall see what effect if any that has. Might start a wave of Lesbianism in the blameless purlieus of Norwood or Finchley. Then we should feel our little extract was the real thing."

He banged down the piano lid and stood up, groping for his brief-case in order to produce a dirty handkerchief wherein to blow his nose. "I'd offer you some," he said "but you wouldn't need it, being a married man of consequence and place." There was no hint of bitterness in his tone—it was simply a light-hearted sally: but to my surprise it stung me. Taken unawares by an overwhelming sense of futility and inadequacy I heard myself saying: "Yes. I am Mr. Benedicta Merlin, no less" in tones of savage irony. Marchant looked at me keenly and with a new sympathy. "I didn't mean anything by what I said," he told me apologetically "truthfully."

"I know you didn't."

"Good."

I poured him a stirrup-cup to show that there were no hard feelings. "Listen," I said "I wonder if later on you would let me pick your brains a bit; indeed you might help me build it. When I've sorted out my library of voices—it will take ages. I wanted to build a sort of sound-bank based on phonetics. I can already build up voices from a sort of sound-bank—based on the vowel-sounds. A sort of embryology of language. Just like Cuvier deducing his whole animal from one bone; some time I'll get around to developing it, but I'd need help on the practical side—the electrical wave-mechanics side. For the moment I'm snowed under with other projects."

"So am I. But of course I will."

"But this is something of my own, outside the firm. I wouldn't, for example, tell Julian about it."

He walked slowly towards the door, brooding. "I wonder Charlock" he said "if you aren't under the same misapprehension as I was; I mean in imagining that he runs the firm. He doesn't you know. He has to fight tooth and nail sometimes for his own ideas about how things should be done, and very often he is overruled by his own boards. No, nobody runs the firm, strictly speaking; it's a sort of snowball with its own momentum now, the bloody organisation. I pity Julian, in fact; to be so powerful and at the same time so powerless."

"Truthfully I am beginning to dislike him" said I.

"Ah! the father-figure" he said cryptically. "I think that's a waste of energy. You are in it now, you are part of it, rowing with the rest of us. Myself I would have got nowhere without the firm; they picked me out of a provincial university. I would have spent my life in a senior common room babbling about Rutherford forever had it not been for them. As it is I am marvellously free to give of my best; once they even gave me three years off to travel. No, Merlin's is a godsend—at least for me."

So might it have been for me, I thought, had I not made the mistake of marrying into it. Or was that really the reason? The whole problem of Benedicta rose like an overtoppling wave and engulfed me. I shook my head doubtfully. "Well," said Marchant shaking my hand "thanks for being decent; and count on me when you want anything."

I watched his slight figure disappearing down the street, with its queer slanting stride. The telephone was ringing. The telephone was ringing.

* * * * *

We always think that we are thinking one thought at a time because we have to put them down one under the other, in a linguistic order; this is an illusion I suppose. Here I was talking to the office while my hands riffled the coloured pages of a weekly magazine which dealt with Iolanthe's new conjugal life in a turreted Hollywood mansion bearing a fair resemblance to parts of "Cathay". Her swimming pool, her bedroom, the expensive scents, the loaded racks of clothes, the press-cuttings, the emptiness of the mirror-world. She herself looked pale and tired, clad in riding boots. Expression of a frail oldfashioned devotion which no longer had any place in our world, but which the screen still perpetuated as a herd-echo. Her husband looked palatable and superficial. I wished her luck. O yes, I did.

Summer passes, autumn comes; and with it the news that Benedicta had produced the intentional man-child, who was to be called Mark. (I was not consulted on this point among others.) Shoals of telegrams like flying-fish, cases of champagne. Moreover she was planning to return for Christmas. Nash pronounced her in excellent health, but advised me to make no move, to let her do things at her own rhythm. "It is maddening and worrying for you, I know that" he added with sympathy. "But it will come right, I am sure, with time." In the meantime there was only one thing to do—to become absorbed in my work, the classical response. My list of trophies mounted gradually, one success following another, but with an ease and rapidity which somehow had the hollowness of an illusion. Entangled in its coils I felt a sort of heartbreak as I found myself harking back nostalgically to the promises which the past had once sanctioned—Istanbul huddled among her veils of mist. All the more poignant because distance in time had cast all these events in the brilliant colours (memory-induced) of half-fictions. Small fragments broken from the bright screen of days passed with a different sort of Benedicta, a woman who might seem forever unreal to me now; naturally with fear comes misunderstanding, with anxiety the sense of separation, of drifting apart. Unless. Unless what? An outside chance of reversing the immortal process.

Hippolyta came to London somewhen about now to nurse a broken ankle. Sitting before the fire, crutches beside her, she was staring bitterly at the face of Iolanthe which adorned the cover of a glossy magazine. It was startling how much she had aged—perhaps the crutches by association made it seem so? No, there were great meshes of white at her temples. Crow's foot, reading glasses and so on. Nor was she the only one for "Charlock, you've changed" she cried: and breaking out, as if from a mask of witch-hazel, her face flowered once more into that of the impetuous inquisitive Athenian. Yes, of course. I had been putting on weight, my hair was badly cut, lustreless and dandruffy, my suit unpressed. "Longer cigars, shorter wind." But we embraced until she winced from the pain of her leg. "Wiser! Sadder? Have you seen this new face?" She pointed ruefully at the star. ("The body dries up, the mind becomes toneless, the soul reverts to chrysalis; only the providing power lives on and on, independent of a dogmatic theology. The only thing that does not wear out is time." Thus Koepgen.) She smiled up at us like a mummy, and tapping her face with her glasses Hippo said, with the same downcast expression, "I get more and more jealous of less; she gets better and better, Felix. She is a real personage now. Have you seen her new film? I've come over for it specially. I shall choke with rage, but I must see it, I must see them all. It's become an obsession. I hunt among her expressions for the traces of Graphos."

"Graphos!"

"Yes. And to think that all that time I didn't know that this common little fiend enjoyed the real thing."

She lit a cigarette with steady hands and blew a great plume of smoke like a denunciation. "And now he's dying slowly, out of reach of everybody. Nobody knows as yet, he is still active. But he knows." She poked up the fire with one of her crutches. I said "Graphos" on a sort of grace-note. She smiled. "He explained it to me. You might say it was hate at first sight—the only form of love they could know; they had the same values, were both frustrated in the same affective field. But they did not have to *pretend* to each other. It lasted like that, for ages and ages. And, to my humiliation, I did not know. Does one ever? I rebuilt his career, poor moonstruck me." She used some very bad language in Greek; brief tears came into her eyes. "And now I am obsessed with her because of it. But never mind, she has made her mistakes, even though she now wears her sex like an expensive perfume. Aha, but the man *she* married creaks, *creaks*. I am glad. There is no joy to be got from *him*. It's malicious, but I can't help being pleased."

"No. That's not you, Hippo."

"It is. It is. And what galls me worse is that she is *articulate* now; I stole some of her letters to Graphos. You see how low one can sink? I can remember parts by heart, like where she says: 'As for me, having been in a sort of clinic of love, a captive when young, and forced by circumstance to take on everyone, young or old, I missed the whole point. My understanding remained unkindled. The sex act misses fire if there is no psychic click: a membrane has to be broken of which the hymen is only a parody, a mental hymen. Otherwise one can't understand, can't receive. So very few men can do this for a woman. You, Graphos, did this for me. Though I never could love you I'm grateful.' "

She banged her crutch on the floor and turned the journal over on its face, her face.

Well we dined there, by the fire, plate on knee; and there was a kind of luxury to talk about the past which for me had become prehistory—yellowing snapshots of the Acropolis or Byzantine Polis. After dinner Pulley and Vibart put in a short appearance, and though our talk gathered a superficial animation we could still feel the hangdog death of Caradoc looming over us. It was a deeply felt physical presence—not only because all his papers were stacked up there on the sideboard. It would only have increased the sense of constraint to have played out his voice upon my machines, so I did not try to. But there was news of Banubula who might be coming soon to London to have his prostate looked at. "In the morning he still retires to the lavatory for an hour with a churchwarden clay pipe and a bowl of soapy water. There he sits in silent rapture blowing huge iridescent bubbles and watching them float out over Athens. In harmony with himself. Only he still moans a good deal about not getting into Merlin's. Otherwise no change."

Vibart had just returned from a visit to Jocas who was also recuperating from a fall and a fractured hip. Picture of him bedridden before a huge fire taking castor-oil out of an oldfashioned soup-spoon; having his toenails trimmed for him by the eunuch. Almost mad with boredom, and unable to read, he had hit upon a solution—a model railway. His little trains ran all round the house, and around half the garden. Carried from point to point in a sedan, he passed his time agreeably in this fashion.

But at last talk lagged; Caradoc ached on like a bad tooth. The decanter was empty. They took their leave, reluctant to leave the evening unachieved, yet realising they could not revive it. Hippo stayed on to gossip and meditate. "Will you come with me? I have located four other films in the provinces in which she plays. I am here for a week—all too short for London." I agreed, feeling curiously stirred by the idea; apart from the brief glimpse on board the vessel of love I had seen nothing of Iolanthe. She pressed my hand; we spoke of other things, and I mentioned the dead boy in Sipple's bed. Who was finally responsible, both for the deed and for hushing the matter up? She did not know; and I could sense that she was telling the truth. "Sipple had threatened to do it because the boy was going to blackmail him. Fifteen all. But later he said it was done while he was out. Thirty fifteen. Yes, it was a brother of Iolanthe, and her father, who was in Athens that week end, had also threatened to punish the boy. Thirty all." She gave a little groan and patted her head. "There seem to be a hundred reasons to account for every act. Finally one hesitates to ascribe any one of them to the act. Life gets more and more mysterious, not less."

"I must say I thought that she herself might have. . . ." I gazed in abstracted fashion at the doe-like face of the world star. "I wonder if the firm knows."

"You must ask Julian."

Later, of course, I did. He said something like: "You know most questions become more macro or micro, more Copernican or Ptolemaic: they don't stay still, the pendulum is always on the move. They change as you watch. And always the answer proposed, particularly by an organisation like the firm, is provisional, short-term. We have to accept that." There was an overwhelming sadness in his voice. I was so touched by his sadness that I almost had a lump in my throat.

"Questions and answers" said she with bitterness. "How should I explain you loving Benedicta Merlin?"

"Easy. It was like breathing in."

"And now?"

"Exactly. I am all confused."

She gave a cruel little laugh. "Ah wait" I said reproachfully. "It still goes, on my side."

"No woman can stand her" she said. "You know that."

Of course I knew that. It wasn't easy to explain the sort of mesmeric influence Benedicta exercised over her witless scientist. "A form of hysteria I suppose; in the Middle Ages it would have been classified as possession."

"They say that the firm has her regularly burgled in order to offset her tremendous expenditure against insurance!"

"Malice" I said.

"Very well, malice."

There was a ring at the door; I had ordered her a taxi, and now slowly and reluctantly I helped her hobble to it. She turned in the street and said: "Shall we tomorrow afternoon? Please."

"Of course we shall." She meant the film of Iolanthe. Away she rolled with a wave of a white glove and a tremulous smile.

All at once the house seemed very old and damnably musty, like some abandoned tomb which the grave-robbers had not spared. I got out one of the firm's calendars—huge meretricious pictures of colonial landscapes—and marked off the days to Xmas. I supposed I should have to make some preparations to receive her. Or should I just leave it to chance, let her walk back naturally into the circle of our common life if you could call it that like one who had only left the room for a few moments? I wondered. I wondered.

But the pilgrimage to the shrines of the love goddess intervened among these preoccupations—poor Hippolyta's week of self-torture and admiration; riding to suburban cinemas in Finchley and Willesden where the sacred mask was being exhibited in a series of hieratic roles which, superposed at such speed one upon the other, and with such variety of age, situation, landscape, hypnotised me hardly less absolutely. Sitting in musty seats, inhaling dusty floors whose peanut shells crackled under foot: in afternoon flea-pits, holding the white glove of Hippo and watching, heart in mouth—well no, I couldn't any longer use the prop of her name as a memory-aid. Iolanthe had slipped away, far beyond me now, out of sight of Number Seven, of Athens, the Nube. She brought to this new silver life a gravity, authority, distinction, even a tender mischievousness which bewitched; she had refined her potential for gesture and expression in some radical fashion. No. No. This creature I did not know at all. I whispered her name once or twice, but it raised no echo. And yet it was with real concern for her true self that I watched this mammoth distortion of Iolanthe into a world-fetich. (Hippo gasping after some great scene, saying "marvellous", touched to the quick.) But my goodness, the responsibility she had taken upon herself was frightening. She lived by the terms of this mock-art, lived a travesty of a life passed in public: as much a prisoner of her image as any of us to the firm. She couldn't walk down a street to post a letter unless she was disguised. I saw in the flash the sad trajectory of her new life, the life of a priestess, with a clarity that no further information could ever qualify. It was all there, so to speak. Even what she told me herself afterwards added only detail—even the worst things, like having to dress up and "really act" when she wanted to be alone, out of the glare of the following pressmen. For example, even to visit their securities in the bank vaults twice a year—a ritual the husband insisted upon: it lulled his sense of insecurity. Then about how one day the child gets locked in a safe, suffocated, brought out dead—all that stuff; and running down the street from the hospital in tears there comes a snap from a street-photographer and a tendered card. "Your picture, lady?" He did not notice the tears under the dark glasses. Well and then pacing a long low-ceilinged room with her new camera-shy walk, so painfully learned from a ballerina, she says piteously: "Why should I not love this life, Felix? It's the only real life I have known."

Indeed. And then Hippo saying savagely: "If it were an art-form she would be really great. Thank God it isn't. I should be even more angry."

"How can we know?"

"Why it's aimed at the mob."

"And?"

"And!"

Then later over repulsive tea and buttered toast in some small café she explained in more detail. "You see, the majority must always be denied the higher pleasures like art etc. which in our age it feels entitled to. It's not a matter of privilege, my dear. Just as literacy doesn't confer the ability to really read—so biologically the many are unfitted for the rarest pleasures which are travestied by Iolanthe; love-making, art, theology, science—they each contain whole lives, silver lives, encapsulated in a form. They exist for the maker and his few subjects. She exists for everyone. When we speak of the destruction of an ethos or a civilisation we are describing the effect on it of the mob-discovery of it. The mob wants it, but it must be made palatable. Naturally the efficacy becomes diluted. There you have Iolanthe."

I was not sure at all about this. I had spilt butter on my tie. But inside I simply ached with vexation at never having met Iolanthe.

But there was no news until the day before Christmas when Nash rang up very chirpy. "Well, here she is at last" he said with his false-sounding heartiness. "All safe and sound."

Flowers! In my benign way I had always thought of her returning to Mount Street; but Nash dispelled the illusion. "No, she's in the country. She wants you to bring Baynes down to her if you will—you will go down this evening won't you?" I said I would, though I had to disguise a distinct pique that Benedicta had neither bothered to inform me of her arrival before the event—nor telephoned me to tell me of her whereabouts. However I swallowed the toad-like thought as best I could, and went out to buy such presents as might be deemed suitable to the season. It was sleeting, the taxi-driver was kindly garrulous; there was, as usual, nothing that I could give Benedicta, for she had everything—nothing, that is, of any real value or worth; things such as paintings or books would not have felt to her like presents. It was going to be an unbridled yuletide.

The shops were all lighted up with a ghastly artificial array of colours and forms which signal the triumphs of commerce over religion. Loudspeakers everywhere were playing "Silent Night", pouring the spirit of the Christchild over everything with this amplified crooning of organs and xylophones: into the frosty streets with their purple-nosed crowds of milling hierophants, busy buying tokens of the miracle—poor pink-witted, tallow-scraping socialist mobs. It was cold. It was biting cold. I was angry. The latest jazz hit sawed at the frosty air, with its oft-repeated refrain:

She's as sweet as a tenderised steak
And I'll conquer the world for her sake.

In all this tremendous tintinnabulation Charlock walks, the "self-inflicted man" of Koepgen's fable, wondering what he might buy as an offering to the season. There's something wrong about a philosophy which doesn't offer the hope of certain happiness. Despite man's estate (tragic?) there should be at least a near-guarantee of happiness to be dug out of the air around us. In Selfridges the air hovered and lapped us, impregnated with the heat of our bodies and breath. Pressed in sardine fashion on all sides I let myself drift slowly down the carpeted streams. Our predispositions reveal themselves very accurately in our *moeurs*. Never mind. I bought some expensive gifts and had them elegantly wrapped; then swollen with these acquisitions waddled back to the doors like a woman at term, crushing up my paper as I went. The crowds milled and swirled. "Freed from the economic whip, we will not steer your bloody ship." Nor could I find another taxi. I had to walk almost all the way back to the office where the duty car was waiting for me. At Mount Street Baynes was waiting, he had already packed for me. I looked around to see if anything had been overlooked, gasping a bit, like a goldfish fallen out of its bowl on to the carpet.

But by now, with the falling evening temperatures everything had become stringently real—for heavy creamy snow was falling, showers of white inhaling the white lights of cars, fluttering like confetti from an invisible proscenium of heavenly darkness. Speed and visibility got into lock-step; we slithered down Putney and away into the spectral ribbons of main road which led us ever deeper into what now slowly became an enchanted forest—a medieval illustration to Malory. To beguile the time I played over some prints of recent voices which were destined for my collection; it was strange to sit watching the snow while Marchant's somewhat squeaky voice... "The war, my boy, meant all things to all men; full employment, freedom from the wife and kids, a fictitious sense of purpose. Blame your neighbour for your own neurasthenia and punish him. It was all real, necessary and yet a phantom. The reason why everyone loved the war was simple: there was no time to think about the even more pressing problem namely: 'Why am I making a mess of my life?' I had had the time, but not the good sense. I threw myself into this delicious amnesia which only wholesale bloodspilling can give. Thirsty Gods! What hecatombs of oxen. Hurrah!"

It was late when we arrived, hush-hushing down the white avenues towards the strange house, where every light seemed to have been lit and left to burn on in tenantless rooms; who went round and turned off all those lights, and at what time? The lake had frozen iron-stiff and here a great fire of oak-logs sparked and hissed in the centre of it, near the island; several dozens of muffled figures skirred about it on skates. There was even a coloured marquee with fairy lights where some were drinking steaming coloured drinks—presumably hot lemonade, since it was past the drinking hour, and even considerations of Christian charity could not be expected to sway the habits of mind of lazy bureaucrats and publicans. Nevertheless it was a grateful and heart-warming scene in this desolate property to have a few villagers amusing themselves. From time to time would come a pistol crack from the ice, and a fissure would trace itself with soft rapidity, like someone running a stick of charcoal across the whiteness. Shrieks and laughter greeted these warnings. Baynes shook a sage head and muttered something like "It's all very well, sir, but a few minutes' thaw and they'll all be in the drink."

The car drew up, the doors opened. The hall and all its galleries were hung with dusty bunting left over from other festivals; there were a few servants about, engaged on unobtrusive tasks, but not many. Yet from the light and the decorations you would have said that Benedicta expected a great company to descend on us. No such thing. Moreover she had gone up already. No glittering cars disgorging madonnas in evening gowns, no monocles glittering, no sheen of top-hats.

I mounted heart-beat by heart-beat. The bed she lay in was like some fat state barge with its squat carved legs and damascened wings of curtain drawn back and secured with velvet cords. The light fell upon the book she was reading, and which she closed with a snap as I entered the room. The child lay in a yellow cot by the chimney-piece—a small indistinct pink bundle, thumb in mouth. We stared at each other for a long moment. Though her regard was sad, almost humble in its directness, I thought I could detect some new quality in it—a new remoteness? She was like some great traveller who had come back finally after many adventures—come back to find that his experiences overshadowed the present. Sitting at the foot of the bed I put my hand upon hers, wondering if she were ever going to speak, or whether we should just sit like this for ever, gazing at each other. "The snow held us up" I said, and she nodded, still staring into my eyes with her sad abstracted eyes. She had made herself up carelessly that evening, and had not bothered to take the make-up off; the pale powdered face looked almost feverish in contrast to the thin scarlet mouth. "You know" she whispered at last "it's like coming back from the dead. It's so fragile as yet—I hardly recognise the world. So tired." Then she took my hand and placed it upon her forehead saying: "But I am not feverish am I?" She trembled as I embraced her softly and went on. "But you know there is something else to be got over now between us. It's very clear. How patient can you be?" She drew down her frowning brows over those wide-awake eyes and stared keenly, sternly at me. Then she pointed at the cot in the corner. "Have you seen?" To temper the ominous intensity of this monologue I crossed the room and stared dutifully at the child. She had turned sideways upon an elbow now, and her concentrated gaze held a strange hungry animal-like quality. She resumed her full voice to say—with a sort of dying fall. "He has come between us now, don't you see? Perhaps for ever. I don't know. I love you. But the whole thing must be thought over from the very beginning."

Over and above the numbness I felt only a sudden rage; like a wild boar I could have turned to rend the world. Benedicta gave a sob, a single sob, and then all at once was smiling again: a smile disinterred from forgotten corners of our common past, full of loyalty and fearlessness. She shook two pellets out of a bottle. They tinkled into a shallow glass which she held out for me without a word. I filled it from the tap in the bathroom. She watched them froth and dissolve before drinking the mixture; then, putting down the glass, she said "The main thing is that I am really back at last." A church bell began to toll from the nearby village, and the clock by the bed chirped. "I must feed it" she said—it seemed to me strange the use of "it". I turned away, muttering something about going downstairs to dine, and then crossed the room with a sudden purposeful swiftness to take up the child. I left her sitting crosslegged in the armchair by the bed, holding "it" to her breast, absorbed as a gipsy.

Downstairs the grizzled Baynes was waiting for me; he had organised my dinner, knocking up a couple of servants from the deeper recesses of the kitchens. I could see he was dying to question me about Benedicta but resisted the impulse like the perfectly trained servant he was. I settled down to this late repast with a sense of anticlimax, but to put a good countenance upon it all—the long solitary table I mean with its coloured candlesticks, the absence of Benedicta—I made some rough notes for a speech I would soon be having to deliver to the Royal Society of Inventors.

Afterwards I betook myself to the log fire in the hall; and while I was sitting there before it, half asleep, I heard the traditional cannonade upon the front-door knocker, followed by the shrill pipe of waits whose voices were raised quaveringly in a painful carol. It was a welcome diversion; I went to the front door and found a small group of village children standing in a snow-marked semicircle outside. Their leader held a Chinese lantern. They were like robins, pink cheeked and rosy. Their infant breath poured out in frosty tresses as they sang. I sent Baynes hot-foot for drinks, cakes and biscuits, and when the first carol ended invited them into the warm hall with its big fire. It was bitterly cold outside, and they were glad to huddle about the blazing logs with small bluish fingers extended to the flame. The teeth of some were a-chatter. But the warm drinks and the sweet cakes soon restored them. I emptied my pockets of small change, pouring it into the woollen cap of their leader, a tough-looking peasant boy of about eleven: blond and blue-eyed. As a parting gesture they offered to sing a final carol right there in the hall and I agreed. They began a ragged but full-throated rendering of "God rest you merry, gentlemen". The house echoed marvellously; and it was only when they were half way through the melody that I saw an unknown figure stalking in military fashion down the long staircase; a tall thin woman with grey hair, clad in a white dressing-gown, which she clutched about her throat with long crooked fingers. Her narrow face was compressed about a mouth set in an expression of malevolent disapproval. "You will wake the child" she repeated in a deep voice. She came to a halt on the first landing. "Who are you?" I said. The waits came to a quavering halt in mid bar. "The nurse, sir."

"What is your name?"

"Mrs. LaFour."

"Can you hear us upstairs?"

She turned back without a word and began to remount the staircase. There was nothing for it but to disband the carol-singers and wish them goodnight.

When I reached my room some time later it was to find pinned to my pillow one of Benedicta's visiting-cards; but there was no message on it. I slept the sleep of utter exhaustion—the kind of sleep that comes only after a prolonged bout of tears; and when I woke next morning everything had changed once more—like the shift of key in a musical score. A new, or else an old, Benedicta was sitting on the foot of the bed, smiling at me. She was clad in her full riding outfit. Every trace of preoccupation had vanished from this smiling reposed face. "Come, shall we ride today? It's so beautiful." The change was breath-taking; for once it was she who leaned down to embrace me. "But of course."

"Don't be long; I'll wait for you downstairs."

I hurried to bathe and dress. Outside the country snowscapes were bathed in a brilliant tranquil light. There was no trace of wind. Occasionally a tall tree let fall a huge package of whiteness which exploded prismatically on the roofs of the house. And now even the house itself seemed suddenly to have woken up, to be full of a purposeful animation. There was a servant actually humming at her dusting; the hall tables were piled with telegrams and packages. This was more like it. The horses were at the door sneezing white spume. Benedicta was giving some last-minute orders to Baynes about lunch. "Julian rang to wish us everything, and so did Nash" she cried happily as she pulled on the close-fitting felt hat with its brilliant jay's feather. She seemed to have restored, with a single smile, a hundred lost familiarities. It was hardly conceivable.

We set off briskly, swinging across the meadows in the snow; though we were upon the path of a traditional ride well known to us, the snow had baffled boundaries and we were forced to work from memorised contours, munching across this abstract whiteness into woods whose trees had become wedding-cakes. And everywhere, as if developed mysteriously from a secret print, we could study the footmarks, trace the movements, of animals which were normally invisible: cuneiform of hare and squirrel and fieldmouse scribbled into the snowcarpet. A whole geodesy of the invisible life which surrounded our own. The shallow ford was frozen, and I dismounted to lead my horse, but with her customary rashness she forced her own mount through revelling in the crunching ice under its hooves. We rode westward towards the Anvil following the long intersecting rides formed naturally by the firebrakes, now outlined and demarcated clearly by the contrasting snow and forest. Once towards the top of the Anvil we turned along the down, and here the going became riskier. A rabbit-warren could have spelt a heavy fall or a broken leg for a horse. But Benedicta defied sweet reason; she turned her flushed face to me and laughed aloud. "Nothing can happen to me any more, now that I have told you the truth, how we must separate. You see, it has freed me to love you again. I am immune from dangers today." And she set herself into a breakneck gallop across the white surface leaning ever closer into the drawn bow of her horse's neck. So we came at last without mishap to the little inn, the Compasses, whose clients, dazed by the bounty of this winter sun in a windless world, were standing about in the snow outside the tap room to drink their brown beer. We tethered at a convenient hitching post and joined them for a few moments to drink hot lime and rum. Benedicta's arm was through mine, pressing softly against me, as we leaned against the fence. "They put me in a huge canvas jacket like a burnous, with long sleeves to wrap around one; it was always when I wanted to write to you. I felt so safe in there. The canvas was heavy—you couldn't poke a needle through. I felt so safe, just like I feel today. Nothing can happen."

"When do we separate? Do you want to divorce me?"

She frowned and reflected for a long moment; then she shook her head. "Not divorce" she said. "I couldn't do that."

"Why?"

"It's hard to explain. I wouldn't like to lose you because of many reasons; the child must have a father, no? And then from the point of view of. . . ." She stopped just in time; perhaps she caught a glimpse of the expression on my face. If she was about to say "the firm", it would have been just enough to make me lose control of myself.

I replaced the glasses on the gnarled counter and paid for the drinks; we remounted and moved off, more slowly now, more soberly. Benedicta's eyes were on her own white hands holding the reins.

"If I stay here until spring you could come at week-ends."

"I suppose so."

"It's only the sleeping business I can't manage; I'm still a little fragile, Felix. Ah but you understand everything—there isn't any need to explain to you. Come, let's gallop again." We broke once more into this breakneck pace, swerving down the long rides, hurling up petals of snow behind us. "I shall leave tomorrow" I called across the few feet which separated us—our labouring horses were neck and neck.

She turned her bright smiling face to me and nodded happily. "Now you understand I have confidence in myself. Tomorrow, then."

The city seemed exhausted and deserted by everyone, abandoned to the snow; not less the rows of empty offices in the Merlin Group's offices. The heating had been turned off or frozen and for a few days I had to content myself with an electric stove trained upon my feet. My secretaries were on leave, as were the servants in the Mount Street house. I had my meals at the club, often staying on as late as I could in the evening, spinning out time with a game of billiards. The late-night ring of footsteps on the iron-bound roads.... But yes, Benedicta sometimes rang, full of afterthoughts and moribund solicitudes; one could feel the heavy ground-swell of the resistances licking the sunken rocks—the steep seas of Nash's little pet, the unconscious. He at least was in town, in bed with a cold; I dined with him once or twice, taking care to admonish him when I did. "Theology is the last refuge of the scoundrel." I had read it somewhere among a friend's papers. I also spent some time on the Koepgen scribbles which yielded their linear B after prolonged scrutiny, thunderous aphoristic flights like: "A great work is a successfully communicated state of mind—*cosa mentale*" and "The poet is master of faculties not yet in his freehold possession—his gift is in trust. He is no didact but an enjoiner." Crumbs, I said to myself, crumbs! And we talk about nature as if we were not part of it. I could see the influence here and there of a writer called Pursewarden. Nor could I interest Master Nash very much in such lucubrations. "You see, my good Nash, reality is there all the time but we are not: our appearances are intermittent. The problem is how much can we swallow before closing time?"

O but it was a miserable period... I lay choking among my frustrations. "I know it is miserable" said the great man. "But sudden swerves aside are part of the pattern. The recovery will go on steadily, you will see. Do nothing to alarm her."

All ye graceful midgets come
Softly foot it bum to bum

I suppose that in an abstracted sort of way I had begun to hate Benedicta! Even now the idea surprises me; indeed it may not be true. A form perhaps of inverted love, a famished ingrown vegetable love fostered by exhaustion and the sense of perpetual crisis. I had several beautiful photographs of her hugely enlarged and framed—for my bedroom at Mount Street as well as for the office. Thus I was able from time to time to rest a reflective eye upon that long grave face with its confederate eyes. Emotions that refused to maintain any stability of pattern.

I went down for several successive week-ends, heart in mouth, briefcase in hand, soft hat on head—to be greeted by the new composed Benedicta; a quiet, kindly, slightly abstracted woman whom I vaguely recognised. All her thoughts were for the infant prawn-like Mark, a mere series of bone-twigs as yet: but upon whose small thoughtful face I seemed already to see etched the first pull, so to speak, of the sparrow-chested intellectual he would doubtless become. They would send him to Winchester, he would be filled with notions, learn to control his emotions as well as his motions, become a scholar. . . . It was desirable, desirable. Later he could help me on lasers. Dear Mark, Matthew, Luke, John, bless the bed that I lie on. We sat on either side of the fire with the cot between us, discussing neutral topics like elderly folk sunning away a retirement. Benedicta. In the emptiness of my skull I howled the name until the echoes deafened me; but nothing came out of my mouth. It was almost with relief that I returned to my papers of a Monday—to the flat in Mount Street where Vibart and Pulley at least were visitors, where Marchant came to expatiate about the power of light to carry sound-waves—the principle which I was afterwards to adopt for Abel. A single laser beam etc. He covered the grand piano in blue chalk formulae and I had to have it French-polished again. But wait, there was one surprise.

Pulley came into my office on tip-toe, pale to the hairline with wild surmise. "Felix" he whispered, waving *The Times* "unless you did it *he's still alive.*"

For a moment I did not follow his drift; then I followed the shaking finger down the column of Personals until, by godemiche, I struck . . . *a mnemon.* I read out in astonishment: *Lazy dwarf with sponge cogs seeks place in animal factor's poem.* I gave a cry. "No, I didn't do it, Pulley. He must be *alive.*" The word rushed about the room like a startled pigeon. Caradoc! But Pulley was speaking so fast now that he was spitting all over the place. "Not so loud" he cried in anguish. "If it's true it means—O the silly fool—that he's escaped; yet how typical not to be able to resist . . . O Felix." His eyes filled with tears, he wrung his long soapy fingers together. "Why?" I cried, and he answered "If Julian sees this—do you think Julian would ever let him go? No, he'd set to work to find him, to inveigle him back, the silly old bugger." I thought furiously. "Nonsense" I said seeing the whole thing in a flash. "We could easily tell Julian. . . ." And the phone started to ring. We looked at each other like schoolboys caught masturbating. Pulley went through an extraordinary contortion, pointing to the phone, then to his own lips as they spelt out a message in dumb show. I nodded. The same idea had come to me. I picked up the instrument.

Julian's quiet warm voice filled the ear-piece; he spoke in a calm, thoughtful, amused tone. "I wondered if you had seen *The Times* as yet? It has one of those oddities of Caradoc's in it today."

"Yes," I said "Pulley and I thought it up as a sort of obituary to an eccentric man." There was a long pause and then Julian yawned. "O well, then. That solves the problem. Naturally I was a bit puzzled." Pulley writhed. I said effusively. "O naturally."

"You see," said Julian dryly "one can be sure of nothing these days. There were several survivors from the crash; we've heard no more about them. Our man on the spot was away. And then of course some of his papers *have* been washed up." I agreed to all this. "Well," he went on, his voice taking a sly tinge "I only wanted to ask." He rang off. We sat on, Pulley and I, discussing this new development in hushed tones. It was not long before the phone rang again and Nathan asked if Pulley was with me, as Mr. P. wanted to talk to him. I ran my fingers across my throat and handed him the instrument. Pulley, all subservience, sibilated his information into it, the sweat starting on his forehead as he spoke. Then he put it down and stared thoughtfully at the blotter before him. "He's not convinced," he said hoarsely "not at all. Wants me to fly out and get at the truth." Then he flew into a characteristic rage and banging the newspaper with his palm said: "And this bloody fool is probably sitting in a brothel in Sydney, thinking he's escaped from the firm. I ask you." He rippled with moral rage.

"You'll have to go."

"I shall have to I suppose."

Go he did. I drove him up to the airport myself next morning grateful for a chance to escape from the office. Pulley was dressed as if for the Pole, his pink stoat's nose aquiver at the chance of having a holiday from an English winter. Dismay and uncertainty had replaced our original excitement, for enquiries had revealed that the mnemon had been posted in New York—perhaps before Caradoc had started on his journey. I watched with affection the gangling figure of Pulley trapesing across the tarmac, turning to give one awkward wave before climbing into the bowels of the aircraft. Outside the bar I saw Nash hanging about, waiting for an incoming flight, and we decided to have a coffee together. He looked at my face quizzically and said: "Things are not going too well as yet are they?" I made a face and briefly sketched an ape swinging from a chandelier. "Frankly, Nash, I have almost made up my mind to get a divorce. Nothing else will meet the case." Nash drew in his breath with a groan of dismay. "O Lord" he said "I shouldn't do that. O No." Then he cheered up and added: "As a matter of fact I don't think you could even if you wanted. Felix be patient awhile."

Patient! But it was really my concern for Benedicta which kept me bound hand and foot. I drove back recklessly, half soliciting a crash—always the weak man's way out. But safely back once more I allowed the tranquil little lift to carry me upwards to my office. My fervent secretary looked up and said: "Promotion has been ringing you every few minutes since I came in." Promotion department consisted of three exophthalmic old Etonians, who lived in a perpetual susurrus of private jokes, and an intrepid Bremen Jew called Baum who smoked cigars and looked freshly circumcised each morning. Between them they schemed up ways of marketing Merlin products. Baum's voice was deep and full of forceful enthusiasm: "You remember the idea of having the biggest Impressionist exhibition of all time at London Airport—sponsored by us?" Vaguely I did. I vaguely remembered the memorandum which began "In our age nothing has proven itself so useful to merchandising as the genuine cultural product. Merlin's has found that nothing pays off so well in terms of publicity as the sponsoring of art exhibitions, cultural gatherings, avant-garde films." The latest of these ideas was to sponsor an Impressionist exhibitions of mammoth dimensions at the air terminal—offsetting these cultural trivia with a huge display of Merlin products. "Well, yes, Baum, what about it?" Baum cleared his throat and said: "Well, guess who we've got to open it? I have the telegram of acceptance before me."

Iolanthe! It seemed extremely improbable. But, "her new film opens in London at the same time and she has agreed to come. Isn't it wonderful?"

It was indeed—a wonderful conjunction of commercial and aesthetic interests. Buy a lawn-mower while you sip your culture. "Good" I said. "Very good. Masterly." Baum crooned. "The entry will be free" he said. I waved my paws and barked like a chow. "What did you say Charlock?" Woof, Woof. Iolanthe's new film was called *Simoun, the Diva.* Somewhere, down deep inside, a new and urgent irritation against Julian had begun to materialise. It had its point of departure in a chance aside of Benedicta's, when she said: "And Julian is in full agreement that he should go to Winchester." He was was he? I studied with savage attention that fluent hand which had engraved a few words upon a recent paper of mine. I tried the old graphologist's trick of tracing the writing with a dry nib, trying to feel my way into the personality of the writer; absent yet omnipresent, what sort of a man could this quiet voice represent? And did he simply regard me, like everyone else, as a sort of catspaw to be telephoned whenever he wished to issue an order? Why would he not meet me? It was insulting—or rather it would have been if everyone else had not been in the same boat. And yet . . . that voice could never tell a lie, one felt; it inspired the confidence of an oracle. Julian was good. I tried to brush aside my annoyance as a trivial and unworthy thing. Who knew what pains and sorrows Julian himself had had to endure? And where would I have been had it not been for his far-sightedness? It was thanks to him that my professional career. . . . Nevertheless it came over me by degrees—the idea that I might force the issue, actually waylay him. Face to face I could discuss Benedicta, and the issues which had grown up around us and were threatening my concentration on the tasks vital to the firm. Damn the firm!

When the office closed that evening I took a taxi to the little square in which he lived—there was nothing secret about his address, it was in *Who's Who.* Sepulchral trees, a little snow. The Rolls and the liveried chauffeur at the door raised my hopes of finding him in; but I did not wait to ask the man, who sat stonily at the wheel with the heating purring. I took the lift to the second floor and rang twice. I was let in, already prepared to see Ali, the Turkish butler—a heavy torpid man with the head of a stag-beetle; prepared too to hear the soft plosive jargon he talked, squeezing the words up into a cleft palate.

He was not sure about Julian's movements, and had received no instructions for the evening. I asked if I might wait awhile. I had already phoned Julian's club to ascertain whether he were dining there or not. There was a fair measure of probability that he might come back here, if only to change for dinner—suppose him to be invited out. It was not late.

I examined the fox's earth with the utmost attention, surprised to find how at home I felt in it. It was a sympathetic and unworldly place—a relatively modest bachelor flat with a fine library of classical and medieval books, opulently bound and tooled. A bright fire of coal burned in the grate. The three armchairs were dressed in brilliant scarlet velvet; on an inlaid card-table with its oasis-green baize centre stood a decanter, a pack of cards, a pipe, and a copy of the *Financial Times*. The tips of his slippers peeped out from under one of the chairs. A sage-looking black cat sat upon a low wicker stool gazing into the blaze. It hardly vouchsafed me a glance as I sat down. So this was where Julian lived! He would sit opposite me over there, in a scarlet chair, wearing slippers and cooling his mind with the arid abstractions of the world markets. Perhaps he even wore a skull cap? No, that would have spoiled everything. The cat yawned. "For all I know *you* might be Julian" I told it. It gave me a contemptuous glance and turned back to the fire.

A small upright piano gleamed in the far corner of the room. A bowl of fresh flowers stood upon it, together with some bundles of sheet music. The tall goose-necked alabaster lamps with red parchment shades made a pair, echoing and chiming with the red velvet chairs. Yes, it was atmospherically a delightful room; the good taste was unselfconscious and unemphatic. The pictures were few but choice. Everything hinted at a thoughtful and eclectic spirit. One felt that its owner was something of a scholar as well as a man of affairs.

So I sat, waiting for him, but he did not come. Time ran on. The servant brought me a cocktail. The fire burned on. The cat dozed. Then I noticed, standing on the little escritoire in the corner, a small framed photograph. It had been clipped from the *Illustrated London News*, and it depicted a group of people leaving St. Paul's after some national memorial service or other. The size of the screen was not very fine and the result was a somewhat vague photo; but I noticed Julian's name among those printed in the caption. At last a picture of him! I went carefully along the second row, name by name, until I came to the fifth figure. It gave me something of a start, for the picture was surely that of Jocas. Or so it seemed. I cleaned my spectacles, and taking up a magnifying glass which lay to hand I subjected it to a close and breathless scrutiny. "But it is Jocas" I exclaimed aloud. It was damnably puzzling—there were the huge hands, even though the face was shaded by the brim of a hat. I found the servant standing behind me, gazing over my shoulder at the picture with an expressionless attention. "Is that really Mr. Julian?" I asked, and he turned a glossy and vacant eye upon me, as if he hardly understood. I repeated the question and he nodded slowly. "But surely it's his brother Mr. Jocas Pehlevi; there's some error."

He moved his tongue about in his mouth and pressed some air up into the cavity below his nostrils. He had never seen Jocas, he said; as far as he knew it was Julian all right. I was nonplussed. Of course it could have been a mistaken ascription, a journalistic error. "You are sure?" I said again, and he nodded expressionless as a totem. He shuffled off and left me staring at this singular picture. I finished my cocktail and set the glass down. Then my eye caught sight of another small door in the further wall. It was ajar. I pushed it open and took an inquisitive look into the tiny adjoining room to which it gave access. It was a little work room, with an overflowing desk. But what surprised me was that on the further wall, beautifully framed, was a gigantic picture of Iolanthe, an enlargement from her Greek film. She stood, looking down, hands gravely clasped, on the temple plinth of the Wingless Victory, with all Athens curving away under her to the sea. I had hardly time to take this all in before a clock struck somewhere. I was dying to explore further—I wanted to see the bedroom, have a look at the clothes in the wardrobe and so on. But the noise startled me in burglarish fashion; I turned, and then the telephone began to ring in the hall. I heard Ali answer it with his gasping and grunting delivery—he must be conveying the fact of my presence. And sure enough, he appeared in the door and beckoned me away from my investigations towards the phone. How familiar were the lazy precise kindly tones. "My dear Charlock, fancy you being there. What a disappointment for me." Sometimes it was Felix, sometimes Charlock. "It was another vain attempt to see you" I said lamely.

"My dear fellow." He spoke mildly and yet with a scruple of genuine pleasure in his tone—as if in some obscure way I had actually conferred a compliment on him by coming here unheralded. "It's the weirdest luck" he went on, and the dramatic pointing, so to speak, of his voice, suggested the presence of a cigar between his teeth. "To miss each other once again. Do you know, I had definitely planned to stay in this evening? Then at the last moment Cavendish rang up about an urgent decision which had to be taken about a merger up north—and dammit here I am at the airport, waiting for a plane." He laughed softly. "But is there anything urgent I can do?" So calm, so friendly, so serene did he sound that I felt all of a sudden guilty: as if I had tried to take an unfair advantage of him in hounding him down. My voice faltered in the instrument as I said, "I wanted to discuss Benedicta with you, in very general terms of course." He coughed and said: "Oh that!" with an evident relief, as though the subject were already trivial, or else out of date. "But I know about all your difficulties from Nash—all of them! I was going to tell you how grateful I was—we all are—that you are treating these unfortunate matters with such patience and conscientiousness. It's heroic. And you have even put aside the notion of divorce for the present—for her sake. My dear chap, what can I say? We will make it up to you in any way we can. All our sympathies are with you."

In the scratchy background I could hear a voice from a loudspeaker intoning plane-numbers—the faintest intonation of a muezzin from a tulip-mosque. I could feel that he had half an ear cocked back, waiting for the flight number of his own plane.

"I wonder why you hide from me?" I said at last, with a sort of graceless aggressiveness. Julian gave his quiet surprised laugh; he sounded so fond, almost tender—as if mentally he had put his arm through mine, or around my shoulders. "My dear Felix" he said with loving reproachfulness. "Answer me" I said. "Go on."

"Above all you mustn't exaggerate" he said. "Once or twice I might have found it inconvenient, but for the most part it was sheer coincidence—like tonight for example."

"Would you have come home if you had known I was here?"

"It's too late to say. The fact remains that coincidence kept us apart tonight; how can I say what I *might* have felt? That would be hypothetical merely." I rapped my knuckles on the polished wood. "Verbiage" I said. "You wouldn't have come; perhaps even you *did* know and deliberately sidestepped me." He clicked his tongue in reproof.

"Come now" he said plaintively.

"No, I wouldn't put it past you; the thing is—*why*? I sometimes wonder what you can have weighing on your mind." He gave a small groan—a satirical small sound. "In the age of the detective story one could hardly do less. But I fear you are building up a house of cards. Just imagine me as real, awfully prosaic, but a trifle shy—almost to the point of eccentricity if you wish. Truthfully."

"No" I said. "It won't fit."

"Good Lord, why not?"

As I had been talking I had been sifting through the silver bowl which stood by the telephone, telling over the thick pile of white pasteboard invitations addressed to him—Embassies and Clubs, individuals and societies. I knew that an office secretary came down every morning from the firm to deal with his social correspondence. He had neatly annotated the top left-hand corner of each card in that beautiful secretary-hand of his. On some he had written "Refuse pl" and on others "Accept pl".

"Not too shy" I said—feeling at the same time a trifle ashamed of myself for prowling around his private domain in this way—"not too shy to accept lunch at Buckingham Palace to meet the Persian Trade Mission." He gave another exasperated chuckle and said, without heat: "But Charlock, for the firm's sake I have to, don't you see? I can't afford to do otherwise: besides an invitation from Buck House is really a command, you know that." Yes, I supposed that I knew that: and yet....

"Come" he said in his coaxing, conciliatory tone, as if he were speaking to a child. "Have some confidence in me, in my good intentions towards you. I haven't failed you yet have I? Have I?"

"Quite the contrary" I said, with very real despair.

"And you know how deeply we are all concerned about Benedicta. Believe me, you are not the only one to care for her. Jocas must have told you about this unhappy pattern which repeats itself, no? But it's intermittent, it never lasts for long. You should base your hopes on that, as we all do. As for our meeting—why, better luck to us both next time, that's all I can really say." I grunted. "Ah, there's my plane coming up." A vague burble of sound from a loudspeaker swelled up slowly behind his silence. "I must be off" he said, with a little sigh. "Will you tell Ali to dismiss the car? Thank you. Well, Felix, goodbye for now . ." A faint click, and we were once more cut off.

I went back to the fire to finish my drink and reflect upon the little picture in its silver frame. The cat had disappeared. I heard the manservant doing something in the kitchen. I sat in bemused fashion, staring into the fire, almost asleep now. Somehow, I thought, I must get a glimpse of Julian's hands, if only to slake my curiosity. At least he could not deny me that! It was strange to feel like a suppliant, like a beggar: and then suddenly again to be overcome by rage or remorse. The moment I heard his voice a wave of sympathy was elicited. I melted. It was baffling this polarity of feelings—and I supposed, to adopt the formulae of Nash, that the whole thing was due to nervous strain, mental weariness which hovered about the central problem of Benedicta. The Victorian word was still the most expressive—brain-fag. Where we cannot establish the aetiology of a disease or of a course of human action—when, for example, the providing brain and the sustaining nerves are out of whack—we can always slap a clinical term on it, give it a name even if the name is meaningless.

I had drunk more than one cocktail from the silver canister before it occurred to me to look at the time; it was not as late as I'd thought. I set out to walk across London to Mount Street. A fresh tormenting wind blew, the parks rustled. In my mood of prevailing despondency I hardly noticed my feet covering the pavements of the capital, between the dark brown houses; slow and regular as breathing. And the half attention I could devote to the life around me cast a curious kind of glow about ordinary realities—making them seem disembodied. In Bond Street the back of a lorry blew down and out fell a hundred gilt chairs. They tumbled out like a river and gave the illusion of dancing with each other on the pavement before subsiding into eighteenth-century curtsies. They had obviously been bound for some Embassy ballroom. Then later, in a narrow street, a woman dropped a big leather purse which exploded on the pavement scattering hundreds of halfpennies. Almost at once the passing crowd, like an ant-file diverted, started to help her gather them up—they had rolled everywhere, even into the centre of the street. Within the space of a breath everyone was transformed into a snail-picker or mushroom gatherer. The woman stood looking vaguely around her, almost tearful, holding her bag open; one by one the kindly helpers filled it with the coin they had gathered. I stood and simply watched. Thence onwards to the dry click of the key in the door, to the ministrations of silent servants, to my tapes and papers. We were still not finished with the Cham, thank goodness. "Modern architecture reflects the dirty vacuum of the suburban mind." Yes, but other voices had to be cleared off the track, vexatious and interfering voices—many of them unidentified; but some of these baffling irruptions were singular enough to be worth preserving. One voice, for example, which said: "When Merlin was dying of GPI he had his Rolls brought out and sat by it in a wheel-chair touching it, as if rubbing cold cream into its glossy velvet skin." Who on earth could that have been?

There remained such a lot to do—so many confusing diversions to be followed up or to be eliminated. In such a chaotic collection, spanning such a long period of time, the problem of ascription had become a formidable one. It was all right where I had captured a distinct voice saying a distinct thing—a voice made recognisable by its familiar timbre—like that of Caradoc. But what of the droning quotations which so frequently supervened; and sometimes even the background noises which gave substance and point to what had actually been recorded? My little dactyls worked loyally enough transcribing all they overheard, but with faulty transmission I was left often with huge sheaves of confusion—speeches one could not faithfully ascribe to one person or another. And yet many of them too good to tear up. It was like some mad accumulator building up its energies to supply a mnemonic museum. . . . Goodness, that was it. Somewhere in the midst of these studies, wallowing in this mountain of white paper, I had the idea which later led to the building-up of Abel, the computer. It was only a germ, then, though in the succeeding months it began to take sharper form. The raw materials of phonology are relatively simple if reduced to an alphabet. But if the actual phoneme—so I thought in my muddled fashion—could be translated, by a conversion table, into vibration . . . why, poor Charlock, in terms of frequency, could sort out the authors of this voice-*fest* and bring scientific order into chaos: not even chaos, just a misnumbering of the data? It was all horribly vague; I still had much to learn from Marchant of electronics. I might even go so far as to make people seem explicit simply by marking down the tonalities of their ordinary speech. Who knows? A new sort of interpretation of the human being in terms of his vocal chords?

At any rate anything would be better, however factitious, than to surrender all this equivocal but often amusing or instructive babble to the dustbin. We were making a beginning with Caradoc, and for a specific purpose. But even here the identification was becoming questionable. It was mixed up with other things—which might have been his—pronounced in other voices, or in different keys. It was in a way as if his personality (now dead) had begun to diffuse around its edges, become less distinct, less easy to grasp in terms of an individual psychology. He was entering into his own mythology now; and of course our own mistakes of ascription might completely falsify him by adding to his massive incunabula of obiter dicta examples of Koepgen or others. These were the irresolute ideas which crossed my mind as I plugged in and watched the little creature begin to sick out her pages for me on to the expensive carpet—a human ticker-tape from the strongrooms of memory, of destiny.

To what degree is pattern arbitrary? Please help me, little faithful dactyl, with your pretty claws, please help me. I marked slowly and with as much conscientiousness as possible the voices that I knew, using a letter of the alphabet for such of my friends as I could. But often these cursed toys had been left running when I was not there. Both Caradoc and Iolanthe had been shown how to play with them. It was no wonder that there were so many puzzles to be sorted out.

Come, a drink, my boy
Winch me in a drink,
Gaff me a zebib,
Harpoon me a gin (C)

an abacus of the
contemporary moods
(K?)

steeplejack
your beanstalks
are the sky
(K?)

Poets; put your
sperm to work
(?)

his death is still fresh
paint Ah do not touch
a mystic who likes his breakfast
in bed would you say? (?)

my balls have bells Wang Shu
while your balls have little
ad hoc bells, so ting a ling
cherished master as you pass
in your swansdown sampan
(C)

Fundamentally every woman
wants to give birth to an
upper-class child, my dear.
(H)

One lesson women teach is that
it is possible to be superb in
mind without being at all
intelligent. (K)

Little gold ear-rings in the
shape of a guillotine darling;
they all wore them under the
Terror. Look how pretty.
(B?)

Eros de-fused will save
the human race. (K)

My ancestors, yogically untrained, died
through the eyes as they say; hence me,
look, a house, a museum, a brothel.
(?)

So the labyrinth of this intermittent record poured out of the little machine to spread themselves on the carpet, to be gathered and stacked like sheaves; later our three bent heads would try to puzzle them out, to listen to them played back, to dispute their authorship. And some which were only holes in sound. For example, simply a sweet long sigh—the unmistakable sigh of Iolanthe in my dark room. She must have had someone there while I was out? A door opens, a match scratches, someone sees the wooden pattens. Graphos' voice—but in a whisper so that I cannot say for certain it is his: but certainly speaking Greek says "These are your shoes, then?" The silence scratches on for an age; the bed creaks. Later came the equally unmistakable clank of the bath-tap and the sound of running water. Yes, some of the scratched parts could themselves be human sighs, luxurious sighs to correspond with simple acts—a voice whispering "Ah" or else (I am not so sure) "Ah mother". Such faulty transcription defies significance; some of those dreadful crepitations could be the sucking of a breast. My little instrument whirrs on transcribing nothing—nothing in darkness. This is one tape I shall be able to destroy without compunction. Iolanthe!

Sitting among the tall columns of blue cigar smoke I meditate on this broken record of a past which is still not too far away to be revived and recaptured; which can still be compared to itself for example—memory against records. Only the faults in human memory cause the doubt and distortion. Where neither memory nor machine is completely sure you often get this kind of tentative ascription on the page. Palimpsest.

after all nature is big-breasted
indiscreet, undiscriminating, ample,
a spender . . . why not you? why not
you?
(C or K)

Zoë Pithou
"the life of the jar"
think of it, for the mind
needs housing-space
(C)

I do not usually like the type
but if he is rich he must be
very nice (H)

the present overtaking the past
bit by bit and falsifying it all
the time, breath by breath;
seeing it through the spectrum of
death one supposes. (K)

such salient facts as self-transformation, the pursuit and identification of dead selves, the accommodation of the idea of death—
these are the capital preoccupations.
All the rest is tinsel.
(K)

you talk of the prodigality
of nature; but the old bitch
in spite of those swollen dugs
is really lean as a bedrail,
all the superfluous fat is
melted off her in her war to
the knife with history.
(C or K)

All change for Moribundia!
ah the beautiful anguish of change!
(C?)

a dialogue in whispers, but
the transcription very faulty;
a few phrases, among them:
"But must he die—can't you make
him disappear?"

O God what have I done?
(?)

Come in. Lock the door.
(?)

I don't know, I shall never
know. (?)

To wake up with a start at two o'clock in the morning, surrounded by these growing hillocks of paper: to switch off and crawl girning up to bed. Only to echo on, I fear, in the dreams and fevers which crowded the skull of the happy weed. Did I say happy? Ah, Charlock infelix—why ever did you let your fancy stray along these unbeaten paths, lured by the idea of razors which sharpen themselves as they cut, of an electronic Braille vibrating through the sensitive fingertips of blind men? All those hybrid voices filtering through my toys afflicted their creator's sleep. A confused jumble of historical echoes —for once dead everything sleeps in the same continuum: a historical reference from Pausanias or a remark by a modern streetwalker— "a public mouth from which the lipstick has been gnawed"; or a line here and there of poetic aphorism—"poetry which modifies uncertainty awhile". Somewhere walking hand in hand with a girl among the great stored stones of Delphi which seem to yawn at post-Christian relics—the Goth of a yawn.

Or as in the film where the Parthenon by celluloid moonlight seems fashioned in a modern soap; and Io's face faceless with the interior preoccupations of the silent stone women with snail-locks. Stone head with ring? "Once a cut lip which kissing gave back salt and wine, pepper and loot". On airless nights in the desert Benedicta and I climbed into cold showers and then without drying took the car to ride over the coiling dunes, to let the moon dry us out. "Death like hair, growing by inchmeal". Voice of Hippo: "Of course they are starving; the humble always have the biggest wombs." And then Julian's chop-logic. (*I must see his hands.*) I awake with a cry, the telephone is ringing; but by the time I reach it it has gone dead, the caller has rung off. Dozing off again I dream that I enter my office to find a loaded revolver lying on my blotter.

Nevertheless ... I nearly had him next day at Crockford's; I had discovered that he often dropped in for a flutter. Indeed that very evening he had lost an impressive sum. But I was just too late; he had been spirited away by a phone-call. There was still the butt of a cigar burning in the silver ash tray by an armchair. The manservant showed it to me as one might show someone the bones of a martyr. I watched the cynical smoke curling upwards in the warm air. The tables were buzzing—all these people had seen him, he had been there standing shoulder to shoulder with them, or sitting smiling over a hand, really existing.

Then again I overheard a clerk telephoning some bookings to Nathan; Julian was going to Paris in the Golden Arrow. I noted the numbers of his reservation and with a light heart (and lighter head) I went into the Strand and, somewhat to my own surprise, bought an automatic with six cartridges. I must have looked vaguely furtive, like a monk buying a french letter. Nor was it anything to do with aggressive notions—rather those of self-defence. But the action puzzled me a little. I sat at my desk and cleaned it respectfully, waiting for the taxi which would take me to Victoria. But once again I was bedevilled by traffic holdups. I burst past the ticket-collector and broke into a ragged gallop for my train was sliding smoothly out of the station. Coach six. Coach six. I redoubled my efforts. A window seat, number twenty-six, about the middle. Panting, I glimpsed the six on the side of a dining car and drew level with it. But the machine had gathered speed now and I had to put on another spurt to gain on the coveted carriage. Right down to the end of the platform I held it, gaining only inches.

Yes, I drew slowly abreast of Julian's seat, but just not enough to see his face; *but I did see his hands*! They were not the hands of Jocas, no. Very fine, small, white, Napoleonic fingers, holding a cigar. The hands of a manipulative surgeon, intricate, subtle fingers; but no face, I could not reach the face. I collapsed on a trolley at the end of the platform. Strangely enough I felt elated and a little frightened, perhaps even a shade triumphant. I had seen his hands, at any rate, or rather one of them. I left the automatic in a litter bin outside the station, burying it under some sodden newspapers. Its existence in my pocket was a puzzle which would not yield to analysis; yet once rid of it, the neuralgic pain between the eyes abated. I went down for a shilling wash and brush-up for the sheer curiosity of examining my face in the mirror. I looked amazingly well and quite handsome in an ugly way.

Yes, it was with a distinctly new feeling of relief that I found my way back to the office, to the plush-carpeted cage where I was surrounded with all the paraphernalia of the creative life. (Some new protos had appeared: I pawed them appreciatively.) The secretaries chirped in that white light (which turned fair powdered skins to buckram) excited by the quaint wheels and cogs. Quite suddenly I had lost all interest in Julian, in his identity; my mind had put him aside. I stood at the window, staring out at the beautiful austerities of my winter London, wondering about the symbiosis of plants, and jingling the change in my pockets. I jest of course, for the backdrop of my consciousness was still crammed with the ominous images of the country house where Benedicta walked, with pale concentration, as if waiting for something to explode. She strained to listen to something which was just beyond the reach of human ears. She might even say "Hush" in the middle of a conversation; and once as I walked across the hall towards her I found her eyes fixed upon something which was behind me, something which advanced towards her as I did. She shrank away from me; then, with an effort of will, shook her head as a swimmer does to clear the water from his eyes, and re-emerged, smiling and normal and relieved.

Then one afternoon I arrived to find a long line of hearse-like buses drawn up outside the office, and the whole staff of Merlin's in a ferment. I thought at first it was a funeral, everyone was dressed up in their best black. Extraordinary characters whom I had never seen before in my life poured out the nooks and crannies of the building—all clad with sepulchral respectability; they represented the differing totem-clans of our establishment—the accounts men like cassowaries, the legal men like warthogs or rhinos, the policy-makers like precious owls. Baum, superbly clad and ringed in a fashion which reminded one of a Blue Admiral flirting its wings, was busying himself with the organisation of this tramping crowd, now rushing to the window to assure himself that the hearses were being filled in an orderly manner, now marching up and down the corridors, tapping on doors and calling hoarsely: "Anybody there?" Clearly someone of national importance had turned up his toes. Baum caught sight of me and started: "You'll be late" he cried tapping his sideburns. "What the devil is it?" I cried, and the good Baum lowering his head to an invisible lectern uttered the reproachful words: "The great Exhibition, Mr. Charlock. You mustn't miss that." I had completely forgotten about the affair. I could see Baum running a reproachful eye up and down my town-clothes. "Come as you are" he said. "There won't be time to change now. I'll tell your chauffeur."

So I set off following this long cortège of apparent mourners across the star-prinkled snow-gashed London, jerked to a halt everywhere by traffic blocks (Baum gesticulating furiously), skidding in mush and viscid mud. Had it been a funeral cortège, whom would we have elected corpse? Fortunately there was a well-stocked cocktail bar in the car, and I reinforced my resolution with a couple of strong whiskies, filled now with a sense of resignation. By the time we reached the white billiard table of the airport the snow had thickened and dusk was falling. The white lights of cars crossed and recrossed caressing each other, as if making recognition signals as insects do with their antennae. Some mad draughtsman had drawn black lines and parabolas everywhere on the whiteness, so that the whole place looked like some plausible but tentative geodetic diagram. We settled on the central building like a flock of starlings. But inside all was light and space and warm air.

The exhibition area was roped off by a silk ribbon. Everywhere stood policemen. Baum had told me that the insurance on the pictures was so huge that practically the whole CID would be needed to guard it. It was very well done I suppose. The hessian walls with their treasures confronted a wall of equal length and height which contained specimens of Merlin's choicest products. I could not help chuckling—perhaps too loudly—and was quenched by the flashing eye of Baum. We clotted up in slow fashion to wait for our guests, milling slowly round, ill at ease. No drinks as yet, no smoking. Much pulling down of waistcoats, shooting of cuffs, adjustment of collars and ties. Some slid on the polished floors. I looked down at the notes my chauffeur had handed me to study a list of the guests. Everyone, literally everyone. Now through the swinging snow-silhouetted doors came the Lord Mayor of London, and the senior members of the diplomatic corps. Ye Gods!

And was that an illuminated address he held in scroll fashion upon his bosom? The police teemed like perspiration. Nor were the Worshipful Companies outdone by this social display—for here come the Fishmongers, Skinners, Cordwainers, Tanners, Logrollers, Straphangers, and God knows who else. All pink, all suitably embaubled, all determined to see justice done to the arts. As for the diplomats, they provided the overture, so to speak—so enormously complacent, so relaxed, so Luciferian in their elegance. They recognised each other in the crowd with little false starts of surprise and mock-cries of astonishment. "Fancy meeting you. . . ." They hugged each other with circumspection like actors who "when they embrace, hold each other's wigs in place". More snow and more lights. I gradually backed away into the crowd, found my way through a curtain into a small bar which was serving the ordinary passengers. Drink in hand I peeped out upon the dark superstitious horde. And Iolanthe? Well, rumours of her impending divorce were in all the papers together with moody pictures. I suppose it must be the same in all fashionable love-affairs conducted in the public eye—when the attraction wears thin you are left with a heap of soapsuds and a film contract. The hum of the company rose up into the glass roofs as if from a hive of bees or: "as sharp-tongued scythes gossiping in the grass". I was feeling unsteady but secure. I yawned.

At last came a swirl of movement outside the great doors; six huge cars settled simultaneously, moth-like, spreading their wings. The police were all expectancy now. A brilliant star-flash of pink light coloured the whole scene—a dense brilliance which gave all out waiting eyes huge shadowed orbits. Cameras began to tattle; the smaller flash of light-bulbs dotted this aurora borealis with harsh white smears. "There she is" cried someone. "Where? Who? There! Who?"

The doors fell back and she advanced slowly in the centre of a semicircle of business-like looking people, perhaps armed guards? A hundred times more beautiful, of course, and set in the pattern of dark-suited men like the corolla of some rare flower. The famous crescent-shaped smile. She walked slowly with soft and hesitant tread, as if unsure of her role, looking about her almost beseechingly. In a twinkling the foyer was brimming with uninvited lookers-on—passengers, desk-employees, hairdressers, pilots. . . . The police started to try and prevent this intrusion. The spacious hall diminished in size until they were all shoulder to shoulder.

Iolanthe advanced with all the shy majesty of a pantomime fairy, certain of her applause and yet still a little diffident about it—I mean the thunderous clapping which swelled up to the roofs. The huge wet false eyelashes set off her features to admiration, giving them shape and grace. Her dress was shot with some sort of bright rayon which made it seem lighted from within. O, she was wired for sense and sound—nor could she escape an expression of alembicated piety as she advanced towards the waiting dignitaries from whom she would unlock the mysteries of Monet, Manet, Pissaro. . . . And this was the girl who had once asked me what a Manet was. ("It says here that she bought a Manet—is it a sort of motor-bike?") I hoped she would tell the Mayor that it was a motor-bike. Vaguely, in a shuffling manner, a line of reception was being formed. I was about to duck back into the bar when Baum appeared and caught me forcibly by the elbow and all but frog-marched me into this forming line, whispering "Please, Mr. Charlock. Please" in an agony of supplication. I hadn't the moral courage to bolt; so found myself elbow to elbow with my fellow slaves in the direct line of march. I closed my eyes for a while to restore my composure and judge how much I might be swaying; but no, I was all right.

The radiance moved inexorably towards us in slow camera-time. It was possible to see how really beautiful she had become—factitious beauty I don't doubt, but very real. The smooth skin had burst from its mask of eggwhite fresh as a chick. Smiling eyes and modelled nose. Moreover she accepted her presentations with a modest distinction which won one as she floated effortlessly down the long line of dignitaries. Kallipygos Io, acting the third caryatid for all she was worth. The cameras traversed lecherously across our numbed faces. I was tempted to close my eyes on the ostrich principle in the hope that she would not see me; but I saw the critical gaze of Baum upon me and refrained. The radiant light was upon me at last and here she was with beautifully manicured fingers extended towards me. "*Xaire* Felix" she said, in a low amused voice, and the little sparks of mischief took possession of the centres of her eyes. Perhaps there was also something a little proudly tremulous there too—she was half pleased and half ashamed of all these trappings of success. I replied hesitantly and in a Pleistocene Age Greek to her greeting. She depressed her cheeks in the faintest suggestion of the old grin and went on, low-voiced, looking about her to judge whether anyone in the line understood what she was saying. "I have been wanting to see you for some time past; I have much to tell you, to ask you." I nodded humbly and said "Very well", which sounded stupid. I could see Baum swelling with pride, however, and this encouraged me to add "As soon as you have time, as you wish." Iolanthe wrinkled her brow briefly and said: "Thank you. Quite soon now." Then she passed slowly along to where the Mayor stood panting and mopping.

She made a speech, brief and wise, and obviously written for her; she did not mention motor-bikes in it. Then with a huge pair of dressmaker's scissors she cut the ribbons. We all poured reverently into the Exhibition behind her. In the heat of battle the mayor had forgotten to deliver his reply to her speech; he stuffed it into his tail-coat and followed manfully. There was nothing further to keep me and I made my way back to the bar for another drink to wait upon her departure—for she might conceivably ask for me again and I didn't want to hurt Baum. Through the curtain I kept a sharpshooter's eye on the proceedings, so intently, indeed, that I hardly heeded a thump on the shoulder from behind. Then, spinning round, I found myself face to face with Mrs. Henniker. "My poy!" The last person in the world I was expecting to see! She extended a hand rough as a motoring glove and pumped mine violently; she spoke with untold vivacity. She had not changed by a day—but yes; to begin with she was dressed in country tweeds and natty brogues, a black pullover and pearls. Neatly smart. Her hair had been cut into roguish curls and dyed reddish. She smelt rather heavily of drink, and there was a slight vagueness of eye and speech which suggested—but this might have been sheer emotion at seeing me again. Her skin was rough and red and windblown. She was carrying several folders and a notebook. She moved up and down on her heels with triumphant delight. To my question about what she might be doing there she jerked her head in the direction of the Exhibition and said: "With her. I am Iolanthe's secretary." Then, draining her glass at a blow: "The minute she could she wired me to come to her. She has been a daughter to me, and I . . ." she broke off to order another round "have been a mother to her." There was no suspecting the deep emotion with which she made me this confidence. "Well I'm damned" I said, and Mrs. Henniker gave a harsh cackle of laughter. "You see?" she said with gleaming eye, raising her glass. "How strange life is?"

We had several more drinks on the strength of this, and it was only when the goddess was leaving that Mrs. Henniker jumped to her feet and exclaimed that duty called. "Can you come to Paris next week? She prefers to meet you there—because of Julian." I jumped.

"Of course I can come to Paris." Mrs. H. shook her red wattles and said "Good, then I'll get in touch with you with all the details. She will have to dress up, you know, and meet you in a café or something. I expect she'll explain everything to you. But she's mobbed wherever she goes. And there's no privacy in the apartment. I'll ring you. Ah my poy, my poy."

I drove back to London with a certain pleasurable perplexity, in the company of Baum who was beside himself with joy at the great success. Full justice had been done both to the painters and also to those superior titillations of the thinking mind like the Merlin lawn-mower. "You must have been very moved to see your work bang opposite the great masters" he said. "And she was so beautiful I felt quite afraid. Do you know she gets a million dollars for every film now? A million dollars!" His voice rose in a childish squark of amazement. "She was like a flower, Mr. Charlock." Yes, an open flower filled with synthetic dew. "A dedicated artist" went on Baum impressively. Indeed. Indeed. Full of the *feu sucré*. I was jealous of her success.

It is all very well to be flippant; the truth was that even from the glimpse I had had of the new Iolanthe I had gathered the impression of a maturity and self-possession which made me rather envious. She seemed to me to be very much her own woman leading a life a good deal more coherent than mine. And yet it had been a pretty good mess had it not? I picked up an evening paper at the corner and took it home to dinner, the better to study the pictures of her and of her husband; it was still in the rumour stage, of course, this impending separation, but it remained undenied, which gave it a certain flavour of validity. Well, all this was nothing to do with me. After dinner Julian rang up and startled me—I mean that I had almost forgotten his existence, and the fact of his voice resurrecting thus caused me a real surprise. He talked about the Exhibition, asked me if it had been a success and so on. I described as much of it as I could; and I had the impression that he positively drank in anything I might have to say about Iolanthe. He seemed to linger over anything concerned with her.

Then he modestly cleared his throat and said, almost humbly: "She was your mistress once, wasn't she?" I replied: "No, not this woman. That was quite another girl. She's completely changed, you know." Julian's voice sank a tone. "Yes, I know," he said "I know." There was a long silence; then he said: "Has she asked to see you? Will you be meeting?" But, made cautious by long doubting, I replied: "No. We have nothing to say to each other now, I don't think there is any point." He grunted, and I could hear him light a match. "I see. By the way, I hear that Benedicta hasn't been too well this last week. Nash has gone down to see her." I supposed that meant some more deep sedation. I said nothing. Benedicta rose with my gorge until I was filled with a sensation of nausea.

"In the meantime" said Julian "I want you to spend a few days in Paris." He gave me the details of some negotiations which were going on; I duly noted them down on my blotter. "Very well" I said. "Very well." And that was that; he sounded as if he were speaking from Dublin or Zürich. I returned to my fire and my cigar, full of a certain mild surmise. (To bow or not to bow, that is the question?) Before going to bed I sent a night letter to Mrs. Henniker, asking her to phone me at the office on the morrow.

But it was Iolanthe's voice which came over the wire, heavy with sleep. "Henniker is off today so I thought I'd ring you . . ." she began, and then switched into Greek, in order, I suppose, not to be understood by the casual switchboard operators. "I want to give you a number to ring when you come—I hope you do. I am here for another month at least. I'm so looking forward to it. When do you think you will come? Friday and Saturday I have free." So the appointment was made, aided and abetted by the chance which was to take me to Paris anyway. My spirits rose at the prospect of a short change from snowgirt London—even though it would mean lodging at the Diego which was owned by the company and where everything was free. I know. Everyone hates the Diego—its spaciousness confers an infernal anonymity upon its residents. But then I had some trivial details about patents to discuss: and this was the ideal place to discuss them, for it boasted of elegantly appointed conference rooms smelling of weary leather and Babylonian cigars. Threading and weaving about its great entrance halls with their flamboyant marquetry were grouped all the traditional denizens of the international world of affairs—Arab potentates with black retainers poring over maps of oilfields, gamesome little bankers from the USA moving on hinges, forgotten kings and queens, gangsters, revivalists and fleshy brokers. The never-stopping hum of critical conversations, anguished bids, political lucubrations, arguments, disagreements, hung heavy on the air. All this variegated business fauna pullulated. The Diego buzzed with a million conflicting purposes, schemes and schisms.

I conducted my business with despatch and moved into the fourteenth where I had once lodged as a youth; it was still there, the old Corneille, though it must have changed hands a hundred times since. Still the same high reputation for general seediness and defective plumbing; but modestly priced, and with rooms backing on to insanitary but romantic courtyards, and tree-tufted. Also there was my old room vacant. It was in reality Number Thirteen, but in deference to public superstition it had been renumbered Twelve A. The old telephones creaked and scratched, half transforming the melodious laugh of Iolanthe when at last I reached her. "Listen" she said "you know my problem about being mobbed—she told you? I daren't show my face except over a cop's shoulder. And so I have to dress up a bit to enjoy any sort of privacy." She sounded however as if she enjoyed it. "And this apartment is useless, here I am watched." I groaned. "O God," I said "not you too. Must we then meet heavily veiled or in false beards? And who watches you anyway?" I groaned again. "Julian!" I said with bitter certainty. She laughed very heartily. "Of course not. It's my husband." Out of the window Paris was in the grip of a magnificent early spring thaw, gutters running, trees leafing, birds loafing. The scent of pushing green in the parks, the last melted drops running from the penis of the stone Pan in the public gardens. "Well what, then?"

"I am going to act Solange" she said gaily.

"Solange?" I was startled. "What do you know about Solange?"

"Your little girl" she said. "Everything you told me about her has stayed in my memory like a photograph."

"I told you about Solange?" This was really surprising; Solange had been a little *grisette* with whom I had lived for one brief summer—actually part of the time here, in this room. But when could I have mentioned her to Iolanthe?

"You have forgotten" she said. "You told me all about her, making unfair comparisons with me. I remember being depressed. She was so this, she was so that. Besides I didn't realise that it was all Paris snobbery. In those days everyone simply had to have a love-affair in Paris or risk being ridiculous. But I didn't know that—you took advantage of my ignorance. Nevertheless I listened carefully, always anxious to learn. And I have never forgotten Solange. And what is more, I shall prove it to you. At eleven-thirty. The Café Argent isn't it?" As a matter of fact it used to be the Café Argent all right; then back here for those tender little manoeuvres which by now I had so completely forgotten that I had to make a real effort to recapture the fleeting expressions on the white peaky face of my little Parisienne. "Good God" I said. It seemed an extraordinary thing to bring up; one never knows what lumber one has shed like this—lumber which has been preserved in somebody's memory. Tons of this detritus thrown off by a single life, flushed away one thinks: but no, someone has recorded it—sometimes a chance remark, sometimes a whole case-history. "Very well" I said with resignation. "Come and act her then."

She did it to such good effect that for a moment I did not quite believe it—of course she could not look exactly like Solange: and there were quite a few young women sitting along the *terrasse* even at that time of day—laid up like trinkets in some pedlar's tray. But then Solange! It was only when the waiter brought me a little slip of torn newspaper with a question mark on it, indicating the sender of the missive by a jerk of his head, that Solange burst out of the tomb and into that warm spring sunlight. Solange of the powder-blue skirt badly cut, the dove-grey shoes much worn, the yellowing mackintosh, colour of an uncut manuscript: cheap beads, crocodile handbag, mauve beret. Rising she came towards me with that heavily whitewashed face and over-made up eye, with that flaunting yet diffident walk. (The diffident part was Iolanthe herself.) "*Je suis libre Monsieur.*" Among those shy students, Germans, Swiss and Americans, the little monotonous whining voice, the dire sadness covered by the deliberately pert smile. "Iolanthe," I exclaimed "for goodness' sake—what next?" She burst into a characteristic peal of common laughter as she sank into the wicker chair beside mine, putting her handbag on the table between us. She clapped her hands to summon a waiter and demand a *coupe* in her marvellous tinfoil tones. "Go on," she said "tell me I can't act. *The Times* says I can't act." But the brilliant impersonation of Solange held me spellbound. Of course she was wigged—brown bobbed hair with two points at her dimpled mouth. Certainly she would never be recognised like this. "You see?" she said, clipping her arm through mine as we sat. "So we can be free to talk. Tell me everything that has happened to you." I should have answered perhaps that while much seemed to have happened in fact catastrophically little had. Where to begin anyway? I tried my hand at a brief sketch of my fortunes; there was much that she already knew. She listened carefully, attentively, nodding from time to time as if what I said confirmed her own inward intuitions. "We are in the same boat" she said at last. "Both rich, celebrated and sick."

"Sick, Iolanthe?"

"In my case physically."

"And mine?"

"You've taken the wrong road—I knew you would even then: always in your cards I found it: and then yourself—you always saw real people as sort of illustrations to things—glandular secretions. I felt that you'd never get free, and then later when I heard you had joined Merlin's my heart went down and down. I know what it has cost me to free myself from them. I knew you'd never do it."

"Why should I?" I said sturdily. "It suits my book very well." She looked at me with dismay, bordering on disgust; and then her expression changed. She realised that I wasn't telling the whole truth. "Merlin's made me what I am" I said sententiously, feeling quite sick to hear myself talk such twaddle. Now she began to laugh. Ouf! It seemed as if the whole conversation were going to take a wrong turning. "Come, let's walk" I said. As we passed the Café Dôme she insisted that I entered it to see if there was any message from Solange on the postboard. Sure enough there was, in typically bad French: she had had it planted by Mrs. Henniker. "This is going too far" I said with poor grace. "Now we better go back to the hotel and. . . ." An expression of sadness came into her eyes for a moment and then was swallowed by her smile. Taking my arm once more she fell into step. So in leisurely fashion we crossed the park, quizzing the statues, talking in low voices now, inhabitants of different worlds. "And so you are free, as you call it? What does it mean to you Iolanthe?"

"Everything; I just needed it. But it has cost me a great deal—in fact my company is hovering on the edge of bankruptcy all the time—thanks to Julian of course. He could not bear to see me free."

"Do you know Julian?"

"I saw him once—just a single look we exchanged, a look to last a lifetime. I knew then that he loved me—indeed in a perverse way all the more for crossing him, for breaking free. With my first money I set up my own firm, chose my own parts. Julian has tried to break us because—again perversely—his only way of getting me would be by owning me, having shares in me." She laughed, not bitterly but ruefully. "If you men didn't prey on women where would you be?" she added smiling. "But Julian's expression was so strange that I even tried to learn to draw in order to reproduce it."

"How did you meet?"

"We didn't; our audience research people said that there was one of my fans who was always there, never missed a single film, often saw them over and over again for weeks. They wanted to make a newspaper story of it; but the journalist was told by his proprietor that Julian had had the story stopped. Then they pointed him out to me at a Fair."

For some reason I felt jealous of this.

Across the Luxembourg, the children's play-pit and so on, slowly down, drawn by the inexorable strings of our Athenian memories. There was much to surprise me; it was like coming upon a bundle of letters one had read in cursory fashion and thrust aside into a cupboard corner—and now on re-reading discovered to be full of things which had escaped notice. For example: "It puzzled me afterwards very much to think how much I thought I loved you then. I did love you, but for singular reasons. Ultimately it was your lack of understanding which enabled you to occupy this place in my mind—your very indifference in a queer way. Since you could be objective, cool, and consequently *considerate.*" (O dear, this is the mere vermiform appendix of love.)

"At times I thought you quite contemptible as a man, but I never wavered. You don't know, Felix, how little a woman hopes for in life—for an iron ration only: *consideration.* We haven't enough confidence in ourselves to believe that we could ever be loved—that would be butter and jam on the bread. But the bread itself? A woman can be won by simple consideration, she will settle for that when she is desperate. Look, you took my arm in the public street, though all Athens knew I was a street-girl. You dared to be seen with me, opened doors for me. What chivalry, I thought! Everyone will believe us to be engaged. But of course later I realised that it had no special connotation for you—it was pure absent-mindedness and ignorance of the mentality of small capitals." She laughed very merrily; I turned her friendly face round to embrace her, but she groaned with pain, and said her wounds were not yet healed. "You used to talk about going from the unproven to the proven in your work; but later I realised that with each new discovery the so-called proven is falsified. It collapses. The whole thing is only a funk-hole process—necessary because you are weak."

I didn't care about all this, inhaling the warm Jupiterian air, the leaves, the crunching passers-by who walked as if upon a tilting deck, or else were dragged widdershins by huge dogs on heat. Intuition can become a conditioned reflex? "And then" she went on "I heard what you'd done, and I crossed my fingers for you. I half believed that you might decide for independence one day like myself. But when I saw your face the other day I knew that you hadn't made a serious effort. You had the same funny stillborn look you always had; I was tempted to kiss you very hard, very triumphantly, simply because Julian was there in the crowd."

"Julian was there?"

"I *think* it was Julian."

I kicked some pebbles about for a moment wondering if I shouldn't become angry. "I don't much like this sort of curtain-lecture coming from you," I said at last "with its boastful idea that you have done something very special; you who supply a surrogate mob-culture with vulgarised versions of classics watered down by pissy-witted cinéastes. . . ." Iolanthe looked at me with delight. She said: "It isn't the point; even if it had only been a small dressmaker's shop in the Plaka instead of a film company. It means living without deceptions, awkward secrets, living in the round. The real freedom. *My own.*"

I laughed contemptuously. "*Real* freedom?" She nodded briskly. "Inevitably you would ask yourself how real you were; you would think that it isn't just the firm which confers an illusory reality upon you. O I'm not saying the firm is anything but benign, it helps you towards what you want to do, to achieve."

"Then why all this quaker-maid nonsense?"

"I've angered you" she said sadly. "Come let's talk about other things. You know Graphos is dying; now he would have been worth the love of some great-hearted woman if his health had not spoiled his mind. It's typical of the cynicism of fate that he should imagine he loved me, and still does. And I like him too much to deny that he does. After all, he educated me, taught me to see—in spite of his perverse habits and tastes."

We had come to the doors of the old hotel; I took my key and we mounted slowly, arm in arm. She chuckled as she gazed round her. "It's typically your sort of room" she said. She went to the grimy window and stared out into the foliage. It was raining now, quite a storm of rain. "Do you remember the spoiled picnic on the Acropolis when the sky seemed to come down in whole panes of molten glass and our footsteps smoked on the marble?" She kicked off her shoes and lay down beside me, setting a pillow in the nape of her neck, lighting a cigarette. It needed only a lighted candle and an ikon. . . . Ikons, the portfolio of the collective sensibility. I imagined them as I dozed. ("There is no God and no plan: and once you accept that you can start to identify"?) She lay quietly with her eyes half shut. I had penetrated again the cardboard, the outer cerements of the worshipped mummy. Above all, one should not make a mythology out of one's longing.

My hand sought out hers and pressed it; we were half dozing, reconstituting like archaeologists with every drawn breath, a past which had long since foundered. The arcane clicks and whistles of the little owls; mountains of gauche leaves blowing in the parks. The firm was like one of those great works of art which perish from over-elaboration. ("The greatest happiness of the highest few is what nature aims at, the great aristocrat.") The white mice I have cut up, starved, tortured on behalf of science—as Marchant might say; some people one can only convince by drawing blood. I kissed the nape of her neck softly and lapsed into inertia, dozing by her side while she quietly talked on and on in sweet leaden tones. "It's a terrible thing to feel that one has come to the end of one's life-experience—that there is nothing fundamentally new to look forward to: one must expect more and more combinations of the same sort of thing—the thing which has proven one a sort of failure. So then you start on the declining path, living a kind of posthumous life, your blood cool, your pulse steady." She pressed my finger to her slow calm pulse. "And yet it is just the fruitful point at which some big new understanding might jump out on you from behind the bushes and devour you like a lion." Small sighs, small silences, we were like people drugged; without any sexual stirring we had reverted to the prehistoric mode of an ancient intimacy.

"It's a sort of curse, you might say, for I've brought little comfort to anyone; and some I have gravely harmed. Not voluntarily, but simply because I was placed at an axis where all their lives intersected. That Hippolyta—I had to act to deceive her. And others, like that poor Sipple. Whenever I am in Polis I look him up as a sort of expiation, though we never mention my brother."

"What on earth about Sipple?"

She rose yawning and stretching to seat herself at the mirror; she took off her wig and began to comb it softly. "I thought you knew about that boy; he *was* my brother; I was obliged to kill him."

It was like a pistol shot fired in the quiet room. She turned round to me smiling, with an air of patient fidelity. "And poor Sipple has had to bear the odium. He is going blind, you know. He has become a perfume-taster. They dab those little flippers of his with scent and he tells them how to mix their perfumes. He is studying to be received into the Catholic Church, of all things."

"But why, Iolanthe? Why on earth?"

"That's the sad thing—in order not to let my father take it upon himself; he was a very rash, violent little man, and he had vowed to punish Dorcas. To the Virgin, you know. I knew that he would be obliged to do it, if only because of his vow. I could not let him go to the grave with that upon his conscience—a man of sixty-five. So I stepped in to shield him; and Graphos had it all hushed up. I suppose the idea of atonement is a lot of conceit really—who can say?"

"As arrows fit the wounds they make!" She crossed to the bed and placed a lighted cigarette between my lips; so we stayed silently smoking for a long while, staring at each other.

Then she began to speak of her father's death. He at least was unaware of what she had done for his sake. The scene rose so vividly before my eyes—the little house with its cobwebs, its table and three chairs before the fireplace. A dying peasant wrestling with a death by tetanus, closing up slowly like a jacknife. "Have you heard someone scream with their teeth firmly locked together—an inhuman screaming like a mad bear?" And stumbling, knocking over the furniture. He would not submit, fought death every inch of the way. And the rigor setting the body in such strange shapes. He was like a man wrestling with riding boots too small for him. And then the candles smoking; but even dead he wouldn't lie down. Up he came each time they pushed him down like a jack-in-the-box. The piercing lamentations of the villagers. But it was no go, he wouldn't fit. Finally the village butcher had to be summoned to break up his bones like a turkey in order to coffin him properly. But now there was sweat on Iolanthe's brow, and she was walking slowly up and down at the foot of the bed. They tied a ribbon, a green ribbon, round his arm before the barber bled him. There was so much blood in that withered old arm. "He wouldn't give in, you see." Then she paused and went on. "The little house is still there, it's mine, but I daren't go back. I left it just as it was, the key in the hole by the coping of the well—but you remember, don't you? If ever you go that way will you visit it and tell me about it? I'm sufficiently Greek to feel that I might return one day when I am much older—but how? Someone must exorcise it for me. Felix, if you did that I should be grateful. Will you?" She was so earnest and so beseeching that I said yes, in my futile way, yes I would. And of course now it's too late, as it always is.

"Meanwhile I am here." she said with a rueful bitterness "the most beautiful woman in the world they say. O God."

She has gone such a long way away now, dissolved among the shadows of time; only her masks are preserved in the tin cans that crowd the lumber rooms of the bankrupt companies. Iolanthe now is an unidentified wave to sadness which reaches out for me whenever I see a slip of blue Greek sky, or a beautiful late evening breaking over the Plaka. And then the horror and sadness of the way in which she said "Look" in a voice of a frightened child; and ripping open the cheap bodice showed me the bandaged breasts plumped out with their surgical wadding, and taped like hot cross buns. "I haven't completely healed up as yet."

"Cancer?" I exclaimed; but she shook her head and replied: "Not yet at anyrate. It's even more ironic. Last year in Hollywood they brought in a new treatment for falling breasts—injections of liquid paraffin. It was all the rage. But mine went wrong though I am not the only one, Felix."

She sat down at the mirror once more to adjust her disguise, saying tonelessly: "Now I have brought you up to date." Subjects of calendar time trapped in the great capitals of the world. I let Iolanthe sink deep into my reveries; down she went and down like a plumb-line, turning and rolling through the subaqueous worlds of memory and desire, dissolving and disappearing from view.

"Come," she said at last "enough of these post-mortems. I have ordered a hire car to wait for us at the office. Let us drive into the country together, have lunch, lie on the grass, forget, pretend."

"Forget" I said, and suddenly remembered Benedicta. "I must just ring the office and see if there is any news of Benedicta; she hasn't been very well of late."

"Benedicta" said Iolanthe. "They say that it is all because she drugs. I heard it ages ago and it may be true. Apparently Julian. . . ."

I felt my scalp tingle with rage; it climbed my spine to burst in the centre of my mind like a black bubble of fury. "I do not want to hear his name any more" I said. "I implore you."

"Very well" she said calmly, and kissed me—the sort of kiss that might soothe a refractory child. I banged Number Thirteen shut behind us as we went downstairs.

We came back in the late evening, and she was careful to adjust her disguise before crossing the pavement to the glass doors of the apartment house. Outside lay the film company's Rolls, with the usual small knot of onlookers hanging about it. Its presence always signified that she was inside and might at any moment emerge to be driven somewhere. It was quite miraculous to see how swiftly the crowd gathered—people seemed to spring from the very pavements: she had only to leave the lift and appear in the soft red light at the end of the corridor for the ferment to begin. Autograph books would flash. It was necessary to clear a track for her. Then as she sat back in the car noses would be pressed grotesquely against the windows; avidly the parched faces would inhale her, drink her up. But little Solange looked like some shabby dressmaker and not a head turned as she unlocked the tall doors and, once safe inside, blew me a kiss and rang for the lift.

I walked for half the night by the river which mirrored the opal-studded floors of the dark heaven powdered by stardust; cold, it was cold. The spring day had foundered back into a subzero night which made me glad of a heavy overcoat. I roamed the deserted bookstalls and the dark ships along the river-front with a sense of confusion and loss; I should have been sobbing, I imagine, but what is one to do if the tears pour inwardly, if the amateur face expresses nothing? All that I deserved was some dirty unknown old woman with a gold tooth and shrunken thighs to drain my semen in an instant, pocket the money and scuttle downstairs again to her lamp-post; but even this seemed merely an act of bravado, an attempt at a self-inflicted wound which hardly penetrated the thick carapace of my narcissism and self-regard. Smelling of dirty underlinen, rubber, and sweat; nor could I assuage the thirsty hounds of introspection which were licking my bones. In a bookshop window I read a phrase from an open volume of Flaubert: "*On ne saura jamais ce qu'il a fallu être triste pour entreprendre de ressusciter Carthage.*" I read it over and over again; perhaps if I had had my wits about me I could also have become a master of corkscrew prose? I walked on and on until my legs would carry me no further; then I took a taxi back to my musty room, to spend the rest of the night sleeplessly doing battle with the giant shapes of a nightmare which paralysed my breathing and my will. My own groans woke me, and I remembered Benedicta saying: "But I suffer from daymares, Felix, *pavor diurnus*, as Nash calls it; it is harder to wake from them." (At midnight the quantity of carbon monoxide in the blood reaches its maximum.) As always when she was talking honestly one had the impression of truth barbed with a ferocious tenderness. Next morning I scribbled a note to Iolanthe promising to visit her again, and pleading that urgent business called me back to London. In some unanalysable fashion our meeting had upset me, had knocked the props from under my self-esteem. It was hard as always to leave Paris—hard, grimy and metallic city where civilisation is always dragging its anchor; harder still to face cold London with the sullen ferocious visages of the young half hidden by hair.

the big syringe
the shrunken penis
is all they offer now
to Venus

No, it won't do; deep in the penetralia of one's self-regard there was an arrow pointing towards something which had remained unrealised and unachieved—though how to formulate it without making a model I knew not. Nor should I let the calculated despair of this realisation drive me towards any violent solutions—violence is for the weak. But then Felix, it is precisely because of your weakness.... Someone said once that Julian was obsessed, not with dying, but with rotting; he could not face the idea of that (was it Iolanthe or Koepgen?). Nor could he submit to having his entrails removed, his body embalmed. He hit upon the notion of having a steel, air-tight coffin built for him by Gantry the famous makers of office safes. I had one in my office which closed with a slight puff. A Gantry with an elaborate combination-system whose code I am always forgetting.

High summer to autumn the year went by, its clock-time not matching the slow accretive growth of the buried decisions I meditated; but they were so inchoate as to have to be disinterred, brushed clean, examined—dug up like the bones of dinosaurs. The flora and fauna belonging to such bones must be imagined, their world visualised. Externally nothing had outwardly changed. Life still held its unhurried glacier-pace. Iolanthe wrote once or twice and I tried to answer, sitting before the blank paper for ages biting a pen. What I most needed to say would not rise to the nib. I gave up the struggle. Banubula, in search of female hormone I suppose, paid me a brief visit and for a few days carried me back to those remote unhurried epochs when we had both time and will to devise, to execute. Also the sacramental whiff of Polis and Athens. Jocas had been shot at by a eunuch and in returning the fire had killed the man; elaborate and exhausting litigation about restitution was still going on. Graphos was much worse; he spent all winter at the Paulhaus now, but the treatment availed him little. Hippo had "gone so white". Well, so had we in a way; both the Count and I found our temples turning. I was sorry to see him go, in spite of his perpetual moaning about not being able to join the firm. ("But why on earth should you *want* to join it?" Banubula stroked his nose. "Well, because of you all; look at you, you are all so happy".)

Benedicta still lay at anchor, not noticeably better or worse; still hovering between white depression and sudden bursts of tender enthusiasm—attacks of almost total lucidity one might have called it. Yet always lying for half the day in the darkened rooms, blinds drawn, candles fuming. "I suddenly realised one day that real people had become shadows—without any substance as egos." It was well expressed, but I was tempted to answer "Except Julian I suppose?" Then self-reproach, of course, and bad dreams in which Julian sat by my bed, a small vampire-snouted man, staring at me with two live coals. I knew of course what all these women lacked—a tablespoon of fresh poet's sperm breathing salt air and seed into them. It can work wonders with a sensitive woman. What we all lacked, it seemed to me —and here I was mentally copying Koepgen with his *ex cathedra* judgements—was the mythological extension of human personality. I remember him saying, in front of a statue of the old king who went on sleeping with his dead wife for months: "And do you dare to imagine that there isn't a real historic personage buried underneath each mythological one?" It was all very well. I went to New York, to Rio, conferring my intellectual bounty on them in well-shaped discourses.

And then, quite unaccountably (or so it seemed, it was so sudden) Pulley walked into the house in Mount Street one evening with an air of rare distraction. He had found the front door ajar as I had been expecting Marchant to come and talk chemicals. A new cadaverous Pulley; without even greeting me he crossed the drawing-room to the sideboard and poured himself a stiff whisky and soda. "Well" I said. He looked at first blush as if he had been beaten up—his forehead was all blue and bruised; moreover his skin was yellow, as if he were just getting over an attack of jaundice. But no, he said, the bruises were due to a fall downstairs and the yellowness due to a bug he had picked up "out there" and for which he had been under treatment by Nash. "Just got back from Zürich this morning to find my digs in an awful mess." He sank into a chair sighing, and giving me a yawning grin with very little grin in it—a funny rictus really.

"Pulley, what have you been up to?"

He shivered a little and said: "They gave me drugs at the Paulhaus, drugs for bugs, old man. And now I don't know what I've told them, at all I don't. I can't remember. It worries me. Did I tell them the truth? I didn't mean to. Anyway, I'm not really sure it was him—Robinson."

"Wait a minute. Stop this babble. Who is Robinson? And where?"

"Sorry" he said with contrition. "Either it was Caradoc or it wasn't Caradoc, and it was only a glimpse. I was sure it was at first; then when I left I suddenly grew doubtful. Maybe it was Robinson after all, the old man. But I'll begin at the beginning. The smell of copra—do you know it? I can't get it out of my nose. Specially rotting copra mixed with a little oil and bilge. Day and night vomiting about in a little boat smelling of singed gym-shoes. I'm not saying it isn't all very beautiful, it is: but I'd prefer to see postcards. The damp in those islands, my boy, the damp winds, damp clouds, steamy jungle. And the diet, chunks of pig and breadfruit inadequately cooked and very badly served on leaves. After about a month I'd had enough. Moreover I'd cleared the few survivors, visited them as from an airline insurance company. There remained a man called Robinson, a de-frocked clergyman they said, who had gone native and retired to a tiny little island miles from anywhere. He had been on the plane, or so the passport people said, and had crawled ashore and disappeared. Presumably he had gone back home again; but the last copra boat had gone ages since and the next wasn't due for a while, so I just had to cool my heels in Pyengo.

"A more godforsaken dump I never hope to see; and if the ladies are kind as they are reputed to be, it's all very well. Only you should smell the local cold cream they use on their bodies. That also takes getting used to. However there was sunshine, there was a sharkless lagoon, and the foodstuffs arrived wrapped in old *Times*, so I made do with it until I could catch the boat for Robinson's little island. Apparently he had quite a tidy copra crop to be collected and some shells. So an occasional visit was on. Anyway there I stuck and waited, slowly getting athlete's foot in my armpits. Nor did such enquiries as I could make offer much hope. In fact the whole thing seemed a waste of time. I didn't sleep very well, the blasted trees make such a noise. Also they said the season would soon be breaking, and I had visions of being stuck altogether. However at last it came, the boat, and the skipper agreed to take me; but he emphasised that Robinson absolutely refused to allow people ashore on any terms whatsoever; the crew were allowed to ship the copra and clear off. There were signs tacked up everywhere saying: 'Strangers forbidden'. I said I would take a chance on it; but I didn't feel too elated as apparently Robinson had a gun and was quite likely to use it. He had once fired at a suffragan bishop who tried to come and draw him back into the fold.

"Well, one has to take risks; and after all that time waiting I felt I really should. The voyage was hell for smell, the sea was oily, everything appeared to be rotting all round us. Three days it took and at last we came to the tiny little island and drew into a rusty iron pier with a crooked crane. The ship tooted to tell Robinson that we had arrived but nobody answered, so the crew just swung off and began to load the copra which was lying around fairly neatly laid out for them; also several big boxes of seashells. I walked up and down for a bit in a hesitant manner, keeping my eyes skinned; but nobody appeared, and the skipper seemed to think that nobody would. It was often like that, he said. He pointed over the hill and said that the village was somewhere over there; and so I started to stroll in the direction he indicated. It was quite pretty and quite green with patches of cultivation here and there; I had been told that the total population of the island was about sixty souls—enough for the harvesting and all that. There was rather an exceptionally large hut standing some way outside the nearest village-shaped cluster and I went towards it, imagining it must be the chief's or Robinson's. All the way along I saw notices tacked to the trees saying: 'Strangers absolutely forbidden. Danger' which didn't sound too reassuring. However on I pressed. As I got nearer to the big hut I saw that there was an old man sitting on the steps, an old man with a mane of white hair. He started when he saw me and gave an inarticulate cry, as if of rage. I waved my hands in a peaceable and pleading manner, like a soldier waving a white flag of truce, and called out in English: 'Is Mr. Robinson here? I have only come for a moment to ask him a question.' My dear Charlock, that was absolutely all. My range was fairly extreme, but I did get a good look at him. He was simply covered in hair, beard to his waist, high-foreheaded sweep of mane backwards, loin-cloth, and rough thonged slippers made of some bark or other. His eyes were small and bloodshot, and at this moment regarded me as a cornered and wounded wild boar might.

"Everything seemed to come together in a confused sort of focus—you know how it is in moments of excitement? And some of the things I saw in that few seconds I didn't take in until afterwards, when I was on the run. For example that he had two small kids at his breasts, *he was giving them suck, old man.* I could even see some of the milk trickling down among the hairs on his breast, white as coconut-milk. It seemed to me that it was Caradoc all right. I mean that at that precise moment it seemed so; later I lost confidence in my judgement. A woman appeared at an upper window, large and rather handsome, and clucked something at him. All this happened in a twinkling. I called his name once in an uncertain sort of way. Then he put down the kids and picked up a gun which was lying beside him and opened fire. A bunch of leaves from above my head fell with a crash on me. There was no time to argue; it was a near miss. I took to my heels with the shells knocking up the stones all around me. Once I thought I had been hit, but it was gravel thrown up by the shots—but it hurt. It must have been a six shot twelve-bore, for he sent all six whistling about my ears, some damn near. I cleared the brow of the hill with thumping heart and galloped down to the pier where they had just finished loading. I took refuge in the deck-house until the ship drew anchor and set off. I feared he might follow me down to the harbour and take a pot shot at me there.

"Well, this whole thing, sort of instant snapshot stuff, had a strange sort of effect on me. It wasn't just the unexpectedness, the fright and so on. I felt as if my mind had been, for one brief second, unfrozen; and even later when it went back into deep freeze again, the experience left something, a nagging something. I'm not much good at expressing these things. Later, of course, when I got very ill I had all sorts of feverish delusions about us all, about the firm. Julian had me flown back to Zürich where they could look after me. But God, the drugs were strong—I'm still woozy from them. And then that old fool, Caradoc or Robinson? Yes, but it *was* Caradoc. It is touching in a way—I saw how clumsily, how shakily he had tried to escape, to leave his body behind so to speak. Why on earth should he do it? The firm is everything to me; it's a livelihood, and a creative way of earning one. And yet, Felix, and yet. . . ."

He gazed at me with sallow concentration from the fireplace, fingering the bruises on his forehead and sucking his teeth. "Another thing I didn't know I'd noticed until after we set sail was the sort of house he was living in there. It wasn't like most of the architecture of the place—it was canted up on piles. You don't remember, do you, how Caradoc used to talk about the theory of Sarasin that the proportions of the Parthenon corresponded in a way to the pile-buildings in Celebes? He used to go on quite a lot about it, and often drew it in the sand for us. No, you've forgotten? Well, anyway, it's this sort of shape if I remember rightly." He took out a coloured pencil and sketched in the following figure on the back of a newspaper.

No, I had never seen it before. "Ah well" said Pulley with resignation. "That was what he had been building for himself. It would prove nothing to anyone else, but to someone who knew Caradoc it would be conclusive. You see, he just could not resist making mnemons and building houses. Try as he would. And he'll always be found out because of it." He paused for a while, finished his drink, and said "I don't know whether I told them all this, I couldn't judge. All that Julian said when he was thanking me was 'Well, the case is closed, then.' But did he mean it, that's the point? Ah! That's the point."

The case is closed. "I don't know" said Pulley. "Perhaps we should act out ourselves more." He strolled about fiddling with things on the tables and mantelpiece. "But I could never dream of trying to get out" he said sadly. "But in your case, Felix, I——"

"Me?" I said with some indignation. "Why pick on me?"

"I wasn't; but somehow I have always wondered about you—from way back at the beginning I mean. Whether you really belonged here, with us."

"Well I'm damned" I said, and the surprise was genuine. It was suddenly borne in upon me that there must, after all, somewhere, be people who didn't belong to the firm. Pulley showed his huge teeth in an infantile grin. "You are one of the few people" he said "one can honestly distrust in this outfit. I would confide anything in you, I think."

"And you feel I should get out somehow?"

"O, I didn't say that exactly. I don't know quite what I feel about anything any more, I'm so damn tired after all this drugging. And I still occasionally get the weeps for nothing at all. So don't ask me leading questions. Besides, Felix, is there really *time* to worry? One minute you are fretting over your income tax, and the next you are staring up from the bottom of a pinewood coffin. Heavens, stay put, old boy, stay put."

"Stay put, you tell me now."

"Well, unless you feel too hampered. Lots of us do. The weak usually resort to acts of senseless violence. I remember old Trabbe—he ran out with a fireman's axe one day and buried it in Julian's car. But they cured him and sent him abroad. And poor Mrs. Trabbe—after she died the servants started wearing her frocks and shoes, surprising everyone and giving pain. O well!" He yawned and stretched. "I must be getting along now. It's been good to see you; we must meet again soon, eh? When things don't feel so damned precarious."

His eyes had a haunted look which somehow I misliked; his walk, too, was the walk of an old man. I accompanied him to the door and suggested that he might like to move in with me for a few weeks, but he shook his head slowly. "Ah thanks" he said. "But no. Cheerio."

I stood at the door and watched him wander off down the street towards the nearest tube station. He did not turn round and wave on the corner as was once his wont.

* * * * *

I had some difficulty in running Julian to earth—if that is the expression—but at last I found him week-ending somewhere in the country. My call caught him in mid yawn. "Ah good, it's you Charlock" he said. "I was wondering who it might be."

"Julian" I said "I've come to a decision which I want to discuss with you. In itself it may not seem very important, but it is extremly so to me." Julian coughed and said: "Well you know you can always count on me." It sounded not at all sententious. I took a breath and went on. "I have decided to give one of my inventions away to the public—to *give* it away, do you see? Simply, unequivocally donate it." He said nothing, and after a pause I went on. "Recently in playing about with some chemistry work in the lab I tumbled upon something which one might really describe as a boon to the ordinary housewife. It costs nothing, or almost nothing to make. It will completely transform washing-up."

"Well, for goodness sake take out a pat——"

"Ah but listen. This I propose to *give* away. I propose to write a letter to *The Times* describing how anyone can, for the price of a pennyworth of common salt, make this. . . ."

The timbre of Julian's attention seemed to shift and deepen. He sighed, and I heard a match click, followed by a puff. "I'm glad you decided to discuss it with me first before doing anything" he said. "What is the point of it, after all? At a penny halfpenny it would still be a boon—as a Merlin patent. Do you think we are dealing hardly by the public? By comparison with other firms I should have thought. . . ."

"That has nothing to do with it. I simply feel that for once in my life I must make this gesture, *give* something freely, you see; something which is the fruit of my thought, so to speak. Can't you see?"

"I follow what you mean" he said coolly. "But nevertheless I can't quite see the motive. You have given the world so much through the firm, Charlock."

"Not given, Julian. That's the point. Sold."

"There is a pleasing touch of religiosity about your idea" he said dryly. "I commend you." He sounded serious but weary.

"I know it sounds trivial; but for me it represents something momentous, something I haven't been able to imagine for years—an act."

"The married man dreams of divorce" he said oracularly, and I recognised a Greek proverb in translation. "And the scientist thinks of science as a pretty girl with two cunts. . . ." He was wandering, playing for time. Then a little more sharply came: "What am I supposed to do about this idea—agree? How can I, Charlock? Indeed I wonder why you consulted me. You know that you are raising much more than a personal question? It smells of precedent. Indeed whatever I said, I doubt if the firm would agree: and I am not the firm, as you know, only one of the camel-drivers, so to speak, in the general caravan. Anyway thanks for being honest enough to tell me what was in your mind."

"I always felt I could talk to you as man to voice" I said.

"Irony was always your long suit, Charlock. Always."

"Anyway, now you know what I've decided."

Julian cleared his throat softly and let a pause intervene; when he came back to the charge he was dreamy, reflective, unincisive. "I wonder if you have really thought about it—no, it's a pure impulse of generosity on your part."

"On the contrary: the fruit of a long interior debate."

"Hum. Have you considered, for example, your articles of association with the firm? This would cut across our agreement which is valid, if I remember, for some twenty years more at least."

"Twenty years." A shiver ran down my spine. Yes, I knew it all right—but uttered out loud like that it produced a chilling effect.

"It wouldn't work" said Julian at last in a more wide-awake voice. "It would lead to some costly and tedious litigation, that's all. And you'd lose, the firm would win. Contractually you are tied for everything."

"We shall see" I said, but I felt my voice falter. Julian went on suavely: "You know don't you that there is a whole string of charities supported by us in part or in full? Merlin's staff are encouraged to contribute to them—why don't you? You could make over the whole of your salary to them if you wished. Ask Nathan to show you the bound volume with the lists."

"I've seen it." I had. There was a huge vellum tome the thickness of the Bible listing all the charities to which the firm contributed.

"Well" said Julian. "Wouldn't that do?"

"No."

"Why not?" He was almost peevish now.

"We get Income Tax relief on those—it's a company ploy."

"I see! My goodness, you are hard to please."

He puffed away another long silence and then asked: "What is the source of all this unrest, Charlock; where does it come from?"

"I have simply come to a point where I must make a gesture, even the feeblest of free gestures, to continue breathing."

"It must be due to some misconception about the nature of the firm. I feel in all you say a funny kind of moral bias—an implied criticism which cannot be wholly just. Are you just being pharisaical, holier-than-thouish?"

"No, I'm being holier-than-meish for a change."

"What I'm trying to say is that the firm isn't just an extension of moral qualities, a product of a wicked human will, of a greedy mercantile spirit. It goes deeper than that. I mean, it has always existed in one form or another. At least I suppose so."

"What a sophistry! The firm is not the world."

"I'm not so sure. I'm not saying it's an easy thing or a gay thing; but it's a fact of nature, man's nature. One can't blink the firm, Charlock."

"Nature!"

"It must correspond to some deep unexpressed need of the human psyche—for it's always been there. We should take it more coolly. It's not in itself malefic, it is just neutral, a *repoussoir*. It's what we make of it. . . ."

"So the slave is born with his chains, is he?"

"Yes. Some can free themselves, but very few. I couldn't. If you believe in free will or predestination, for example——"

"Cut out the homilies" I said.

"Well, who imposed the firm on you, then?"

"I did. Out of ignorance."

"Not really; everything was clear from the beginning; your eyes were wide open."

"Like a three-day kitten."

"I don't see how you can want to back down at this stage."

"Even in prison they get remission for good behaviour."

"But damn it, you might wake up one day and find yourself in charge of the firm, or most of it; Jocas and I won't live for ever, you know."

"God forbid!"

Julian said "Ach!" in an exasperated sort of way and then became mild again. "The firm isn't inflexible" he said, with a faint tinge of reproach. "Despite its size it is a pretty fragile thing, a bundle of long wires stretching out around the world. But it is all based on one slender item—the spinal column of the matter: that is the sanctity of contractual obligation. If you abrogate that you begin to damage the essential fabric of the thing. Naturally it will try to protect itself like any other organism."

"I *must* do this thing, I tell you."

"You will end up by building up a delusional system about being persecuted by the firm—the poor thing does not merit it."

I ground my teeth.

"Anyway," he went on "there is no pressure the firm can bring upon you in the immediate sense; but it would certainly counter any such move as the one you have outlined. It's strange, you still seem to think of it in terms of personalities; but it has long ago outgrown the personalities which created it—Merlin, Jocas, myself: we are already merely ancestors. The firm is self-subsisting now, rolling down its appointed path with a momentum which neither you nor I can alter. Of course he that is not with it is against it, and so on. In other epochs it might have taken other forms. But man rests, unchangeable, unteachable, and the firm is cast in his mould—*your mould, Charlock*! Ask and it shall be answered! Prod the old sow with a stick and it grunts." He paused and his voice sank softly into the tones of a twilit resignation. Under his breath, in a whisper which I could just catch,

I heard him say: "And Iolanthe is dying?" He sighed, he was talking to himself. A long silence fell.

"You are still there, Charlock?"

"Yes."

"Well, I think all this must come from your sense of impotence aggravated by success; such feelings always result in rash moral judgements. You have never succeeded in doing the abstract work for which you pined—though that was not our fault. And you have worked up a grudge against the firm in telling yourself that it is caught up in the nets of base matter, is exploring and adapting matter, expropriating matter."

"And the results?"

"My dear, I can do nothing, nobody can. Yes, we can make small adjustments of stress or direction or emphasis. But the wheel turns in spite of one. Come, grow up, Charlock. The firm won't bite, you know."

"I am still waiting to be convinced" I said grimly. "All this is special pleading."

It was, of course; and yet in another way it wasn't. It made sense on one level. nonsense on another. I had not yet succeeded in penetrating to the basic fallacy in these contentions. In a funny way, too, I thought him—Julian personally—innocent of any intention to delude. He believed what he said, and consequently it was true, not for me, but for him. Perhaps even objectively true? My reason was spinning like a top. The vertiginous sense of failure was so intense that it had got mixed up with my breathing. I was suffocated. I heard Julian put down the receiver and walk away a few steps; then in the silence I heard some music begin to play—the opening bars of a Schumann concerto. "As an honourable man," he said "who abhors all exaggeration, I do not know what to tell you."

How many of these ideas would remain waterproof? I wondered. Julian was sighing again. "What about Iolanthe?" I said cruelly. (Marchant said that ideas were simply nags; one rode about on them until one tired of them, then tied them to a tree and fucked them.) "Iolanthe" he repeated slowly, accenting the word wrongly. "What of her?" In my almost drunken state I could not resist a further threat. "A creation of the soap-flakes mind" I said. "Nobody would believe it to see her picture in your flat." Julian smiled invisibly. "An artist" he said, and "A smile to make one rise in one's stirrups."

"I might even leave England," I said "where the national sloth has reached the brain cortex."

Julian coughed. All of a sudden his voice became bony and determined; a sort of cold fury possessed it: "There is only one solution for you—to stop inventing altogether; to retire on your winnings—I will not call them earnings, for without us you would be penniless today. Abandon the game altogether." Then his voice changed again; it sank into a lower register, it became merciful, tender, calm. He whispered almost to himself. "Who can gauge the feeling of a man in love who is forced to sit and look on at the steady deterioration of a fine mind and lovely body? We must celebrate the people who set us on fire."

"Julian" I cried. "Is this your last word?"

"What else?" he said with such world-weariness, such inexpressible sadness, that I felt a lump come into my throat. Yet at the same time gusts of rage and frustration were still there in my mind, I could not still them. "Mountebank! Actor!" I jeered. Yet he did not seem to have heard me—or at any rate the insults produced no recognisable reflection in his tone.

"Graphos" he said "could only love a weeping girl. If she did not weep she must be made to—so he said." All of a sudden I recalled a chance remark of Io's to the effect that only the free man can really be loved by a woman; I wondered which of us she might have in mind? Ah which?

I had said it before I knew the words were out of my mouth—without any premeditation whatsoever. "Julian, for how long has Benedicta been your mistress, and what is the name of the drug?" I heard him draw his breath sharply as if I had run a thorn under his fingernail. "Do you hear me?" I said lurching about drunkenly and laughing coarsely. Silence from his end. It was war now to the very knife, I felt it. Yet the silence prolonged itself into infinity as I stood there. "Julian," I said again "you don't need to tell me; I shall find out from her." There was the dry crisp click of the receiver going down, that was all; and I stood with the sea-shell of emptiness to my ear, mumbling to myself; for somehow these stupid remarks had set fire to my mind, illuminating a whole new area of unmapped action. The key—*of course*—the key to everything was Benedicta! I could do nothing that did not encapsulate her consent, her agreement. Before any problem could be settled I must settle the problem of this wife of mine. "By God" I said to myself as suddenly the fact dawned upon me. "Of course." How unjust I had been to her! I was filled with remorse all of a sudden. I had never really talked to her, explained to her, tried to enlist her support for my plans . . . I must rush to her side to explain everything.

But by the time I reached her Benedicta had already taken one of her characteristic leaps forward into triumphant unreason, eluding more successfully than ever the vain pursuit of her doctors or her lovers.

The slim three and a half litre Lethe lay outside the office—a birthday present from the firm; its glossy black snout pointed down-street like a lance laid in rest. This elegant missile could sway silently through traffic, and climb effortlessly into the hundreds with a faint blue snarl. For the most part it made only the noise of cremated silk—which is to say, no noise whatsoever. Its brief insistent horn copied the note of a trumpeting goose. I tell you the intoxication of driving this deft shooting-star across London soothed away my anxieties. Cool winds came off the river at Hammersmith; cloudy sunshine feathered out the last of the daylight. It would be dark before I arrived. It was dark when I did.

The house presented its usual aspect of tenantless animation—as if the owners had gone out to the pub for a drink leaving all the lights on, the radio on, the fires unguarded. It was the servants' day off no doubt. The lake was still. In the vague enthusiasm of my self-discovery (that I still had the power to conceive of independent actions) I was ill prepared for anything out of the ordinary. I could think about nothing but my own feelings: about how to make them clear to poor Benedicta. So much so that I hardly took in at first the bloody spoor which here and there marked the scarlet staircase-carpet; nor the trail of dummy books which lay anyhow on the landings—an obscure paperchase of empty titles like *Decline and Fall* and *Night Thoughts* and *The Consolations of Philosophy*. Up I went and up: not sufficiently attentive to be alarmed, more puzzled. Yet here and there—it was like following a wounded lion to its lair—I came upon a red pug-mark freshly impressed in the carpet. What could it mean? How on earth could I guess that Benedicta had been at that double toe of hers with a kitchen knife?

Well, the bedroom door was ajar and pushing it softly open I entered, to stand upon the threshold and contemplate the new Benedicta in her latest yet oldest role. I vaguely surmised that her period had surprised her, that was all. But everything was quite different. She was standing on the bed naked, her arms raised in rapture, her face burning with gratitude and adoration; it was clear that the ceiling had burst open to reveal the heavens, clouded and starry, with its vast frieze of angels and demons—figures of some great Renaissance Annunciation. The ceiling had withdrawn, had become the inverted bowl of the heavens. She was talking to the figures—at least her lips were moving. In the heavy pelt of the bed you could not discern the torn foot. She was surrounded by an absolute snowdrift of paper, torn up very small. Most of it was my transcripts I suppose—I recognised the paper I use for dactyl. But there were other things, letters on lined paper. Cupboards hung open with clothes pouring from them. Her dressing table was cluttered with fallen cosmetics. The elegant little leather boxes with trees—her *postiche* and wig boxes—lay about poking their tongue out at us. It was memorably silent. The trance could have been indefinitely prolonged, one felt; the figures in the frieze held up their hands to bless, or to point to breasts, or crowns of thorns. But they were benign, they were on her side, and her tears flowed down her cheeks in gratitude. In the bubble of this enormous concentration there was simply no room for me, nor for my preoccupations. I stood gaping at this tableau until she caught sight of me out of the corner of her eye and turned slowly in a puzzled way—the wonder widening in concentric rings upon her white face, as if I had thrown a stone into a pool. I suppose I must have stammered out something for she stared keenly at me and then put a finger to her lips. A look of sudden panic intervened now with astonishing rapidity and clutching her ears she screamed one: "I've gone deaf." Then just as suddenly dropped her hands, calmed and smiled wickedly.

This called for restraint of some sort, though nothing could be more angelic than the cool sweet smile of the demon. Underneath it, too, far down below the surface one recognised the look of a wounded animal, say a cat which tries to say: "I have a thorn in my foot. Please help." Borne on a clumsy tide of scattered and conflicting emotions I surged awkwardly forward, mumbling, arms outspread in the travesty of an embrace, unsure what the contents of my gesture might be—to embrace, to restrain, to comfort? All three, I suppose. In the corner there was a telephone torn out of the wall which hinted at strength which that slender body did not appear to own. "You see how it is?" she whispered, and slipped from the bed to elude my arms. The operation was more delicate and awkward than I had supposed; like when a swallow flies into a room and one tries to expel it without damaging or frightening the creature. Well, so we walked round, full of an awkward stateliness. Once or twice I almost caught up with her; her attention jumped for a moment from me to other objects in the room. But it was never absent for long, and she continued to elude me in a deft unhurrying fashion. And so out on the landing, with only a pause to topple a small statuette; and down the long staircase, saturated in the loneliness of this dreadful situation. Where the devil was everyone? Normally the house was full of servants. She slipped through doors, shutting them behind her to delay me; as I entered I would see her leaving the room from the far end, still looking at me over her shoulder to make sure I followed, expressionlessly seductive. She was heading steadily across the mansion towards the eastern side—towards, in fact, the old gunroom with its glass cases stocked with weapons. My concern deepened, my pace increased, but she held her distance. Then, as she disappeared into the gunroom she managed to find a key to turn. I was locked out. Under the noise of my impotent banging and cajoling I could hear the sliding doors of the glass cases being opened; then a crackle of paper and carton which instantly translated itself into a vision of Benedicta stripping a cartouche of shells. There were several drawers full of them. I began to sweat; then I remembered that there was a second door, a mere hatch, which led into a tiny bar built into the corner of the room. This was a swing-door, and I rushed for it; but the delay had given her just enough time, and when I barged through it was to see her quietly slipping out from the further end of the room with a gun under her arm.

She had chosen the second ballroom—the huge gilt one—now polished like a skull and empty of everything but its mirror and grand piano. She was standing in the centre of it, waiting for me to appear in the doorway, quite calm and composed. A few streaks of blood only—toes are relatively bloodless—marked her progress across the polished floor. But there she lounged, as if waiting for the machine to flick clay pigeons into the sky. It was no use calling her name. Inevitably, too, I feared at that instant that her target would be myself, framed by the gilt doorway in all my ineffectualness. But if by any chance the idea had not entered her head, I did not wish to provoke it by a sudden move. I stood rooted, expecting to receive the twelve-bore charge in the stomach; but she swung up and away and round, confronting the long chain of mirrors which lined the sombre room. As she let fly she began to recite the Lord's Prayer in a shaky broken voice—a small thread of sound among the explosions. "Our Father which art" (bang) "in heaven hallowed" (bang) "be thy name" (bang). And so forth. She had picked upon a repeating pump-gun, a six-shot. The noise of the smokeless shots was deafening, wit-scattering. I felt dizzy and faint, all my impressions fused together in a dazzle; and yet with the part of one's mind which remains attentive and critical I could not help noticing the voluptuous thwack with which the charge bust into the mirrors, embedding itself deep in the reality of the non-mirror world, shattering her image. A plump sound like someone beating up a swansdown pillow.

The rest doesn't translate so very well. I had picked up, I don't know how or where, a short ashplant—perhaps with some vague instinct of self-defence. I suppose I rushed at her—but it must have been with the toppling sliding motions of someone on ice, for the floor was glossy. Vaguely something in the nature of a football-tackle. I locked my arms round the defiant nakedness and together we stumbled and fell to the ground, the gun pressed between us. Indeed, the last discharge went off as we were falling and its hot breath burned my forehead; the barrel was fiendish hot too. So we rolled over and over until she released it and sent it skittering across the floor. Then to my surprise I began to beat her with my own weapon, but beat her precious hard across the back and buttocks. A sort of voluptuous rage must have possessed me—I was beating Julian, I suppose. And for her part she lay, pale and with an expression of content almost, eyes shut, lips moving in prayer—like someone accepting a well-merited punishment. It was frightening, also sexually exciting in a dim sort of way. But an end was soon put to this disgraceful scene, for by now the room was filling up with people.

The two governesses were upon us, witch-like and purposeful in their rusty black clothes; they hardly spoke as they set about separating and shackling us. Then frightened supers like Baynes, gobbling and swallowing. And lastly fussy Nash with his calamitous concern.

I was sick and feverish and upset—and now very much out of place in all this babble. Nor was the solace of strong drink very much in keeping with so hysterical a mood. I could not sleep in spite of it. I lay awake most of the night, listening to the faint sounds which betokened more purposeful activities than my own in other parts of the house; the telephone ringing, the voice of Nash. "Yes, he's here. I've put him to bed." I laughed grimly to myself and shook my fist at the ceiling. It did not need much imagination to translate the keening of rubber tyres on gravel in the first dawn-light; that would be the limousine with the drawn blinds. Soon Benedicta would be beginning that eternally repeated journey back to the land of the archetypes. "Our Father which art in heaven". By craning my head out of the window I could verify these hypotheses. The child would be in front with the harpies. Benedicta would be carried, heavily veiled, like a statue of the Virgin Mary. I don't say it wasn't all for the best. I don't say it wasn't all for the best. *Om.*

* * * * *

VI

Human attention is fragile and finite; won't be mastered; can't be bribed; is always changing. . . . Ah, for one moment of that total vision which might reorder the whole field and make it significant. I suppose from the outside it must have seemed like a progressive melancholia —I mean, resigning from the firm (no reaction to this) and locking myself up in the country in a desperate attempt to abdicate, along the lines suggested by Julian. *Not to invent any more.* Somehow one day one must try and stop being one's own little hero—eh Charlock? You can do it for a year or two at most without faltering. It's all very well, solitude and misanthropy. The beard I grew was patched with white; it gave me a startled look. I had to buy heavier lenses for my glasses. I was drinking a good deal and smoking too much. But it was a pleasure to let my appearance run to seed, to wear torn pullovers and knee-bulged grey bags. Nor was I completely cut off, except from Julian; he was biding his time, I supposed. I spoke to others on the phone, long conversations full of *non sequiturs*, yes, and common-room pleasantries. And all the time, unknown to my conscious me, that bloody old mass of wires I have called Abel was maturing. A certain resignation set in, too, walking about in the snow, hammering out Bach, skating in a deep muse upon the frozen waters of the lake. Well, so be it; if I must occupy myself, what better way? Besides, who would ever understand poor Abel, his foggy calculus of human potentials based upon the first cave-man chirp of the human voice? I was also preparing my revenge on Julian.

You may say that such an instrument could not possibly predict; but the future is only the memory of the past extended into the future. The backside of the moon of memory, if you like. The prediction of stars in the sky as yet undiscovered by the lens—that is a fair analogy. From the birth-cry to the death-rattle most lives can be plotted. I shall spare myself the eight lines of maths which resume this statement—crisp pothooks, shell of the cosmic egg. How little one needs to divine the human potentials in a single given life; translate through vibrations back to memory and thence to situation. Something the pundits of the firm will not fathom. When they take Abel apart they will be left with a mute collection of wires, like a human skeleton. Where is the soul of the machine? they will cry. Ah me! An invention as singular, original and definitive as the telescope. *E pur si muovi*, and so on.

The proof was in the pudding; and I had a pitifully small abacus to work with—just the people who had collided with me like rogue stars: just their sayings, visions, and the few facts I knew about them. I took over the big musicians' gallery for my keyboard, mounting the long and complicated panel of my fascia in the manner of some huge cinema organ; behind it was the library with its transmuting system. What is better than reading the stars? Why, listening to them in their transports of love and pain, music of the spheres echoed by diluted animals. It all grew out of my little magnetic boxes—a lot of it scratchy as hell. Sitting there in the tremendous loneliness of the silent house (I had sent most of the servants away) I sat, a lean and bearded man, switching from life to life. It took ages, of course; more than three years before I managed to obtain the first coherent response to my data. In this way I hoped to prosecute the opening moves of my war upon Julian—my persecution of this hidden man. I had thought of other things, but they were schoolboy pranks—messages in invisible ink slowly printing themselves on astonished blotters. But Abel was better. With him I could scry and scan. Much of it was not very palatable—but is truth ever palatable? I discovered much too about myself, about my inadequacy with women. O it was terrible to see the real truth about Benedicta; she was to be pitied, not to be hated. And the quiet Iolanthe's death-bed cry: "How little I have managed to live, and that always in hotels. There never seemed to be enough time, and now. . . ." I should have carried off these women in my teeth to devour them at leisure on a piece of waste ground. But then women cannot help being predatory—to take up with one is to inherit a mink farm.

Mark came, my son—how strange the word sounds! But he sheered away from me, sneaking round corners to avoid encounters.

I saw him, a pale thin little creature with sticking-out ears, walking solemnly to church between those two black harpies, as if between warders. It was clear that they had had their instructions. The boy was doing some sort of preparatory work for an entrance exam though still barely out of kindergarten. I could pick him up on Abel, but dimly. I saw him, *heard* him, sitting at my desk in Merlin's—a pale small-boned young man with a widow's peak. But that lay far ahead as yet, after my own . . . disappearance. This was foggy, with more than a hint of suicide about it. But talking of suicide, since the word has cropped up, I remember Mark's own little effort. I was working very early one morning when I happened to glance out of a window in time to see him walking down towards the lake. The earliness of the hour struck me—it was barely light. He had a slice of bread in his hand and was apparently about to feed the swans. I was about to turn away when something about his walk aroused my curiosity; it was so stiff and stilted, as if he were forcing himself to advance by sheer will-power. A moment later and he has walked right into the icy water, wading slowly outwards. Heavy sleet was falling. I shouted twice but he did not turn. Suddenly the comprehension of what he was doing dawned upon me and I raced for the door. The cold struck one amidships. He was moving steadily into the deeper reaches, already almost up to his neck. In spite of the blazing freeze I plunged after him, gasping with pain. I just reached his head as the water rose to his mouth, and grabbed him. He was blue and contorted with cold, crying and snickering. I half pushed the little creature into my shirt and crawled laboriously back to land with him, myself half fainting from the cold. Through his little blue prawn lips he was saying "They are trying to keep me away from you." Over and over again. I plunged for the downstairs bathroom with its hot taps, in a delirium of cold and anguish; plunging him into the hot water to soothe his numbed limbs. Then I slumped down on the bidet opposite him and wept; I wept my way right back to my solitary childhood, back to the breast, back into the very womb which is the only memory we know about. He wept too, but commiseratingly; and presently I felt his small pale hand touching my head, patting me, consoling me. I did not need to ask who or what was trying to keep him from me. So we sat for an age, staring at each other. Then I towelled his pink frail body back to life, alarmed at his slenderness, his shallow lungs. Our clothes fumed upon the radiators. Waiting for them to dry I said "Would you like to work with me on Abel?" and his eye lit with a frail gleam. He sighed: "They wouldn't let me." "Then they mustn't know, Mark, that is all. You must find times like this, too early or too late for them."

And so it was, he became my famulus, sneaking down before first light to spend two engrossing hours among my lights and wires. It was difficult at first to teach him the first principles of the thing; but later he mastered the whole system and crawled about my organ-loft like a powder-monkey.

"What is Abel really?"

"Well, one day you will want to know about us all, about your past and mine, about your future."

"Will I?"

"Almost certainly. Everyone does. Here look at the programme manual—do you see the different bays marked 'When' 'Who' 'Why' 'Where' and 'If'."

"*If*?" he said with surprise. "Why *If*?"

"It's the most important question of all in a way—it can change all the others: just one tiny grain of *If*."

It was a pleasure too to have someone to talk to; and as we worked I gave him the whole pedigree of Abel, starting with the *Theaetetus* and its block of wax in the human soul eager to imprint itself with every perception, thought, emotion; the whole theory of Platonic memory and all that blubber to which the child listened with wonder and a certain understanding. The only thing was that I had to warn him against the Julian dossier—how to be careful; because when I had finished with Julian I knew he would walk into my trap and come down to find out what there was to know about himself. What man could resist reading a secret report on himself? It was the second panel on the left with an inviting red button. I pushed it open for Mark—in order to make certain that he understood—and together we stared into the barrels of the loaded twelve-bore I had lashed to a stand and wired for action. I would leave this behind me when I left. Mark gazed at it wonderingly, and then at me, his small blue eyes narrowed as he tried to assess the meaning of this present.

But he said nothing. "You won't give me away?" I said, feeling so sure of his love for me. He shook his head proudly.

So we opened up several of the channels and completed the elaborate programmes which would bring them to life—if that is the scientific word. I don't know when I have been so happy. Nor was the business kept a secret; Nash came and had it all explained to him. He looked very strange, declared that he understood, and tiptoed away again. If he did not tap his head significantly before my eyes he perhaps did it before the eyes of others. Marchant also came—but he turned pale and gnawed his lip, whether from jealousy or contempt I do not know. Yes I do, though. I had pitifully little on him and I hadn't really assorted the field with any thoroughness but up in the predicter came the word "plagiarism". I wanted all this guff to filter back slowly to Julian, and it did. But that was only the beginning.

Then unluckily Mark was caught; one of the harpies in a wizard's dressing-gown stood sibilating in the doorway of the gallery. "Mark, you have been *told* over and over *again.*" She reached out a hand like a spade. I watched with a sort of recondite insolence, tipping the bottle of lemonade to my lips. Mark allowed himself to be led tamely away, head high, lips white, ears pink—the captive rabbit. It seemed useless to protest, so I did nothing, secure in his confidence. He stepped high and proud, and did not turn his head to say goodbye.

Well: and then what? Why, a whole winter lay before me of ordering and scrying—on a much firmer wicket than John Dee ever was. Fires blazed everywhere, the snow blanketed everything. And now *Julian* was being persecuted. His *own* voice was ringing him up! "Is that Julian?" "Yes." "This is Julian too." It had been pretty largely given out that Abel was some sort of electronic hoax; but truth is relative. It was far less accurate than I would have liked to hope, but nevertheless I found I could use it. After all, the planchette is no good without the hand, the crystal ball without the sorcerer's eye. Yes, I could see backwards and forwards along the tragic ellipse of these segmented lives, to come up now and again with partial fragments of truth. At times my nets were full; at times I had to empty the small fry back into the stream. Goodness, but enough came up to fill Julian with alarm. He tried to ring me several times, and I was delighted by the concealed agitation in his tones. How did I know what I knew? Truth to tell, by the merest divination in the name of Abel. It took hardly any time to convince and disturb him because I fell upon some trivia which proved themselves accurate within days of Julian's voice telling him. Perhaps all this might prove a useful guide to the stock market or the race-course? I made Julian ask Julian this in a slightly bitter tone. But then inexorably I began to edge towards his private life—the field of his emotions and hopes. Ah, I wanted to reduce him slowly, with infinite slowness; already I scented his weakness. He was like a drowning man. At times too I was overcome with remorse to be so brutal, for now he was really suffering. And I brought the whole weight of my tortures to bear upon the sick Iolanthe, upon her silent native death. He had heard enough by now to suspect that the rest might well become true. And then Graphos too: the sad footsteps of Hippo echoing on the lino of some gravid hospital corridor. The ignominy of the acetone breath, the legs gradually filling up, turning gangrenous. So carefully kept, those legs, in grey woollen socks. He had been *warned* not to try and cut his own toenails, for the slightest wound. . . . But Graphos was not used to obeying others. He always knew better.

I had written to Iolanthe, promising to exorcise her house provided she came with me; but the letter arrived too late and she burned it along with many others. All this comes of a strange meeting I was to have with Mrs. Henniker on the Zürich plane. Her face had been hollowed out by suffering, scaled and pared to the bone by the sleepless nights she had spent at the bedside of Io. The tall steel bed against a window full of Alpine stars and tumultuous grass. One candle burning before an ikon—no need to say which. Shaken by a kind of involuntary sobbing which contained no more tears—she had used them all up. At first nobody knew except Julian *of course.* Whenever she was ill she was registered at three different clinics in order to enjoy some peace and anonymity at a fourth. Well, there by candlelight reciting her past and peering with those wild enlarged eyes into the fastnesses of the future, the pinewood coffin. *Tunc.*

It was so slow, the simple declining into the final pens of sleep, without too much pain, too many numbed regrets. Rolling down the green slopes of death, moving faster and ever faster, turning through the slow spirals of consciousness towards the heart of the fire opal. All night long now Mrs. Henniker sat beside the bed, her stone-coloured eye fixed upon the face of the white woman who had become her daughter; all night upright in an uncomfortable steel chair, the whole building silent around her, save for the shuffling shoes of the night-nurse—one for the whole floor. From time to time the patient's eyes would open and wander about the ceiling as if seeking for something. Her lips might move a little, perhaps even tenderly smile. I would have liked to think—I *did* think—that she was picturing both of us crossing to her father's island in the blue fishing-boat. A church, cypresses, sand-coloured jetty, box-dwellings of coloured whitewashes, the pink-toed pigeons crooning. Up and ever up to the abandoned barn where his whole life had been lived, had completed its simple circle. The well overgrown with moss now, the marble well-head grooved by the cable which for centuries had drawn up the sweet water. One loose stone extracted revealed the hiding-place of the key. Let us suppose we entered on tip-toe—entered the smelly gloom of the apple-charmed room full of unbroken cobwebs—the room he died in. Somewhere along the line, at this exact point, everything about my life threatens to become successful; everything takes a turn for the better. A fresh wind fills the sails—so Abel tells me, but always adding the rider "a delusion like so many others, that's all". Then the field goes blank again and the hints about suicide come up. It would not last, you see: could not last.

Well, on and on she sits, Mrs. Henniker with her hanky screwed up in her hand, her red horse-face gleaming with sweat. If I could convey with how much dazzling longing I gazed upon the face of Iolanthe dead—why everything would burst apart, catch fire, disintegrate. The little green book which fell from the bed had no underlining in it to serve as a guide-line to her last thoughts—perhaps she did not have many. Henniker carried it away for me, together with a lock of that famous hair—the sentimental relics which human children so cherish: the evidences of memory which are supposed to endure as long as the last unshed tear. Her eyes, did they fall upon the passage which I was now reading out, my own lips moving stiffly along the lines? "*Vous êtes liê fatalement aux meilleurs souvenirs de ma jeunesse. Savez-vous qu'il y a plus de vingt ans que nous nous connaissons? Tout cela me plonge dans les abîmes de rêverie qui sentent le vieillard. On dit que le présent est trop rapide. Je trouve, moi, que c'est le passé qui nous dévore.*"

Perhaps it was the eyes of Julian rather which traced and retraced these faltering lines written in the hand of the ageing Flaubert; for Julian inevitably was there. He came in silently, unannounced, just after midnight, softly putting his briefcase on the floor. In her confusion Henniker saw only a batlike figure in a black suit and a soft black hat. He motioned her to silence and indicated that she might leave the patient to be guarded by him. Without a word all was understood. With a sigh Henniker crossed to the low divan and plunged into a deep sleep. One thing only she noticed. Iolanthe did not open her eyes at all, but all of a sudden her face quivered and her hand came softly across the white sheet towards Julian's small, childlike hand. So they sat silently with her feverish fingers resting upon his. Of course I asked how he *looked*, but her answers were vague; she had received a dozen conflicting impressions. Terribly tired and old, an ashen face, the crater of an extinct volcano; or else some great quivering bat of pain clinging by his wings to the steel-tubed chair. Or else.... But it is useless, useless. Whenever it is really necessary Julian appears, and one knows it: but often only after he has gone.

The night wore on and on into the milky opaqueness of dawn; the white fangs of snowscape glittered in all their fruitless splendour. All nature dozed and even Julian felt his head drooping. It must have been after one of these transitory cat-naps that he woke to feel the full massiveness, the charged weight, of her changed status. Death had made her fingers so heavy, it seemed, that he almost had to prize his own out from under them. Just that. He did not move any more. Mrs. Henniker snored faintly. He continued to stare intently at the white profile she presented to him with such motionless intentness. Even when a drowsy fly settled on the eyeball he could not move.

But they were not to be spared the final indignities which the press reserves for events such as these. Somehow the secret of her whereabouts had leaked out. The clinic was ill-equipped to protect itself against sixty such persecutors, especially at such a time of day. They burst through the swing doors with all the vulgar assurance of the tribe, overwhelming the dazed duty nurse, deaf to all protest. Some even climbed over the balcony from the garden. The candle-lit silence of the room was filled now by their hoarse reverent breathing, the shuffle of their feet, the hiss and splash of their bulbs. Even now Julian did not move; he sat exhausted in his chair. And in some singular way they did not notice him, for not a single glance or question was addressed to him; and in all the photographs which smeared the dailies of the world there was no trace of his presence—the chair seemed to be empty. Why go on? The planned obsolescence of the human body etc. Mrs. Henniker slept right through it and was only woken by a banged door. Julian had gone. "The unlucky thing" he said later "was her loving you; it was completely unsuitable, and anyway you did not care." I cannot answer these charges any more. A fearful horror and exhaustion seizes me. I am guilty of nothing—in fact that's really what I am guilty *not of*. Then later in the gutter-press to read of her grave being robbed. They said that fans had done it—it is true that fans will stop at nothing. At any rate it could hardly have been Julian; nor ordinary robbers, for her jewelry had not been touched. Hair, though; there is a high market value for the hair of a goddess. What she sought was not love but the frail combining of hopes with someone—but how was Henniker to know this? She had choked me with a phrase and I sat there staring at her feeling as if I had swallowed a toad.

It is very still here. *Om*. I said *Om*.

* * * * *

VII

It has been wearing, this brief period of lonely inertia in Athens, waiting for Koepgen to appear. I don't know why I felt I ought to see him before . . . before getting on with it. I kept an eye on the favourite tavern; that too is much the same. One window has fallen in, and the vine had got mildew. The widow is dead, but her son carries on. I have been walking about a good deal at night . . . the brutal velvet Athenian night with its harsh rancorous music and game-smells. I can't record thoughts any more, the spool seems to have run out. The whole bloody thing has begun to seize up in my head like an engine. And then, bang, tonight I ran into him—the pocket Silenus in the monkish gear. A streak of brindle in his hair. But no surprise at seeing me. We sat silently for a while devouring each other with our eyes; I noticed he was rather drunk and hastened to join him in that blessed state. "I knew you'd come." Nodding owlwise and tipping the blue tin can. "You want to hear about me, my story." I did actually. A vague nervous curiosity had possessed me, for in spite of my fairly extensive data upon Koepgen I could hardly get anything out of Abel except fictitious-sounding aphorisms. "The ikon and all that . . your farty fairy-tale." His eyes danced, he leaned his back against the whitewashed wall of the tavern. "My God, Charlock," he said "I am really free. I took ages to earn it, but I stuck it out and got an honest discharge. Free, my lad!"

I raised the wine can and almost let him have it on the crown of his head—so sick was I of the meaningless four-letter. "They've treated me very well" he said. "But that isn't the strangest thing. Yes, I found my ikon at last—and what I took to be some sort of mystical awakening waiting for me turned out to be the most prosaic thing imaginable." He laughed very heartily. "My father's will was gummed into the back of it, together with the deeds for our property in Russia—if ever they decide to give it back to us."

"Where, though?"

"Another fantastic thing—Spinalonga."

"The leper island? The one off Crete?"

"The very same. I got the Church to post me there when Jocas told me and sure enough I found it there. It was the damnedest thing. And it wasn't all. There was a little old man, one of the lepers, who was dying and I was asked to help send him down with all the usual formalities. But he took ages to die; and in his delirium he talked away whole nights. You know, he was English; he told me—what next? He told me he was *Merlin* himself."

"The devil he did."

"It was certainly his name; but how could I tell if he was THE Merlin or just someone of that name? Eh? But he knew a great deal about us all, about Benedicta, about you; and indeed he twice sent you a message through me. I am not lying, Charlock. Wait a second and let me recall." He guzzled some more wine with its bitter twang. Wiped his lips with bread and went on. "He said '*The firm only exists to be escaped from. Tell Charlock.*' What do you make of that? Then on another occasion he said: '*There are two kinds of death open to the living. Tell Charlock.*' " I sat looking incredulously at him, but feeling somehow cheered up in a confused way. We clapped hands for another beaker of the thought-provoker. "In his view he said the firm was something different for each of us; it was something like memory for you—its banked funds too great to be exhausted by promissory notes."

"To the devil with it all."

"I know what is in your mind" said Koepgen seriously. "But you ought to visit the little house before you decide. And you ought to realise that such an act——"

"Shut up, Koepgen" I growled, baring my fangs.

"I know, I apologise. The free should never moralise to the bound. Let's talk of something else. Let me tell you about a stroke of luck I have had; you remember the translations you helped me with? Of my poems? I sent them in anonymously to an agent. They have been accepted without any *piston* whatsoever. Straight off. Like that! I received the contract today. Look!" I took the wad of paper from him and glanced at it. Then I looked at him in slowly dawning horror.

The firm was Vibart's. The contracts were signed by Vibart's partner. Was it possible that the fool did not know? I stared keenly, reverently, tenderly into the eyes of the poor foolish little man and swallowed my Adam's apple a number of times. Should I tell him? "No" cried my *alter felix*. "Not a word."

"Well, we must drink another one on this", and Koepgen echoed my clanking pledge with his own, his eyes full of the tears of fulfilment. We sat until very late, until the violet sky went lilac and started to bleed; until the waiters were snoring on window-sills. Then we clambered down the hill past the Acropolis.

Well, I had made my decision. I would visit Io's house before deciding how and when.

* * * * *

Nash was always at a loss to account for the depression which welled up in him as his car turned slowly along the axis of the hill, along the double avenue of elms. But the man in the dark suit who sat beside him looked at it all with a studied coldness; Julian had been relatively silent for the first part of the journey down. But in the last few miles he had begun to muse again after his usual fashion. "It isn't beautiful" he said, as if reading Nash's thoughts. "I agree. The grandeur is too Byzantine. It could never be a home for anyone, I suppose." Nash changed gear, shaking his head. A frown anointed his cock-robin's face. "It's not her fault" he said. "She has made a wonderful recovery, you must agree; in spite of so much bad news, the death and so on."

Julian lit a cigar and said: "Presumption of death isn't quite the same thing. Without a body to show for it. You need as much body to die as to live. In the case of Charlock—we will have to wait upon the evidence. At any rate the Mediterranean always gives up its bodies. I think we'll find him, if he is to be found. It's only a matter of waiting awhile." He coughed and settled himself deeper in his seat. They had come down to inspect the curious toy in the musicians' gallery. ("An abacus of the intuition—can you make one?") That and other little matters had to be gone into. Julian went on softly "It's like those legends of the Hesychasts—to die and leave an empty grave. One must beware of Charlock."

"Oh dear, I don't know" said Nash and Julian replied coolly.

"You are not expected to know; you are expected to exist, to be."

"That's the whole trouble."

The lake was of dark and dirty jelly. The swans floated about like white lanterns. The paint had peeled along the benches. Under this lowering sky the skin of wet leaves lagged his tyres. Nash was fastidious as a cat when it came to his car; he could not bear things sticking to his paws. He found a stick to poke at them while Julian stood in the drive, debating heavily. "We will deal with the child first" he said softly. "He may know how the thing is booby-trapped, as obviously it must be. At least we can ask." Nash grunted. He had found a bracelet on the gravel, which he put into his overcoat pocket. The manservant let them in with a silent inclination of the head and they passed together down the long corridors and up the spiral staircase to the room where Julian proposed to interrogate Mark. Nash thumped heavily along behind him, puffing a little on the landings, with a curious air of fugitive derision on his face. "I'll go and see Benedicta, then" he said, and turning left where the landings intersected, marched away towards the bedrooms.

As usual Julian, that master of effect, had chosen a place of interrogation worthy of a practised inquisitor. It was an old cobwebby boxroom with a single uncurtained window looking out across the park. Here an oldfashioned high-backed chair had been placed facing the window—a chair with so tall a back that when Mark did come hesitantly into the room all he could see of Julian was a pair of white hands lying softly, negligently on the arms of the chair. Nothing else. The high back hid even his head. Mark had been marched down the corridors of the east wing by a nurse and introjected into the room at a given signal. He stood now, anxious and pale, with his feeble countenance made whiter than usual by the daylight outside. "Yes, Uncle Julian?" he said when his name was uttered. "Yes?"

Julian put on his slow, sauve reptilian voice, letting the words uncoil by themselves, musingly. "Mark, you helped our dear Felix build Abel, didn't you?"

"Yes."

"Is there a booby-trap of any sort in it: something that might explode and injure someone?"

Mark began to breathe very heavily and his face took on an unwonted expression of determination, of awkward resolution. The man in the tall-backed chair stayed heavily, ominously silent as if he wished to give time for some reaction to these inappropriate emotions to set in.

"I won't tell you. I promised" said the boy at last.

"Then if someone should get hurt you might be to blame?"

"I promised."

"Then if someone should get hurt you might be to blame?"

Mark watched the slow spirals of cigar smoke rise in the eddyless air of the musty room. "I am asking you" said Julian suddenly in a voice so sharp that the boy started. "I am asking you." Mark hung his head. He was hovering on the edge of tears now. Julian resumed his suave impartial voice. "Mark," he said with infinite slowness "you know the story of the Princes in the Tower?" Mark nodded and breathed out his "Yes" into the silent room. "Very well," said Julian "I'm glad you do. It's not a pretty story. Now, Mark, I am going to ask you something else. Is there any safe way of dismantling the trap?"

After a long interior struggle Mark once more delivered himself of his half-choked affirmation. "Good," said Julian "and you know how to do it, don't you?"

"Yes, Uncle Julian."

"And you will help us, won't you? We cannot afford to lose that machine by some clumsy accident."

"There's a switch" said Mark haltingly. "I was shown it."

Julian heaved a great sigh of relief. "Then that settles it" he said. "You will do it for us, won't you? You see, Professor Marchant and I want to have a look at the machine. It's a very beautiful and original work—the best thing Felix ever did. The firm can't afford to lose it. If you would do that this morning, I could come down this week with him and we could put it into motion."

A long, deafening silence fell. Mark stared at the spirals of smoke curving upwards towards the dirty ceiling.

"Very well, Uncle Julian. I'll do it now, if you wish."

"That's my boy" said Julian with relief. "That's a good boy."

"Can I go now?" said Mark.

"Of course you may."

"Goodbye, Uncle Julian."

"Goodbye, Mark, and thank you very much."

* * * * *

Benedicta was still convalescent, still only half up, half out of bed. She was forbidden to move about too much in case the palpitations set in again. Nash sat by the bed full of hopeful optimism. "You are very much better" he said, and reached for his small prescription pad and fountain pen. "We'll have you up and about in a day or two." She watched him carefully as he wrote with small feathery strokes of his pen. Her pale long face was set in a helmet of unkempt blonde hair. She was dressed in greensleeves fashion—a vague smock-gown with a gold rope sash round her slender waist: the attire of a Victorian poetess, one would have said. A small heart-shaped watch ticked on her breast, attached by a brooch in the form of an octopus. She half reclined, surrendering her pulse to Nash, brooding heavily the while.

"Marchant rang me up" she said abstractedly. "About all the tapes by Felix which they found on the beach with his clothes. He has been through them very carefully. The last one is a bit of a puzzle though. He says that there is something recorded which one *could* take for the sound of oars, a squeaky rowlock. But it's all very hazy. Do you think that Felix is really . . . ?"

"We can't think anything" said Nash hastily. "I was discussing it with Julian today. "We must wait. We have all the time in the world now, all the time in the world."

But it was when the dark shade of Julian stood before her, gazing at her from the foot of the bed, that Benedicta recovered some of her wonted animation of look; her eyes stared into his with a sweet burning intensity. His mere presence seemed to ignite her, to return her to the order of coherent things; her indisposition slid from her like a mummy-wrapping. "Julian" she said, and her voice took on a thrilling resonance.

"Mark is going to cooperate" he said in his lazy musing way.

"And that is one point we have cleared. Now then, for the rest, Benedicta: Nash and I both feel that as you have made such a splendid recovery we must take advantage of it. I have spoken to Jocas and he is quite on our side. You must have a decent rest. Go to Polis for a while and leave us to settle up all the details at this end. Will you?"

"If you wish" she said. "If you wish, Julian."

He rested his elbows on the end of the bed and looked down abstractedly at her pale beautiful face. "You could also be useful to us if you wish" he went on slowly. "There is a young German baron, a botanist, travelling about in Turkey with his yacht. He has found a flower which he says could give us something like perfect insect control in a natural way . . . I won't bore you with the details. But the firm must try and secure him. You could take the provisional contracts with you when you go, so that Jocas can get to work persuading him. He seems rather doubtful about joining."

"Of course I will" she said with a curious furtive, wolfish look, beginning to bite her nails as she listened.

"But there's no hurry" said Julian. "We have all the time in the world, all the time in the world."

The sound of a distant report, muffled by the heavy walls of the building, was barely loud enough to pierce the hard integument of Julian's abstraction or of hers. She still stared at him with admiration and pity, and he gazed down at her as he had always done—his eyes full of an impenetrable sadness. It was left to Nash to sit up in his chair and say: "Surely that was a shot?"

AUTHOR'S NOTE

By intention this is the first deck of a double-decker novel. Here and there in the text attentive readers may discern the odd echo from *The Alexandria Quartet* and even from *The Black Book*; this is intentional.